The Midwestern
Junior League Cookbook

THE PARTICIPATING JUNIOR LEAGUES INCLUDE:

The Junior League of Greater Alton, Illinois
The Junior League of Battle Creek, Michigan
The Junior League of Cedar Rapids, Iowa
The Junior League of Champaign-Urbana, Illinois
The Junior League of Chicago, Illinois
The Junior League of Cincinnati, Ohio
The Junior League of Columbus, Ohio
The Junior League of Dayton, Ohio
The Junior League of Des Moines, Iowa
The Junior League of Evansville, Indiana
The Junior League of Fargo-Moorhead, North Dakota/Minnesota
The Junior League of Flint, Michigan
The Junior League of Grand Rapids, Michigan
The Junior League of Indianapolis, Indiana
The Junior League of Kansas City, Kansas
The Junior League of Milwaukee, Wisconsin
The Junior League of Peoria, Illinois
The Junior League of Rockford, Illinois
The Junior League of Saginaw, Michigan
The Junior League of St. Paul, Minnesota
The Junior League of Sioux City, Iowa
The Junior League of South Bend, Indiana
The Junior League of Springfield, Illinois
The Junior League of Toledo, Ohio
The Junior League of Wichita, Kansas
The Junior League of Youngstown, Ohio

. . . .

Illustrations by Lauren Jarrett

. . . .

The Midwestern Junior League Cookbook

. . . .

Edited by Ann Seranne

. . . .

David McKay Company, Inc.
New York

Library of Congress Cataloging in Publication Data
Main entry under title:

The Midwestern Junior League cookbook.

Includes index.
1. Cookery, American—Middle West.   I. Smith, Margaret Ruth, 1914–
TX715.M636   641.5   78–9522
ISBN 0–679–51204–7

Manufactured in the United States of America

10   9   8   7   6   5   4   3   2

Preface

The purpose of the Junior League is exclusively educational and charitable and is to promote voluntarism; to develop the potential of its members for voluntary participation in community affairs; and to demonstrate the effectiveness of trained volunteers.

Proceeds from the sale of Junior League cookbooks go into the Community Trust Funds, which finance the Leagues' community programs.

To find out how to obtain a particular Junior League's own book of recipes, turn to pages 595–599.

Contents

Metric Equivalent Chart

LENGTH

1 inch (in)	=	2.5 centimeters (cm)
1 foot (ft)	=	30 centimeters (cm)
1 millimeter (mm)	=	.04 inches (in)
1 centimeter (cm)	=	.4 inches (in)
1 meter (m)	=	3.3 feet (ft)

MASS WEIGHT

1 ounce (oz)	=	28 grams (g)
1 pound (lb)	=	450 grams (g)
1 gram (g)	=	.035 ounces (oz)
1 kilogram (kg) or 1000 g	=	2.2 pounds (lbs)

LIQUID VOLUME

1 fluid ounce (fl. oz)	=	30 milliliters (ml)
1 fluid cup (c)	=	240 milliliters (ml)
1 pint (pt)	=	470 milliliters (ml)
1 quart (qt)	=	950 milliliters (ml)
1 gallon (gal)	=	3.8 liters (l)
1 milliliter (ml)	=	.03 fluid ounces (fl. oz)
1 liter (l) or 1000 ml	=	2.1 fluid pints or 1.06 fluid quarts
1 liter (l)	=	.26 gallons (gal)

Appetizers

Spinach Balls

2 10-ounce packages frozen spinach
2 cups packaged stuffing mix
1 cup grated Parmesan cheese
6 eggs, beaten
¾ cup butter, softened
Salt
Pepper

Cook spinach according to package directions and drain very well.

Combine all ingredients, mix well, and roll into balls the size of walnuts. Freeze.

Before serving, and while still frozen, place balls on cookie sheet and bake at 350° for 10 minutes.

YIELD: 60–70 BALLS

Soupçon
THE JUNIOR LEAGUE OF CHICAGO, ILLINOIS

· · · · · · · · · · · · · · · · · · · ·

Sauerkraut Balls

½ pound pork sausage, finely crumbled
¼ cup finely chopped onion
1 14-ounce can sauerkraut, drained and chopped
2 tablespoons bread crumbs
3 ounces cream cheese
2 tablespoons chopped parsley or dry flakes
1 teaspoon prepared mustard
¼ teaspoon garlic salt
⅛ teaspoon pepper
¼ cup flour
1 egg, beaten well
¼ cup milk
¾ cup bread crumbs

Cook sausage and onion until lightly browned. Drain. Add sauerkraut and 2 tablespoons bread crumbs. Combine cream cheese, parsley, mustard, garlic salt, and pepper. Stir into meat mixture and chill.

Shape mixture into small balls and coat with flour. Combine egg and milk. Roll floured balls in egg mixture and then in ¾ cup bread crumbs. Fry in hot oil until lightly browned, about 3–5 minutes.

May be made ahead and warmed in oven before serving time.

YIELD: 3 DOZEN SMALL BALLS

THE JUNIOR LEAGUE OF YOUNGSTOWN, OHIO

.   .   .   .

Cocktail Meat Balls

1 pound ground beef
1 pound ground sausage meat
2 eggs, beaten
½ cup cracker crumbs
¼ cup grated Parmesan cheese
½ package dry French dressing mix
1 14-ounce bottle catsup
½ cup brown sugar
1 10-ounce jar grape jelly
½ teaspoon garlic powder

Combine beef, sausage, eggs, cracker crumbs, and cheese. Shape into 1-inch balls. Place balls in shallow baking pan and bake at 375° for 20 minutes, shaking pan occasionally to turn balls. Drain.

Combine remaining ingredients and pour over balls. Cover and simmer 20 more minutes.

Serve hot.

YIELD: 7 DOZEN

THE JUNIOR LEAGUE OF TOLEDO, OHIO

.   .   .   .

Swedish Hors D'oeuvre Balls

3 pounds ground beef
1 pound ground pork
4 eggs, beaten
2 slices bread, soaked in water
8 tablespoons minced onions
6 tablespoons chopped parsley
1 teaspoon grated lemon peel
2 teaspoons lemon juice
2½ teaspoons salt
1 teaspoon dill weed
Freshly ground pepper to taste
1 stick butter
4 cups beef stock or consommé
8 tablespoons flour
3 tablespoons drained capers
Dash sherry
1 pint sour cream

With wet hands, combine beef, pork, and eggs. Wring out bread, shred, and add to meat along with onions, parsley, lemon peel, lemon juice, salt, dill, and pepper. Mix well and shape into 1-inch balls; brown quickly on all sides in a skillet in the butter.

Bring beef stock or consommé to a simmer. Drop in balls and simmer for 15 minutes.

To butter remaining in skillet, stir in flour to make a smooth roux. Cook roux, stirring constantly, until golden brown in color.

With slotted spoon, remove meat balls from consommé to a chafing dish. Strain the consommé into the roux and cook, stirring, over low heat until sauce is smooth and thickened. Stir in capers, sherry, and sour cream.

Pour sauce over meat balls and serve with plenty of toothpicks for spearing.

YIELD: ABOUT 12 DOZEN

THE JUNIOR LEAGUE OF ROCKFORD, ILLINOIS

Ham Balls in Cranberry-Orange Sauce

2 pounds fully-cooked ham, ground
2 cups bread crumbs
½ cup milk
1 teaspoon prepared mustard
2 teaspoons horseradish
2 eggs, lightly beaten
Fresh parsley for garnish

Mix all ingredients except parsley, roll into 1-inch balls, and bake on lightly greased cookie sheet at 375° for 15–20 minutes.

Pour Cranberry-Orange Sauce over hot ham balls and serve in chafing dish. Garnish with fresh parsley.

CRANBERRY-ORANGE SAUCE:
½ cup sugar
2 tablespoons cornstarch
1 cup orange juice
¼ cup vinegar
1 1-pound can cranberry sauce
1 cup diced orange

Mix first four ingredients. Stir in cranberry sauce and orange. Heat, stirring, until cranberry sauce melts.

YIELD: 90–100 BALLS

THE JUNIOR LEAGUE OF COLUMBUS, OHIO

Glazed Ham Balls

1 pound fully-cooked ham, ground
½ pound ground beef
¾ cup soft bread crumbs
1 egg
½ cup milk
¾ cup unsweetened pineapple juice
½ cup maple or maple-flavored syrup
2 tablespoons cornstarch

Combine ham, ground beef, bread crumbs, egg, and milk; mix well. Shape into 1½-inch meat balls. Place in baking dish and bake, uncovered, in 350° oven for 20 minutes.

Meanwhile, in small saucepan, combine pineapple juice, maple syrup, and cornstarch. Cook and stir until thickened and bubbly. Pour over meat balls and bake 20 minutes more.

Keep warm and serve as hors d'oeuvres with toothpicks for spearing.

YIELD: 18 BALLS

THE JUNIOR LEAGUE OF YOUNGSTOWN, OHIO

• • • • • • • • • • • • • • • • • •

Hamburger Dip

2 pounds ground beef
1 medium onion, chopped
½ cup taco sauce
½ cup catsup
Garlic powder to taste
1 1-pound can kidney beans, drained, rinsed, and mashed
1 bunch fresh green onions, chopped
6 ounces cheddar cheese, shredded
½ cup olives with pimento, sliced

Brown ground beef and onion in skillet. Add taco sauce, catsup, garlic powder, and kidney beans. Heat. Layer in a chafing dish—first some of the beef mixture, then fresh onions, cheese, and olives. Repeat layers.

Serve with king-sized corn chips or in taco shells with shredded lettuce and chopped tomato.

YIELD: 12 SERVINGS

THE JUNIOR LEAGUE OF ST. PAUL, MINNESOTA

Party Pizza

1 pound hot sausage meat
1 pound processed cheese, cubed
1 teaspoon Worcestershire sauce
½ teaspoon garlic salt
1 teaspoon soy sauce
2 loaves party rye bread

Cook sausage but do not drain. Add remaining ingredients. Spread on bread. (Freeze at this point, if desired.) Bake in 350° oven for 15 minutes, until brown.

YIELD: 60–80 PIZZAS

Bluff City Cooks
THE JUNIOR LEAGUE OF GREATER ALTON, ILLINOIS

Beer-Cheese Dip

3 6-ounce rolls sharp cheese, softened
1¼ ounces Roquefort cheese
2 tablespoons butter, softened
1 medium onion, minced
2 medium cloves garlic, minced
1 teaspoon Worcestershire sauce
½ teaspoon Tabasco
½–1 cup beer, heated and slightly cooled
1 round loaf rye bread

Mix all ingredients except beer and bread with electric mixer; gradually add beer until good consistency for dipping bread chunks. Refrigerate.

Make serving bowl by hollowing out center of rye bread, leaving a 1-inch-thick shell. Tear bread into chunks. Just before serving, pour dip into the bread shell and serve surrounded by bread chunks.

YIELD: 10–12 SERVINGS

Cincinnati Celebrates
THE JUNIOR LEAGUE OF CINCINNATI, OHIO

. . . .

Hot Appetizer Dip

8 ounces cream cheese
2 tablespoons milk
¾ cup finely diced dried beef
2 tablespoons minced onions
2 tablespoons finely chopped green pepper
⅛ teaspoon pepper
½ cup sour cream
¼ cup chopped walnuts or pecans

Mix all ingredients except nuts. Spread mixture in an 8-inch pie plate and sprinkle with nuts. Bake at 350° for 15 minutes.

Serve hot with crackers.

YIELD: 6–8 SERVINGS

THE JUNIOR LEAGUE OF ROCKFORD, ILLINOIS

Three-Layer Appetizer Pie

8 ounces cream cheese
1½ ounces blue cheese
½ teaspoon Worcestershire sauce
1 tablespoon minced parsley
1 4–5–ounce can deviled ham
2 tablespoons pickle relish
4 hard-boiled eggs, chopped
1 tablespoon chopped pimento
¼ teaspoon salt
Dash pepper
2 tablespoons mayonnaise
Parsley for garnish

Cream cheeses with Worcestershire sauce and parsley and pack into bottom of an 8-inch pie plate, spreading evenly. Cover with a mixture of the ham and relish. Add a third layer of egg combined with pimento, seasonings, and mayonnaise.

Chill pie for several hours.

Serve garnished with parsley and surrounded with crackers.

YIELD: 8 SERVINGS

THE JUNIOR LEAGUE OF CHAMPAIGN-URBANA, ILLINOIS

Daffodil Dip

8 ounces cream cheese, softened
⅓ cup mayonnaise-type salad dressing
1 teaspoon parsley flakes
1 hard-boiled egg (use white only, finely diced)
2 tablespoons chopped green onion
¼ teaspoon garlic salt
Dash pepper
1 teaspoon lemon juice
1 hard-boiled egg yolk

Beat softened cream cheese until smooth. Add salad dressing by hand, then stir in all remaining ingredients except egg yolk.

Spoon into serving dish and crumble egg yolk on top.

YIELD: 1 PINT

THE JUNIOR LEAGUE OF YOUNGSTOWN, OHIO

•   •   •   •   •   •   •   •   •   •   •   •   •   •   •   •   •   •   •

Parsley Tree

Cover a 3-inch styrofoam ball with foil. Poke holes in the ball with a toothpick and stick pieces of parsley into the holes until the whole ball is covered. Put the ball on a short piece of doweling, and stick the dowel into a piece of cork stuck in a low candlestick holder.

Onto this topiary tree attach any of the foods listed below, or any combination of them, with toothpicks.

Radish roses
Celery brooms
Carrot curls
Olives
Cooked shrimp
Gherkin slices
Cucumber wheels
Pickled onions
Cauliflower buds

This makes a beautiful hors d'oeuvre centerpiece to place on the coffee table when entertaining. Allow about an hour to assemble it; it cannot be done ahead and will hold at the longest 4–5 hours. It will be very top-heavy, so careful attention should be paid to placement of the vegetables so it does not topple.

Serve with Michigan Ginger or Dill Weed Dip.

MICHIGAN GINGER DIP:
1 cup mayonnaise
2 teaspoons vinegar
4 teaspoons soy sauce
½ teaspoon ground ginger
1 tablespoon grated onion

Mix all ingredients and chill.

YIELD: 1 CUP

DILL WEED DIP:
1 teaspoon dill weed
1 teaspoon dill seed (optional)
3 tablespoons instant minced onion
1 cup sour cream
Salt to taste (about ¼ teaspoon)

Recipe continues . . .

Mix all ingredients together. Make ahead of time and refrigerate.

YIELD: 1 CUP

Tested, Tried, and True
THE JUNIOR LEAGUE OF FLINT, MICHIGAN

· · · · · · · · · · · · · · · · · · ·

Cheese Ball

8 ounces cream cheese
½ pound sharp cheddar cheese, shredded
½ teaspoon minced dehydrated onion
2 teaspoons Worcestershire sauce
1 teaspoon lemon juice
1 teaspoon dry mustard
½ teaspoon paprika
½ teaspoon seasoned salt
¼ teaspoon salt
2 tablespoons finely chopped pimento, thoroughly drained
About ⅔ cup finely chopped nuts, preferably pecans

Soften cream cheese in mixer bowl, beating well with electric mixer. Beat in cheddar cheese and remaining ingredients except nuts.

Cover and refrigerate for several hours, or until cheese mixture is firm enough to handle.

Shape cheese into one large ball or two smaller ones and coat evenly with chopped nuts. Wrap in moistureproof material and refrigerate until ready to serve.

YIELD: 1 LARGE OR 2 SMALL BALLS

THE JUNIOR LEAGUE OF CHAMPAIGN-URBANA, ILLINOIS

· · · · · · · · · · · · · · · · · · ·

Holiday Cheese Ball

2 6-ounce jars sharp cheddar cheese, at room temperature
8 ounces cream cheese
3 ounces blue cheese
1 teaspoon Worcestershire sauce
1 green onion, chopped
Pecans, chopped
Parsley

Mix the cheeses together. Beat in Worcestershire sauce and onion. Chill until firm enough to handle. Roll into a ball, then roll in pecans mixed with parsley.

YIELD: 1 LARGE BALL

THE JUNIOR LEAGUE OF CHAMPAIGN-URBANA, ILLINOIS

Cheese and Chutney Spread

8 ounces cream cheese
1 8-ounce package shredded cheddar cheese
1 teaspoon curry powder
½ teaspoon salt
2 tablespoons dry vermouth
1 5-ounce bottle chutney, chopped
4–5 green onions, chopped

Soften cheeses and then blend with curry, salt, and vermouth. Shape on plate any way you wish, but preferably not more than 1 inch thick. Refrigerate.

Just before serving, spread chutney on top and sprinkle with chopped onion. Serve with wheat crackers.

YIELD: 12 SERVINGS

THE JUNIOR LEAGUE OF TOLEDO, OHIO

Olive Curry Spread

1 4½-ounce can ripe olives, chopped
¼ cup sliced green onions
¾ cup shredded cheddar cheese
¼ cup mayonnaise
Dash salt
¼ teaspoon curry powder
2 tablespoons parsley
Party-size rye bread or toast rounds

Mix all ingredients together and spread on snack rye or toast rounds. Bake at 350° for 12 minutes.

YIELD: 36 CANAPÉS

THE JUNIOR LEAGUE OF ST. PAUL, MINNESOTA

· · · · · · · · · · · · · · · · · · · ·

Cream Cheese and Caviar

12 ounces cream cheese, softened
3–4 hard-boiled eggs, chopped
1 teaspoon Worcestershire sauce
¾ tube anchovy paste
1 6-ounce jar red caviar
Lemon juice

Mix all ingredients together except caviar and, using large spoon, work mixture into a nest. Fill center with caviar and sprinkle with lemon juice.
    Serve with crackers or party rye.

YIELD: 8 SERVINGS

THE JUNIOR LEAGUE OF SPRINGFIELD, ILLINOIS

· · · · · · · · · · · · · · · · · · ·

Turner's Alley Shrimp

2-2½ pounds fresh or frozen shrimp
½ cup celery tops
¼ cup mixed pickling spices
1 tablespoon salt
1½ cups salad oil
¾ cup wine vinegar
3 tablespoons capers and juice
2½ teaspoons celery seed
1½ teaspoons salt
Dash Tabasco
2 cups sliced onions
7–8 bay leaves

Simmer shrimp for 5 minutes in boiling water to which celery tops, pickling spices, and 1 tablespoon salt have been added. Cool, shell, and remove intestinal veins.

For pickling marinade, combine salad oil, vinegar, capers and juice, celery seed, 1½ teaspoons salt, and Tabasco. Mix well.

Alternate the shrimp, onions, and bay leaves in shallow glass baking dish or bowl and cover with marinade. Chill at least 24 hours, spooning marinade over shrimp occasionally.

Pickled shrimp, covered with marinade, may be kept in refrigerator at least a week.

If desired, serve with mayonnaise or shrimp sauce.

YIELD: 6–8 SERVINGS

The Cook's Book
THE JUNIOR LEAGUE OF CEDAR RAPIDS, IOWA

Clam Dip

½ green pepper, chopped
1 small onion, chopped
3 tablespoons butter
1 10-ounce can minced clams, drained
¼–½ pound processed cheese
4 tablespoons catsup
1 tablespoon Worcestershire sauce
1 tablespoon sherry
⅛ teaspoon pepper

Sauté green pepper and onion in butter for 5–10 minutes. Add remaining ingredients and stir over low heat until cheese melts.

Keep warm in chafing dish and serve with rye rounds.

YIELD: 8 SERVINGS

THE JUNIOR LEAGUE OF SPRINGFIELD, ILLINOIS

Swiss Seafood Bites

1 6–7-ounce can flaked crabmeat
1 tablespoon sliced green onions
1 cup shredded Swiss cheese
½ cup mayonnaise
1 teaspoon lemon juice
Party rye slices

Combine all ingredients except rye slices. Mix well. Spread on rye slices and broil about 6–8 inches from heat for 3–4 minutes, or until cheese melts and bubbles.

Serve warm.

YIELD: 30 BITES

THE JUNIOR LEAGUE OF SAGINAW, MICHIGAN

Crabmeat Canapés

1 tablespoon minced green onions
3 tablespoons butter
3 tablespoons flour
¾ cup cream or half and half
¼ cup dry vermouth
¾ teaspoon salt
Dash cayenne
½ pound canned or frozen crabmeat, flaked
½ cup grated Parmesan cheese
Toast rounds

Sauté onions in butter until wilted. Blend in flour and gradually add cream and vermouth, stirring constantly until sauce comes to a boil. Cook over low heat for 5 minutes.

Mix in salt, pepper, and crabmeat.

Spread on toast rounds and sprinkle with Parmesan cheese. Bake at 425° for 5 minutes.

YIELD: 8–12 SERVINGS

THE JUNIOR LEAGUE OF SPRINGFIELD, ILLINOIS

· · · · · · · · · · · · · · · · · · · ·

Hot Mushroom Spread

2 medium onions, chopped
¼ pound butter
8 ounces cream cheese, softened
1 pound mushrooms, chopped
¼ teaspoon garlic salt
½ teaspoon Worcestershire sauce

Sauté chopped onions in butter. Add to the cream cheese. Blend well, then

Recipe continues . . .

add chopped mushrooms, garlic salt, and Worcestershire sauce and mix. Spoon into an ovenproof dish and bake at 375° for 15–20 minutes.

Serve hot with crackers or party rye bread. This may be made ahead and heated before serving.

YIELD: 8 SERVINGS

THE JUNIOR LEAGUE OF YOUNGSTOWN, OHIO

· · · · · · · · · · · · · · · · · · · ·

Marinated Mushrooms and Artichokes

½ cup tarragon or red wine vinegar
¼ cup oil
¼ cup chopped parsley
2 teaspoons salt
½ teaspoon thyme
½ teaspoon oregano
¼ teaspoon pepper
⅛ teaspoon garlic powder
1 pound mushrooms, sliced
1 8-ounce can artichoke hearts, drained and quartered
1 medium red onion, sliced

In a large bowl, combine first eight ingredients. Add mushrooms, artichokes, and onion. Marinate, covered, in refrigerator for 24 hours, stirring occasionally.

Drain well and serve on individual plates as a first course.

YIELD: 8–10 SERVINGS

Be Our Guest
THE JUNIOR LEAGUE OF MILWAUKEE, WISCONSIN

· · · · · · · · · · · · · · · · · · ·

Nutty Stuffed Mushrooms

24 medium mushrooms
2 tablespoons butter
1 teaspoon instant minced onion
½ cup dry bread crumbs
¼ cup sliced almonds or brazil nuts
2 strips crisply cooked bacon, crumbled
¼ teaspoon salt
6 tablespoons canned chicken broth or consommé

Rinse and pat dry mushrooms. Remove stems and chop them, reserving caps. Heat butter and in it, sauté stems for 2 minutes. Add onion and sauté 2 minutes longer.

Combine mushroom stems and onion with bread crumbs, nuts, bacon, and salt. Add chicken broth and mix well. Stuff mixture into mushroom caps. Place mushrooms in shallow buttered baking dish. Bake at 350° for 8–10 minutes, or until heated through.

YIELD: 24 MUSHROOMS

THE JUNIOR LEAGUE OF ROCKFORD, ILLINOIS

· · · · · · · · · · · · · · · · · ·

Mushroom Cocktail Strudel

2 tablespoons finely chopped onion
6 tablespoons butter
1 pound mushrooms, finely chopped
Salt and pepper to taste
2 tablespoons sherry
½ teaspoon dried tarragon
½ cup sour cream
½ pound phyllo pastry
1 cup fine dry bread crumbs
½ cup melted butter

Recipe continues . . .

Cook onion in butter until soft. Add mushrooms, salt, pepper, sherry, and tarragon. Cook, stirring occasionally, until most of the liquid has evaporated and the mixture is mushy. Cool slightly. Stir in sour cream.

Spread out one phyllo pastry sheet on work surface and brush with melted butter. Sprinkle with a few bread crumbs and cover with another sheet of pastry. Place some mushroom filling along the long edge and roll up jelly-roll fashion. Brush with melted butter. Repeat with remaining leaves.

Place the rolls on a greased cookie sheet and bake at 375° for 15–20 minutes until golden brown. Cut into 1-inch slices.

YIELD: 10–12 SERVINGS

THE JUNIOR LEAGUE OF INDIANAPOLIS, INDIANA

· · · · · · · · · · · · · · · · · · · ·

Hungarian Pastry Sticks

1 cup warm mashed potatoes
1 cup flour
½ cup butter
½ teaspoon salt
1 egg yolk, slightly beaten
1 tablespoon milk
4 tablespoons sesame seeds
2 teaspoons caraway seeds
3 tablespoons grated Parmesan cheese

In a bowl, mix potatoes, flour, butter, and salt to form a smooth dough. Shape into a ball on a floured board. Roll out ¼ inch thick. Brush dough with beaten egg yolk mixed with milk.

Cut dough into quarters. Sprinkle two sections of dough with sesame seeds and two sections with caraway seeds. Then sprinkle one sesame and one caraway section with grated Parmesan cheese.

Cut into sticks ½ inch wide and 3 inches long. Place on greased baking sheet and bake in preheated 375° oven for 12 minutes.

Serve warm. May be made ahead, refrigerated, and baked when needed.

YIELD: 6 SERVINGS

Tested, Tried, and True
THE JUNIOR LEAGUE OF FLINT, MICHIGAN

· · · · · · · · · · · · · · · · · · · ·

Cheese Batons

⅓ pound Gruyère cheese
12 very thin slices white bread
Dijon mustard

Cut cheese into twelve strips about 3¼ x ⅓ x ⅓-inches. Trim crusts from bread. Flatten slices of bread between sheets of wax paper with a rolling pin. Spread mustard on one side of each slice and arrange cheese strip along one edge of each slice. Roll the slices tightly and roll the rolls in individual squares of foil as tightly as possible.

Chill rolls for at least 1 hour. Remove foil and, in a deep-fat fryer, fry rolls in deep oil (375°) for 2–3 minutes, or until golden. Drain on paper towels and serve hot.

YIELD: 12 BATONS

THE JUNIOR LEAGUE OF KANSAS CITY, KANSAS

· · · · · · · · · · · · · · · · · · · ·

Cheese Blintz Hors D'oeuvres

3–4 slices white bread
8 ounces soft cream cheese, whipped
½ cup melted margarine
Sugar and cinnamon mixture

Recipe continues . . .

Remove crusts from bread. Roll bread with rolling pin to flatten and spread with cream cheese. Roll each slice of bread tightly and cut into two or three pieces.

Dip each piece into melted margarine, then dip into sugar and cinnamon mixture. Bake in a 350° oven for 8–10 minutes, or until brown.

Serve with a dip of applesauce and/or sour cream.

YIELD: 8–12 HORS D'OEUVRES

THE JUNIOR LEAGUE OF ROCKFORD, ILLINOIS

•   •   •   •   •   •   •   •   •   •   •   •   •   •   •   •   •   •   •

Cheese Samplers

1 5-ounce jar sharp cheese spread
¼ cup butter
½ teaspoon salt
¼ teaspoon paprika
½ cup flour
Pimento olives (optional)
Vienna sausage (optional)
Spicy sausage (optional)
Water chestnuts (optional)

Thoroughly cream cheese and butter. Add dry ingredients and mix well. Form balls, either plain or wrapped around one of the optional ingredients.

Chill thoroughly. Place on greased baking sheet and bake for 10 minutes at 400°. These can be frozen. Allow at least 5 more minutes baking time after removal from freezer.

YIELD: 18–20 CANAPÉS

THE JUNIOR LEAGUE OF DES MOINES, IOWA

•   •   •   •   •   •   •   •   •   •   •   •   •   •   •   •   •   •   •

Cheese Bits

45 slices sandwich bread
4 5-ounce jars sharp cheese spread
1 pound margarine or butter
1 teaspoon Tabasco
1 teaspoon onion powder
1½ teaspoons Worcestershire sauce
Dash cayenne
1 teaspoon Beau Monde seasoning
1 teaspoon dill weed

Trim crusts from bread. Beat all remaining ingredients together to make a smooth, soft spread. Using three slices for each sandwich, spread cheese mixture between slices, reserving enough mixture to ice tops and sides, then cut each sandwich into thirds both ways, making nine small cubes.

Ice sides and top of each cube (not bottom). Place on cookie sheets and freeze. Once frozen, store in plastic bags in freezer.

When needed bake at 350° for 20 minutes, or until brown.

YIELD: 135 CANAPÉS

THE JUNIOR LEAGUE OF TOLEDO, OHIO

. . . .

Parmesan Puffs

1 10-ounce package frozen, ready-to-bake patty shells, thawed
1 egg, lightly beaten
½ cup grated Parmesan cheese

Heat oven to 425°. Place patty shells, slightly overlapping, on lightly floured board. Roll out to a 9 x 18-inch rectangle. Brush with egg.

Sprinkle half the pastry with 2 tablespoons of the cheese; fold other half over to form a square. Roll out to a 12 x 16-inch rectangle. Brush

Recipe continues . . .

with egg and sprinkle with remaining cheese. Cut lengthwise into 1¾-inch-wide strips, then cut on a diagonal to make diamond-shaped pieces.

Place pieces ½ inch apart on ungreased cookie sheets. Bake 10–12 minutes, or until puffed and golden brown. Serve hot.

Store in airtight container if made ahead. To reheat, place on cookie sheet and heat at 425° for 5 minutes, or until crisp.

YIELD: 4 DOZEN

THE JUNIOR LEAGUE OF DES MOINES, IOWA

· · · · · · · · · · · · · · · · · · · ·

Cheese Puffs

2 cups shredded sharp cheddar cheese
2 cups shredded mild cheddar cheese
2 cups flour
2 sticks margarine, softened
¼ teaspoon hot red pepper
¼ teaspoon garlic salt

Combine cheeses and stir in flour, margarine, and spices. Mold into small balls about 1 inch in diameter.

Place balls on a cookie sheet and put in freezer. Once frozen, remove and store in plastic bag.

When ready to use, place on cookie sheet and bake in 350° oven until cheese is browned and melted.

YIELD: 36 PUFFS

VARIATION: Place an olive in center of cheese ball before freezing.

THE JUNIOR LEAGUE OF ST. PAUL, MINNESOTA

· · · · · · · · · · · · · · · · · · · ·

Cheese Thing 'A'mabob

2 sticks margarine
2½ cups shredded cheddar cheese
2 cups flour
2 cups crispy rice cereal
2 dashes cayenne

Combine all ingredients and shape into balls the size of marbles. Flatten each ball in palm of hand and arrange on ungreased baking sheet. Bake 4–7 minutes at 475°. Watch!

YIELD: 6 DOZEN

THE JUNIOR LEAGUE OF EVANSVILLE, INDIANA

· · · · · · · · · · · · · · · · · · · ·

Cheesies

2½ cups flour
1 cup butter
1 cup sour cream
1 teaspoon salt
3 cups shredded cheddar cheese
Paprika

Combine flour, butter, and sour cream in mixing bowl. Mix well. Divide into four portions. Chill until firm.

Roll out dough, one portion at a time, into a rectangle 12 x 16 inches. Sprinkle with salt and ¾ cup shredded cheese. Starting with 12-inch side, roll up jelly-roll fashion. Seal edges.

Place seam down on ungreased cookie sheet. Using sharp knife, cut

Recipe continues . . .

rolls halfway through at 1-inch intervals. Sprinkle with paprika. Bake at 350° for 30–35 minutes, or until golden brown. Serve warm.

YIELD: ABOUT 45 APPETIZERS.

Bluff City Cooks
THE JUNIOR LEAGUE OF GREATER ALTON, ILLINOIS

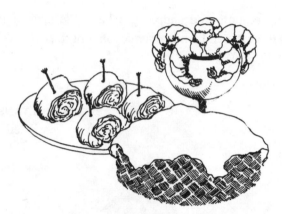

Deviled Nuts

½ pound blanched almonds, pecans, or chestnuts
1½ tablespoons butter
Salt
Paprika
Worcestershire sauce
Tabasco

Sauté nuts in butter in heavy skillet until golden brown, stirring constantly over low heat to prevent burning. Season to taste with remaining ingredients. Toss until coated.

Serve cold.

YIELD: ½ POUND

Bluff City Cooks
THE JUNIOR LEAGUE OF GREATER ALTON, ILLINOIS

Salted Pumpkin Seeds

Pumpkin
Vegetable oil
Salt (optional)

Remove seeds from pumpkin and separate from stringy fibers. Wash seeds, drain, and let dry thoroughly on paper toweling, preferably in the sun, but a warm room is all right. Then put seeds in a bowl and pour just enough vegetable oil over them to coat them. Mix well. Add salt to taste and stir.

Spread oiled seeds on a cookie sheet and put in a 250° oven. Stir occasionally and roast until seeds have begun to turn brown. Remove from oven and turn out onto paper toweling to cool.

VARIATION: If desired add some garlic powder, celery seed, or any other spices and herbs that strike your fancy. Or don't use salt, but instead add sugar or honey and pumpkin pie spice to taste for a sweet treat.

Tested, Tried, and True
THE JUNIOR LEAGUE OF FLINT, MICHIGAN

· · · · · · · · · · · · · · · ·

Cold Filet Appetizer with Sour Cream Sauce

1 carrot, chopped
1 stalk celery, chopped
1 medium onion, chopped
6 tablespoons butter
2 pounds filet of beef
Salt and pepper to taste
1 teaspoon fresh chopped parsley

In a small roasting pan, sauté the carrot, celery, and onion in 2 tablespoons of the butter until the vegetables are soft and the onion transparent.

Recipe continues . . .

Sprinkle the filet with salt, pepper, and chopped parsley. Place the filet on top of the vegetables and dot with the remaining 4 tablespoons butter.

Roast in preheated 500° oven for 20–25 minutes. Remove from the oven and cool in the pan for at least 1 hour. Transfer the meat to a serving platter. Strain and reserve the pan juices.

Cut a V-shaped piece 1-inch deep the entire length of the filet. Fill the resulting trough with Sour Cream Filling. Cover filet with a foil tent and refrigerate for ½ hour. Trim the removed V of meat by cutting off the point of the V, leaving a flat piece of filet. Place the flat piece on top of the filling and refrigerate until ready to serve.

To serve, slice the chilled filet into ½- or ¾-inch slices and garnish the platter with fresh parsley.

SOUR CREAM FILLING:
½ pound bacon, cut in small pieces
1 clove garlic, minced
1 cup sour cream
2 tablespoons pan juices reserved from filet
1 tablespoon grated onion
1 tablespoon chopped chives
1 teaspoon chopped fresh parsley
½ teaspoon horseradish (optional)
¼ teaspoon tarragon
¼ teaspoon dill weed
Salt and white pepper to taste

In a skillet, sauté the bacon with the garlic until the bacon is crisp. Remove the bacon bits with a slotted spoon and drain on paper toweling. In a bowl, combine the sour cream with bacon and remaining ingredients.

YIELD: 10–12 SLICES

Discover Dayton
THE JUNIOR LEAGUE OF DAYTON, OHIO

. . . .

Chicken Wings

¾ cup grated Parmesan cheese
1½ teaspoons parsley
¾ cup herb-seasoned bread crumbs
½ teaspoon garlic salt
16 chicken wings, split at joint
½ cup melted butter

Combine cheese, parsley, bread crumbs, and garlic salt. Dip wings in butter and roll in crumbs mixture. Bake at 350° for 18 minutes or 450° for 15 minutes.

YIELD: 16 APPETIZERS

THE JUNIOR LEAGUE OF DES MOINES, IOWA

· · · · · · · · · · · · · · · · ·

Sweet and Sour Chicken Wings

40 chicken wings
SAUCE:
1 14-ounce bottle catsup
1 8-ounce can tomato sauce
1 cup apple cider vinegar
Dash Worcestershire sauce
1 teaspoon dry mustard
1 teaspoon ginger
1 cup brown sugar
1 cup white sugar

Cut off tips of wings and discard. Cut joints of wings in two and put in rectangular baking dish in a single layer.

Recipe continues . . .

Mix sauce ingredients and pour over wings. Bake, uncovered, at 350° for 2 hours, or until sauce cooks down and the wings are well glazed.

Be sure to have enough sauce to cover the wings before baking. If there isn't enough, fix half the sauce recipe again.

YIELD: 8–10 SERVINGS

Sunflower Sampler
THE JUNIOR LEAGUE OF WICHITA, KANSAS

· ·

Chicken Breast Sandwich

2 tablespoons oil
2 tablespoons butter
4 chicken breasts, halved and skinned
Salt, pepper, and paprika to taste
½ teaspoon salt
¼ teaspoon pepper
¼ teaspoon paprika
⅛ teaspoon garlic salt
½ pound fresh mushrooms, sliced
⅔ cup white wine
3 tablespoons cornstarch
½ cup cold water
8 slices Canadian bacon
8 bread rounds

In the oil and butter, brown chicken seasoned with salt, pepper, and paprika. Remove chicken to a covered casserole and bake in a 350° oven for ½ hour, or until chicken is tender.

Meanwhile, add the additional salt, pepper, and paprika, and the garlic salt and mushrooms to the fat remaining in frying pan. Stir in wine.

Dissolve cornstarch in water and slowly stir into the wine mixture. Stir gently and simmer until thick. Add additional water to give proper consistency to gravy (about ¾ cup).

Brown bacon and toast bread rounds. Bone chicken breast.

On each plate place a toast round; top with a slice of bacon and a chicken breast. Spoon gravy over all and serve.

YIELD: 8 SERVINGS

Bluff City Cooks
THE JUNIOR LEAGUE OF GREATER ALTON, ILLINOIS

· · · · · · · · · · · · · · · · · · · ·

Midwest Pizza

1 10-ounce package frozen patty shells
¼ cup chopped green onions
1 tablespoon butter or margarine
½ cup canned spaghetti or pizza sauce
½ teaspoon oregano
1 egg yolk
1 teaspoon water
16 slices pepperoni
8–10 ounces cooked ham, shaved or thinly sliced
8–10 ounces mozzarella cheese, cut in ½-inch strips

Thaw patty shells slightly, about 30 minutes. Place patty shells in two slightly overlapping rows on a lightly floured board. Roll into a 16 x 9-inch rectangle. Cut into two strips, 16 x 5 and 16 x 4 inches. Place both strips on a cookie sheet and chill.

Recipe continues . . .

Sauté onion in butter until soft. Add spaghetti sauce and oregano; cook until slightly thick, about 5 minutes.

Mix egg yolk with water and brush mixture down center of 16 x 4-inch dough strip. Spoon sauce down center, leaving 1-inch margin around edges. Next layer pepperoni, ham, and cheese on strip. Carefully place 16 x 5-inch strip on top, pressing top and bottom edges together with a fork. Brush top with egg yolk mixture. Make three or four slits in top pastry. Bake in 425° oven for 25 minutes, or until golden brown.

May also be prepared a few hours ahead, covered with a damp cloth, and refrigerated.

Delicious served with a green salad as a late supper dish or cut into narrow slices as an appetizer.

YIELD: 10–12 FOR APPETIZER; 4 FOR LUNCH OR SUPPER

THE JUNIOR LEAGUE OF INDIANAPOLIS, INDIANA

· · · · · · · · · · · · · · · · · · · ·

Barbecued Ham On Egg Rolls

¾ cup onion, chopped
⅓ cup celery, chopped
1 clove garlic, minced
½ cup butter
3 tablespoons parsley flakes
1 bay leaf
3 tablespoons Worcestershire sauce
⅛ teaspoon thyme
1 tablespoon vinegar
¼ teaspoon allspice
1 14-ounce bottle catsup
1 cup water
5 pound ham, sliced wafer-thin
100 cocktail egg roll buns

To make the saute: sauté the onion, celery, and garlic in butter until tender Add parsley, bay leaf, Worcestershire sauce, thyme, vinegar, allspice, catsup, and water. Cook all together in deep kettle for at least ½ hour. May simmer 2–3 hours or it can be made the day before and then reheated.

Add meat and simmer for 2 more hours.

Serve in cocktail egg roll buns.

YIELD: 50 SERVINGS (2 ROLLS EACH)

Sunflower Sampler
THE JUNIOR LEAGUE OF WICHITA, KANSAS

Chipped Ham Barbecue Sandwich Spread

¼ cup vinegar
½ teaspoon dry mustard
2 tablespoons water
2 tablespoons dark jelly such as blackberry
¼ teaspoon paprika
2 tablespoons brown sugar
¾ cup catsup
1 pound spiced ham, chopped

Mix all ingredients and heat.

YIELD: FILLING FOR 12 SANDWICHES

THE JUNIOR LEAGUE OF YOUNGSTOWN, OHIO

Puffed Open-face Sandwiches

2 tablespoons butter
1 tablespoon prepared horseradish
4 slices raisin bread
½ pound corned beef or ham, thinly sliced
½ cup mayonnaise
1 teaspoon prepared mustard
1 cup shredded cheddar cheese
½ teaspoon Worcestershire sauce
3 tablespoons chopped ripe olives
2 tablespoons finely chopped green onions

Combine butter and horseradish; spread on bread. Cover with corned beef or ham.

Combine rest of ingredients and spread evenly on top of the four open-face sandwiches. Broil until cheese melts.

YIELD: 4 SERVINGS

THE JUNIOR LEAGUE OF INDIANAPOLIS, INDIANA

·　·　·　·　·　·　·　·　·　·　·　·　·　·　·

Baked Corned Beef Sandwich Loaf

1 1-pound loaf white bread, unsliced
1 cup mayonnaise or mayonnaise-type salad dressing
2 tablespoons prepared mustard
1 tablespoon horseradish
2 12-ounce cans corned beef, chilled
½ pound Swiss cheese, sliced
2 cups sauerkraut, well drained
Melted butter

Cut bread in twenty slices, almost but not through bottom crust. Combine mayonnaise, mustard, and horseradish; spread facing sides of every other slice with mixture. Cut each can of corned beef into five slices; insert a corned beef slice, cheese slice, and sauerkraut in each sandwich.

Tie loaf with string; brush top and sides with melted butter or margarine. Place on baking sheet and toast at 350° for 20–25 minutes.

Cut through unbuttered slices to serve.

YIELD: 10 SANDWICHES

Peacock Pie and Other Perfections
THE JUNIOR LEAGUE OF BATTLE CREEK, MICHIGAN

. . . .

Heywood's Beef Barbecue

3 pounds beef chuck roast
Water
1 teaspoon salt
½ teaspoon pepper
1 large onion, chopped
1 cup chopped celery, including leaves
1 teaspoon garlic salt
1 bay leaf
1 teaspoon chili powder
1 clove garlic, minced
2 medium onions, chopped
¼ cup butter or margarine
¼ cup brown sugar
¼ cup lemon juice
¼ cup vinegar
2 cups canned tomatoes
1 8-ounce can tomato purée
⅛ teaspoon red pepper
2 teaspoons chili powder
1 teaspoon prepared mustard
1 cup chopped celery
Several drops liquid smoke (optional)
Tabasco to taste

Recipe continues . . .

Put beef in deep pan; add water to 1 inch above meat. Add salt, pepper, 1 onion, 1 cup celery, garlic salt, bay leaf, and chili powder. Bring to a rapid boil, then simmer 2–3 hours.

Pour half the liquid from pan, reserving liquid. Cool, then shred meat, discarding gristle and fat. Put meat with half the liquid in shallow 3-quart baking dish.

To make sauce, combine remaining ingredients with 1 cup liquid reserved from meat in a 1½-quart saucepan, bring to a boil, and simmer for 40 minutes. Pour sauce over meat and bake at 350° until most of liquid is absorbed.

This can be made three days before serving and it freezes well. The sauce is also good with spareribs baked in the oven or grilled.

YIELD: 16–18 SANDWICHES

Cincinnati Celebrates
THE JUNIOR LEAGUE OF CINCINNATI, OHIO

· · · · · · · · · · · · · · · ·

Stroganoff Steak Sandwiches

⅔ cup beer
⅓ cup salad oil
1 teaspoon salt
¼ teaspoon garlic powder
¼ teaspoon pepper
1 2-pound flank steak
2 tablespoons butter
½ teaspoon paprika
Dash salt
4 cups sliced onions
12 slices French bread, toasted
1 cup warm sour cream
1 teaspoon prepared horseradish
Paprika

Combine beer, oil, salt, garlic powder, and pepper. Place flank steak in mixture, cover, and marinate overnight in refrigerator; drain.

Broil steak 3 inches from heat for 5–7 minutes on each side for medium-rare.

Meanwhile, melt butter; blend in paprika and dash salt. Add sliced onions. Cook until tender but not brown.

To serve, slice meat on the diagonal across grain. For each serving, arrange meat slices over two slices toasted French bread. Top with cooked onions. Combine warm sour cream with horseradish; spoon mixture onto sandwiches and sprinkle with paprika.

YIELD: 6 SERVINGS

Cincinnati Celebrates
THE JUNIOR LEAGUE OF CINCINNATI, OHIO

· · · · · · · · · · · · · · · · · · · ·

Stromboli Sandwiches

2 pounds ground beef
2 tablespoons chopped onion
1 cup tomato sauce
1 cup catsup
4 tablespoons Parmesan cheese
¼ teaspoon garlic powder
½ teaspoon fennel seed
¼ teaspoon oregano
12 slices mozzarella cheese
12 hamburger buns

Recipe continues . . .

Brown beef and onion. Add all ingredients except mozzarella cheese. Cook 20 minutes.

Put meat mixture and mozzarella cheese on hamburger buns and wrap in foil. Heat in 350° oven for 15 minutes.

YIELD: 12 SANDWICHES

THE JUNIOR LEAGUE OF DES MOINES, IOWA

· · · · · · · · · · · · · · · · · · ·

Sloppy Joes

1 pound ground beef
½ medium onion, finely chopped
1 10½-ounce can chicken gumbo soup, drained
¼–½ cup catsup
1 teaspoon prepared mustard
½ teaspoon salt
¼ teaspoon pepper
¼ teaspoon garlic powder
Dash Tabasco (optional)

Brown beef and onion together in a skillet. Drain off excess fat. Drain and reserve liquid from can of soup. Add soup and remaining ingredients. Simmer 10 minutes.

Serve on buns with pickles, mustard, and catsup.

If you want sloppier Sloppy Joes, add about ¼ cup of the reserved liquid.

YIELD: 4–8 SERVINGS

THE JUNIOR LEAGUE OF KANSAS CITY, KANSAS

· · · · · · · · · · · · · · · · · · ·

Paul Bunyan Burgers

1 pound ground beef
1 6-ounce can tomato paste
1 1½-ounce package sloppy joe seasoning mix
1¼ cups water
¼ cup grated Parmesan cheese
½ teaspoon oregano
1 loaf Italian bread
1 6-ounce package mozzarella cheese slices

Brown ground beef and spoon off excess fat. Add tomato paste, seasoning mix, water, Parmesan cheese, and oregano. Mix well. Bring to a boil, stirring constantly. Reduce heat and simmer 10 minutes.

Cut lengthwise slice from top of bread and reserve. Scoop out center of loaf to form a shell. Cut mozzarella slices in half and place half of them on the bottom of shell; fill with beef mixture. Cover with remaining cheese slices and top with the reserved slice of bread. Wrap in foil. Bake at 400° for 8–10 minutes.

Cut into sandwiches.

YIELD: 6 SERVINGS

THE JUNIOR LEAGUE OF INDIANAPOLIS, INDIANA

·   ·   ·   ·   ·   ·   ·   ·   ·   ·   ·   ·   ·   ·   ·   ·   ·   ·

Chili Burgers

1 onion, chopped
1 pound ground beef
⅓ cup cider vinegar
1 tablespoon Worcestershire sauce
1 teaspoon dry mustard
2 tablespoons sugar
½ cup catsup
¾ teaspoon salt
¼ teaspoon chili powder (or more to taste)

Recipe continues . . .

Brown together onion and beef. Pour off excess fat and add remaining ingredients. Simmer, uncovered, 30 minutes.

Serve on hamburger buns.

YIELD: 8 SERVINGS

THE JUNIOR LEAGUE OF SPRINGFIELD, ILLINOIS

· ·

Corn Dogs or "Pronto Pups"

¾ cup yellow corn meal
1 teaspoon salt
2 tablespoons sugar
¾ cup boiling water
1 egg
½ cup milk
2 tablespoons shortening, melted
1 cup flour
1½ teaspoons baking powder
1 quart vegetable oil
16 (2 pounds) hot dogs
16 wooden skewers

Combine corn meal, salt, and sugar. Slowly stir in boiling water, cover, and let stand for 10 minutes. Beat egg, milk, and shortening; add to corn meal mixture. Sift flour and baking powder; stir into batter with a minimum of strokes.

Heat oil to 375°, or until a drop of water splatters when dropped into it. Spread batter evenly over each hot dog; drop gently into hot fat and let brown, turning with tongs. (Do about three at a time.)

Drain and keep warm in a low oven (200°) until all are ready.

Serve on wooden skewers with condiments.

YIELD: 8 SERVINGS

Cookbook
THE JUNIOR LEAGUE OF GRAND RAPIDS, MICHIGAN

· ·

Easy Sandwich Filling

½ pound medium-sharp cheese
4–6 strips bacon, fried
2 hard-boiled eggs
½ green pepper (optional)
1 small onion
⅓ bottle chili sauce
6–8 hamburger buns

Grind together all ingredients except chili sauce. Mix ground ingredients with chili sauce.

Broil on half buns.

Serve hot.

YIELD: 6–8 SERVINGS

THE JUNIOR LEAGUE OF YOUNGSTOWN, OHIO

·   ·   ·   ·   ·   ·   ·   ·   ·   ·   ·   ·   ·   ·   ·   ·   ·   ·   ·

Cheese-filled Coneys

6 hard-boiled eggs, chopped
1 6-ounce can tomato paste
½ pound American cheese, shredded
1 8-ounce can ripe pitted olives, chopped
½ cup finely chopped onion
18 coney buns

Mix first five ingredients together in mixing bowl. Fill buns with mixture and wrap in wax paper. Bake at 300° for 20 minutes.

If freezing is desired, do so before baking.

YIELD: 18 CONEYS

THE JUNIOR LEAGUE OF DES MOINES, IOWA

·   ·   ·   ·   ·   ·   ·   ·   ·   ·   ·   ·   ·   ·   ·   ·   ·   ·   ·

Frosted Sandwich Loaf

1 day-old loaf sandwich bread, unsliced
Butter
2 cups egg salad filling
2 cups ham filling
2 cups chicken salad filling
9 ounces cream cheese, softened
5 tablespoons light cream
Hard-boiled eggs, almonds, and parsley for garnish

Remove crusts from bread and slice loaf lengthwise into four slices. Butter one side of three slices and set aside.

Make the three fillings.

Spread one slice of buttered bread with egg salad filling, top with second slice of buttered bread and spread with ham filling. Top with third slice of buttered bread and spread with chicken salad filling. Top with the unbuttered slice of bread.

Beat cream cheese and cream until mixture is soft and fluffy and frost top and sides of the sandwich loaf. Decorate as desired with slices of hard-boiled eggs, almonds, and parsley.

Chill loaf for several hours before serving. It will keep in the refrigerator for several days but cannot be frozen.

YIELD: 12 SERVINGS

The Discovery Shop Cookbook
THE JUNIOR LEAGUE OF SIOUX CITY, IOWA

Hot Tuna Salad on Bun

¼ pound (1 cup) American cheese, cubed
3 hard-boiled eggs
1 7-ounce can tuna
2 tablespoons chopped onion
¼ cup pickle relish
½ cup mayonnaise
8 hamburger buns

Combine cheese, eggs, tuna, onion, relish, and mayonnaise and mix lightly. Split hamburger buns and fill with mixture. Place in shallow pan and cover with aluminum foil.

Heat in 250° oven for 30 minutes.

YIELD: 8 SERVINGS

THE JUNIOR LEAGUE OF KANSAS CITY, KANSAS

·   ·   ·   ·   ·   ·   ·   ·   ·   ·   ·   ·   ·   ·   ·   ·   ·   ·

Broiled Tuna and Cheese Sandwich

2 tablespoons French dressing
3 ounces cream cheese
1 7-ounce can tuna
6–8 rusks
2 tomatoes, sliced
6–8 slices American cheese
Stuffed olives for garnish

Blend together the French dressing and cream cheese. Mix in the tuna.

Recipe continues . . .

Spread on rusks slices and top each with a tomato slice. Broil about 5 minutes, not too close to heat. Top with cheese slices and broil until the cheese melts.

Garnish with olives.

YIELD: 6–8 SERVINGS

THE JUNIOR LEAGUE OF SPRINGFIELD, ILLINOIS

Soups

Sleepy Legume Soup (13 Bean Soup)

4 quarts water
1½ cups dried navy beans
1½ cups dried great northern beans
1 tablespoon dried split peas
1 tablespoon dried black-eyed peas
1 tablespoon dried kidney beans
1 tablespoon dried gazpacho beans
1 tablespoon dried marrow beans
1 tablespoon dried cranberry beans
1 tablespoon dried pinto beans
1 tablespoon dried mung beans
1 tablespoon dried black beans
2 tablespoons dried lima beans
1 tablespoon lentils
1 tablespoon barley
12–15 peppercorns
4–5 carrots, diced
4–5 celery stalks, diced
4 tablespoons sugar or 6 tablespoons honey
1 clove garlic, minced
3 bay leaves
2 onions, chopped
2 tomatoes, peeled and chopped
1 pound smoked ham or salt pork, diced and lightly sautéed
Salt and pepper
Milk or water

Bring water to a rapid boil (no salt added). Keep it boiling rapidly while gradually adding all the beans, lentils, and barley. Boil covered for 1–2 hours. Add peppercorns, carrots, celery, sugar or honey, garlic, bay leaves, onions, and tomatoes and continue boiling at least 1 hour, adding additional boiling water if needed. Remove from heat and let beans soak in the liquid overnight.

If beans are soft, take one-third and put through food mill or food processor until almost puréed and return to soup. If beans are not soft, continue to boil until they are and then proceed similarly.

Slowly bring back to the boil and add smoked ham or salt pork. Simmer for at least 1 hour longer. Add salt and pepper to taste (needs *very* little salt). Thin with milk or boiling water if necessary.

Freezes well in ½-gallon containers.

YIELD: 24–30 SERVINGS

THE JUNIOR LEAGUE OF COLUMBUS, OHIO

·   ·   ·   ·   ·   ·   ·   ·   ·   ·   ·   ·   ·   ·   ·   ·   ·   ·

Midwestern Chili Bean Soup

1½ pounds ground beef
1 medium onion, chopped
1 28-ounce can tomatoes
1 1-pound can tomato sauce
¾ cup water
2 1-pound cans chili beans
½ teaspoon salt
¼ teaspoon paprika or cayenne

Cook ground beef and onion in saucepan until meat loses color and onion is transparent. Add tomatoes, tomato sauce, water, and chili beans. Add salt, paprika or cayenne, and other seasonings to taste.

Simmer for at least 1 hour.

YIELD: 6 SERVINGS

THE JUNIOR LEAGUE OF EVANSVILLE, INDIANA

·   ·   ·   ·   ·   ·   ·   ·   ·   ·   ·   ·   ·   ·   ·   ·   ·   ·

Beef-Noodle Soup with Caraway Dumplings

1½ pounds very meaty beef soup bones
8 cups water
1 onion, sliced
1 bunch celery tops and leaves, unchopped
1 stalk celery, sliced
2 teaspoons salt
2 cloves garlic, minced
2 bay leaves
½ teaspoon savory
¼ teaspoon pepper
1 cup uncooked noodles
½ cup (or more) frozen peas

CARAWAY DUMPLINGS:
1 cup flour
1 tablespoon parsley flakes
1½ teaspoons baking powder
1 teaspoon caraway seeds
¼ teaspoon salt
1½ tablespoons margarine
½ cup milk

In kettle, combine bones, water, onion, celery tops and leaves, sliced celery, and seasonings. Cover and simmer for 3 hours or until meat is very tender.

Discard bones, bay leaves, and most celery tops. Add noodles and peas.

For dumplings, mix flour, parsley, baking powder, caraway seeds, and salt; cut in margarine until mixture is crumbly. Add milk; stir just until moistened. Drop 6 spoonfuls of dumpling batter on top of bubbling soup. Cover and steam for 15 minutes; do not peek.

YIELD: 6 SERVINGS

Soupçon
THE JUNIOR LEAGUE OF CHICAGO, ILLINOIS

Ski Warmer-Upper

1½ pounds soup bones
1 pound beef brisket or other soup meat, trimmed and
cut into bite-size cubes
2 tablespoons shortening
4 cups water
1 1-pound can tomatoes
1 cup chopped onion
2 tablespoons minced parsley
1½ tablespoons sugar
1 clove garlic, minced
½ bay leaf, crumbled
2 teaspoons salt
1 teaspoon celery salt
¼ teaspoon crushed basil
¼ teaspoon paprika
¼ teaspoon pepper
½ medium cabbage, shredded (about 2 cups)
1 large fresh beet, peeled and diced
½ cup lemon juice
½ cup sour cream
Freshly ground pepper

Brown meat cut from bones and the brisket in hot shortening in a large kettle. Add bones, water, tomatoes, onion, and next nine ingredients. Simmer, covered, 1½–2 hours, or until meat is tender. Discard bones.

Add cabbage, beet, and lemon juice. Cover and cook 30 minutes longer, or until vegetables are tender.

Ladle into large soup bowls. Top with a spoonful of sour cream, then sprinkle with freshly ground pepper.

YIELD: 4–6 SERVINGS

THE JUNIOR LEAGUE OF ST. PAUL, MINNESOTA

Quick Beet Soup

2 1-pound cans undrained julienne-style beets
2 10½-ounce cans beef broth
1 tablespoon chopped fresh dill
2 tablespoons instant minced onion
1 cup chopped raw cabbage
1 clove garlic, minced
1½ teaspoons salt
6 tablespoons lemon juice
3 tablespoons light brown sugar
1½ cups water
Sour cream

In a 6-quart saucepan, combine beets, broth, dill, onion, cabbage, garlic, salt, lemon juice, sugar, and water. Over medium heat, bring to a boil. Reduce heat and simmer, uncovered, for 15 minutes.

Serve hot, each serving topped with a spoonful of sour cream.

YIELD: ABOUT 8 CUPS

THE JUNIOR LEAGUE OF SAGINAW, MICHIGAN

· · · · · · · · · · · · · · · · · · · ·

Korean Brisket Soup

1 pound beef brisket
3 quarts (12 cups) water
2–4 green onions, chopped
2½ tablespoons soy sauce
½ teaspoon monosodium glutamate
½ teaspoon minced garlic
½ tablespoon toasted sesame seeds
1½ tablespoon sesame oil
Dash pepper
Additional chopped green onions for garnish

Cover brisket with the water. Simmer over low heat about 2 hours, skimming off scum as it forms.

When meat is tender, remove and cut into thin pieces. Return meat to broth and add remaining ingredients. Bring to a boil, adding more soy sauce and salt to taste.

Garnish each serving with green onions.

YIELD: 4 SERVINGS

THE JUNIOR LEAGUE OF KANSAS CITY, KANSAS

·   ·   ·   ·   ·   ·   ·   ·   ·   ·   ·   ·   ·   ·   ·   ·   ·   ·   ·   ·

Broccoli Chowder

2 pounds fresh broccoli
2 12½-ounce cans chicken broth
3 cups milk
1 cup chopped, cooked ham
2 teaspoons salt
¼ teaspoon pepper
1 cup half and half
½ pound Swiss cheese, shredded
¼ cup butter

Cook broccoli, covered, in 1 can chicken broth until tender. Remove broccoli from broth. Cool. Chop coarsely.

Add remaining chicken broth, milk, ham, salt, and pepper and bring to a boil. Stir in remaining ingredients and the chopped broccoli.

Heat to serving temperature.

YIELD: 2½ QUARTS

THE JUNIOR LEAGUE OF FARGO-MOORHEAD, NORTH DAKOTA/MINNESOTA

·   ·   ·   ·   ·   ·   ·   ·   ·   ·   ·   ·   ·   ·   ·   ·   ·   ·   ·   ·

Cream of Broccoli Soup

½ cup chopped onion
2 stalks celery, finely chopped
4 tablespoons butter
2 bunches broccoli, trimmed
1 quart beef bouillon
1½ teaspoons salt
½ teaspoon Tabasco
1½ cups half and half
Fresh parsley for garnish

Sauté onion and celery in butter in large heavy saucepan.

Cut broccoli in 2- to 3-inch pieces. Add broccoli, bouillon, salt, and Tabasco to sautéed vegetables. Simmer 20 minutes over medium heat. Purée in blender.

Before serving, stir in half and half and heat gently. Garnish with sprig of fresh parsley.

YIELD: 2 QUARTS

Be Our Guest
THE JUNIOR LEAGUE OF MILWAUKEE, WISCONSIN

Cheese Soup

2 tablespoons butter
1 tablespoon flour
2½ cups milk
¾ cup shredded sharp cheddar cheese
2 tablespoons shredded carrot
2 tablespoons finely chopped green pepper
2 tablespoons finely chopped celery
2 tablespoons grated onion
2 cups chicken stock
Salt and pepper to taste
Paprika

In saucepan, melt butter; stir in flour. Gradually stir in milk and cheese and cook, stirring, until cheese sauce is smooth and thickened.

In the meantime, cook the vegetables in the chicken stock until tender.

Combine sauce and vegetables and correct seasoning with salt and pepper. Sprinkle each serving with paprika.

YIELD: 6 SERVINGS

THE JUNIOR LEAGUE OF SAGINAW, MICHIGAN

Beer-Cheese Soup

¼ cup chopped onion
2 tablespoons butter
2 tablespoons flour
1 tablespoon cornstarch
⅛ teaspoon paprika
½ teaspoon salt
Dash white pepper
2 cups milk
2 cups chicken broth
½ cup diced sharp cheddar cheese
2 tablespoons chopped parsley
¾–1 cup beer or to taste

Sauté onion in butter until onion is wilted. Stir in next five ingredients to make a thick paste (roux). Gradually stir in milk and broth. Simmer 15 minutes. To this point, soup can be made ahead.

Before serving, reheat and stir in cheese. Add parsley and beer to taste.

YIELD: 4 SERVINGS

THE JUNIOR LEAGUE OF ST. PAUL, MINNESOTA

· · · · · · · · · · · · · · · ·

Chicken Soup

2½ pounds chicken pieces
1 onion, chopped
3 potatoes, diced
4 carrots, sliced
2 stalks celery, sliced
3 tablespoons soy sauce
½ teaspoon Tabasco
1 teaspoon salt
3½ cups water

Combine all ingredients in a slow cooker. Set temperature on "low"; cook 10–12 hours.

Discard bones and dice chicken meat before serving.

YIELD: 6–8 SERVINGS

THE JUNIOR LEAGUE OF EVANSVILLE, INDIANA

· ·

Chicken Spaghetti

1 large, fat chicken
½ lemon
1 large onion, coarsely chopped
6 cloves
1 tablespoon salt
2 large onions, chopped
3 cloves garlic, minced
2 tablespoons butter
1 pint tomato juice
½ pound mushrooms, chopped
1 1-pound 2-ounce can peas
Salt and cayenne to taste
8–12 ounces spaghetti
Grated Parmesan cheese (optional)

Boil chicken in plenty of water seasoned with the lemon, the coarsely chopped onion, cloves, and 1 tablespoon salt.

After chicken is done, remove from bones and cut in small pieces. You should have at least 1 quart of liquid left in the pot the chicken was boiled in.

For the sauce: sauté the chopped onions and garlic in butter until lightly browned. Add tomato juice, mushrooms, peas, salt, and cayenne. Add the chicken liquid and the chicken. Heat until blended.

Meanwhile, cook the spaghetti in boiling salted water until tender. Drain and add to soup. Serve cheese on the side if desired.

Recipe continues . . .

This is more of a soup than a spaghetti dish, so the amount of spaghetti you use depends on how much you want in each bowl.

YIELD: 4–6 SERVINGS

THE JUNIOR LEAGUE OF ST. PAUL, MINNESOTA

. . . .

Hearty Clam Chowder

4 slices bacon, diced
3 green onions and tops, chopped
5 medium-size potatoes, peeled and cut into ½-inch cubes
1 stalk celery, sliced
1 carrot, finely sliced
1 clove garlic, mashed or minced
2 cups water
1 teaspoon salt
½ teaspoon pepper
1 teaspoon Worcestershire sauce
4 drops Tabasco
2 cups chopped clams with juice
1 pint light cream

In a large heavy kettle, sauté bacon until crisp; add green onions and tops, potatoes, celery, carrot, and garlic. Pour in water and season with salt, pepper, Worcestershire sauce, and Tabasco. Cover and simmer 15 minutes, or until potatoes are tender. Mash mixture slightly with a potato masher.

In a separate pan, heat clams in their juice for 3 minutes or until tender. Add clams to vegetable mixture and pour in cream. Stir well, then heat just until piping hot, but do not boil.

Good with dark bread, a tray of cheese, and a bowl of fruit on a cold winter evening.

YIELD: 4 SERVINGS AS A MAIN COURSE

The Discovery Shop Cookbook
THE JUNIOR LEAGUE OF SIOUX CITY, IOWA

. . . .

Quick Clam Chowder

6 slices bacon, diced
1 medium onion, chopped
2 stalks celery, chopped
½ cup flour
4 cups milk
2 7½-ounce cans minced clams with juice
½ teaspoon dill weed
Salt and pepper to taste
1 1-pound bag frozen hash brown potatoes

Sauté bacon until almost done, add onion and celery, and cook until vegetables are tender. Stir in flour and cook over low heat but don't allow to brown. Slowly add milk and stir until boiling.

Add clams and juice and seasonings. Return to boil. Simmer for 15 minutes. Add potatoes and simmer 15 minutes more.

YIELD: 6 SERVINGS

Tested, Tried, and True
THE JUNIOR LEAGUE OF FLINT, MICHIGAN

. . . .

Corn Chowder

4 slices bacon, finely chopped
1 medium onion, thinly sliced
4 cups peeled, diced potatoes
1 cup water
4 cups fresh corn kernels or 2 10-ounce packages frozen corn, defrosted
1 cup heavy cream
1 teaspoon sugar
½ stick butter
2½ teaspoons salt
¼ teaspoon white pepper
2 cups milk

Recipe continues . . .

Sauté bacon until crisp. Add onion, potatoes, and the water. Cover, bring to boil, and simmer 10 minutes, or until potatoes are tender but not mushy. Remove cover and set aside.

In medium saucepan, combine corn, cream, sugar, and butter. Simmer, covered, over low heat for 10 minutes.

Add to potato mixture with remaining ingredients. Cook, stirring occasionally, over low heat until heated through. *Do not boil.*

YIELD: 4 SERVINGS

THE JUNIOR LEAGUE OF FARGO-MOORHEAD, NORTH DAKOTA/MINNESOTA

Crab Bisque

1 tablespoon onion, finely chopped
1 tablespoon butter
¼ teaspoon dry mustard
1 tablespoon flour
1 7-ounce can crab flakes
2 cups milk
1 cup light cream
1 hard-boiled egg, minced
1 teaspoon salt
1 teaspoon parsley
½ cup sherry (or to taste)

Sauté onion in butter until onion is tender. Stir in mustard and flour to make a roux. Stir in remaining ingredients, bring to a simmer, and cook over low heat for 5 minutes.

If desired, reserve some of the egg and/or parsley to garnish.

YIELD: 3 LARGE SERVINGS

THE JUNIOR LEAGUE OF ST. PAUL, MINNESOTA

Curry Consommé

1 small apple
1 medium onion, chopped
⅛ teaspoon curry powder (or to taste)
2 tablespoons butter or margarine
2 10½-ounce cans condensed beef consommé
1 cup cream for whipping
Chopped parsley for garnish

Pare, halve, core, and chop the apple. Sauté with onion and curry powder in butter or margarine until onion is soft.

Spoon into an electric blender container. Add 1 can of the consommé. Cover and blend on high speed for several minutes, or until smooth. Pour back into saucepan. Stir in remaining can of consommé and cream. Heat slowly until hot.

Serve in cups with a sprinkling of chopped parsley for color.

YIELD: 6 SERVINGS

Tested, Tried, and True
THE JUNIOR LEAGUE OF FLINT, MICHIGAN

· ·

Easy Michigan Gazpacho

2 cucumbers, peeled and seeded
2 avocados, peeled and seeded
1 red onion
5 cups tomato juice
3 tablespoons salad oil
2 tablespoons wine vinegar
Limes

Recipe continues ...

Finely chop the cucumbers, avocados, and red onion. Add the vegetables to the tomato juice mixed with the salad oil and wine vinegar.

Chill for several hours and serve with lime wedges.

YIELD: 6 SERVINGS

THE JUNIOR LEAGUE OF SAGINAW, MICHIGAN

Fruit Soup

5 cups water
6 tablespoons quick tapioca
⅔ cup sugar
Dash salt
1 16-ounce can sliced peaches and juice
2 8-ounce cans mandarin oranges, drained
1 12-ounce package frozen strawberries and juice
1 16-ounce can grapefruit sections and juice
2–3 bananas, sliced

Bring half the water to a rolling boil. Stir in tapioca, sugar, and salt and cook, stirring, for 3 minutes. Add remaining water and the fruit.

Chill thoroughly and stir before serving. May be served at brunch from a punch bowl.

YIELD: 1 GALLON

The Discovery Shop Cookbook
THE JUNIOR LEAGUE OF SIOUX CITY, IOWA

Greek Egg-Lemon Soup

6 cups chicken broth
½ cup rice
1 teaspoon salt
6 eggs
2 tablespoons water
Juice of 1½ lemons
Parsley for garnish

Combine chicken broth, rice, and salt in a large saucepan. Bring to a boil, then reduce the heat. Cover and simmer until the rice is just tender. Long-grain rice should cook in 15 minutes. Remove pan from heat.

In a bowl, beat eggs until fluffy and pale yellow, adding water. Beat in lemon juice. Slowly pour about 2 cups of the hot broth into the egg-lemon mixture, beating vigorously so the eggs don't curdle.

Pour this mixture back into the rest of the broth and stir over low heat 1 minute. Remove from heat, stirring occasionally, until ready to serve.

Garnish each serving with a sprig of parsley; serve with cheese crackers.

YIELD: 6–8 SERVINGS

Tested, Tried, and True
THE JUNIOR LEAGUE OF FLINT, MICHIGAN

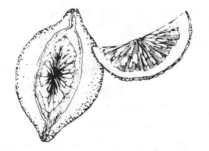

Minestrone Soup al Pesto

1 7-ounce package minestrone soup mix
5 slices bacon, diced
1 large onion, chopped
1 cup diced carrots
1 cup diced celery
2 10½-ounce cans beef consommé
2 10½-ounce soup cans water
1 soup bone
Salt and pepper to taste
1 clove garlic, minced
1 cup elbow macaroni, ditalini, or thin spaghetti
1 1-pound jar Italian cooking sauce
1 16-ounce can Italian-style zucchini, diced

Follow instructions for soaking the minestrone soup mix.

In a large pot, combine bacon, onion, carrots, celery, beef broth, water, soup bone, salt, pepper, and garlic. Simmer for about 45 minutes. Add minestrone soup mix and cook until beans are tender. Add spaghetti, Italian cooking sauce, and zucchini and simmer about 25 minutes longer.

Top each serving of hot soup with a large dab of Pesto.

YIELD: ABOUT 3½ QUARTS

PESTO:
¼ cup soft butter
¼ cup grated Parmesan cheese
½ cup finely chopped parsley
1 clove garlic, minced
1 teaspoon basil
¼ teaspoon marjoram
¼ cup olive oil
¼ cup chopped pine nuts or walnuts

Thoroughly blend butter with cheese, parsley, garlic, basil, and marjoram.

Use a mortar and pestle if available and gradually work in oil and nuts to make a smooth paste.

THE JUNIOR LEAGUE OF INDIANAPOLIS, INDIANA

· · · · · · · · · · · · · · · · · ·

Cream of Mushroom Soup

1½ pounds fresh mushrooms
9 tablespoons butter
2 scallions, finely chopped
6 tablespoons flour
6 cups fresh or canned chicken stock
2 egg yolks
¾ cup heavy cream
Salt
White pepper

Separate caps and stems of mushrooms. Slice half of the caps ⅛ inch thick. Chop the other half along with the stems.

Melt 2 tablespoons butter in an 8–10-inch enamel or stainless skillet. When foam subsides, put in sliced mushrooms and stir with wooden spoon until lightly colored. Then remove with a slotted spoon and set aside in a bowl. Add 2 tablespoons more butter to skillet and cook chopped mushrooms and scallions for 2 minutes. Set skillet aside.

In a heavy 4- to 6-quart saucepan, melt remaining butter. Remove from heat and stir in flour. Cook over low heat, stirring constantly, for 1–2 minutes. Do not brown. Remove from heat and let cool a little.

Pour in chicken stock. Return mixture to stove and whisk constantly over moderate heat until it boils. It will thicken. Add chopped mushrooms and scallions. Simmer for 15 minutes.

Purée soup through food mill and return to saucepan. Whisk egg yolks and cream. Whisk in ½ cup of the soup, 2 tablespoons at a time, to the

Recipe continues . . .

yolks and cream. Then whisk this mixture into the large portion of the soup. Bring the soup to a boil for 30 seconds, stirring constantly.

Remove from heat and season to taste. Add sliced mushrooms and serve. This can be made the day before and reheated.

YIELD: 8 SERVINGS

The Discovery Shop Cookbook
THE JUNIOR LEAGUE OF SIOUX CITY, IOWA

Rockford French Onion Soup

4 large yellow onions, thinly sliced
1 stick butter
2 10½-ounce cans beef consommé
1 soup can water
1 soup can dry white wine
6 slices 1-inch-thick French bread, toasted
¾ cup mixed grated Parmesan and shredded Gruyère cheese

Sauté onions in butter until lightly browned. Add consommé, water, and wine. Simmer until onions are tender.

Spoon soup into earthenware or other ovenproof individual bowls. Top each serving with toasted French bread. Sprinkle with cheeses. Broil until cheese is melted and golden brown.

YIELD: 6 SERVINGS

THE JUNIOR LEAGUE OF ROCKFORD, ILLINOIS

Sioux City French Onion Soup

4 tablespoons butter
2 tablespoons vegetable oil
4 cups thinly sliced yellow onions
1 teaspoon salt
¼ teaspoon freshly ground black pepper
½ teaspoon Worcestershire sauce
3 tablespoons flour
½ cup dry sherry
8 cups fresh or canned beef stock
French bread
Olive oil
1 clove garlic, peeled and split
3 cups shredded Swiss cheese

Melt butter and oil in heavy 4- to 5-quart saucepan or soup kettle over moderate heat. Add onions; sprinkle with seasonings. Mix well, then cook, uncovered, over low heat, stirring occasionally, until onions are a rich golden brown.

Sprinkle with the flour, stir again, and cook another 2–3 minutes. Add the sherry and the broth, bring to a boil, then simmer over low heat, partially covered, for 30–40 minutes. Skim off the fat once in a while. Taste for seasoning and add more salt if necessary.

Cut thick slices of French bread, allowing 2–3 slices per person. Place bread on a baking sheet and bake for 15 minutes in preheated 325° oven. Brush with olive oil, then turn and bake another 15 minutes. The bread should be lightly browned and completely dry. After the croutons come from the oven, rub each slice well with a cut clove of garlic. Set aside.

To serve, place 2 croutons in each heated soup bowl, sprinkle liberally with cheese, ladle soup over it all and sprinkle with more cheese. If desired, put each bowl of soup under the broiler for a couple of minutes to melt the top cheese.

YIELD: 6 SERVINGS

The Discovery Shop Cookbook
THE JUNIOR LEAGUE OF SIOUX CITY, IOWA

Passatelle

7 tablespoons bread crumbs
1⅓ tablespoons butter
2 eggs
Dash nutmeg
½ teaspoon grated lemon peel
6 cups broth, chicken or beef
3 tablespoons Parmesan cheese

In a bowl, mix first five ingredients to a dough consistency. Bring broth to boil in a large kettle. Shape dough into small balls and add to broth, or if you have a large-size cake decorator, squeeze dough into broth through it and cook for 2 or 3 minutes.

Sprinkle each serving with Parmesan cheese.

YIELD: 4 SERVINGS

Peacock Pie and Other Perfections
THE JUNIOR LEAGUE OF BATTLE CREEK, MICHIGAN

. . . .

Swedish Pea Soup

2 cups yellow split peas
3 quarts soft water
1 onion, sliced
2 pounds lean pork butt or loin
1 bay leaf
1 clove
6 peppercorns
½ teaspoon thyme
½ teaspoon marjoram
Salt to taste
1 tablespoon brown sugar
2 tablespoons vinegar

Soak peas overnight in water. Next day boil the peas in the same water, skimming occasionally. Add remainder of ingredients except sugar and vinegar and boil for 2–2½ hours. Stir and skim occasionally.

Remove meat, cut into small pieces, and return to soup. Just before serving, stir in brown sugar and vinegar.

YIELD: 8 SERVINGS

The Discovery Shop Cookbook
THE JUNIOR LEAGUE OF SIOUX CITY, IOWA

· · · · · · · · · · · · · · · · · · ·

Curried Pea Soup

½ stick butter
2 tablespoons flour
1 tablespoon curry powder
5 cups fresh or canned chicken stock
Additional chicken bouillon cubes if necessary
3 cups fresh purée of peas
1 cup milk
Salt to taste

Melt butter in saucepan. Add flour and curry powder and stir over low heat for 5 minutes, or until flour is cooked. Stir in the chicken stock, and if not strong enough, add bouillon cubes (watch the salt). Simmer a moment or two and add the purée of peas. Again, bring to a simmer, stirring.

Stir in the milk and continue to simmer for a few minutes. Add salt if needed.

YIELD: 6–8 SERVINGS

THE JUNIOR LEAGUE OF FARGO-MOORHEAD, NORTH DAKOTA/MINNESOTA

· · · · · · · · · · · · · · · · · · ·

German Potato Soup

4 large potatoes, peeled and chopped
½ cup finely chopped celery
½ cup finely chopped onion
1 stick butter
Salt, pepper, and dill to taste
6 cups chicken stock or canned chicken broth
½ cup sour cream

Sauté potatoes, celery, and onions in butter until onion is transparent. Add salt, pepper, dill, and chicken stock. Simmer, covered, for at least ½ hour.

Just before serving, pour a portion of the soup into a bowl and stir in the sour cream. When mixed, combine with the remaining soup.

YIELD: 6–8 SERVINGS

THE JUNIOR LEAGUE OF YOUNGSTOWN, OHIO

· · · · · · · · · · · · · · · · · ·

Cold Spinach Soup

½ cup chopped green onions
3 tablespoons butter
2 10-ounce packages frozen spinach
2 13¾-ounce cans chicken broth
1 teaspoon salt (or to taste)
⅛ teaspoon pepper
Dash nutmeg
1 8-ounce package cream cheese, cubed
2 hard-boiled eggs, chopped

Sauté onion in butter until wilted. Add spinach, cover tightly, and braise for 10 minutes over low heat. Add broth, seasonings, and cream cheese and bring to a boil.

Put a small amount at a time into blender container and blend until smooth. Chill.

Serve cold with chopped hard-boiled egg on top for garnish.

YIELD: 8 SERVINGS

THE JUNIOR LEAGUE OF YOUNGSTOWN, OHIO

· ·

Russian Summer Soup

2 cups thinly sliced radishes
2 cups thinly sliced young white turnips
2 cups thinly sliced green onions
3 large cucumbers, sliced but not peeled
4 cups finely shredded leaf lettuce
1 12-ounce can beer
2 quarts buttermilk
Salt and pepper to taste
Fresh dill to taste

Combine ingredients in a large earthenware or glass bowl rubbed generously with garlic. Cover tightly and refrigerate for at least 4 hours.

Serve cold with rye bread and butter.

YIELD: 6–8 SERVINGS

THE JUNIOR LEAGUE OF KANSAS CITY, KANSAS

· · · · · · · · · · · · · · · · · · · ·

Tomato Sipper Soup

2 10½-ounce cans condensed tomato soup
2 10½-ounce cans beef consommé
1 cup water
⅓ cup thinly sliced onion
4 peppercorns
½ teaspoon salt
1 tablespoon lemon juice
¼ teaspoon nutmeg
½ cup sherry
1 tablespoon chopped parsley

Combine all ingredients except sherry and parsley in 3½-quart saucepan, mixing well. Bring just to boiling point, reduce heat, and simmer, covered, for 30 minutes.

Strain, discarding onion and black peppers. Return to heat; add sherry. Bring to serving temperature, stirring constantly.

Sprinkle each serving with chopped parsley.

YIELD: 6–8 SERVINGS

THE JUNIOR LEAGUE OF INDIANAPOLIS, INDIANA

· · · · · · · · · · · · · · · · ·

Hearty Tomato Soup

1 veal knuckle
2 medium onions, chopped
2 carrots, peeled and chopped
¼ cup butter
¾ cup flour
2 quarts hot chicken broth
2–3 pounds chicken backs and wings
3 leeks, sliced
2 stalks celery, chopped
6 large tomatoes, peeled
4 cups tomato purée
1 clove garlic, mashed
8 white peppercorns
1½ teaspoons salt
1 tablespoon sugar
1 cup heavy cream
1 tablespoon butter
Milk

Parboil veal knuckle in salted water for 15 minutes; drain and reserve. Sauté onions and carrots in butter in 6- to 8-quart kettle. Blend in flour and cook, stirring constantly, until roux turns golden. Add chicken broth and cook, stirring, until mixture is smooth and slightly thickened. Add chicken and veal knuckle.

Stir in remaining ingredients except cream, butter, and milk. Simmer 2 hours, skimming as needed. Remove bones and press soup through food mill or fine sieve.

Before serving, add cream and butter and thin to desired consistency with milk.

YIELD: 3–4 QUARTS

Be Our Guest
THE JUNIOR LEAGUE OF MILWAUKEE, WISCONSIN

Good Woman Soup

9 quarts water
3 pounds beef, plus shank soup bone
1 bunch pascal celery
2 onions, cut in half
3 tablespoons seasoned salt
1 teaspoon garlic salt
1½ teaspoons sweet basil
1 teaspoon chervil
1 teaspoon thyme
1 teaspoon oregano
1 tablespoon pepper
4 tablespoons sugar
8–10 carrots, scraped and sliced in ¼-inch rounds
1 small bunch green onions (tops and all), chopped
1 1-pound 13-ounce can tomatoes
1 1-pound 13-ounce can tomato juice
1 10-ounce package each, frozen peas, cauliflower, corn,
green beans, lima beans, and okra

In a 4-gallon pot or roasting pan put water, beef, top half of the celery, including the leaves, the halved onions, salt, seasonings, and sugar. Bring to a boil and cook over medium heat for 3½ hours or until meat is completely tender and falling off bones. Remove meat. Trim off all fat and cut meat into bite-size pieces. Strain broth through colander. Skim off most of the fat. Return broth and meat to soup pot and add carrots, green onions, remaining celery, chopped, and the tomatoes and juice. Cook over medium heat, uncovered, for 2 hours. Add frozen vegetables and continue cooking until vegetables are tender.

This takes 4 hours one day (refrigerate overnight and skim fat), and 3–4 hours cooking time the next day.

Serve with cheese, crackers, crisp pickles, and hot apple pie.

YIELD: 26 HEARTY SERVINGS FOR A ONE-DISH MEAL

Marigolds to Munch On
THE JUNIOR LEAGUE OF PEORIA, ILLINOIS

Steak and Vegetable Soup

1 stick butter
1 cup flour
2 quarts water
1½–2 pounds ground beef
1 cup coarsely chopped onions
1 cup sliced carrots
1 cup sliced celery
2 cups frozen mixed vegetables
1 15-ounce can tomatoes
1 tablespoon monosodium glutamate
2 tablespoons granulated instant beef bouillon
1 teaspoon ground black pepper

In largest soup pot (at least 1 gallon), melt butter and whip in flour to make a smooth paste. Heat until bubbly, then stir in water until there are no more lumps. Continue cooking until mixture comes to a boil, then reduce heat to a simmer.

Meanwhile, brown ground beef in skillet, drain off excess fat and add meat to soup liquid. Add onions, carrots, and celery to soup and simmer for 20 minutes. Add rest of the ingredients and simmer for a minimum of 10 more minutes, making sure vegetables are all cooked. Do not salt. Serve.

This soup can be served immediately or refrigerated and reheated. It can also be frozen in family-size portions and then reheated.

YIELD: 1 GALLON

THE JUNIOR LEAGUE OF SOUTH BEND, INDIANA

German Vegetable Soup with Dumplings

2–3 pounds beef arm roast or other soup meat
2 quarts water
1 49-ounce can tomato juice
8 potatoes, peeled and coarsely cut
8 carrots, scraped and coarsely cut
1 onion, sliced
2 stalks celery, coarsely cut
½ cup dried beans
¼ cup dried peas
¼ cup dried lentils
2 tablespoons salt
1 teaspoon pepper
2 teaspoons parsley flakes
2 16-ounce cans mixed vegetables, or leftover diced vegetables

Using a large 10-quart soup kettle, cook meat in water on medium heat for 2 hours. Skim off fat. Remove fat and bones from meat. Add tomato juice, potatoes, carrots, onion, and celery. Add dry ingredients. Cook 4–5 hours on low heat. During last ½ hour add mixed vegetables.

Make dumpling batter and 15 minutes before serving, bring soup to a rolling boil. Drop dumpling dough from a large spoon into the soup. Cover tightly and cook for 10 minutes. Surprise! Your drops of dough will double in size. Serve immediately.

This soup is always better the next day, so make ahead.

YIELD: 14–16 SERVINGS

DUMPLINGS:
1 dozen eggs
1 teaspoon salt
3–4 cups flour

Beat eggs until well mixed. Stir in salt and flour until mixture is sticky and stringy and will fall from a spoon.

THE JUNIOR LEAGUE OF SOUTH BEND, INDIANA

· · · · · · · · · · · · · · · · ·

Cold Zucchini Soup

1 pound young zucchini, seeded, cooked, and chilled
2 cups chilled chicken broth
2 cups chilled, unflavored yogurt
½ teaspoon curry powder or crushed dill weed
½ teaspoon salt
1 teaspoon grated green pepper
Lime wedges, flaked crabmeat, or sour cream
Chopped parsley

Blend all of the ingredients except the last two briefly in a blender and adjust seasoning to taste.

Garnish each serving with a lime wedge, crabmeat, or a dollop of sour cream plus parsley.

Serve cold.

YIELD: 8 SERVINGS

THE JUNIOR LEAGUE OF SPRINGFIELD, ILLINOIS

· · · · · · · · · · · · · · · · · · · ·

Zucchini Soup

4 cups water
1 beef bouillon cube
1 10½-ounce can beef bouillon
4 pounds zucchini
6 slices bacon
Salt and pepper
Garlic salt
Grated Parmesan cheese

In large pan, heat 1 cup water and dissolve the bouillon cube in it. Wash and cut up zucchini, add to bouillon and cook, covered, until tender.

Recipe continues . . .

Fry bacon until crisp; crumble and add to zucchini. Empty zucchini into blender container and blend, adding three remaining cups of water to make a smooth purée. Combine purée in pan with canned bouillon and heat.

Season to taste with salt, pepper, and garlic salt.

Serve with Parmesan cheese sprinkled on top of each serving.

YIELD: 3 QUARTS

Sunflower Sampler
THE JUNIOR LEAGUE OF WICHITA, KANSAS

·   ·   ·   ·   ·   ·   ·   ·   ·   ·   ·   ·   ·   ·   ·   ·   ·

Matzo Soup Balls

4 medium- to large-size eggs
1 teaspoon salt
1 scant cup matzo meal

Beat eggs well and add salt. Fold in matzo meal gradually with rubber spatula. Refrigerate 1 hour.

Shape into small balls and drop into boiling salted water. Cook, covered, ½ hour to 45 minutes.

Drain and warm in chicken broth to serve.

YIELD: 24 BALLS

The Discovery Shop Cookbook
THE JUNIOR LEAGUE OF SIOUX CITY, IOWA

·   ·   ·   ·   ·   ·   ·   ·   ·   ·   ·   ·   ·   ·   ·   ·   ·

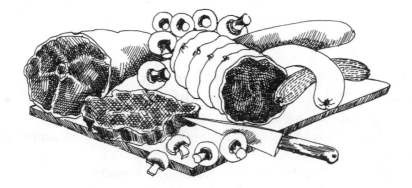

· ·

Beef

· ·

Perfect Rib Roast

Rib roast (bone in)
Salt and pepper

Roast should be room temperature. Bake in open roaster pan 1¼ hours, fat side up, in 375° oven. Turn off oven but do not open oven door. Leave meat in unopened oven for about 2 hours.

Forty-five minutes before serving, sprinkle with salt and pepper and turn oven to 300°.

This recipe is fine for any size roast over 4 pounds. Count on ½ pound per person. All the slices will be the same shade of pink.

YIELD: APPROXIMATELY 2 SERVINGS PER RIB

Sunflower Sampler
THE JUNIOR LEAGUE OF WICHITA, KANSAS

. . . .

Foolproof Roast Beef

Standing rib roast, any size
Salt and pepper

Let roast stand at room temperature at least 30 minutes per pound before baking. Season with salt and pepper. Place the roast, ribs down, uncovered, in shallow baking pan; put in oven thoroughly preheated to 500°. Cook 5 minutes per pound, then turn off heat and leave meat in the *unopened* oven for at least 2 hours. Roast will be crusty and brown outside and evenly rare and juicy inside.

The important things are to have the roast at room temperature and to leave the oven closed for at least 2 hours. The roast may remain in closed oven for up to 3 hours.

YIELD: 2 SERVINGS PER RIB

Cincinnati Celebrates
THE JUNIOR LEAGUE OF CINCINNATI, OHIO

. . . .

Beef Standing Rib with Herbs

Beef is the number-one meat in the Midwest. Here is a delicious way to prepare that favorite: standing rib roast.

1 clove garlic
4–5 pounds standing rib roast
3 tablespoons lemon juice
1 teaspoon dry mustard
1 teaspoon ground ginger
1 teaspoon onion powder
1 teaspoon salt
½ teaspoon cayenne

MIXED HERBS:
1 tablespoon savory
1 tablespoon sweet basil
1 tablespoon celery flakes
1 tablespoon dried parsley
1 tablespoon marjoram
1 tablespoon rosemary
1 tablespoon tarragon

Sliver garlic clove; insert slivers into beef, making deep slits in the meat with a sharp knife. Pour lemon juice over meat. Sprinkle with the spices.

Combine the herbs and sprinkle beef with 1 tablespoon of the mixture. Reserve rest for future use. Place roast on foil-lined broiling pan and broil for 12 minutes on each side.

Wrap roast tightly in foil. Bake at 400° or until meat thermometer registers 140° for rare.

YIELD: 6–8 SERVINGS

Soupçon
THE JUNIOR LEAGUE OF CHICAGO, ILLINOIS

Broiled Tournedos with Sauce Béarnaise

Not an old traditional Midwest dish, but typical of the French cuisine Chicago Junior League hostesses often serve at formal, sit-down dinner parties.

3 pounds beef filet
12 slices bacon
1 cup fresh sliced mushrooms
½ cup chopped onion
2 tablespoons chopped shallots
2 tablespoons butter
8 toast rounds

Cut beef filet in eight slices. Sauté bacon until half done. Drain; wrap 1½ bacon slices around each tournedo, securing with wooden picks or string. Brush meat with bacon drippings.

Sauté mushrooms, onion, and shallots in butter until tender. Keep warm.

Broil tournedos 6 inches from heat for 2–3 minutes on each side for medium-rare.

Set each tournedo on a toast round. Top with mushrooms, onions, and Sauce Béarnaise. Keep warm.

YIELD: 8 SERVINGS

SAUCE BÉARNAISE:
¼ cup tarragon vinegar
¼ cup dry white wine
1 tablespoon chopped shallots
1 tablespoon fresh tarragon or 1½ teaspoons dried tarragon
3 egg yolks
2 tablespoons butter
½ cup butter, melted
2 tablespoons chopped parsley
¼ teaspoon salt
¼ teaspoon pepper

Combine vinegar, wine, shallots, and tarragon in saucepan. Bring to a boil; cook until reduced by half, about 3–4 tablespoons.

Put egg yolks and butter in top of double boiler over hot water. Beat until thick. Strain vinegar mixture into egg mixture. Gradually add melted butter, beating constantly, until thickened; add seasonings.

Serve over tournedos.

YIELD: ABOUT 1½ CUPS

Soupçon
THE JUNIOR LEAGUE OF CHICAGO, ILLINOIS

Grilled Beef Tenderloin

¾ cup soy sauce
½ cup sugar
½ cup toasted crushed sesame seeds
¼ cup oil
¼ cup flour
2 green onions, sliced
1–2 cloves garlic, mashed
¼ teaspoon pepper
3–4 pounds beef tenderloin

Combine all ingredients except meat. Slice beef into six filets.

Fifteen minutes before grilling, spread mixture on filets. Grill to desired doneness.

YIELD: 6 SERVINGS

Be Our Guest
THE JUNIOR LEAGUE OF MILWAUKEE, WISCONSIN

Beef Tenderloin with Bordelaise Sauce

3 pounds beef tenderloin, trimmed
3 cloves garlic, minced
3 tablespoons salt
Watercress for garnish

Preheat oven to 450°. Meanwhile, tie tenderloin with string at ½-inch intervals down the entire length.

In small bowl, combine garlic and salt. Work together with metal spoon until paste forms. Spread on all surfaces of meat.

Put meat on baking sheet and bake 30–35 minutes in preheated oven until outside is crispy brown and inside is pink.

Garnish with watercress. Slice and serve with Bordelaise Sauce.

YIELD: 6 SERVINGS

BORDELAISE SAUCE:
1 shallot, minced
1 onion, sliced
2 carrots, sliced
Sprig of parsley
6 peppercorns
1 clove garlic
½ bay leaf
2 tablespoons butter
2 tablespoons flour
1 10¾-ounce can beef bouillon
¼ teaspoon salt
⅛ teaspoon pepper
¼ cup dry red wine
1 tablespoon chopped parsley

The day before serving, sauté shallot, onion, carrot, parsley sprig, peppers, garlic, and bay leaf in butter until onion is golden and tender. Add flour and cook, stirring, over low heat until roux is lightly browned.

Stir in bouillon. Simmer, stirring, until sauce is thickened. Strain. Add salt, pepper, red wine, and chopped parsley.

Refrigerate and reheat when needed.

THE JUNIOR LEAGUE OF DES MOINES, IOWA

· · · · · · · · · · · · · · · · · · ·

Marinated Beef

4 pounds sirloin tip roast
1⅓ cups oil
½ cup red wine vinegar
¼ cup capers
2 tablespoons chopped parsley
2 teaspoons tarragon
2 teaspoons chopped chives
2 teaspoons dry mustard
2 teaspoons salt
1 teaspoon ground pepper
1 teaspoon sugar
½ teaspoon garlic powder
Several dashes Tabasco
¾ pound fresh mushrooms, sliced
2 red onions, sliced
Parsley and cherry tomatoes for garnish

Roast meat to rare (1–1½ hours) and slice thinly. Set aside.

Combine remaining ingredients except mushrooms, onions, and garnish; mix well. Pour over meat, mushrooms, and onions. Cover; marinate in refrigerator 4–6 hours. Drain meat and vegetables.

Arrange on serving platter. Garnish with parsley and cherry tomatoes. Serve on or with crusty rolls.

YIELD: 8–10 SERVINGS

Be Our Guest
THE JUNIOR LEAGUE OF MILWAUKEE, WISCONSIN

· · · · · · · · · · · · · · · · · · ·

German Sauerbraten

4 pounds rump roast
1 clove garlic
2 cups mild vinegar
2 cups water
½ cup sugar
3 bay leaves
1 tablespoon peppercorns
2 onions, sliced
Flour
4 slices bacon
1 large onion, chopped
6–8 beef bouillon cubes
4 tablespoons flour
¾ cup water
½ cup heavy cream

Rub meat well with garlic. Heat vinegar, water, sugar, bay leaves, pepper-corns, and sliced onions; do not boil.

Place meat in a deep bowl; pour hot mixture over it. Cover tightly and refrigerate at least 4–5 days, turning once daily.

When ready to cook meat, drain and reserve marinade. Flour meat. In Dutch oven render bacon; brown meat slowly in bacon drippings. Add chopped onion and brown. Add marinade; cook slowly on top of stove at least 2 hours, or until well done.

Remove meat. Let the sauce cool slightly. Pass sauce through food mill; skim off fat. If sauce is too sour add more sugar. Add beef bouillon cubes.

Just before serving, thicken sauce with the 4 tablespoons flour mixed with water. Stir in cream.

Serve with buttered parsley noodles and red cabbage.

YIELD: 6–8 SERVINGS

Soupçon
THE JUNIOR LEAGUE OF CHICAGO, ILLINOIS

· · · · · · · · · · · · · · · · ·

Beer Brisket

3–4 pounds beef brisket
Salt and pepper
1 onion, sliced
¼ cup chili sauce
2 tablespoons brown sugar
1 clove garlic, minced, or garlic powder
1 12-ounce can beer
2 tablespoons flour
½ cup water

Trim excess fat from brisket (important), season with salt and pepper, and place in 9 x 13-inch baking dish; cover with onion slices.

In bowl, combine chili sauce, brown sugar, garlic, and beer; pour over meat. Cover tightly with foil. Bake in preheated 350° oven for 3½ hours. Uncover and bake 30 minutes more, basting occasionally.

Set meat on platter. Skim excess fat from liquid; measure remaining liquid and add enough water to make 1 cup. Pour into saucepan. Blend flour and ½ cup water; combine with liquid and cook, stirring constantly, over medium heat until thickened and bubbly.

Cut meat across grain . . . pass beer gravy.

Leftovers make good cold sandwiches.

YIELD: 8–10 SERVINGS

Sunflower Sampler
THE JUNIOR LEAGUE OF WICHITA, KANSAS

Beef Brisket

3–4 pounds beef brisket
Garlic cloves, halved
Whole allspice
Salt and pepper
1 cup water

Punch holes 1 inch apart on fat side of the brisket and insert in each ½ clove garlic and 1 whole allspice. Sprinkle top side with salt and pepper.

Place brisket in heavy casserole with the water and cook, covered, in 350° oven for 3 hours.

Remove meat from liquid. Cool; carve into thin slices, diagonally, against the grain, and return to liquid. Heat when ready to serve.

Leftover meat may be served as sandwiches on rye bread.

YIELD: 6–8 SERVINGS

The Cook's Book
THE JUNIOR LEAGUE OF CEDAR RAPIDS, IOWA

·   ·   ·   ·   ·   ·   ·   ·   ·   ·   ·   ·   ·   ·   ·   ·   ·

Marinated Beef Brisket

6–8 pounds beef brisket
Salt and pepper
1 clove garlic
1 8-ounce bottle French dressing
1 12-ounce bottle chili sauce
1 cup sherry
3 onions, sliced
½ pound fresh mushrooms or 1 4-ounce can sliced mushrooms

Season beef with salt, pepper, and garlic. Place in a shallow dish, cover with French dressing, and marinate several hours or overnight in refrigerator, turning meat occasionally.

Place brisket and marinade in a large roasting pan and cook at 325° allowing 30 minutes per pound. When roast is half cooked, add chili sauce, sherry, and sliced onions.

Remove roast from pan, cool, and slice. Add mushrooms to gravy remaining in pan. Return sliced meat to pan and heat at 325° for 30 minutes.

Leftovers may be frozen for later use and reheated.

YIELD: 10–12 SERVINGS

THE JUNIOR LEAGUE OF SOUTH BEND, INDIANA

· ·

Smoked Beef Brisket

3–5 pounds beef brisket
4 tablespoons liquid smoke
1 teaspoon each celery, onion salt, and garlic salt
Several dashes Worcestershire sauce

Place a strip of heavy foil in a shallow pan; put meat on foil. Combine seasonings and brush on meat; seal foil around it and refrigerate overnight.

Bake, still sealed in foil, at 275° for 5–5½ hours. Let stand 15–30 minutes before unsealing.

To serve, slice meat across the grain.

Leftover meat, combined with a bottled barbecue sauce, makes wonderful sandwiches.

YIELD: 4–6 SERVINGS

THE JUNIOR LEAGUE OF DES MOINES, IOWA

· ·

Illinois Pot Roast

1 cup sliced onions
1 cup chopped celery
¼ cup sliced carrots
¼ cup chopped parsley
1 clove garlic
2 tomatoes, sliced
3–4 pounds beef roast
1½ cups beef broth or consommé
1 cup dry red wine
Flour or cornstarch (optional)

Grease bottom of roasting pan. Add onions, celery, carrots, parsley, garlic, and tomatoes, covering bottom of pan with vegetables. Put roast on top. Roast in 450° oven, uncovered, for 45 minutes, or until meat is seared and vegetables are brown.

Lower oven to 325° and add the consommé and wine. Cover and simmer for about 2 hours. Remove meat to platter and strain gravy. Purée strained vegetables and return to the gravy. Thicken gravy if desired with a little flour or cornstarch mixed with enough water to make a thin paste.

YIELD: 6–8 SERVINGS

Bluff City Cooks
THE JUNIOR LEAGUE OF GREATER ALTON, ILLINOIS

· · · · · · · · · · · · · · · · · ·

Italian Rump Roast

2 teaspoons red pepper
1 teaspoon oregano
2 teaspoons basil
Garlic powder to taste
1 envelope onion soup mix
6 pounds rolled rump roast
3 cups water

Mix all spices and soup mix and pat on roast. Put roast into heavy casserole, add water, cover, and roast at 325° for 3½ hours.

This may be kept in the refrigerator in the juices up to 3 days. Reheat before serving.

YIELD: 6–8 SERVINGS

Bluff City Cooks
THE JUNIOR LEAGUE OF GREATER ALTON, ILLINOIS

Steak Bake

Flour
1–2 pounds beef stew chunks
1 medium onion, sliced
2 tablespoons shortening
1 tablespoon soy sauce
1 29-ounce can tomatoes
1½ tablespoons molasses
½–1 pound mushrooms, sliced
1 10-ounce package French-style green beans, cooked

Flour beef chunks and brown with onion in shortening. Add remaining ingredients, cover, and simmer for 2½–3 hours, the longer the better.

Serve with rice or noodles.

YIELD: 4–6 SERVINGS

THE JUNIOR LEAGUE OF YOUNGSTOWN, OHIO

Steak Singapora

3 tablespoons salad oil
2 cloves garlic, minced
3 stalks bok choy, chopped
1½ cups sliced mushrooms
3 green onions, sliced
3 cups chicken broth
3 tablespoons soy sauce
1 tablespoon sugar
Salt and pepper
2 teaspoons dry sherry
2 tablespoons cornstarch
¼ cup water
½ cup bamboo shoots
½ cup water chestnuts, sliced
½ cup snow pea pods
3 pounds sirloin steak

Heat oil in skillet or wok; add garlic and bok choy. Stir-fry 4–5 minutes. Add mushrooms, green onions, chicken broth, soy sauce, sugar, salt, pepper, and sherry. Stir and bring to boil.

Mix cornstarch with the water to make a thin paste. Add slowly to mixture, stirring all the time. Add bamboo shoots, water chestnuts, and pea pods. Keep warm on low heat.

Broil the steak, then pour the sauce over the cooked meat and slice at the table.

YIELD: 4 SERVINGS

Tested, Tried, and True
THE JUNIOR LEAGUE OF FLINT, MICHIGAN

Pizza Steak

1 teaspoon garlic powder
Salt and pepper
1 cup grated Parmesan cheese
2 pounds round steak, ½-inch thick, cut into serving pieces
2 tablespoons oil
½ cup water
1 10½-ounce can tomato purée
½ teaspoon oregano
1 8-ounce package shredded mozzarella cheese
Tomatoes and mushrooms for garnish

Use meat pounder and pound garlic powder, salt and pepper, and ¼ cup Parmesan cheese into steak. Brown meat on both sides in oil in large skillet.

When meat is browned, add water and heat until bubbly. Add tomato purée, oregano, then the remaining Parmesan cheese and the mozzarella. Bake in a 350° oven for 45 minutes to 1 hour.

Garnish each piece with tomato slice and fresh sliced mushrooms.

YIELD: 4–6 SERVINGS

THE JUNIOR LEAGUE OF COLUMBUS, OHIO

Teriyaki Chuck Roast

2½ pounds boneless chuck roast
1½ teaspoons meat tenderizer
3 cloves garlic, minced fine
¼ cup soy sauce
1 tablespoon vegetable oil
2 tablespoons water
3 tablespoons brown sugar, firmly packed
½ teaspoon ground ginger
½ teaspoon pepper
1 tablespoon honey
½ teaspoon seasoned salt

Cut chuck roast into 1½-inch cubes. Sprinkle with tenderizer; cover and refrigerate overnight.

Combine the remaining ingredients and pour over meat the following day. Let the meat marinate 1–2 days in the refrigerator, turning several times. Grill on skewers or as individual pieces until done to taste.

YIELD: 4–6 SERVINGS

THE JUNIOR LEAGUE OF SPRINGFIELD, ILLINOIS

Grilled Flank Steak

1½–2 pounds flank steak
1 8-ounce bottle Italian dressing
1 5-ounce bottle soy sauce
½ cup lemon juice
¼ cup Worcestershire sauce
2 teaspoons garlic powder
¼ teaspoon dry mustard
Natural meat tenderizer

Score steak diagonally. Combine all ingredients except meat tenderizer and marinate the steak in them for 24 hours.

Tenderize just before broiling and broil 10–15 minutes on each side, basting with marinade frequently.

Slice diagonally for serving.

Any marinade left keeps well in the refrigerator.

YIELD: 3–4 SERVINGS

Marigolds to Munch On
THE JUNIOR LEAGUE OF PEORIA, ILLINOIS

·   ·   ·   ·   ·   ·   ·   ·   ·   ·   ·   ·   ·   ·   ·   ·   ·   ·

Flank Steak in Wine Sauce

1½ pounds flank steak
1 small onion, finely chopped
1 4-ounce can sliced mushrooms, drained
2 tablespoons butter or margarine
1½ teaspoons seasoned salt
1 teaspoon herb meat seasoning
½ cup dry red wine
2 beef bouillon cubes
½ cup water

Slice flank steak ⅛-inch thick and set aside.

Sauté onion and mushrooms in butter until slightly browned. Add meat and brown quickly. Reduce heat to low. Add salt, seasoning, wine, bouillon cubes, and water. Simmer 15 minutes, stirring occasionally.

Serve over cooked rice or noodles.

This dish may be made in advance and reheated before serving.

YIELD: 4 SERVINGS

THE JUNIOR LEAGUE OF SOUTH BEND, INDIANA

·   ·   ·   ·   ·   ·   ·   ·   ·   ·   ·   ·   ·   ·   ·   ·   ·   ·

Grilled Flank Steak with Red Wine and Shallot Sauce

1½–2 pounds flank steak
Soy sauce
Freshly ground black pepper
1 teaspoon dried thyme, crumbled
1¼ cups chopped shallots (can substitute green onions,
but less successful)
1¼ cups red Bordeaux or Burgundy
8 tablespoons butter
Rock salt
Pepper
2 tablespoons finely chopped parsley

Brush steak with soy sauce and sprinkle with pepper and thyme (no salt—it draws *out* juices). Turn over and repeat. Brush again with soy sauce and broil 3–4 minutes on each side.

In saucepan, bring shallots and wine just to boiling point. Add butter and several dashes of freshly ground salt and pepper; stir until butter is just melted. Add parsley.

With a very sharp knife, slice steak very thinly on the diagonal. Ladle sauce over steak slices on serving platter.

YIELD: 4 SERVINGS

THE JUNIOR LEAGUE OF COLUMBUS, OHIO

·   ·   ·   ·   ·   ·   ·   ·   ·   ·   ·   ·   ·   ·   ·   ·   ·

Lynn's Grilled Flank Steak

1½–2 pounds flank steak
Soy sauce
Salt, pepper, and thyme

Brush steak with soy sauce and sprinkle with salt, pepper, and a generous amount of thyme. Let stand for an hour or more.

Grill about 3 minutes on each side or until medium-rare.

Carve on the diagonal and serve with Red Wine Butter Sauce.

YIELD: 3–4 SERVINGS

RED WINE BUTTER SAUCE:
1 cup chopped green onions
1 cup red wine
½ stick butter
Salt
2 tablespoons chopped parsley

In saucepan, combine onions and red wine. Bring just to boiling point. Add butter and salt to taste.

Add parsley and spoon over steak slices.

THE JUNIOR LEAGUE OF CHAMPAIGN-URBANA, ILLINOIS

·   ·   ·   ·   ·   ·   ·   ·   ·   ·   ·   ·   ·   ·   ·   ·   ·

Good and Easy Flank Steak

1–2 pounds flank steak
⅓ cup soy sauce
⅓ cup sherry
½ teaspoon ground ginger
½ teaspoon dry mustard
1 clove garlic, crushed

Lightly score flank steak on both sides.

Combine remaining ingredients and pour over steak, turning to wet both sides. Marinate overnight in refrigerator.

Grill quickly over high heat, about 3 minutes per side, to rare or medium-rare stage. Do not overcook.

Slice thinly on the diagonal to serve.

YIELD: 4–6 SERVINGS

THE JUNIOR LEAGUE OF INDIANAPOLIS, INDIANA

·   ·   ·   ·   ·   ·   ·   ·   ·   ·   ·   ·   ·   ·   ·   ·   ·

Scrumptious Swiss Steak

6 tablespoons flour
2 teaspoons salt
¼ teaspoon pepper
2 pounds round steak, 1 inch thick
4 medium onions, sliced
6 tablespoons shortening
½ cup chopped celery
1 clove garlic, minced
¾ cup chili sauce
¾ cup water
1 green pepper, sliced

Combine flour, salt, and pepper; rub into both sides of steak, or pound in with a meat mallet. Cut into serving portions.

In preheated skillet, cook onions in half the shortening until golden brown. Remove onions from skillet and set aside.

Add remaining shortening and brown steak on both sides. Reduce heat. Add celery, garlic, chili sauce, and water. Cover and simmer for 1 hour.

Add pepper and cooked onions to skillet. Continue cooking for 30 minutes, or until meat is tender.

YIELD: 8 SERVINGS

THE JUNIOR LEAGUE OF YOUNGSTOWN, OHIO

Swiss Steak with Mushrooms and Sherry

½ cup flour
Salt and pepper
2 pounds round steak, 1-inch thick
3 tablespoons shortening
1 medium onion, chopped
1 clove garlic, minced
1 cup finely chopped celery
1 8-ounce can tomato sauce
½ cup sherry
1 8-ounce can mushrooms, stems and pieces

Pound flour mixed with salt and pepper well into steak. Cut in serving pieces.

In large, heavy skillet heat shortening. Brown meat well; add remaining ingredients. Cover and bake at 350° for 1½ hours or until tender. Turn and baste occasionally. Water may be added if sauce becomes too thick.

YIELD: 6 SERVINGS

Peacock Pie and Other Perfections
THE JUNIOR LEAGUE OF BATTLE CREEK, MICHIGAN

Rouladen

1 cup chopped onion
4 tablespoons butter
½ cup chopped parsley
2½ pounds trimmed round steak, cut in 3 x 5-inch strips
½ pound sliced bacon, halved
¼ cup shortening
Salt
Pepper
3 cups water or stock (or half red wine)
2 tablespoons cornstarch
¼ cup cold water

Sauté onion in butter until transparent; add parsley. Spread 1 tablespoon on each strip of beef and cover with ½ slice of bacon. Roll up meat and secure with toothpick or string.

Brown meat rolls in shortening in large Dutch oven. Season with salt and pepper. Pour water or stock over meat; cover and simmer until tender, at least 2½ hours. Add additional stock or water as needed during the cooking time. (When regular oven is used, bake at 325° for the same length of time.)

Remove rouladen and thicken liquid with cornstarch mixed with ¼ cup cold water. Bring to a boil; correct seasoning by adding salt to taste. Return meat to pot. Reheat at time of serving.

Can be made ahead and can be frozen after cooking.

YIELD: 6 SERVINGS

Cookbook
THE JUNIOR LEAGUE OF GRAND RAPIDS, MICHIGAN

Round Steak Roll-Ups

2 pounds round steak
2 tablespoons butter

FILLING:
¼ cup chopped onion
¼ cup butter
1 egg
1 tablespoon chopped parsley
Seasoned salt and pepper
2 or 3 slices of bread, broken into small pieces

SAUCE:
1 10½-ounce cream of mushroom soup
½ cup red wine or sherry
Freshly ground pepper

Pound steak well on both sides and cut into serving pieces. Set aside.

To make filling, sauté onion in butter until onion is transparent. Mix egg, seasoning, and bread together and add to onion.

Place 1 tablespoon of filling on each piece of steak. Roll up and skewer with toothpicks.

Brown rolls in a skillet with 2 tablespoons butter; remove and place in baking dish.

To make sauce, put soup and wine in skillet used for browning steak rolls and heat through. Sprinkle with fresh pepper.

Pour sauce over rolls. Cover and bake at 325° for 1¼ hours.

YIELD: 6 SERVINGS

THE JUNIOR LEAGUE OF EVANSVILLE, INDIANA

Pepper Steak

1½ pounds top sirloin, 1 inch thick
¼ cup vegetable oil
1 clove garlic, crushed
1 teaspoon salt
1 teaspoon ginger
¼ teaspoon pepper
2 green peppers, seeded and sliced
2 large onions, thinly sliced
¼ cup soy sauce
½ teaspoon sugar
1 cup beef bouillon
1 8-ounce can water chestnuts, sliced
4 green onions cut in ½-inch pieces
2 tablespoons cornstarch
¼ cup cold water
2 firm tomatoes, peeled and cut into eighths

Freeze steak for at least 1 hour. When ready to cook, cut meat into ⅛-inch-thick slices.

Heat oil in skillet and add garlic, salt, ginger, and pepper. Sauté until garlic is golden.

Add steak slices and brown lightly. Remove meat.

Add green peppers and onions. Cook 7–10 minutes.

Return beef to pan. Add soy sauce, sugar, bouillon, water chestnuts, green onions, and cornstarch mixed with water. Simmer, stirring, for 3 minutes, or until sauce thickens. Add tomatoes and heat.

Serve over hot rice. Top with soy sauce if desired.

YIELD: 4–6 SERVINGS

Sunflower Sampler
THE JUNIOR LEAGUE OF WICHITA, KANSAS

Curried Pepper Steak

2 pounds well-trimmed top round steak
2 tablespoons olive oil
1 clove garlic
2 large green peppers, seeded and cut into strips
2 large onions, coarsely chopped
½ pound mushrooms, sliced
½ teaspoon black pepper
2 teaspoons salt
1 clove garlic, finely minced
¾ cup red wine
1½ teaspoons curry powder

Cut steak into ½-inch strips. Brown well in oil with garlic. Discard garlic clove.

In a second skillet, sauté green peppers and onions until tender; add mushrooms, pepper, salt, and minced garlic.

Mix vegetables with meat and add red wine. Cook slowly, covered, for ½ hour. Add curry powder, and simmer for another hour.

This dish may be cooked ahead and reheated. The flavor is even better the second day.

YIELD: 6–8 SERVINGS

THE JUNIOR LEAGUE OF EVANSVILLE, INDIANA

Quick Pepper Steak

2 tablespoons oil or shortening
1 pound round or flank steak
1 teaspoon salt
⅛ teaspoon pepper
2 tablespoons minced onion
1 clove garlic, minced
1 can beef bouillon
1 cup drained canned tomatoes or 3 tomatoes, quartered
2 green peppers, seeded and cut in strips
1½ tablespoons cornstarch
2 teaspoons soy sauce
¼ cup water

Melt oil or shortening in skillet.

Cut meat into 1-inch strips; sprinkle with salt and pepper. Brown meat with onion and garlic in the hot fat. Add bouillon, cover, and cook for 30 minutes to 1 hour.

Add tomatoes and green peppers; simmer 5 minutes. Combine cornstarch, soy sauce, and water; add to meat mixture and cook 5 minutes, stirring constantly.

YIELD: 4 SERVINGS

THE JUNIOR LEAGUE OF FARGO-MOORHEAD, NORTH DAKOTA/MINNESOTA

Korean Deep-Fried Beef Strips

½ pound flank steak
1 egg
¼ cup water
6 tablespoons cornstarch
½ teaspoon salt
3 cloves garlic, minced
2 green onions, finely chopped
3 cups oil for frying

Slice the flank steak thinly into 1 x 2-inch strips.

Beat together the egg and water in a bowl. Add the cornstarch and salt and beat with a fork until smooth. Add garlic and green onions, then the beef strips and mix well until all sides of the beef are coated.

Heat oil to about 400°. Drop the beef strips one by one into hot oil and fry for 1 minute; remove with a slotted spoon or strainer.

Return the beef to the cornstarch mixture and again coat on all sides. Fry a second time in oil until brown. When the meat strips float to the top, they are done. Drain on paper toweling.

YIELD: 2–4 SERVINGS

THE JUNIOR LEAGUE OF KANSAS CITY, KANSAS

Beef Oriental

2 pounds choice round or sirloin tip steak, sliced ¼ inch across
the grain and trimmed of fat
2 tablespoons oil
½ cup soy sauce
½–1 cup water
1 tablespoon sugar
1 teaspoon monosodium glutamate
1 6-ounce can mushrooms with liquid
1 cup celery, thinly sliced on the bias
1½ cups onions, thinly sliced on the bias
2 tablespoons cornstarch
1 cup water

Brown steak in oil for 1–2 minutes. Pour soy sauce and enough water to barely cover over meat; add sugar and monosodium glutamate. Cover and cook until meat is tender.

Add mushrooms and mushroom liquid. Add celery and onions last so vegetables are crisp-cooked.

Add cornstarch mixed with 1 cup of water. Cook, stirring, until sauce is thick.

Serve with wild rice or a rice dish, but not on top of rice as chop suey.

YIELD: 6–8 SERVINGS

Tested, Tried, and True
THE JUNIOR LEAGUE OF FLINT, MICHIGAN

Perfect Beef Stroganoff

2 pounds beef filet
6 tablespoons butter
1 cup chopped onion
1 clove garlic, chopped
½ pound fresh mushrooms, sliced
3 tablespoons flour
2 tablespoons meat extract paste
1 tablespoon catsup
½ teaspoon salt
⅛ teaspoon pepper
1 10½-ounce can beef bouillon
¼ cup dry white wine (optional)
1 tablespoon snipped fresh dill or ¼ teaspoon dried dill weed
1 ½ cups sour cream

Trim fat from beef and cut into thin ½-inch strips. Melt 2 tablespoons butter in heavy skillet and sear beef quickly on all sides (do only enough at one time to cover bottom of pan). Set beef aside.

In remaining butter, sauté onion, garlic, and mushrooms until onion is golden. Remove from heat and add flour, extract, catsup, salt, and pepper, and stir until smooth. Gradually stir in bouillon; bring to a boil, stirring. Reduce heat and simmer 5 minutes. To this point the dish may be made ahead of time.

Over low heat, add wine, dill, and sour cream, stirring until well combined. Add beef and simmer just until sauce and beef are hot.

Serve over rice.

If desired, sprinkle 2 tablespoons dill or parsley over top.

YIELD: 6 SERVINGS

Sunflower Sampler
THE JUNIOR LEAGUE OF WICHITA, KANSAS

Quick Beef Stroganoff

1½–2 pounds sirloin steak, sliced into strips ¼ inch thick
2 tablespoons shortening
1 red or Bermuda onion, chopped
1 tablespoon flour
Salt and pepper to taste
1 cup hot water
2 beef bouillon cubes
1 3-ounce can mushrooms with liquid
¼ cup sherry
8 ounces sour cream

In skillet, brown meat in shortening. Add onion and cook until onion is tender.

Sprinkle flour over meat and onions. Blend well and season with salt and pepper. Add hot water and bouillon cubes. Stir until a gravy forms. Add mushrooms with liquid and simmer for 15 minutes, or until thickened, stirring occasionally. Stir in sherry and sour cream.

Serve over rice.

YIELD: 4 SERVINGS

THE JUNIOR LEAGUE OF EVANSVILLE, INDIANA

Paprika Stew

2 pounds lean beef
2 tablespoons margarine
2 large red onions, sliced
2 teaspoons salt
1 tablespoon paprika
1 3-ounce can tomato paste
½ teaspoon caraway seeds
½ cup dry red wine
1 10½-ounce can beef bouillon
6 medium par-boiled potatoes, cut into pieces
1 tablespoon butter
½ teaspoon paprika
2 tablespoons warm water

Cut beef into 1½-inch cubes.

In large skillet, melt margarine, and in it sauté onions and beef until brown, stirring. Season with salt and 1 tablespoon paprika.

Add tomato paste, caraway seeds, red wine, and enough bouillon to cover. Simmer, covered, for 2–3 hours, adding more bouillon and wine if needed.

When meat is tender, add potatoes and mix. Cook 10 minutes more.

Just before serving, melt butter in small saucepan and stir in ½ teaspoon paprika and warm water, a tablespoon at a time. Stir into stew and serve.

YIELD: 4–6 SERVINGS

Sunflower Sampler
THE JUNIOR LEAGUE OF WICHITA, KANSAS

Bavarian Braised Beef

2½ pounds lean beef, cut in 1-inch cubes
2 tablespoons cooking oil
3 cups sliced onions
2 cloves garlic, peeled and minced
½ cup beef consommé
1 tablespoon brown sugar
1 bay leaf
1½ teaspoons salt
¼ teaspoon pepper
¼ teaspoon thyme
1 12-ounce bottle beer
1½ tablespoons water
1½ tablespoons cornstarch
Parsley for garnish

In heavy pan, brown beef cubes in oil. Don't crowd; brown on all sides and remove from pan.

Add onions and cook until soft; move to side of pan, add garlic, and cook 30 seconds. Return beef to pan and add consommé, sugar, seasonings, and beer. Bring to a boil, cover, and simmer gently on low heat until beef is tender, about 2 hours.

Blend water with cornstarch until smooth; stir into meat mixture and simmer gently until sauce is thickened.

Serve over noodles or rice sprinkled lightly with parsley.

YIELD: 6–8 SERVINGS

Cincinnati Celebrates
THE JUNIOR LEAGUE OF CINCINNATI, OHIO

Busy-Day Oven Stew

PART I:

1 28-ounce can tomatoes
¾ cup beef consommé
½ cup white wine
4 tablespoons tapioca
1 tablespoon brown sugar (optional)
1 bay leaf
2 teaspoons salt
1 teaspoon monosodium glutamate
1 teaspoon Beau Monde seasoning
½ cup prepared bread crumbs
3–4 potatoes, peeled and quartered (optional)

PART II:

3 pounds stew meat
3 large carrots, cut in chunks
1 16-ounce can small onions, drained*
1 16-ounce can tiny peas, drained*
1 16-ounce can small green beans, drained*

Stir together in a Dutch oven all ingredients listed in Part I. Place ingredients listed in Part II on top but don't stir. Cover with a tight lid and cook in preheated 250° oven for 7–8 hours.

YIELD: 8 SERVINGS

*NOTE: Do not drain onions, peas, and beans if potatoes are used.

Sunflower Sampler
THE JUNIOR LEAGUE OF WICHITA, KANSAS

Herb Beef Stew

4 pounds lean beef, cut in 1½-inch cubes
¼ cup oil
6 onions, chopped
1 pound fresh mushrooms, sliced
1 10-ounce can beef consommé
2 1-pound 13-ounce cans tomatoes
2 cloves garlic, crushed
1 teaspoon dried dill weed
¾ teaspoon basil
2 bay leaves, crushed
¼ teaspoon freshly ground pepper
½ teaspoon powdered savory
1 pound white onions, peeled
1 bunch cleaned carrots, chopped
6 tablespoons flour
½ cup cold water
Parsley or cooked peas for garnish

Brown beef cubes in Dutch oven in the oil. Remove meat and sauté chopped onions and mushrooms until tender. Return meat and add consommé, tomatoes, and herbs. Simmer, covered, 1½ hours, or until meat is tender.

Add white onions and carrots and cook 45 minutes, or until vegetables are done. Mix flour with ½ cup cold water, add gradually, and cook, stirring constantly, until gravy is thickened.

Serve in a big tureen. Garnish with a circle of parsley or cooked frozen peas.

YIELD: 8–10 SERVINGS

Marigolds to Munch On
THE JUNIOR LEAGUE OF PEORIA, ILLINOIS

· · · · · · · · · · · · · · · ·

Starchwork's Stew

1 pound round steak, cut into 1½-inch cubes
2 tablespoons butter
1 large onion, sliced
1 tomato, cut into chunks
½ green pepper, coarsely chopped
¼ teaspoon dry mustard
1¼ teaspoons paprika
2 tablespoons brown sugar
1¼ teaspoons salt
1 tablespoon Worcestershire sauce
2 tablespoons red wine vinegar
6 tablespoons catsup
2 cups water

Brown meat in butter; add onion and brown. Add remaining ingredients and simmer until meat is tender, about 2 hours.

If necessary, thicken liquid with a little cornstarch mixed with water. Serve over hot well-buttered noodles.

YIELD: 4 SERVINGS

The Cook's Book
THE JUNIOR LEAGUE OF CEDAR RAPIDS, IOWA

. . . .

Easy Beef Carbonnade

1½ cups catsup
1 12-ounce bottle beer
½ cup brown sugar
Salt and pepper
4 pounds lean beef, cubed
3 onions, chopped

Recipe continues . . .

Combine catsup, beer, and brown sugar; mix well. Season to taste with salt and pepper. Pour over meat and onions in a 3-quart casserole. Cover and bake at 300° for 2–3 hours, or until meat is tender. Thicken gravy if desired with a little cornstarch mixed with water.

YIELD: 10 SERVINGS

Be Our Guest
THE JUNIOR LEAGUE OF MILWAUKEE, WISCONSIN

. . . .

Denise's Slow-Cooked Stew

2½ pounds pot roast, cut into 1½-inch cubes
1 1-pound can stewed tomatoes
½ cup red wine
2 tablespoons brown sugar
1 teaspoon salt
Ground pepper to taste
6 or 8 carrots, coarsely cut
8 stalks celery, coarsely cut
Pinch each rosemary and thyme

Combine all ingredients in slow cooker and cook at least 12 hours or overnight.
   Serve over rice.

YIELD: 6 SERVINGS

THE JUNIOR LEAGUE OF FARGO-MOORHEAD, NORTH DAKOTA/MINNESOTA

. . . .

Oriental Supper Bowl

1 pound lean round steak, cut into 1-inch cubes
1 pound lean pork steak, cut into 1-inch cubes
Meat tenderizer
2 eggs
1 cup flour
1 teaspoon salt
1 teaspoon ginger
½ cup water
Salad oil for frying

SAUCE:
1 1-pound 14-ounce can pineapple cubes
2 chicken bouillon cubes
½ cup brown sugar
¼ cup molasses
½ cup vinegar
⅓ cup cornstarch
¼ cup cold water

VEGETABLES:
2 cups sliced carrots (may use canned)
2 green peppers, seeded and cut into chunks
16 cherry tomatoes
1 1-pound can sweet potatoes
1 1-pound can whole green beans, drained

Cut away fat on meats. Sprinkle with meat tenderizer.

Beat eggs, flour, salt, ginger, and water to a smooth batter. Dip meat cubes in batter and fry in 1 inch of salad oil for 10–15 minutes. Drain off excess fat.

Make sauce as follows: Drain syrup from pineapple into measuring cup. Add enough water to make a total of 2 cups liquid. Heat to boiling with bouillon cubes, brown sugar, molasses, and vinegar in a large frying

Recipe continues . . .

pan. Stir in cornstarch smoothed to a paste with ¼ cup water. Cook, stirring constantly, until sauce thickens and boils for 3 minutes.

Cook carrots, if not using canned carrots.

Arrange beef and pork in center of large frying pan. Put pineapple cubes, carrots, peppers, tomatoes, sweet potatoes, and green beans in separate piles around meat. Pour sauce over and cover. Simmer 20 minutes.

Serve with rice.

YIELD: 6 SERVINGS

Tested, Tried, and True
THE JUNIOR LEAGUE OF FLINT, MICHIGAN

·   ·   ·   ·   ·   ·   ·   ·   ·   ·   ·   ·   ·   ·   ·   ·   ·   ·

Beef Stew with Buttermilk Dumplings

1 beef bouillon cube
2½ cups water
2½ pounds beef stew meat
3 tablespoons bacon drippings
2 teaspoons salt
¼ teaspoon pepper
½ teaspoon garlic powder
4 tablespoons flour
¼ teaspoon marjoram
¼ teaspoon oregano
4 medium onions, peeled
5 carrots, scraped and chopped
1 cup Burgundy

Dissolve bouillon cube in water and reserve.

Brown meat in hot drippings in a skillet. Add salt, pepper, and garlic powder. Remove meat to heavy pot with tight cover.

Stir flour into the drippings in skillet, then add bouillon and herbs. Pour sauce over meat. Add onions, carrots, and wine.

Stew 2 hours tightly covered. About ½ hour before serving, make dumplings. Drop batter by spoonfuls into the stew and cook, covered, for 12–15 minutes.

DUMPLINGS:

½ cup buttermilk
1½ cups flour
¾ teaspoon salt
1½ teaspoons baking powder
½ teaspoon baking soda
1 egg, beaten
3 tablespoons oil

Add buttermilk to dry ingredients. Then add beaten egg mixed with the oil. Beat well, until just blended.

YIELD: 5 SERVINGS

THE JUNIOR LEAGUE OF SAGINAW, MICHIGAN

· · · · · · · · · · · · · · · · · · · ·

Boeuf Bourguignonne

8 slices bacon, diced
3 pounds sirloin tip roast
1½ cups flour, seasoned with 2 teaspoons freshly ground salt
and 1 teaspoon freshly ground black pepper
4 tablespoons butter
2 large onions, sliced
1 pound fresh mushrooms, sliced
3 cups dry red Burgundy
2 10½-ounce cans beef consommé or 2½ cups bouillon

In large skillet, cook bacon crisply and remove to large platter.

Cut beef into 1-inch cubes (or larger if desired*), removing as much fat and gristle as possible. Roll in flour mixture and brown in the hot bacon drippings. Remove pieces as they are browned on all sides and put on bacon platter.

Melt butter and add sliced onions and mushrooms. Sauté gently until they begin to wilt. Add 1 cup Burgundy and simmer for 2–3 minutes.

Recipe continues . . .

Pour contents of skillet into a heavy kettle or Dutch oven. Add 2 more cups wine and the bouillon. Bring to a boil and add cooked beef and bacon. Simmer, stirring, for 2–3 minutes. Cover and cook over low heat for 2–3 hours. Add additional wine or bouillon to taste if sauce thickens too much.

Excellent served with a mixture of white and wild rice.

It freezes well.

YIELD: 12 SERVINGS

* NOTE: If meat cubes are bite-size, this dish is good for buffet service with plates on laps and no need for knives at mealtime.

THE JUNIOR LEAGUE OF COLUMBUS, OHIO

·   ·   ·   ·   ·   ·   ·   ·   ·   ·   ·   ·   ·   ·   ·   ·   ·   ·   ·

Beef in Burgundy

16 small white onions
6 slices lean bacon, diced
¼ cup butter
4 pounds beef chuck, cut in 1½-inch cubes
1½ teaspoons salt
¼ teaspoon pepper
2 cups Burgundy
2 cloves garlic, peeled and chopped
2 cups small whole or sliced fresh mushrooms
1½ cups water
1 or 2 sprigs parsley
1 celery top, chopped
1 carrot, coarsely cut
1 bay leaf
1 sprig fresh thyme or 1 teaspoon dried thyme
6 tablespoons flour
½ cup cold water

Brown onions with bacon and butter in Dutch oven. Remove onions and bacon with slotted spoon and set aside. Add meat to pan and brown. Add remaining ingredients except flour and the ½ cup water. Cover and simmer 1½ hours.

Mix flour and cold water to thicken gravy, if necessary.

Pour stew into casserole, cover tightly, and bake at 350° for 35 minutes.

YIELD: 8 SERVINGS

Tested, Tried, and True
THE JUNIOR LEAGUE OF FLINT, MICHIGAN

·   ·   ·   ·   ·   ·   ·   ·   ·   ·   ·   ·   ·   ·   ·   ·   ·   ·

Beef Roulades

¾ pound ground beef
1 medium onion, finely chopped
1 4-ounce can sliced mushrooms
2 tablespoons butter
½ teaspoon salt
Pepper
1 teaspoon dry mustard
2 cloves garlic, minced
1 tablespoon steak sauce
½ cup dry sherry
1 teaspoon parsley
1 teaspoon oregano
1 teaspoon rosemary
1 bay leaf, crushed
Paprika
2 cups shredded sharp cheddar cheese
1 cup grated Parmesan cheese
8 crepes
Melted butter
16 thin slices mozzarella cheese

Recipe continues . . .

Brown beef, onion, and mushrooms in butter. Add salt, pepper, mustard, and garlic; simmer 5 minutes. Add steak sauce, sherry, herbs, cheddar cheese, and half of the Parmesan cheese.

Remove from heat and spread on crepes; roll up each crepe and place in greased baking dish. Sprinkle with the remaining Parmesan cheese and drizzle with a bit of melted butter. Top with mozzarella slices and heat at 400° for about 5 minutes, or until cheese is melted. Brown under broiler if desired.

YIELD: 4–6 SERVINGS

CREPES:
1 cup sifted flour
1 tablespoon sugar
Dash salt
1 cup cold milk
3 eggs, beaten
2 tablespoons melted butter
½ teaspoon butter

Mix and sift flour, sugar, and salt. Add milk and blend until smooth, then add beaten eggs and butter. Let stand for 2 hours.

Melt ½ teaspoon butter in a 7-inch skillet and pour in thin layer of batter, tipping pan to spread. When set and brown on underside, turn and brown lightly on other side.

YIELD: 8 CREPES

Marigolds to Munch On
THE JUNIOR LEAGUE OF PEORIA, ILLINOIS

Beef Turbans

⅓ cup sherry
⅓ cup fresh bread crumbs
3 tablespoons chopped chives
½ teaspoon seasoned salt
½ teaspoon lemon pepper seasoning
1¾ pounds ground sirloin or round steak
1 10-ounce package frozen patty shells, thawed
1 egg, lightly beaten
1 tablespoon water
6 whole mushrooms, sautéed in butter

Combine sherry, bread crumbs, chives, and seasonings. Add beef and mix well. Shape into six thick patties. Broil or grill close to heat about 3 minutes on each side, just until browned but not thoroughly cooked. Chill.

Roll patty shells, one at a time, on a lightly floured surface to a diameter of about 8 inches. Place a dollop of meat mixture on the center of each pastry circle. Fold dough around it by pleating; pinch dough together at top.

Combine egg with water and lightly brush over each "turban." Bake at 425° for 20–25 minutes, or until pastry is nicely browned.

Top each "turban" with a sautéed whole mushroom. Serve with Mushroom Sauce.

YIELD: 6 SERVINGS

MUSHROOM SAUCE:
2 cups sliced mushrooms
2 tablespoons butter
⅓ cup sherry
1½ tablespoons cornstarch
1¼ cups condensed beef broth
1 teaspoon lemon juice

Recipe continues . . .

Sauté mushrooms in butter. Mix sherry and cornstarch and add to mushrooms along with beef broth.

Simmer 2–3 minutes. Stir in lemon juice.

THE JUNIOR LEAGUE OF INDIANAPOLIS, INDIANA

Poor Girl's Stroganoff

1 large onion, sliced
3 tablespoons butter
1 pound ground chuck
3 cups dry noodles
3 cups tomato juice
1 teaspoon salt
1 teaspoon celery salt
2 teaspoons Worcestershire sauce
¼ teaspoon ground fresh pepper
1 cup sour cream

Sauté onion in butter. Remove from skillet and set aside. Brown the ground beef; return the onion.

Lay dry noodles over the meat and onion mixture. Do not stir.

Over all, pour tomato juice mixed with salt, celery salt, Worcestershire sauce, and pepper. Cover and simmer 15 minutes, then stir. Cook covered 15 minutes more.

Add sour cream; stir well. Heat but do not boil.

YIELD: 6 SERVINGS

Marigolds to Munch On
THE JUNIOR LEAGUE OF PEORIA, ILLINOIS

Stuffed Cabbage Rolls with Cranberry Sauce

2 medium heads of cabbage

CRANBERRY SAUCE:
1 1-pound can jellied cranberry sauce
1 8-ounce can tomato sauce
1 cup water
2 tablespoons lemon juice
¼ cup sugar
½ cup raisins

MEAT MIXTURE:
2 pounds lean ground beef
3 saltines, soaked in water and squeezed dry
1 medium onion, grated
3 tablespoons uncooked rice
¼ cup water mixed with 2 tablespoons catsup
1 egg, beaten
Salt and pepper to taste

Core the cabbages and place in a large kettle. Cover with boiling water and cook for 10 minutes. Remove from heat and run cold water over cabbages. Separate leaves and reserve the best leaves from each cabbage.

To make Cranberry Sauce, combine all ingredients except raisins in a saucepan and bring to a boil. Add raisins and simmer for 5 minutes. Remove from heat and set aside.

Combine all meat mixture ingredients in a large bowl. Fill cabbage leaves with heaping teaspoons of the mixture (as much as the leaves can take but not so much that meat escapes when leaves are rolled). Trim off any excess cabbage on either side of the meat.

Place filled and rolled leaves in a roasting pan; cover with Cranberry Sauce and simmer on top of the stove, covered, for 1 hour. Then bake in a 350° oven, uncovered, for 1 hour, or until the cabbage is tender. Baste occasionally.

Recipe continues . . .

It is best to refrigerate the rolls for several hours before serving so the fat will congeal and can be removed. Reheat before serving in 350° oven for 1½ hours.

The cabbage rolls will keep several days in the refrigerator, and they freeze well.

YIELD: 25–30 CABBAGE ROLLS

VARIATION:

For a little extra zip, add a little lemon juice and sugar to the sauce while reheating.

Discover Dayton
THE JUNIOR LEAGUE OF DAYTON, OHIO

Indiana Meat Loaf

2 slices rye bread
2 slices white bread
1 cup water
1 pound ground beef
1 medium onion, chopped
4 sprigs parsley, chopped
3 tablespoons grated Parmesan cheese
1 egg
1 teaspoon salt
¼ teaspoon pepper
2 tablespoons butter
1 8-ounce can tomato sauce
1 teaspoon oregano

Put bread in bowl and pour water over it. Let it soak, then mash with a fork. Add meat, onion, parsley, and cheese.

Beat egg lightly and add. Add salt and pepper and mix well.

Pack into 8 x 4-inch loaf pan, dot with butter, and bake at 375° for 30 minutes. Then pour tomato sauce and oregano on top and bake another 20 minutes.

YIELD: 5 SERVINGS

THE JUNIOR LEAGUE OF SOUTH BEND, INDIANA

Michigan Meat Loaf

2 eggs, beaten
¾ cup soft bread crumbs
½ cup tomato juice
2 tablespoons parsley
½ teaspoon oregano
3 teaspoons salt
¼ teaspoon pepper
Small clove garlic, minced
2 pounds lean ground beef
8 thin slices boiled ham
1½ cups shredded mozzarella cheese
1 8-ounce package sliced mozzarella cheese

Combine eggs, bread crumbs, tomato juice, parsley, oregano, salt, pepper, and garlic; mix with beef.

On a large sheet of foil, place beef mixture and flatten out to a 10 x 12-inch rectangle. Arrange ham on the meat and sprinkle with shredded cheese. Starting at the short end of the meat, roll up jelly-roll style using the foil to lift the edges and ends.

Place the meat loaf, seam side down, in 9 x 13-inch pan. Bake for 1¼ hours at 350°.

Recipe continues . . .

Just before serving, put sliced mozzarella over top to melt slightly. This recipe can be made ahead and frozen, unbaked.

YIELD: 8 SERVINGS

Cookbook
THE JUNIOR LEAGUE OF GRAND RAPIDS, MICHIGAN

Barbecued Meat Loaf

1½ pounds ground beef
1 onion, finely chopped
1 cup fresh bread crumbs
1 egg, beaten
1½ teaspoons salt
½ teaspoon pepper
2 8-ounce cans tomato sauce
½ cup water
3 tablespoons vinegar

Mix together beef, onion, crumbs, egg, salt, pepper, and ½ can tomato sauce. Firm into loaf and place in a loaf pan.

Combine rest of tomato sauce with remaining ingredients and pour over loaf.

Bake at 350° for 1¼ hours, basting occasionally.

YIELD: 4–6 SERVINGS

THE JUNIOR LEAGUE OF INDIANAPOLIS, INDIANA

Pinwheel Meat Loaf

1½ pounds ground beef
1½ teaspoons salt
¼ teaspoon pepper
½ onion, finely chopped
1 egg, lightly beaten
2 tablespoons evaporated milk
½ cup bread crumbs

Mix meat, salt, pepper, and onion. Add egg, milk, and crumbs to meat and mix well.

Roll meat mixture out on a sheet of wax paper with a wet rolling pin to about ½-inch thickness. Spread with Savory Dressing. Roll like a jelly roll.

Place in baking pan and bake in moderate oven (350°) for 1 hour.

YIELD: 6 SERVINGS

SAVORY DRESSING:
¼ cup butter
½ onion, finely chopped
¼ cup finely chopped celery with leaves
3 tablespoons parsley flakes
3 cups soft bread crumbs
¾ teaspoon salt
½ teaspoon poultry seasoning
⅛ teaspoon pepper
1 tablespoon water

Melt butter in a skillet. Add onion, celery, and parsley. Cook slowly for 5 minutes. Mix with crumbs, seasonings, and water.

Tested, Tried, and True
THE JUNIOR LEAGUE OF FLINT, MICHIGAN

. . . .

Individual Meat Loaves with Sherry Wine Sauce

1½ pounds ground beef
1 cup soft bread crumbs
1 egg, beaten
2 tablespoons grated onion
1½ teaspoons salt
½ teaspoon pepper
½ cup tomato sauce

Mix all ingredients together lightly; shape into six small meat loaves. Place in greased shallow pan. Bake in 250° oven for 1 hour.

Drain fat from pan. Pour Sherry Wine Sauce over loaves and bake for ½ hour longer at 350°, basting frequently.

YIELD: 4–6 SERVINGS

SHERRY WINE SAUCE:
1 tablespoon cornstarch
½ cup brown sugar
½ cup tomato sauce
¼ cup sherry
¾ cup beef consommé
1 teaspoon prepared mustard
1 tablespoon wine vinegar

Mix cornstarch and sugar in saucepan. Add remaining ingredients, mixing until smooth. Stir over medium heat until sauce boils and thickens.

The Discovery Shop Cookbook
THE JUNIOR LEAGUE OF SIOUX CITY, IOWA

Lemon Barbecued Beef Loaves

1½ pounds ground beef
¼ cup lemon juice
½ cup water
1 egg, lightly beaten
4 slices stale bread, finely diced
¼ cup finely chopped onion
2 teaspoons seasoning salt
⅓ cup brown sugar
½ cup catsup
1 teaspoon dry mustard
¼ teaspoon ground cloves
6 thin slices lemon

Mix together meat, lemon juice, water, egg, bread, and onion; form six individual loaves. Place in a shallow pan and bake at 350° for 15 minutes.

Mix salt, brown sugar, catsup, mustard, and cloves. Spread over loaves and place a thin slice of lemon on each.

Bake an additional 40 minutes, basting occasionally with pan juices.

YIELD: 6 SERVINGS

Marigolds to Munch On
THE JUNIOR LEAGUE OF PEORIA, ILLINOIS

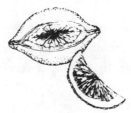

Meat-Stuffed Pumpkin

1 small pumpkin, 8–10 inches in diameter
Salted water
Salt
2 tablespoons cooking oil
2 pounds ground beef chuck
1 pound ground ham (may be smoked)
2½ cups finely chopped onion
1 green pepper, finely chopped
2½ teaspoons salt
2 teaspoons olive oil
2 teaspoons oregano
1 teaspoon vinegar
1 teaspoon pepper
2 large cloves garlic, mashed
1 cup raisins
½ cup diced apple
1 8-ounce can tomato sauce
3 eggs, beaten

Cut circular top from pumpkin, reserving for lid. Scoop out seeds and scrape sides of pumpkin clean. Place in large pan, cover with salted water, add lid, and bring to a boil. Simmer about 30 minutes, or until pumpkin is almost tender but firm enough to hold shape well. Drain and sprinkle inside of pumpkin with salt.

In oil in large skillet, cook beef, ham, onion, and green pepper, stirring until meat is brown and crumbly; remove from heat. Add all remaining ingredients except eggs and stir. Cook, covered, over low heat for about 15 minutes, stirring occasionally.

Cool slightly, then mix in beaten eggs thoroughly.

Fill pumpkin with meat mixture, packing in firmly. Cover with pumpkin lid, place in shallow baking pan, and bake at 350° for 1 hour.

Serve in wedges (pumpkin shell and filling), eating pumpkin as well as filling.

Can be prepared early in the day and baked just before serving. This is a variation of a Jamaican dish using more available ingredients.

YIELD: 8 SERVINGS

Cincinnati Celebrates
THE JUNIOR LEAGUE OF CINCINNATI, OHIO

· ·

Chow Mein Hot Dish

1 pound ground beef
⅓ cup soy sauce
1 cup chopped onion
1 10½-ounce can mushroom soup
1 3-ounce can mushrooms
2 cups chopped celery
1 cup uncooked rice
½ teaspoon salt
½ teaspoon pepper
2½ cups boiling water
chow mein noodles

Brown meat and add remaining ingredients except noodles. Empty into a large casserole, cover, and bake at 350° for 1½ hours.

Sprinkle with chow mein noodles before serving.

YIELD: 4 SERVINGS

The Discovery Shop Cookbook
THE JUNIOR LEAGUE OF SIOUX CITY, IOWA

· ·

Male Chauvinist Chili

6 slices bacon
10 ounces hot Italian sausage, cut into 1-inch slices
10 ounces lean ground beef
1 large Spanish onion, cut into chunks
1 green pepper, cut into large pieces
2 cloves garlic, minced
½ jalapeño chili pepper, diced
1 cup red wine
½ cup Worcestershire sauce
1 teaspoon hot dry mustard
1 teaspoon celery seed
1½ teaspoons chili powder
½ teaspoon salt
1½ teaspoons freshly ground pepper
6 cups Italian (pear-shaped) tomatoes
1 15-ounce can kidney beans
1 15½-ounce can garbanzo beans (chick peas)

Brown bacon in a large cast-iron pot or 4½-quart Dutch oven. Drain and crumble bacon and set aside. Pour bacon drippings from pot, leaving only a film. Brown sausage in pot; set aside with bacon. Pour sausage drippings from pot, again only leaving a film. Brown ground beef; drain and set aside. Pour excess fat from pot.

Cook onion, pepper, garlic, and chili pepper over low heat 2–3 minutes. Stir in wine and Worcestershire sauce; simmer, uncovered, for 10 minutes. Stir in mustard, celery seed, chili powder, salt, and pepper; simmer for 10 minutes.

Mash tomatoes; add (with liquid) to onion mixture along with meats. Heat to boiling; reduce heat and simmer, covered, for ½ hour, stirring occasionally.

Stir beans (with liquid) into chili. Heat to boiling, reduce heat, cover, and simmer for 1 hour.

This recipe is best made a day ahead and reheated, as flavors will meld to their spicy best.

Serve with cooked rice.

YIELD: 10 SERVINGS

Tested, Tried, and True
THE JUNIOR LEAGUE OF FLINT, MICHIGAN

Reuben Casserole

A variation of the Reuben sandwich.

1 16-ounce can sauerkraut, drained
1 2¼-ounce package sliced corned beef
1½ cups shredded Swiss cheese
3 tablespoons Thousand Island dressing
2 medium tomatoes, sliced
1 cup crushed rye crackers
2 tablespoons butter
¼ teaspoon caraway seeds

Layer sauerkraut, corned beef, and cheese in 1½-quart casserole. Spoon dressing over cheese; top with tomatoes.

Sauté cracker crumbs in butter; stir in caraway seeds. Spoon over tomatoes.

Bake at 425° for 30 minutes.

YIELD: 4 SERVINGS

Be Our Guest
THE JUNIOR LEAGUE OF MILWAUKEE, WISCONSIN

Quick Crescent Taco Pie

1–1¼ pounds ground beef
1 1½-ounce package taco seasoning mix
½ cup water
1 8-ounce package crescent dinner rolls
1½–2 cups crushed corn chips
1–2 tomatoes, sliced (optional)
1 cup sour cream
1 cup shredded cheddar cheese

Brown beef in skillet and drain off excess fat. Stir in seasoning mix and water; simmer 5 minutes.

Separate dinner rolls into eight triangles. Place triangles in ungreased 9- or 10-inch pie pan; press to form crust. (Use fewer rolls if a thinner crust is preferred.)

Sprinkle 1 cup corn chips over bottom of crust. Spoon meat over chips. Add a layer of tomatoes, if desired. Spread sour cream over top, cover with cheese, and sprinkle with remaining chips.

Bake at 375° for 20–25 minutes, or until crust is golden brown.

YIELD: 6–8 SERVINGS

THE JUNIOR LEAGUE OF INDIANAPOLIS, INDIANA

Oven Stew

2 pounds round steak or chuck steak, cubed
2 cups thickly sliced carrots
1 4-ounce can water chestnuts, drained and sliced
1 cup thickly sliced celery
2 medium onions, sliced into thick rings
1 6-ounce can mushrooms, drained and sliced
½ teaspoon sweet basil
¼ teaspoon black pepper
3 tablespoons flour
1 tablespoon sugar
1 tablespoon salt
1 1-pound can tomatoes
1 cup Burgundy

Put meat and all vegetables into a heavy casserole or Dutch oven and sprinkle with sweet basil and pepper.

Combine flour, sugar, and salt and sprinkle over meat and vegetables. Pour tomatoes and Burgundy over all. Break up tomatoes; mix lightly. Cover and bake for 4 hours at 325°. It will make its own gravy.

YIELD: 6 SERVINGS

THE JUNIOR LEAGUE OF ST. PAUL, MINNESOTA

Quick Lasagne

½ pound ground beef
½ cup chopped onion
2 cloves garlic, minced
2 teaspoons crushed oregano
2 10½-ounce cans tomato soup
½ cup water
2 teaspoons vinegar
½ pound plain lasagne noodles, cooked and drained
1 pint cottage cheese or ricotta cheese
½ pound mozzarella cheese, thinly sliced
Grated Parmesan cheese

In pan, cook beef with onion, garlic, and oregano until onion is transparent. Add soup, water, and vinegar. Simmer 30 minutes, stirring occasionally.

In shallow 2 x 8 x 12-inch baking dish, arrange three alternate layers of noodles, cottage or ricotta cheese, meat sauce, and mozzarella for a total of twelve layers. Sprinkle with Parmesan. Bake at 350° for 30 minutes.

Let stand 10 minutes before serving.

YIELD: 6 SERVINGS

THE JUNIOR LEAGUE OF FARGO-MOORHEAD, NORTH DAKOTA/MINNESOTA

· · · · · · · · · · · · · · · · · · ·

Lazy Woman's Lasagne

6 lasagne noodles
1 pound ground beef
1 package sloppy joe mix
1 1-pound can tomatoes
8 ounces cream cheese
Sliced green or black olives

Cook noodles according to package directions. Drain and rinse.

Brown beef; stir in sloppy joe mix and tomatoes.

Whip cream cheese until smooth. Layer noodles in a 1½-quart baking dish with meat and cheese. Garnish with olive slices. Bake in a 350° oven for 20 minutes or until bubbly.

YIELD: 4 SERVINGS

THE JUNIOR LEAGUE OF FARGO-MOORHEAD, NORTH DAKOTA/MINNESOTA

·　·　·　·　·　·　·　·　·　·　·　·　·　·　·

Lasagne Milanese

A northern Italian lasagne without tomato sauce.

MEAT SAUCE:
2 large carrots, finely chopped
2 medium onions, finely chopped
2 stalks celery, finely chopped
¼ pound bulk pork sausage
¼ cup oil
2 tablespoons butter
1½ pounds ground beef
1½ cups red wine
1 teaspoon salt
½ teaspoon pepper
2 16-ounce cans tomatoes

WHITE SAUCE:
½ cup butter
½ cup flour
1 teaspoon salt
3 cups milk
10 ounces lasagne noodles
8 ounces shredded mozzarella cheese
Grated Parmesan cheese
Butter

Recipe continues ...

Cook carrots, onions, celery, and sausage in oil and butter until vegetables are tender. Add ground beef and cook gently for 20 minutes; drain. Stir in wine, salt, and pepper; cook until wine evaporates. Add tomatoes and simmer for 1 hour.

Prepare the white sauce using butter, flour, salt, and milk. Cook in a saucepan over low heat until smooth and set aside.

Cook lasagne noodles according to package directions; drain. Place one-third of the noodles in the bottom of greased 3-quart baking dish. Spread with half the meat sauce and mozzarella cheese; sprinkle with Parmesan cheese. Spoon on half the white sauce and dot with butter. Repeat layers, ending with final third of lasagne. Brush with white sauce and more butter.

Bake at 425° for 35–45 minutes, or until top is golden and lasagne is hot and bubbly.

Let stand 10 minutes before serving.

YIELD: 6–8 SERVINGS

Be Our Guest
THE JUNIOR LEAGUE OF MILWAUKEE, WISCONSIN

Michigan Lasagne

½ pound mild Italian sausage
½ pound ground beef
1 teaspoon salt
1 1-pound can tomatoes
1 12-ounce can tomato paste
10 ounces lasagne noodles
3 cups creamy cottage cheese
¼ cup grated Parmesan cheese
¼ cup grated Romano cheese
2 tablespoons parsley flakes
2 eggs, beaten
1 teaspoon salt
½ teaspoon fresh ground pepper
1 pound mozzarella cheese, thinly sliced

Brown meat slowly in skillet; drain off excess fat. Add salt, tomatoes, and tomato paste. Simmer, uncovered, for 30 minutes.

Cook lasagne noodles in large amount of salted water approximately 8–10 minutes, then drain.

Combine cottage cheese, Parmesan, Romano, parsley, eggs, salt, and pepper.

In a 9 x 13 x 2-inch baking dish, place in order: half meat sauce, half noodles, half mozzarella cheese, and then half of egg and cheese mixture. Repeat layers. Bake in a 375° oven for about 45 minutes.

Best made a day ahead for optimum flavor. Can be frozen.

YIELD: 12 SERVINGS

Tested, Tried, and True
THE JUNIOR LEAGUE OF FLINT, MICHIGAN

· · · · · · · · · · · · · · · · · · ·

Lasagne Napoli

1 pound ground beef
1 medium onion, finely chopped
1 clove garlic, minced
1 4-ounce can sliced mushrooms
1 8-ounce can tomato sauce
1 6-ounce can tomato paste
1 teaspoon salt
Oregano to taste
1 13¾-ounce can chicken broth
1 egg
1 10-ounce package frozen spinach, thawed
1 cup creamy cottage cheese
1 8-ounce package sliced mozzarella cheese
1 8-ounce package lasagne noodles, cooked in salt water until done
⅓ cup Parmesan cheese

Brown meat and onion; blend in garlic, mushrooms, including liquid, tomato sauce, tomato paste, salt, oregano, and broth. Simmer about 1 hour, or until thick.

Meanwhile, mix egg, spinach, and cottage cheese.

Arrange layers in a baking dish as follows: one-third of the meat sauce, half the mozzarella, half the lasagne noodles, all the spinach mixture, another one-third of the meat sauce, remaining lasagne noodles, remaining mozzarella, and last one-third of the meat sauce. Top with Parmesan and bake about 45–60 minutes in a 350° oven.

Let stand 10 minutes before serving.

YIELD: 6–8 SERVINGS

THE JUNIOR LEAGUE OF DES MOINES, IOWA

Cannelloni with Meat Filling

½ cup onion, chopped
1 clove garlic, minced
1 carrot, grated
2 tablespoons olive oil
1 pound ground beef
¼ pound pork sausage
1½ teaspoons salt
½ teaspoon ground pepper
½ cup dry red wine
1 cup beef broth
1 tablespoon tomato paste
2 egg yolks, beaten
¾ cup grated Parmesan cheese
8 manicotti shells, cooked
1 cup hot medium white sauce
1 8-ounce package mozzarella cheese, shredded
2 tablespoons margarine

Sauté onion, garlic, and carrot in hot oil for 3 minutes. Add beef and sausage; cook over high heat until brown, stirring to keep lumps from forming.

Stir in salt, pepper, wine, broth, and tomato paste. Cover and cook over low heat for 1 hour, stirring often.

Drain meat and reserve wine sauce. Cool meat a few minutes, then mix with egg yolks and half the Parmesan cheese. Stuff shells with mixture and arrange in shallow casserole in single layer. Pour wine sauce over them.

Combine white sauce and mozzarella cheese. Pour this sauce over stuffed shells. Sprinkle with rest of grated Parmesan, dot with butter or margarine, and bake in 350° oven for 20 minutes or until cheese sauce bubbles.

YIELD: 8 SHELLS (APPROXIMATELY 4 SERVINGS)

Sunflower Sampler
THE JUNIOR LEAGUE OF WICHITA, KANSAS

· · · · · · · · · · · · · · · · · · ·

Cheese and Pasta in a Pot

2 pounds ground beef
2 medium onions, chopped
1 clove garlic, minced
1 14-ounce jar spaghetti sauce
1 1-pound can tomatoes
1 3-ounce can mushrooms
8 ounces macaroni
2 cups sour cream
½ pound provolone cheese, sliced
½ pound mozzarella cheese, sliced

Cook meat; drain off fat. Add onions, garlic, spaghetti sauce, tomatoes, and mushrooms. Simmer for 20 minutes, or until onions are soft. Cook macaroni and drain.

In 3-quart casserole, layer half macaroni, half sour cream, half meat sauce and provolone cheese. Repeat, ending with mozzarella cheese.

Cover casserole and bake at 350° for 35–40 minutes. Uncover and continue cooking until cheese melts and browns.

YIELD: 8 SERVINGS

Cookbook
THE JUNIOR LEAGUE OF GRAND RAPIDS, MICHIGAN

Spaghetti Pie

6 ounces spaghetti
2 tablespoons butter
⅓ cup grated Parmesan cheese
2 eggs, well beaten
1 pound ground beef
½ cup chopped onion
¼ cup chopped green pepper
1 8-ounce can tomatoes, chopped
1 6-ounce can tomato paste
1 teaspoon sugar
1 teaspoon oregano
2 teaspoons garlic salt
1 cup cottage cheese
1 cup shredded mozzarella cheese

Cook spaghetti according to package directions. Stir butter into hot spaghetti. Stir in Parmesan cheese and eggs. Form spaghetti into a "pie crust" nest in a 10-inch pie plate.

Cook beef, onion, and green pepper until vegetables are tender and meat loses all color. Drain off fat. Stir in undrained tomatoes, tomato paste, sugar, oregano, and garlic salt. Heat through.

Spread cottage cheese over spaghetti and fill pie with tomato mixture. Bake in a 350° oven for 20 minutes. Sprinkle with mozzarella and bake 5 more minutes.

YIELD: 6 SERVINGS

THE JUNIOR LEAGUE OF FARGO-MOORHEAD, NORTH DAKOTA/MINNESOTA

Mimi's Goulash

8 ounces noodles
1½ pounds ground beef
3 stalks celery, sliced
2 large onions, chopped
2 10½-ounce cans tomato soup
½ cup water
2 4-ounce cans mushrooms
1 tablespoon salt
¼ teaspoon pepper
4 tablespoons butter or margarine
2 cups cracker crumbs

Cook noodles according to package directions; drain and rinse.

Cook ground beef until it loses color. Drain and mix with noodles and all other ingredients except butter and crumbs. Empty into a 9 x 13-inch pan.

Melt butter in skillet. Stir in cracker crumbs and cook, stirring, until brown. Spread crumbs on top of meat mixture. Bake in a 350° oven for 25–30 minutes, or until bubbling.

YIELD: 4 SERVINGS

THE JUNIOR LEAGUE OF SPRINGFIELD, ILLINOIS

·　·　·　·　·　·　·　·　·　·　·　·　·　·　·

Company Casserole

1 8-ounce package noodles
1 pound ground beef
2 8-ounce cans tomato sauce
1 cup cottage cheese
8 ounces cream cheese
¼ cup sour cream
½ cup chopped green onions and tops
1 tablespoon finely chopped green pepper
2 tablespoons melted butter

Boil noodles according to directions on package. Drain and rinse.

Brown meat. Stir in tomato sauce and turn off heat.

Combine remaining ingredients except butter. Spread half the noodles in a 3-quart casserole. Cover with all the cheese mixture. Put remaining noodles on casserole and pour the melted butter over all. Spread meat mixture on top.

Bake at 350° for 30 minutes.

May be frozen.

YIELD: 6–8 SERVINGS

Marigolds to Munch On
THE JUNIOR LEAGUE OF PEORIA, ILLINOIS

.   .   .   .

Kansas-Style Beef Liver

1 tablespoon bacon drippings
1 large onion, sliced in rings
1 pound beef liver, cut into thin pieces
Salt and pepper to taste
Flour
1 16-ounce can tomatoes
1 teaspoon Worcestershire sauce
3–4 dashes Tabasco
3 tablespoons catsup
3 tablespoons water

Heat bacon drippings in heavy skillet. Add onion and cook until transparent. Remove onion and set aside.

Sprinkle liver slices with salt and pepper and dredge in flour. Place in a pan and brown on both sides. Cover with onion rings.

Combine the rest of the ingredients and pour over liver. Cover and cook over low heat for 30 minutes.

YIELD: 4 SERVINGS

THE JUNIOR LEAGUE OF KANSAS CITY, KANSAS

.   .   .   .

Lamb and Veal

Marinated Roast Leg of Lamb

½ cup olive oil
2 teaspoons salt
1 teaspoon black pepper
Juice of 2 lemons
1 clove garlic
Thyme, parsley, oregano and onion flakes to taste
1 bay leaf
2 cups red or white wine
1 6-pound leg of lamb

Combine olive oil, salt, black pepper, lemon juice, garlic, thyme, parsley, oregano, onion flakes, and a bay leaf. (Use plenty of herbs—lamb is exceedingly friendly to herb flavoring.) Add to this the wine, either red or white. Place lamb in glass or crockery container, pour herb marinade over it, and marinate for 24 hours in refrigerator to let it absorb all the goodness of the mixture. Turn several times during the marinating period.

Remove the leg of lamb from the marinade and roast in a preheated slow oven (300°) until the meat thermometer registers 165°—the lamb will be pink and juicy and tender. Approximately 22–26 minutes per pound is right for medium well-done lamb. If there is a nice layer of fat on the leg, you will not need to baste the roast at all while cooking.

Remove lamb to a hot platter and serve on hot plates. Skim fat from liquid in pan and serve the brown juices over the roast.

A good bottle of wine is wonderful with this dinner, but don't serve mint jelly if you serve wine.

YIELD: 8 SERVINGS

Gourmet Gab
THE JUNIOR LEAGUE OF SAGINAW, MICHIGAN

Des Moines Leg of Lamb Roast

1 6-pound leg of lamb
Salt and pepper to taste
1 large onion, sliced in slivers
2 or 3 cloves garlic, sliced lengthwise
½–¾ 10-ounce bottle Worcestershire sauce
Small peeled potatoes (optional)

Wash leg of lamb with cold water and pat dry. Cut small slashes into meat at several places on leg.

Rub in salt and pepper on all sides of lamb. Insert small slivers of onion and garlic in slashes.

Roast for about 1 hour at 350°, then cover lamb with Worcestershire sauce and continue cooking for another 1–1½ hours.

During last hour of cooking, surround lamb with small potatoes if desired. When meat is done, remove from pan. Make gravy, if desired, by adding a little cornstarch mixed with water to pan juices and cooking until thickened.

YIELD: 8 SERVINGS

THE JUNIOR LEAGUE OF DES MOINES, IOWA

·　·　·　·　·　·　·　·　·　·　·　·　·　·　·　·　·

Butterflied Grilled Leg of Lamb

1 6-pound leg of lamb, butterflied by butcher
½ cup soy sauce
2 tablespoons olive oil
Juice of 3 lemons
4 green onions, chopped
3 or 4 sprigs chopped fresh mint

Marinate lamb in a covered glass or enamel-lined container with mixture of remaining ingredients for about 12 hours, turning meat occasionally.

Recipe continues . . .

Barbecue meat on a charcoal grill approximately 20 minutes per side. Lamb should be pink in the middle. Slice in thin strips.

YIELD: 6–8 SERVINGS

Cincinnati Celebrates
THE JUNIOR LEAGUE OF CINCINNATI, OHIO

· · · · · · · · · · · · · · · · · · · ·

Parmesan Lamb Chops

Onion salt
Freshly ground pepper
4 lamb chops
3 tablespoons grated Parmesan cheese
⅓ teaspoon garlic powder
¼ teaspoon oregano

Sprinkle onion salt and pepper on lamb chops. Broil chops 7–10 minutes; turn and broil 8 minutes more.

Combine Parmesan cheese, garlic powder, and oregano. Sprinkle over chops. Cook 2 minutes longer.

YIELD: 2 SERVINGS

VARIATION:
For a less expensive meal, try the same thing on lamb patties.

Marigolds to Munch On
THE JUNIOR LEAGUE OF PEORIA, ILLINOIS

· · · · · · · · · · · · · · · · · · · ·

Fresbi Lamb Shanks

4 lamb shanks
1 teaspoon dill weed
½ teaspoon oregano
1 teaspoon rosemary
1 clove garlic
1 large onion, thinly sliced
1 8-ounce can stewed tomatoes
¼ cup brown sugar
1 cup white wine
1½ teaspoons salt
⅛ teaspoon pepper

Place shanks and all ingredients in covered roaster and bake for 3 hours at 300°. Remove cover and continue to cook for 30 minutes.

When done, remove lamb to serving platter and pour pan juices into saucepan. Reduce by half over high heat. Pour over meat and serve.

YIELD: 4 SERVINGS

Cookbook
THE JUNIOR LEAGUE OF GRAND RAPIDS, MICHIGAN

Ragout of Lamb

3 pounds very lean boneless lamb, cut into 1-inch cubes
¼ cup flour
1½ teaspoons salt
⅛ teaspoon freshly ground pepper
¼ cup olive or salad oil
2 cups chicken broth, or 1½ cups broth and ½ cup dry sherry
2 cloves garlic, crushed
¼ teaspoon marjoram
¼ teaspoon savory
2 tablespoons finely chopped parsley
1 tablespoon lemon juice
½ tablespoon grated lemon rind
Cooked small carrots and onions (optional)
Watercress (optional)

Dredge lamb in flour seasoned with ½ teaspoon salt and the freshly ground pepper.

Heat the oil in oven-type skillet (one with tight-fitting lid and heat-proof handle) and brown lamb on all sides. Add chicken broth, garlic, marjoram, savory, and the remaining 1 teaspoon salt. Cover tightly and place in a moderate 350° oven for about 1½ hours, or until lamb is tender.

If there is more than 1 cup of broth at the end of cooking time, remove cover and boil rapidly over direct heat to reduce the gravy to 1 cup. Just before serving, stir in the parsley, lemon juice, and rind. Garnish, if desired, with clusters of tiny cooked carrots, whole onions, and sprigs of watercress.

YIELD: 6 SERVINGS

Peacock Pie and Other Perfections
THE JUNIOR LEAGUE OF BATTLE CREEK, MICHIGAN

Spring Lamb Hunter-Style

2 tablespoons oil
⅓ stick butter
2 pounds lamb shoulder, cut in 2-inch pieces
1 teaspoon salt
½ teaspoon pepper
¼ teaspoon sage
¼ teaspoon thyme
¼ teaspoon rosemary
2 tablespoons flour
2 cloves garlic, crushed
1 cup dry white wine
1 cup beef consommé
2 tablespoons wine vinegar
½ pound mushrooms, sliced
1 green pepper, cut in julienne strips

In a heavy Dutch oven, heat oil and butter; add lamb, sprinkled with salt, pepper, sage, thyme, and rosemary. Brown lamb well on all sides. Sprinkle with flour; add garlic, wine, consommé, and vinegar. Cover and simmer for 45 minutes, stirring occasionally.

Add mushrooms and green pepper and cook 20–30 minutes longer, or until meat is tender. If sauce is too thin, remove cover and let it cook down.

This dish may be prepared in advance up to the point where mushrooms and green pepper are added and frozen. When ready to cook, bring back to simmering heat, add mushrooms and peppers, and cook until meat is tender.

YIELD: 4–6 SERVINGS

Cincinnati Celebrates
THE JUNIOR LEAGUE OF CINCINNATI, OHIO

Baked Hash

Leftover cooked lamb or beef (1 cup per serving)
1–2 potatoes
2 carrots
1 small onion
Leftover gravy or broth

Grind leftover meat, potatoes, carrots, and onion. Moisten with gravy or broth.

Bake in covered casserole at 350° for about 1 hour. If hash is too moist, remove cover for an extra 10–15 minutes.

Serve with pickle relish.

This can also be served with a poached egg on each portion.

THE JUNIOR LEAGUE OF COLUMBUS, OHIO

Veal Piccata à la Milanese

1 pound veal, thinly sliced
Flour
1 egg, beaten
Bread crumbs
3 tablespoons butter
2 tablespoons olive oil
Rosemary
Pepper
Lemon wedges

Trim any fat or gristle off meat and cut veal into about 2 x 4-inch pieces. Pound with flour until very thin.

Dip the floured meat in egg and then bread crumbs. Put butter and olive oil in heavy frying pan. Add a pinch of rosemary and dash of pepper. Sauté veal slowly until golden brown.

Serve with lemon wedges and the pan drippings.
Can be made ahead and reheated in the pan.

YIELD: 4 SERVINGS

Cookbook
THE JUNIOR LEAGUE OF GRAND RAPIDS, MICHIGAN

·   ·   ·   ·   ·   ·   ·   ·   ·   ·   ·   ·   ·   ·   ·   ·   ·   ·

Braised Veal Rosemary

⅓ cup flour
¾ teaspoon salt
⅛ teaspoon pepper
2 teaspoons paprika
½ teaspoon monosodium glutamate
1½ pounds veal round or cutlet
3 tablespoons butter or oil
2 onions, thinly sliced
¼ teaspoon rosemary
⅓ cup water
¾ cup sour cream

Blend flour with salt, pepper, paprika, and monosodium glutamate. Cut the veal in bite-size pieces, about 1½ inches square. Rub each piece with the seasoned flour.

Melt 2 tablespoons of butter in a heavy skillet. Add pieces of veal and brown on all sides.

While the veal is browning, melt the remaining 1 tablespoon butter in a small skillet; add sliced onions and cook slowly until the onions are light golden in color.

Sprinkle each portion of meat with the rosemary; arrange the onions over the seasoned pieces of veal. Add about ⅓ cup water. Cover and

Recipe continues . . .

simmer for about 1 hour, or until the veal is tender. Add more water if necessary so the meat does not get dry.

Blend sour cream into the liquid in the skillet just before serving.

YIELD: 4 SERVINGS

THE JUNIOR LEAGUE OF FARGO-MOORHEAD, NORTH DAKOTA/MINNESOTA

Veal in Wine

1½–2 pounds veal cutlets, cut in ½ x 2-inch strips
3 tablespoons olive oil
1 16-ounce can tomatoes
1 onion, thinly sliced
1 green pepper, cut into thin strips
1 8-ounce can sliced mushrooms, drained
¼ teaspoon garlic powder
⅛ teaspoon oregano
½ cup grated cheese (mozzarella, Parmesan, or your favorite)
Salt and pepper to taste
¾ cup white wine

Brown veal in olive oil. Drain and arrange veal in baking dish. Add tomatoes, including juice, sliced onion, green pepper, mushrooms, garlic powder, oregano, cheese, and salt and pepper. Pour wine over all.

Cover and bake at 325° for 45 minutes.

Serve on cooked noodles or rice.

YIELD: 6 SERVINGS

THE JUNIOR LEAGUE OF KANSAS CITY, KANSAS

Tarragon Veal

¼ cup butter
4 pounds boneless veal shoulder, cut in 1-inch cubes
⅓ cup flour
1½ cups dry white wine
1¾ cups boiling water
2 teaspoons salt
¼ pound mushrooms, sliced and sautéed
4 teaspoons dried tarragon or ¼ cup chopped fresh
2 medium onions, chopped
4 egg yolks
¼ cup tarragon vinegar
1 cup sour cream
¼ cup chopped parsley

Melt butter in large, heavy skillet and brown meat cubes, removing them when brown; do not crowd skillet.

Return all meat to skillet when the last pieces are browned. Sprinkle flour over meat and stir until flour is absorbed. Add wine and water gradually, stirring constantly. Add salt, mushrooms, tarragon, and onions; cook 1 minute and transfer to a large casserole. Cover tightly and bake for 2 hours at 275°.

Mix egg yolks with tarragon vinegar and sour cream; remove casserole from oven, stir in sour cream mixture, and return to oven for 5–10 minutes, uncovered, to thicken sauce.

Sprinkle with parsley before serving.

YIELD: 10–12 SERVINGS

Cincinnati Celebrates
THE JUNIOR LEAGUE OF CINCINNATI, OHIO

Veal Loaf

1½ pounds ground veal
½ pound ground pork
1 small onion, chopped
1 small green pepper, chopped
1 teaspoon salt
¼ teaspoon pepper
1 egg
1 6-ounce can tomato sauce
½ package stuffing mix
4 slices bacon

Mix together all ingredients except bacon. Pack into a 2-pound loaf pan and cover with bacon strips.

Bake at 350° for 1 hour.

YIELD: 6 SERVINGS

Bluff City Cooks
THE JUNIOR LEAGUE OF GREATER ALTON, ILLINOIS

. . . .

Grilled German Bratwurst

4 bratwurst
Cooking oil
1½ cups chopped onion
1 12-ounce bottle beer
2 tablespoons butter
½ teaspoon onion salt
4 frankfurter buns
½ cup shredded sharp cheddar cheese
4 slices bacon, fried and crumbled

Brown bratwurst over medium heat in a little oil. Add onion and beer. Simmer, uncovered, for 20–30 minutes.

Stir together butter and onion salt; spread on buns.

Make a lengthwise cut in each bratwurst to within ½ inch of end and spoon on drained cooked onion; sprinkle with cheese. Place in a foil "boat," leaving sides open. Broil 4 inches from heat for 2 minutes. Top with crumbled bacon.

This dish can be done ahead except for the final heating, which can also be done on an outside grill; put bratwurst on a baking sheet and cover grill a few minutes. Watch so they do not burn on the bottom.

Serve with German potato salad.

YIELD: 4 SERVINGS

Soupçon
THE JUNIOR LEAGUE OF CHICAGO, ILLINOIS

· · · · · · · · · · · · · · · · · ·

Sweetbreads with Beef

2 pounds calf's sweetbreads
1 teaspoon salt
1 tablespoon lemon juice
2 3-ounce packages dried beef (not smoked)
5 tablespoons butter
5 tablespoons flour
2 cups light cream or milk
2 cups chicken broth
1 pound fresh mushrooms or canned equivalent
(if canned, use juice in cream sauce)
½ cup diced green onion with stems
¼ cup diced green pepper
1 tablespoon butter
Sherry

Soak sweetbreads in ice water for 2 hours, changing water several times. Put sweetbreads in saucepan with 4 cups water, the salt, and lemon juice.

Recipe continues . . .

Bring water to a boil and simmer for 15 minutes. Drain and plunge sweetbreads into cold water. Discard outer tissue and connecting tubes and cut sweetbreads into bite-size pieces.

Pull apart dried beef and frizzle in butter until butter begins to brown. Sprinkle flour over dried beef and stir until light brown. Carefully add cream and chicken broth; correct for thickness after sufficient cooking.

In separate pan, toss mushrooms, green onion, and green pepper and cook briefly in butter.

Combine sweetbreads, dried beef sauce, and mushroom mixture. Add sherry to taste.

If recipe is to be frozen, substitute vermouth for sherry. Add salt if needed. Serve over thin buttered toast.

YIELD: 8–10 SERVINGS

The Cook's Book
THE JUNIOR LEAGUE OF CEDAR RAPIDS, IOWA

• • • • • • • • • • • • • • • • • •

Mary's Lamb

4 lamb steaks
Salt and pepper
Butter
Rind of ½ lemon, grated
1 4-ounce can mushrooms
1 onion, chopped
⅓ cup Burgundy
1 beef bouillon cube
1½ cups water
Cornstarch
Salt to taste
1 10-ounce package frozen peas

Season steaks with salt and pepper, brown in butter, and transfer to a casserole. Sauté lemon rind, mushrooms, and onion; add wine and bouillon cube which has been dissolved in 1½ cups water.

Thicken sauce with small amount of cornstarch and add salt to taste.

Bring to a boil and pour over meat. Bake for 30 minutes, covered, in 325° oven.

Add frozen peas and bake an additional ½ hour.

YIELD: 4 SERVINGS

The Cook's Book
THE JUNIOR LEAGUE OF CEDAR RAPIDS, IOWA

Pork

Austrian Pork Roast

4½-pound boneless loin of pork
2 tablespoons salad oil
1 cup chopped onion
1 cup chopped carrot
1½ teaspoons salt
1 teaspoon paprika
¼ teaspoon pepper
1 cup chicken broth
2 tablespoons flour
¼ cup water
1 cup sour cream
1 tablespoon chopped parsley
2 teaspoons caraway seeds
1 teaspoon minced capers
Parsley for garnish

Brown pork loin on all sides in salad oil in large Dutch oven or heavy kettle. Remove pork and set aside.

Sauté onion and carrot in same pan just until onion is golden. Stir in salt, paprika, pepper, and chicken broth. Return pork to kettle. Heat liquid to boiling. Cover tightly and roast at 350° for 2½ hours, basting occasionally, until meat is thoroughly cooked and tender.

Remove pork to heated serving platter and make gravy: strain liquid and vegetables into a saucepan, pressing down hard on vegetables before discarding them. Skim fat and discard. Combine flour and water to a smooth paste and stir into liquid in saucepan. Cook, stirring constantly, until gravy thickens and boils—about 1 minute. Slowly blend in sour cream. Add parsley, caraway seeds, and capers.

Let pork stand about 15 minutes, then slice into ¼–½-inch slices; drizzle with part of sauce.

Garnish platter with sprigs of parsley. Serve remaining sauce in a sauceboat.

YIELD: 8 SERVINGS

Cookbook
THE JUNIOR LEAGUE OF GRAND RAPIDS, MICHIGAN

. . . .

Jeweled Crown Pork Roast with Wild Rice Stuffing

1 crown roast of pork (16 ribs)
3 tablespoons lime juice
1 tablespoon flour
1 teaspoon ginger
1 teaspoon salt
½ teaspoon freshly ground pepper
2 cups champagne or dry white wine
3 chicken bouillon cubes
2 tablespoons flour
Parsley
Clusters of green grapes
Small red crab apples
8 preserved kumquats

Place roast on rack in baking pan; pour lime juice over it. Mix flour, ginger, salt, and pepper; sprinkle over meat. Roast at 350° for 35 minutes per pound.

Meanwhile, combine all stuffing ingredients.

After first hour of roasting, remove meat from oven. Drain fat from pan; remove rack and fill center of crown with stuffing. Return roast to pan; cover stuffing with foil. Continue baking until done (170° on meat thermometer).

Cook remaining stuffing in a tightly covered casserole along with the roast for about 1 hour.

Drain off all fat but 3 tablespoons from pan. Heat 1½ cups wine with bouillon cubes, stirring until cubes are dissolved. Mix flour and remaining

Recipe continues . . .

½ cup cold wine and stir into pan drippings over low heat. Then add hot wine. Cook, stirring, until thick.

To serve, place pork on a platter; surround with a wreath of parsley. Place bunches of green grapes on top of parsley. Place red crab apples between the clumps of grapes. Spear kumquats on every other rib.

YIELD: 8 SERVINGS

STUFFING:
1 cup finely chopped onion
½ cup crushed pineapple, drained
4 slices bacon, cooked and crumbled
½ cup ripe pitted olives, chopped
1 cup chopped fresh mushrooms
2 eggs, beaten
2 tablespoons chopped parsley
1 cup finely chopped celery, lightly sautéed in butter
2 cups cooked wild rice
1 teaspoon marjoram
½ teaspoon thyme

Soupçon
THE JUNIOR LEAGUE OF CHICAGO, ILLINOIS

· · · · · · · · · · · · · · · · · · ·

Roast Loin of Pork English-Style

¼ cup softened butter
½ teaspoon crumbled thyme
1 bay leaf, crumbled
½ teaspoon salt
¼ teaspoon freshly ground pepper
1 teaspoon Dijon mustard
4–5 pound loin of pork (7–8 chops)
1 tablespoon flour
1 tablespoon butter
Watercress or parsley for garnish

Mix ¼ cup softened butter with seasonings; rub well into pork several hours before roasting and let stand at room temperature to absorb flavors.

Place roast in a shallow pan, fat side up, and brown at 450° for 15 minutes. Reduce oven temperature to 350° and continue to roast until done, about 30–35 minutes per pound.

Transfer roast to serving platter. Remove excess fat from pan and thicken pan drippings with flour kneaded with butter.

Garnish roast with watercress or parsley and serve with the pan gravy.

Delicious with potatoes roasted in pan with meat for last hour, turned occasionally until brown and crusty.

YIELD: 4–6 SERVINGS

Cincinnati Celebrates
THE JUNIOR LEAGUE OF CINCINNATI, OHIO

· · · · · · · · · · · · · · · · · · ·

Pork Tenderloin

1 cup soy sauce
1 tablespoon brown sugar
1½ ounces bourbon
Whole pork tenderloin

Combine soy sauce, sugar, and bourbon and marinate the pork tenderloin in the mixture for 2 hours.

Bake at 300° for 1 hour, basting every 5 minutes with the marinade.

YIELD: 8 SERVINGS

Marigolds to Munch On
THE JUNIOR LEAGUE OF PEORIA, ILLINOIS

· · · · · · · · · · · · · · · · · ·

Pacific Pork and Pineapple

1 1-pound 4 ounce can crushed pineapple
2 10¾-ounce cans cream of celery soup
1 package herb stuffing mix
¼ cup finely chopped green pepper
2 tablespoons melted butter
4–5 pound loin of pork, cut into slices but not all the way through
¼ teaspoon ginger

Drain pineapple; reserve juice. Combine ¾ cup pineapple, 1 can soup, the stuffing mix, green pepper, and butter. Mix well. Spoon between chops. Tie loin lengthwise.

Place on rack in shallow pan, fat side up. Cover with foil and bake at 325° for 1½ hours. Uncover and bake 1½ hours more.

Combine remaining can soup, ¼ cup pineapple juice, 2 tablespoons pan drippings, and the ginger. Heat and serve with pork.

YIELD: 8–10 SERVINGS

THE JUNIOR LEAGUE OF COLUMBUS, OHIO

. . . .

Chinese Roast Pork

⅓ cup soy sauce
2 tablespoons lemon juice
¼ cup sugar
1 small onion, sliced
4 green onions, cut in 1-inch lengths
¼ teaspoon ground ginger
4 cloves garlic, crushed
½ cup water
3-pound rib roast of pork
2 tablespoons cornstarch

Combine soy sauce, lemon juice, sugar, onions, ginger, garlic, and water in a mixing bowl. Place roast in the marinade, cover, and refrigerate 8–10 hours.

Remove roast and place on a rack in a roasting pan. Roast in preheated 325° oven for 1½ hours or until meat thermometer registers 182°.

Remove roast to a heated platter and combine pan juices with remaining marinade. Skim off fat. Add water to make 2 cups and thicken with cornstarch.

Simmer over medium heat until sauce thickens and boils. Slice roast, serve, and pass sauce in a gravy boat.

YIELD: 6 SERVINGS

Discover Dayton
THE JUNIOR LEAGUE OF DAYTON, OHIO

·   ·   ·   ·   ·   ·   ·   ·   ·   ·   ·   ·   ·   ·   ·   ·   ·

Baked Pork Tenderloin with Mustard Sauce

2½–3-pound fresh pork strip tenderloin

MARINADE:
¼ cup soy sauce
¼ cup bourbon
2 tablespoons brown sugar

MUSTARD SAUCE:
⅓ cup sour cream
⅓ cup mayonnaise
1 tablespoon dry mustard
1 tablespoon finely chopped green onion
1½ teaspoons vinegar
Salt to taste

Recipe continues . . .

Marinate meat for several hours at room temperature in mixture of soy sauce, bourbon, and brown sugar, turning occasionally. Remove from marinade and bake in slow oven at 325°, basting frequently with marinade, for 1 hour, or until tender.

Carve the tenderloin on the diagonal in thin slices and serve with Mustard Sauce.

To make the sauce, mix together sour cream and mayonnaise. Stir in remaining ingredients.

YIELD: 6 SERVINGS

Cookbook
THE JUNIOR LEAGUE OF GRAND RAPIDS, MICHIGAN

·   ·   ·   ·   ·   ·   ·   ·   ·   ·   ·   ·   ·   ·   ·   ·   ·   ·

Pork Tenderloin Braised in Wine

4-pound pork tenderloin
2 tablespoons rendered pork fat
⅓ cup currant jelly
Grated rind of 1 lemon

MARINADE:
3 cups dry red wine
2 large onions, coarsely chopped
1 carrot, coarsely chopped
1 large clove garlic, crushed
1½ tablespoons tarragon vinegar
½ teaspoon peppercorns
4 whole cloves
1½ teaspoons salt

Mix marinade ingredients and simmer 20–30 minutes. Cool. Place pork in a glass or earthenware container, pour over the cooled marinade, cover, and refrigerate 2–3 days, turning occasionally.

Remove pork from marinade, reserving the marinade, and blot dry with paper towels.

In heavy casserole, brown pork quickly in hot fat. Add marinade, cover, and cook slowly for 2–2½ hours, or until tender.

Remove meat. Strain liquid, bring to a boil, and reduce to about 1 cup by boiling rapidly. Add jelly and lemon rind to liquid and simmer a few minutes longer.

Pour a little of the sauce over the pork and serve the remainder in a sauceboat.

YIELD: 6–8 SERVINGS

THE JUNIOR LEAGUE OF INDIANAPOLIS, INDIANA

· · · · · · · · · · · · · · · · · · · ·

Pork Chops and Kraut Bavarian

2 large or thick-cut pork chops
1 tablespoon bacon drippings
½ medium onion, chopped
¼ teaspoon salt
¼ teaspoon paprika
½ teaspoon caraway seeds
½ cup light beer
1 tablespoon brown sugar
1 Rome Beauty apple, peeled and sliced
1 8-ounce can sauerkraut, drained

Brown chops well in bacon drippings. Remove chops and add onion. Brown lightly and add other ingredients.

Return chops to pot, cover, and simmer for 2 hours. Add additional beer during cooking if more liquid is needed.

Serve with green beans, dark bread, and beer.

YIELD: 2 SERVINGS

THE JUNIOR LEAGUE OF FARGO-MOORHEAD, NORTH DAKOTA/MINNESOTA

· · · · · · · · · · · · · · · · · · ·

Clean Stove Pork Chops

Salt and pepper
4 thick pork chops
Thyme or oregano
Milk or light cream
Parsley

Salt and pepper the pork chops and rub them well with thyme or oregano. Arrange them in a baking dish and cover with milk or light cream. Bake at 350° until the chops are tender—about 1 hour.

Sprinkle liberally with chopped parsley.

YIELD: 4 SERVINGS

Marigolds to Munch On
THE JUNIOR LEAGUE OF PEORIA, ILLINOIS

· ·

Broiled Pork Chops Stuffed with Apricots

6 rib pork chops, 1½ inches thick, with pockets cut
Salt and pepper
1 17-ounce can apricot halves
2 tablespoons chopped onion
2 tablespoons cooking oil
1 tablespoon lemon juice
¼ cup catsup
½ teaspoon dry mustard

Season pockets of chops with salt and pepper.

Drain apricots, reserving ½ cup of syrup. Insert 2 apricot halves in each pocket and secure with toothpicks.

Grill chops over medium coals for 35 minutes, turning once.

In the meantime, cut remaining apricots into small pieces. In a saucepan, mix onion, oil, lemon juice, catsup, dry mustard, ½ cup apricot syrup, and diced apricots. Heat to boiling, reduce heat, and let simmer for 15 minutes.

Cook chops 5 minutes more, constantly basting with the sauce. Pass remaining sauce with chops.

Try these chops with fresh corn on the cob and a tossed spinach salad for a sensational backyard barbecue.

YIELD: 6 SERVINGS

Discover Dayton
THE JUNIOR LEAGUE OF DAYTON, OHIO

. . . .

Country Pork Chops

4 pork chops
1 10¾-ounce can cream of mushroom soup
½ can water
¼ teaspoon thyme
1 medium onion, chopped
6 medium carrots, sliced round

In skillet on medium-low heat, lightly brown chops. Add other ingredients. Cover and cook 45–60 minutes.

Serve on wide noodles or rice.

YIELD: 4 SERVINGS

THE JUNIOR LEAGUE OF CHAMPAIGN-URBANA, ILLINOIS

. . . .

Paprika Pork Chops

6 center-cut loin pork chops, ¾ inch thick
Salt
Pepper
Paprika
1 large onion, thinly sliced

Season chops on both sides with salt, pepper, and paprika. Place chops together to resemble a loin roast, tucking several onion slices between each chop. Tie together with string.

Place on rack in roasting pan, fat side up. Sprinkle top generously with paprika. Roast at 325° for 2 hours.

Cut string and separate chops. Serve onion slices with each. If desired, make brown gravy from the drippings.

YIELD: 6 SERVINGS

Bluff City Cooks
THE JUNIOR LEAGUE OF GREATER ALTON, ILLINOIS

. . . .

Drunken Pork Chops

6–8 pork chops
Salt and pepper to taste
1 12-ounce can beer
⅓ cup catsup
¼ cup brown sugar

Sauté chops until nicely brown on both sides. Season with salt and pepper. Add mixture of beer, catsup, and brown sugar.

Simmer uncovered for 30–40 minutes, depending on thickness of chops.

YIELD: 6 SERVINGS

THE JUNIOR LEAGUE OF INDIANAPOLIS, INDIANA

. . . .

Sour Cream Pork Chops

Flour
4 thick pork chops
½ tablespoon pork fat or shortening
4 thinly sliced potatoes
2 onions, thinly sliced
1 clove garlic, minced
1½ cups sour cream
1½ teaspoons salt
½ teaspoon dry mustard

Flour pork chops and brown in hot fat.

Lay potato slices in greased 2-quart baking dish. Arrange browned chops on top of potatoes. Put onion slices on top of meat and sprinkle with garlic. Blend sour cream, salt, and mustard and pour on top of everything.

Bake, covered, for 1½ hours in 350° oven.

YIELD: 4 SERVINGS

THE JUNIOR LEAGUE OF SPRINGFIELD, ILLINOIS

Pork Chops and Cheesey Potatoes

1 11-ounce can cheddar cheese soup
½ cup sour cream
¼ cup water
3 tablespoons chopped parsley
4 cups thinly sliced potatoes
Salt and pepper
2 medium onions, thinly sliced
¾ cup chopped green pepper
6 pork chops, ¾ inch thick
¼ cup flour
2 tablespoons oil
6 green pepper rings, ½ inch thick
6 canned, spiced apples

Combine soup, sour cream, water, and parsley.

In 2-quart shallow casserole, alternate layers of potatoes sprinkled with salt and pepper, onions, chopped pepper, and soup mixture. Bake, uncovered, in 375° oven for 30 minutes.

Trim excess fat from pork chops and dust lightly with flour. Sauté in oil until nicely browned on both sides.

Stir potato mixture and put chops on top. Cover casserole and return to oven for 1 hour. Uncover and top with pepper rings and apples. Cover loosely and return to oven for 20 minutes more.

YIELD: 6 SERVINGS

THE JUNIOR LEAGUE OF ROCKFORD, ILLINOIS

Pork Chop and Sausage Casserole

4 loin pork chops
4 bratwurst or smoked sausages
Cooking oil
8–12 small new potatoes
1 1-pound can sauerkraut
1 cup beer

In a skillet, brown pork chops and sausage in small amount of oil. Transfer meat to 8 x 13-inch baking dish.

Brown potatoes lightly in oil remaining in skillet and add to the meat.

Sauté sauerkraut in same skillet, stirring until hot, and pour over meat and potatoes. Add beer.

Cover pan with aluminum foil and bake at 350° for 1 hour.

YIELD: 4 SERVINGS

THE JUNIOR LEAGUE OF ROCKFORD, ILLINOIS

·   ·   ·   ·   ·   ·   ·   ·   ·   ·   ·   ·   ·   ·   ·   ·

Tender Pork Chops

6 pork chops, ½ inch thick
Salt and pepper
2 tablespoons rosemary
2 beef bouillon cubes
½ cup white wine or white vermouth

Season chops with salt, pepper, and rosemary. Dissolve bouillon cubes in enough water to cover the bottom of a large frying pan by about ½ inch. Place chops in pan, cover and steam them in the bouillon, and cook for 30–40 minutes.

Recipe continues . . .

Drain off any remaining liquid. Add wine, turn up heat, and cook until wine is almost evaporated.

Serve with cooked rice.

YIELD: 6 SERVINGS

THE JUNIOR LEAGUE OF ST. PAUL, MINNESOTA

· · · · · · · · · · · · · · · · · · · ·

Pork Chops with Cream and Mustard Sauce

6 center-cut chops, 1½ inches thick
Salt and freshly ground pepper
Flour
2 tablespoons margarine
3 tablespoons vegetable oil
1½ cups onion, thinly sliced
3 tablespoons white wine vinegar
Bouquet garni (1 tablespoon parsley, 2 bay leaves)
Chicken stock or broth
¾ cup heavy cream
2 teaspoons Dijon mustard
1 tablespoon lemon juice
Parsley

Season chops with salt and pepper; dip in flour.

Melt margarine and oil in skillet. Brown chops for 3 minutes on each side, or until golden. Remove to casserole that will hold them in one layer.

Pour off all but a thin film of fat from skillet and add onion. Sauté for 5 minutes, or until soft and lightly browned. Add vinegar and bring to a boil, scraping off all the brown bits from sides and bottom of pan. Reduce to half; pour over the chops and add bouquet garni.

Bake in 325° oven for 10 minutes and then baste. If more liquid is needed, add 2–3 tablespoons chicken stock. Bake another 10 minutes, turn chops and bake for another 10 minutes. Baste again.

Test the chops: if done, remove to platter and keep warm and covered in 200° oven.

Remove excess fat from juices in baking dish, pour what remains into the skillet and add the cream. Bring to a boil over high heat. Stir constantly. When the sauce is thick enough to coat a spoon, remove from heat and add mustard and lemon juice to taste.

Strain the sauce, if desired, before serving. Garnish chops with parsley.

YIELD: 6 SERVINGS

Sunflower Sampler
THE JUNIOR LEAGUE OF WICHITA, KANSAS

·　·　·　·　·　·　·　·　·　·　·　·　·　·　·　·　·　·　·　·

Pork Chops with Spinach

6 pork chops
2 tablespoons shortening or fat
½ cup finely chopped onion
1 clove garlic, minced
3 cups tomato juice
⅓ cup mushroom pieces
½ teaspoon thyme
½ teaspoon marjoram
½ teaspoon rosemary
1 teaspoon sugar
1 teaspoon salt
Dash pepper
2 cups cornflakes
1 10-ounce package frozen chopped spinach, cooked and drained
½ teaspoon salt
1 egg, slightly beaten
1 tablespoon melted butter
¼ cup grated Parmesan cheese
Additional cheese (optional)

In a skillet, brown chops in hot fat. Spoon off all but 1 tablespoon of fat and sauté onion and garlic in the same pan.

Recipe continues . . .

Combine tomato juice, mushrooms, herbs, sugar, 1 teaspoon salt, and pepper and pour over chops in skillet. Cover and simmer 30 minutes.

Crush cornflakes into fine crumbs. Combine with spinach, ½ teaspoon salt, egg, butter, and cheese.

Place a mound of spinach mixture on each chop; cover and simmer 30 minutes longer.

Serve with additional cheese if desired.

YIELD: 6 SERVINGS

Peacock Pie and Other Perfections
THE JUNIOR LEAGUE OF BATTLE CREEK, MICHIGAN

. . . .

Hungarian Goulash

6 slices bacon, diced
3 large onions, sliced
2½ pounds pork tenderloin, cut into 1-inch cubes
1 large garlic clove, crushed
1 teaspoon dill seed
1 teaspoon caraway seeds (optional)
1 teaspoon paprika
1 teaspoon salt
1 teaspoon pepper
1 1-pound 13-ounce can sauerkraut, drained
2 tablespoons brown sugar
1 pound veal steak, cubed
2 cups sour cream

One day in advance, fry diced bacon until crisp. Remove to a casserole dish. Sauté onions in bacon drippings until golden and add to casserole along with cubed pork, garlic, and seasonings.

Cover these ingredients with sauerkraut. Sprinkle with brown sugar. Cover tightly and bake at 350° for 1 hour.

Remove cover, add veal, and mix thoroughly. Cover and bake another 45 minutes. Refrigerate, covered, overnight.

When ready to serve, reheat at 350° for 20–30 minutes, or until heated through. Top with sour cream for the last 15 minutes.

YIELD: 8 SERVINGS

Soupçon
THE JUNIOR LEAGUE OF CHICAGO, ILLINOIS

· · · · · · · · · · · · · · · · · ·

Hunters Stew

This is the national dish of Poland.

¼ cup flour
1 teaspoon paprika or caraway seeds
1 pound lean beef, cubed
1 pound lean pork, cubed
2 tablespoons butter
2 pounds sauerkraut, rinsed and drained
2 medium onions, sliced
12 ounces kielbasa (Polish sausage) or 6 smoked link sausage,
cut in 1-inch pieces
1 4-ounce can mushrooms with juice
½ cup dry white wine
Chopped parsley (optional)
Small cooked potatoes (optional)

Combine flour and paprika and coat meat with the mixture.

Heat butter in a heavy kettle or Dutch oven. Add meat and brown on all sides. Add sauerkraut, onions, sausage, mushrooms, and wine; mix. Cover and cook over low heat for 1½–2 hours.

Garnish each serving with parsley and potatoes if desired.

YIELD: 6–8 SERVINGS

THE JUNIOR LEAGUE OF KANSAS CITY, KANSAS

· · · · · · · · · · · · · · · · · ·

Stuffed Ribs

¼ cup chopped onion
½ stick butter
1 medium apple, peeled and diced
4 slices bread, torn
1 28-ounce can sauerkraut
1 teaspoon caraway seeds
4 4-rib racks pork back ribs
Salt and pepper
2 tablespoons brown sugar
¼ cup soy sauce

Cook onion in butter until transparent. Add apple, bread, sauerkraut, and caraway seeds; mix.

Sprinkle both sides of ribs with salt and pepper. Spread stuffing on inside of two racks, cover with remaining two racks, and tie each double rack together in 2–3 places.

Place on rack in roasting pan and brush with half the brown sugar mixed with soy sauce. Bake for 1½ hours at 350°, or until tender when pierced with a fork. Turn when half baked and brush other side with remaining sugar–soy sauce mixture.

Cut in serving-size sections and serve.

YIELD: 4 SERVINGS

The Discovery Shop Cookbook
THE JUNIOR LEAGUE OF SIOUX CITY, IOWA

Marinated Spareribs

2½ pounds spareribs or country ribs, cracked and cut into 2-inch pieces
1 slice onion
Water
¾ cup sugar
2 tablespoons cornstarch
½ teaspoon curry powder
⅛ teaspoon ground cloves
¾ cup water
⅓ cup cider vinegar
2 tablespoons soy sauce
1 clove garlic, crushed

Place ribs in pan, add slice of onion, cover with water, and simmer for 50 minutes; drain and chill.

Mix together sugar, cornstarch, curry powder, and cloves. Add the ¾ cup water, vinegar, soy sauce, and garlic. Cook, stirring constantly, until thick and boiling. Boil for 3 minutes.

Pour sauce over ribs and bake at 350° for 45 minutes.

YIELD: 6 SERVINGS

Cincinnati Celebrates
THE JUNIOR LEAGUE OF CINCINNATI, OHIO

·   ·   ·   ·   ·   ·   ·   ·   ·   ·   ·   ·   ·   ·   ·   ·   ·

Barbecued Country Ribs

2½ pounds spareribs or country ribs
4 tablespoons oil
Salt

Brown ribs in oil in hot skillet. Salt each one and place in 9 x 13-inch baking pan. Cook in oven at 325° for 1 hour. Pour off fat.

Recipe continues . . .

Pour sauce over ribs and continue cooking in oven for ½ hour more. If desired, lower oven temperature so ribs don't get too brown. Baste occasionally. Ribs can continue to cook for a long time on low heat if you're not ready to serve them.

YIELD: 6 SERVINGS

SAUCE:
½ onion, finely chopped
1 tablespoon butter
½ cup vinegar
¾ cup water
½ cup catsup
½ teaspoon each pepper, paprika, and dry mustard
4 tablespoons sugar

In saucepan, stew onion in butter over low heat for 5 minutes. Add remaining ingredients, bring to a boil, and boil for about 3 minutes.

THE JUNIOR LEAGUE OF ST. PAUL, MINNESOTA

· · · · · · · · · · · · · · · · ·

Finger Spareribs

2 tablespoons prepared mustard
6 tablespoons chili sauce
¼ teaspoon garlic powder
1 teaspoon hot pepper (or less)
4 pounds spareribs, cut into individual ribs
½ cup flour
3 teaspoons salt
½ teaspoon pepper
1 teaspoon thyme
4 tablespoons melted shortening

Mix together mustard, chili sauce, garlic, and hot pepper. Brush mixture on all sides of the ribs.

Mix flour, salt, pepper, and thyme. Shake ribs in this flour mixture. Brown the ribs in shortening, transfer to a shallow baking dish, and bake at 350° for 1 hour, or until ribs are crunchy.

YIELD: 4 SERVINGS

Cookbook
THE JUNIOR LEAGUE OF GRAND RAPIDS, MICHIGAN

· ·

Tender Barbecued Spareribs

2 4-rib racks spareribs cut into 2-bone portions
Salt and pepper
1 cup commercial barbecue sauce
½ cup water

Arrange ribs in a roasting pan and sprinkle with salt and pepper. Place pan, uncovered, in preheated 450° oven and bake until ribs are brown, about 40 minutes. Remove all melted fat from the pan with a squeeze-type baster. Add water. Cover pan and replace in oven for ½ hour. This steams and tenderizes ribs.

Brush the ribs on all surfaces with barbecue sauce. Place pan, uncovered, in oven for ½ hour, basting frequently.

Serve with cold apple sauce and tossed salad.

YIELD: 4 SERVINGS

Marigolds to Munch On
THE JUNIOR LEAGUE OF PEORIA, ILLINOIS

· ·

Special Honey-Barbecued Ribs

5 tablespoons sugar
3 tablespoons honey
3 tablespoons soy sauce
1 cup hot chicken broth (canned or bouillon)
2 tablespoons catsup
1 teaspoon salt
4 4-rib racks country-style ribs

Combine first six ingredients and pour over ribs in a roasting pan. Marinate at room temperature for 2–3 hours, turning ribs several times.

Bake, uncovered, 2–3 hours at 300°, turning occasionally.

YIELD: 4–6 SERVINGS

THE JUNIOR LEAGUE OF SPRINGFIELD, ILLINOIS

· · · · · · · · · · · · · · · · ·

Ham and Egg Rolls

¼ cup chopped green pepper
2 tablespoons chopped onion
1 clove garlic, minced (optional)
2 tablespoons butter
¼ cup bread crumbs
6 hard-boiled eggs, chopped
½ cup mayonnaise-type salad dressing
1 teaspoon dry mustard
Salt and pepper to taste
18 ham slices (cooked ham sliced by butcher is recommended)
½ cup shredded sharp cheddar cheese
¼ cup shredded Swiss cheese

Sauté green pepper, onion, and garlic in butter. Add and mix the next six ingredients. Spread mixture on ham slices and roll up.

Place in flat, buttered casserole and sprinkle with both cheeses.

Bake at 400° for 20 minutes.

For a brunch idea, serve with Bloody Marys and miniature danish.

YIELD: 9 SERVINGS

Tested, Tried, and True

THE JUNIOR LEAGUE OF FLINT, MICHIGAN

Ham and Broccoli Roll-Ups

5 thin slices cooked ham
1 10-ounce package frozen broccoli spears, cooked and drained
½ cup mayonnaise
3 tablespoons flour
½ teaspoon salt
Dash cayenne
1½ cups milk
½ cup shredded cheddar cheese
Fine bread crumbs

Roll ham around broccoli spears and arrange in shallow casserole.

In small saucepan, stir together mayonnaise, flour, salt, and cayenne. Gradually stir in milk. Cook over low heat until thickened. Add cheese and cook, stirring, until cheese is melted.

Pour cheese sauce over roll-ups, sprinkle with bread crumbs, and bake at 325° for ½ hour.

YIELD: 5 SERVINGS

THE JUNIOR LEAGUE OF DES MOINES, IOWA

Ham and Green Noodle Casserole

1 11-ounce can cheddar cheese soup
1 cup sour cream
¼ cup dry white wine
1 teaspoon Dijon mustard
¼ teaspoon white pepper
2 cups green noodles, cooked and drained
2 cups cooked ham, diced
¼ pound fresh mushrooms, sliced
½ cup sliced ripe olives
½ cup chopped dry roasted peanuts
1 cup shredded sharp cheddar cheese

Mix soup, sour cream, wine, mustard, and pepper. Place a thin layer of mixture in a greased 12 x 8 x 2-inch casserole; top, in layers, with half the noodles, half the ham, all the mushrooms.

Stir olives and peanuts into remaining sauce and spread half of it over the mushrooms. Layer again with noodles, ham, and remaining sauce. Sprinkle with grated cheese. Bake at 350° for 30 minutes.

Casserole can be prepared ahead, refrigerated, then baked 20 minutes covered and 20 minutes uncovered.

YIELD: 6 SERVINGS

Cincinnati Celebrates
THE JUNIOR LEAGUE OF CINCINNATI, OHIO

Cabbage Rolls

1 pound lean ground beef
½ pound bulk pork sausage
1 medium onion, chopped
1 egg
½ cup cooked rice
1 head cabbage, cored
1 16-ounce can stewed tomatoes
1 8-ounce can tomato sauce

Combine first five ingredients and form into egg-size balls.

Cook cabbage in boiling water for about 7 minutes. Drain, cool, and carefully remove leaves one by one.

Wrap leaves around meat balls and arrange in 8 x 13-inch baking dish.

Mix stewed tomatoes and tomato sauce and pour over cabbage rolls. Cover with aluminum foil. Bake at 350° for 1 hour.

YIELD: 8 SERVINGS

THE JUNIOR LEAGUE OF ROCKFORD, ILLINOIS

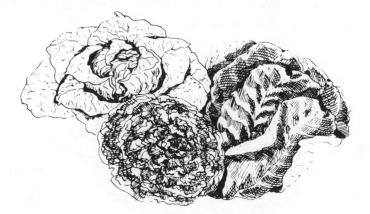

Stuffed Cabbage

A dish popular with the Polish and other Eastern Europeans who came in great numbers to the Midwest.

1 large cabbage (Savoy is best)
1½ pounds sausage meat
3 onions, chopped
½ cup milk
½ cup bread crumbs (can substitute rice)
1 egg
Salt and pepper
Chives
¼ pound bacon
1 10½-ounce can beef broth
Chopped carrot, onion, and celery
1 10½-ounce can water

Blanch whole cabbage in simmering water for 7–10 minutes. Drain on a towel. Open cabbage carefully by laying back each leaf until you almost reach the center, but do not remove the leaves.

To make stuffing, combine sausage, onions, milk, bread crumbs, egg, and seasonings. Spread some stuffing over each leaf, reforming the cabbage as you go. Tie the cabbage back into a head.

Place the bacon in the bottom of a Dutch oven, covering the whole surface. Add the cabbage, the beef broth, the cut-up vegetables, and 1 can water. Cover and simmer slowly for 3 hours.

Serve with boiled potatoes and beer.

YIELD: 6 SERVINGS

Soupçon
THE JUNIOR LEAGUE OF CHICAGO, ILLINOIS

Fourth Street Loaves

1 pound ground ham
1 pound pork sausage
⅓ cup fine cracker crumbs
2 tablespoons finely chopped green onion and stems
1 tablespoon finely chopped green pepper
2 tablespoons finely chopped fresh parsley
¾ cup hard cider
1 egg, lightly beaten
¾ teaspoon thyme
½ teaspoon dry mustard
1 teaspoon dark brown sugar
1 8-ounce can pitted ripe olives, sliced
Salt and pepper to taste
Flour
1 cup light brown sugar
3 tablespoons tarragon vinegar
1 teaspoon Dijon mustard
1 truffle, sliced (optional)

Mix first twelve ingredients thoroughly with salt and pepper to taste; divide into six portions. Form each portion into a uniform loaf. Place loaves on baking sheet, sprinkle each with small amount of flour, and bake in 350° oven until loaves are done and firm on top, about 20–25 minutes.

Bring mixture of light brown sugar, vinegar, and mustard to a hard boil and boil briefly.

Decorate each loaf with sliced truffle and spoon a little of the sauce mixture over them. Return loaves to oven and bake until tops are glazed, basting with remaining sauce once or twice during final baking period.

YIELD: 6 INDIVIDUAL LOAVES

The Cook's Book
THE JUNIOR LEAGUE OF CEDAR RAPIDS, IOWA

Ham Balls

1 pound ground ham
1 pound ground pork
¾ cup dry bread crumbs
2 eggs, beaten
1 cup milk
1½ cups brown sugar, packed
½ cup white vinegar
½ cup water
1 teaspoon dry mustard

Combine meats, bread crumbs, eggs, and milk. Shape into 1-inch balls. Place in 9 x 13-inch baking dish.

Combine brown sugar, vinegar, water, and mustard in small saucepan. Bring to a boil; boil for 2 minutes. Pour over meat balls.

Bake at 350° for 1¼ hours, turning occasionally. Remove excess fat with baster.

YIELD: 30 HAM BALLS

Be Our Guest
THE JUNIOR LEAGUE OF MILWAUKEE, WISCONSIN

.   .   .   .

Glazed Ham Loaf

1 pound ground ham
1 pound ground pork
2 cups bread crumbs
1 cup milk
2 eggs, beaten
1½ cups brown sugar
½ cup water
½ cup vinegar
½ teaspoon mustard

Combine ham, pork, bread crumbs, milk, and eggs. Shape into a rounded loaf and place in a shallow baking pan.

Mix remaining ingredients in saucepan and cook until sugar is melted. Pour sauce over loaves and bake at 350° for 2 hours, basting occasionally with liquid in pan.

YIELD: 6 SERVINGS

THE JUNIOR LEAGUE OF ROCKFORD, ILLINOIS

. . . .

Baked Ham Loaf

1½ pounds ground smoked ham
1½ pounds ground lean pork butt
1½ cups dry oatmeal
1½ cups soft white bread crumbs
1 11-ounce can tomato soup
3 eggs, beaten
1 cup milk

Mix all of the ingredients in a large bowl.

Pack into 9 x 13-inch pan and bake at 350° for 60–75 minutes.

YIELD: 8 SERVINGS

THE JUNIOR LEAGUE OF SPRINGFIELD, ILLINOIS

. . . .

Little Ham Loaves

1½ pounds pork steak
1 pound ham
1 cup cracker crumbs
1 cup milk
2 eggs, beaten
¼ teaspoon pepper

Recipe continues . . .

SAUCE:

1½ cups brown sugar
½ cup vinegar
½ cup water
1 teaspoon dry mustard

Grind together pork steak and ham and mix with cracker crumbs, milk, eggs, and pepper. Shape into eight individual loaves. Put into a 9 x 13-inch pan. Bake at 375° for 30 minutes.

Boil all sauce ingredients together for 5 minutes. Pour over baked ham loaves. Turn oven to 300° and cook loaves for another hour, basting every 15 minutes.

YIELD: 8–10 SERVINGS

Sunflower Sampler
THE JUNIOR LEAGUE OF WICHITA, KANSAS

·   ·   ·   ·   ·   ·   ·   ·   ·   ·   ·   ·   ·   ·   ·   ·   ·

Sausage-Filled Crepes

3 eggs, beaten
1 cup milk
1 tablespoon cooking oil
1 cup all-purpose flour
½ teaspoon salt
1 pound bulk sausage
¼ cup chopped onion
½ cup processed cheese
3 ounces cream cheese
¼ teaspoon marjoram
½ cup sour cream
¼ cup butter

For the crepes, combine eggs, milk, and oil. Add flour and salt; beat until smooth. Pour 2 tablespoons of batter into greased crepe pan; tilt to distribute batter. Cook on one side; invert on paper toweling. Repeat until batter is used. Set crepes aside.

For the filling, cook sausage and onion, stirring to break up sausage, until onion is transparent and sausage is well cooked. Drain off excess fat. Add cheese, cream cheese, and marjoram; mix.

Spread each crepe with 2 tablespoons sausage filling and roll up. Arrange side by side in greased 7½ x 11¾ -inch baking dish. Cover and chill.

Bake, covered, in 375° oven for 40 minutes. Mix sour cream and butter; spoon over baked crepes and bake, uncovered, an additional 5 minutes.

These may be kept for several days in the refrigerator before baking. They may also be frozen.

YIELD: 16 CREPES

THE JUNIOR LEAGUE OF SOUTH BEND, INDIANA

Poultry

Chicken with Grapes

12 whole chicken breasts, split
Flour
1 cup butter
¾ cup chopped onion
2 cups Sauterne
4 cups halved mushrooms
2 cups seedless grapes
1 cup light cream
Salt and pepper
Chopped parsley

Bone and skin chicken breasts and coat with flour. In skillet, brown floured chicken breasts in butter. As breasts brown, transfer them to heavy pot or Dutch oven. Sauté onion in butter remaining in skillet until tender. Spoon over chicken breasts along with any butter and juices left in skillet.

Add wine and mushrooms, cover, and cook gently until done, about 20 minutes. Add grapes and cook 3–5 minutes. Remove breasts and stir in cream. Season with salt and pepper, spoon over chicken and sprinkle with parsley.

YIELD: 24 SERVINGS

Peacock Pie and Other Perfections
THE JUNIOR LEAGUE OF BATTLE CREEK, MICHIGAN

Mozzarella Chicken

3 whole chicken breasts, split, skinned, and boned
2 eggs, beaten
1 teaspoon salt
⅛ teaspoon pepper
¾ cup Italian bread crumbs
½ cup vegetable oil
2 cups tomato sauce
1 teaspoon basil
⅛ teaspoon garlic powder
1 teaspoon margarine
½ cup grated Parmesan cheese
1 8-ounce package sliced mozzarella cheese, cut into triangles

Pound each chicken breast to ¼ inch thick. Combine eggs, salt, and pepper. Dip chicken in egg mixture, then roll in crumbs.

Heat oil very hot in large frying pan. Brown both sides of chicken quickly. Remove to baking dish. Pour off the excess oil and combine tomato sauce, basil, and garlic powder in pan. Heat to boiling and simmer for 10 minutes, or until thickened. Stir in margarine. Pour over chicken and sprinkle with Parmesan cheese. Cover and bake in 350° oven for 30 minutes. Uncover, top with triangles of mozzarella cheese, and return to oven until cheese is melted.

YIELD: 6 SERVINGS

Bluff City Cooks
THE JUNIOR LEAGUE OF GREATER ALTON, ILLINOIS

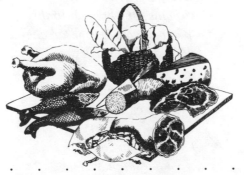

Parmesan Chicken

3 whole chicken breasts, boned
½ cup dry bread crumbs
¼ cup Parmesan cheese
1 teaspoon dried leaf thyme or ¼ teaspoon powdered thyme
1 teaspoon dried basil leaves
1 teaspoon salt
⅓ cup melted butter

Cut chicken breasts into six to eight 1½-inch squares. Combine bread crumbs, cheese, herbs, and salt. Dip chicken into melted butter and then into bread crumb mixture.

Arrange chicken in baking pan in single layer. Bake in 400° oven for about 30–40 minutes.

YIELD: 4 SERVINGS

THE JUNIOR LEAGUE OF EVANSVILLE, INDIANA

. . . .

Chicken Saltimbocca (Jump in the Mouth)

12 slices prosciutto or ham
¼ pound Swiss cheese, cut in 12 slices
6 whole chicken breasts, split, skinned, boned, and flattened
½ cup flour
2 eggs, lightly beaten
½ cup fine, dry bread crumbs
4 tablespoons grated Parmesan cheese
½ teaspoon garlic salt
½ teaspoon tarragon
4 tablespoons butter
½ cup chicken broth
½ cup sherry
1 tablespoon cornstarch
1 tablespoon water

Lay one slice ham and one slice cheese on each chicken breast. Roll and secure with a wooden pick. Roll in flour, dip in egg, and roll in crumbs mixed with cheese, garlic, and tarragon.

Brown rolls in butter. Put in baking dish and add chicken broth and sherry. Bake, uncovered, at 350° for 30 minutes.

Drain cooking juices into a saucepan and bring to a boil. Blend in a paste of cornstarch and water and cook until thickened. Pour sauce over chicken.

YIELD: 8–10 SERVINGS

Cookbook
THE JUNIOR LEAGUE OF GRAND RAPIDS, MICHIGAN

· · · · · · · · · · · · · · · · · · ·

Chicken Breasts in Creamy Grape Sauce

4 large whole chicken breasts, split, skinned, and boned
Salt and white pepper
Coriander
Flour
4 tablespoons butter
2 tomatoes, peeled, seeded, and coarsely chopped
½ cup chicken stock
¼ cup dry white wine
1 cup heavy cream
1 teaspoon coriander
Salt and white pepper
Chopped parsley
48 seedless grapes
Small bunch grapes for garnish

Remove tendon from chicken breasts and flatten slightly. Season with salt, white pepper, and coriander and dust lightly with flour.

Heat butter in skillet and cook the breasts over moderate heat for

Recipe continues . . .

about 3 minutes on each side, or just until breasts are springy to the touch. Remove.

Put chopped tomatoes in pan and sauté for a minute or two. Add chicken stock and wine and cook over high heat until reduced and syrupy. Add heavy cream and seasonings and cook until of desired consistency.

Return chicken to the pan. Spoon sauce over. Sprinkle with chopped parsley and add grapes to heat through. Garnish with a small bunch of grapes.

YIELD: 8 SERVINGS

Cookbook
THE JUNIOR LEAGUE OF GRAND RAPIDS, MICHIGAN

Chicken-Artichoke Rolls

1 8½-ounce can artichoke hearts, drained and chopped
8 ounces cream cheese
Lemon juice
1 8-ounce package shredded sharp cheddar cheese
5 whole chicken breasts, split, skinned, and boned
Flour
3 tablespoons butter
1 10¾-ounce can cream of chicken soup

Mix artichoke hearts with cream cheese, lemon juice, and cheddar cheese. Roll half the mixture into ten small balls.

Pound each half breast between pieces of wax paper until thin. Place a cheese and artichoke ball in the center of each flattened chicken breast. Roll chicken breasts and secure with wooden picks. Flour each chicken roll and sauté in butter until lightly browned. Arrange in casserole dish.

Mix leftover cheese and artichoke mixture with undiluted chicken soup and pour over chicken rolls.

Bake at 350° for 1 hour.

This dish freezes well.

YIELD: 6 SERVINGS

Discover Dayton
THE JUNIOR LEAGUE OF DAYTON, OHIO

Chicken Breasts Deluxe

4 whole chicken breasts, split, skinned, and boned
1 10¾-ounce can cream of chicken soup
1 10¾-ounce can cream of celery soup
½ cup sherry
¾ cup shredded sharp cheddar cheese
3 green onion tops, finely sliced

Arrange chicken in a 2-quart buttered baking dish. Combine soups and sherry. Stir in cheese and green onion; pour over chicken breasts.

Bake, uncovered, in preheated 300° oven for 1½ hours. Remove from oven 10 minutes before serving.

YIELD: 6–8 SERVINGS

Discover Dayton
THE JUNIOR LEAGUE OF DAYTON, OHIO

Chuck's Chicken

2 cups sour cream
¼ cup lemon juice
4 teaspoons Worcestershire sauce
4 teaspoons celery salt
2 teaspoons paprika
¼ teaspoon garlic powder
1 teaspoon onion juice
Pepper to taste
4–8 whole chicken breasts, split, skinned, and boned
Italian bread crumbs
1½ sticks butter

Mix sour cream, lemon juice, Worcestershire sauce, celery salt, paprika, garlic powder, onion juice, and pepper. Marinate chicken breasts in the mixture in refrigerator overnight, turning occasionally.

Next day remove from refrigerator 2–3 hours before cooking. When ready to cook, roll chicken breasts in bread crumbs and arrange in shallow roasting pan.

Melt the butter and pour half of it over the chicken. Bake at 350° for 45 minutes. Pour the rest of the butter over the chicken and bake another 10 minutes, or until crisp.

YIELD: 8–14 SERVINGS

THE JUNIOR LEAGUE OF TOLEDO, OHIO

Chicken Siciliano

4 whole chicken breasts, split, skinned, and boned
Salt, pepper, and Italian seasoning
Dijon mustard
1 8-ounce package sliced mozzarella cheese
Flour
Olive oil
1 bunch green onions, chopped
½ pound fresh mushrooms, sliced
3 ripe tomatoes, peeled, seeded, drained, and chopped
1 clove garlic, crushed
1 cup white wine
Parsley for garnish

Flatten chicken breasts between pieces of wax paper with meat pounder or side of a heavy cleaver. Season with salt, pepper, and Italian seasoning. Spread with Dijon mustard. Place a slice of mozzarella cheese on each breast; roll up and pinch together. Season outside with salt and pepper, roll in flour, and sauté in olive oil over medium heat for 6–8 minutes, or until cooked. Remove from pan.

Scrape loose brown bits from pan and add green onions and mushrooms. Add a little more oil and cook for 2–3 minutes. Add chopped tomatoes, garlic, and additional salt, pepper, and Italian seasoning to taste.

Return chicken to pan and pour in wine. Spoon sauce over chicken until wet.

Sprinkle parsley over chicken and serve with rice or noodles.

YIELD: 4 SERVINGS

THE JUNIOR LEAGUE OF INDIANAPOLIS, INDIANA

Hot Chicken Salad

3 whole chicken breasts, diced
2 6-ounce cans mushroom pieces, drained (reserve juice)
6 ounces pimento, chopped
1 cup chopped onion
¼ cup flour
1 cup mayonnaise
1 cup milk
½ teaspoon salt
⅛ teaspoon pepper
⅛ teaspoon garlic salt

Combine first four ingredients. Stir flour into mayonnaise and add to chicken mixture. Combine milk with enough mushroom juice to make a total of 1½ cups liquid. Add seasonings and mix with chicken.

Empty into buttered baking dish; cover and bake for 1 hour at 350°. Serve over Chinese noodles or in patty shells.

YIELD: 6 SERVINGS

THE JUNIOR LEAGUE OF DES MOINES, IOWA

. . . .

Chicken Orientale

¼ cup butter
4 whole chicken breasts, split
1 9-ounce can pineapple chunks with juice
½ cup brown sugar
2 tablespoons cornstarch
1 teaspoon salt
½ teaspoon Worcestershire sauce
¼ cup vinegar
2 tablespoons chili sauce
⅓ cup catsup
1 teaspoon soy sauce

Melt butter in shallow roasting pan. Roll pieces of chicken in butter until coated. Leave skin side up.

Mix pineapple juice with rest of ingredients (reserve chunks). Cook until thickened, stirring constantly.

Spread half the sauce over chicken. Add pineapple chunks to remaining half of sauce. Bake chicken at 350° for ½ hour, covered, and 30–40 minutes uncovered, basting often with remaining sauce and chunks.

YIELD: 4–6 SERVINGS

Tested, Tried, and True
THE JUNIOR LEAGUE OF FLINT, MICHIGAN

· · · · · · · · · · · · · · · · · ·

Chicken Breasts Alfredo

1 large onion, chopped
1 large green pepper, chopped
¾ cup butter
2 cloves garlic, crushed
2 whole chicken breasts, split and skinned
¾ cup white wine
1 16-ounce can tomato sauce
2 tablespoons basil
½ teaspoon oregano
Salt and pepper
1 cup sliced mushrooms
¼ cup soy sauce
6 ounces mozzarella cheese, cut in strips

Sauté onion and pepper in ½ cup butter. Add crushed garlic and cook about 5 minutes over low heat, or until vegetables are limp. With slotted spoon, remove onion, pepper, and garlic from butter and reserve.

Brown chicken breasts in butter remaining in pan; replace onion, pep-

Recipe continues . . .

per, and garlic. Add wine, tomato sauce, basil, oregano, salt, and pepper. Cover and cook for about 30–45 minutes, or until chicken is tender.

While chicken is cooking, sauté mushrooms in soy sauce and remaining butter for about 15 minutes or until tender.

Just before serving, cover chicken with cheese strips. When cheese begins to melt, top with mushrooms. Serve with sauce from pan.

YIELD: 4 SERVINGS

Sunflower Sampler
THE JUNIOR LEAGUE OF WICHITA, KANSAS

. . . .

Coq au Riesling

6 whole chicken breasts, split
Flour
Salt and pepper to taste
¼ cup butter
2 tablespoons vegetable oil
Dash nutmeg
1 teaspoon thyme
1 leek, well washed
1 sprig parsley
1 onion, stuck with 2 whole cloves
⅓ cup cognac, slightly warm
1½ cups Riesling or other dry white wine
2 slices salt pork
1½ tablespoons butter
12 mushroom caps
18 small white onions, peeled
¼ cup butter
Sugar
Salt
3 egg yolks
¾ cup heavy cream
Chopped parsley

Dredge chicken pieces in flour seasoned with salt and pepper. Brown chicken on both sides in ¼ cup butter and oil in a Dutch oven or iron casserole. Add nutmeg, thyme, leek, parsley, and onion. Pour warmed cognac over all and ignite. When flame dies down, add wine and bring to a boil. Reduce heat to simmer, cover, and cook gently 20–25 minutes, or until chicken is tender.

While chicken is cooking, dice salt pork and sauté in a little butter. When just golden, add to chicken.

Sauté mushrooms in same pan. In separate pan, sauté onions in ¼ cup butter. Sprinkle with a little sugar to glaze and season with salt. Cover pan and steam gently until onions are tender. Keep warm.

When chicken is done, remove to a hot platter, garnish with sautéed onions and mushrooms, and keep warm.

Discard onion, leek, and parsley from casserole and reduce sauce to 1½ cups. Beat egg yolks with cream and beat in a little sauce. Add to sauce slowly, cooking over very low heat. Cook and stir until smooth and creamy. Do not boil.

Serve sauce separately. Garnish chicken with parsley. Serve with buttered noodles.

YIELD: 8 SERVINGS

Cookbook
THE JUNIOR LEAGUE OF GRAND RAPIDS, MICHIGAN

Kansas Chicken Kiev

½ cup softened butter
1 large clove garlic, crushed
2 teaspoons chives
2 teaspoons parsley
½ teaspoon salt
½ teaspoon crumbled rosemary
⅛ teaspoon pepper
1–2 eggs, lightly beaten
1 tablespoon water
4 small whole chicken breasts, skinned and boned
⅓ cup flour
Oil for frying

In small bowl, combine butter, garlic, chives, parsley, salt, rosemary, and pepper; blend well. Lay on sheet of wax paper; fold paper over top, then pat into ¾-inch-thick roll. Freeze until very hard.

In another bowl, thoroughly blend egg and water and set aside.

With edge of plate or rolling pin, pound each chicken breast to ¼-inch thickness.

Cut hard roll of butter mixture into four equal pieces. Lay one piece on each chicken breast and roll up in the chicken, tucking in ends. Secure with skewer or toothpick. Dip chicken rolls in flour, then egg mixture, then flour again.

Heat oil in a deep skillet and fry for about 15 minutes, turning occasionally. Drain on paper towels.

Remove skewers and serve hot.

YIELD: 4 SERVINGS

THE JUNIOR LEAGUE OF KANSAS CITY, KANSAS

Jeanne's Chicken au Gratin

4 whole chicken breasts, split
½ pound fresh mushrooms, sliced
2 tablespoons butter
½ cup butter or margarine
½ cup flour
2 cups chicken broth
½ cup milk
2 cups (8 ounces) shredded cheddar cheese
2 tablespoons finely chopped onion
¼ teaspoon thyme
1 cup sour cream
10 mashed potato nests, heated

Cook chicken; cool. Remove skin and bones and dice meat. Chill thoroughly.

Sauté mushrooms in the 2 tablespoons butter; drain and set aside. Melt ½ cup butter in 3-quart saucepan; blend in flour. Slowly stir in broth and milk and cook, stirring, until sauce boils and thickens; simmer 5 minutes. Stir in cheese until melted. Add chicken, mushrooms, and remaining ingredients except potato nests. Heat 20–25 minutes over low heat, stirring frequently.

Spoon into potato nests.

YIELD: 10 LUNCHEON SERVINGS

Be Our Guest
THE JUNIOR LEAGUE OF MILWAUKEE, WISCONSIN

Crab-Stuffed Chicken Breasts

4 whole chicken breasts, split, skinned, and boned
Salt and pepper
½ cup chopped onion
½ cup chopped celery
3 tablespoons butter
3 tablespoons dry white wine
1 7-ounce can crabmeat, drained, or 1 package frozen
cooked crab, thawed and drained
½ cup herb-seasoned stuffing mix
2 tablespoons flour
½ teaspoon paprika
2 tablespoons melted butter
2 envelopes hollandaise sauce mix
1½ cups milk
¼ cup dry white wine
1 cup (4 ounces) shredded Swiss cheese

Pound chicken between pieces of wax paper to flatten. Sprinkle with a little salt and pepper.

Cook onion and celery in 3 tablespoons butter until tender; remove from heat. Add 3 tablespoons wine, crabmeat, and stuffing mix; toss.

Divide mixture onto flattened chicken breasts, roll up, and secure with toothpicks.

Combine flour and paprika; coat chicken rolls. Place in baking dish and drizzle with 2 tablespoons melted butter. Bake, uncovered, at 375° for 1 hour. Transfer to serving platter.

Blend hollandaise sauce mix and milk; cook and stir until thick. Add the ¼ cup wine and cheese; stir until cheese melts. Spoon a little of the sauce over the chicken and serve remaining sauce separately.

YIELD: 6 SERVINGS

Cincinnati Celebrates
THE JUNIOR LEAGUE OF CINCINNATI, OHIO

· · · · · · · · · · · · · · · · · ·

Chicken-Crab Divan

2 10-ounce packages frozen or 2 15-ounce cans artichoke hearts
4 whole chicken breasts, split and boned
¼ cup butter
1 6½-ounce can crabmeat, drained
¼ cup dry sherry
Salt and pepper
3 tablespoons butter
½ cup small whole mushrooms
¼ cup finely chopped onion
3 tablespoons flour
1⅓ cups heavy cream
1 cup milk
½ cup chopped parsley
Dash cayenne
¼ cup grated Parmesan cheese
Paprika

Arrange well-drained artichokes (halved, if desired) in bottom of greased 8 x 12-inch baking dish.

In large skillet, sauté chicken in ¼ cup butter for 15 minutes, or until lightly browned on both sides. Add chunks of crabmeat; cook 5 minutes. Add sherry and cook until wine is evaporated. Season with salt and pepper. Remove chicken and crab from skillet; keep warm while preparing sauce.

Add 3 tablespoons butter to drippings in pan and sauté mushrooms and onion. Sprinkle with flour; stir until smooth. Gradually add cream and milk, stirring constantly. Stir in parsley and cayenne. Remove from heat and blend in Parmesan cheese.

Recipe continues . . .

Cover artichokes in baking dish with half the sauce. Arrange chicken and crab over sauce and pour remaining sauce on top. Sprinkle with paprika. Bake at 375° for 20 minutes.

Serve with white or wild rice.

YIELD: 6–8 SERVINGS

Be Our Guest
THE JUNIOR LEAGUE OF MILWAUKEE, WISCONSIN

Chicken Chatelaine

3 10-ounce packages frozen asparagus
8 whole chicken breasts, cooked and boned
2 10¾-ounce cans cream of chicken soup
2 cups mayonnaise
2 cups sour cream
¼ cup white wine
½–1 teaspoon curry powder
Grated Parmesan cheese
Paprika
½ pound mushrooms, sliced
2 tablespoons butter
1 2¼-ounce package slivered almonds, toasted

Line two 9 x 13-inch baking dishes with asparagus spears. Top with large chicken pieces. Combine soup, mayonnaise, sour cream, wine, and curry powder. Pour over asparagus and chicken. Sprinkle with cheese and paprika.

Bake at 325° for 30–45 minutes.

Sauté mushrooms in butter. Serve side dishes of almonds and mushrooms for garnish.

YIELD: 12 SERVINGS

VARIATION:
Broccoli spears may be substituted for asparagus spears.

Be Our Guest
THE JUNIOR LEAGUE OF MILWAUKEE, WISCONSIN

· ·

Chicken Breasts Supreme with Bacon

1 3-ounce package chipped beef
Salt and pepper
4 whole chicken breasts, split and boned
8 slices bacon
2 10¾-ounce cans cream of mushroom soup
1 cup sour cream
Fresh mushrooms, sliced (optional)

Grease a 9 x 13-inch pan and line the bottom with chipped beef. Lightly salt and pepper each chicken breast, then wrap with a bacon slice and secure with wooden pick. Place breasts in pan side by side with skin sides up.

Combine soup and sour cream, mixing well; pour over chicken. Bake, uncovered, for 3 hours at 300°.

Sprinkle with fresh mushrooms 15 minutes before end of baking time.

YIELD: 6–8 SERVINGS

THE JUNIOR LEAGUE OF SOUTH BEND, INDIANA

· · · · · · · · · · · · · · · · · · · ·

Chicken in Wine Sauce

2 whole chicken breasts, split and boned
3 tablespoons butter
1 teaspoon oil
8 small onions
¼ pound (fresh) mushrooms
½ cup dry sherry
¼ cup dry white wine
¼ teaspoon savory
¼ teaspoon thyme
¼ teaspoon rosemary
1 teaspoon salt
Pepper to taste
1 tablespoon cornstarch
1 cup heavy cream

In large skillet, sauté breasts for 10 minutes in butter and oil. Add onions and mushrooms; cover and cook for 20–30 minutes. Add sherry and white wine, herbs, salt and pepper to chicken and cook for 20 minutes longer.

Mix cornstarch in a small amount of the cream. Stir cornstarch and rest of cream into chicken. Simmer and stir for 5 minutes, or until sauce is thickened.

YIELD: 4 SERVINGS

THE JUNIOR LEAGUE OF COLUMBUS, OHIO

"Easy" Chicken Breasts in Mushroom Sauce

4 whole chicken breasts, split and boned
Salt
Paprika
Garlic powder
1 10½-ounce can mushroom soup
1 cup heavy cream
¼ cup sweet sherry
1 3-ounce can mushrooms
Chopped parsley

Heat oven to 350°. Sprinkle both sides of chicken with salt, paprika, and garlic powder. Arrange chicken in a shallow baking dish skin side up. Mix soup, cream, sherry, and mushrooms. Pour over chicken and sprinkle with parsley.

Bake, covered with foil, for 45 minutes. Remove foil and cook for 15 more minutes.

Serve with cooked long-grain and wild rice.

YIELD: 6 SERVINGS

THE JUNIOR LEAGUE OF COLUMBUS, OHIO

·   ·   ·   ·   ·   ·   ·   ·   ·   ·   ·   ·   ·   ·   ·   ·   ·   ·   ·

Aunt El's Chicken Mornay

4 whole chicken breasts, split and boned
½ cup flour
1 teaspoon salt
⅛ teaspoon pepper
⅛ teaspoon ginger
½ cup butter
1 cup water

Recipe continues . . .

SAUCE:

4 tablespoons butter
4 tablespoons flour
1 teaspoon salt
½ cup light cream
½ cup milk
1 cup liquid from skillet
1 cup shredded American cheese
1 cup diced canned mushrooms

Coat chicken with flour combined with salt, pepper, and ginger. Brown on all sides in butter in heavy skillet. Cover and cook over low heat 30–45 minutes, or until tender; a little water may be added if necessary. Remove chicken in shallow casserole.

Add 1 cup water to juices remaining in pan and cook, stirring in all bits of glaze from sides and bottom of pan. Set aside.

Melt butter in saucepan; remove from heat. Add flour and salt; blend thoroughly. Add cream and blend. Add milk and liquid from skillet. Return to low heat and cook, stirring constantly, until thickened. Add half the cheese and stir until melted. Add mushrooms.

Pour sauce over chicken. Sprinkle remaining cheese over top and bake for 25–30 minutes in 350° oven, or until cheese melts and browns lightly.

Serve with rice and a fruit salad.

YIELD: 8 SERVINGS

THE JUNIOR LEAGUE OF COLUMBUS, OHIO

Walnut-Orange Chicken

3 whole chicken breasts, split, boned, and skinned
2 tablespoons salad oil
1 6-ounce frozen orange juice concentrate
1 teaspoon poultry seasoning
1½ teaspoons salt
½ cup water
2 tablespoons cornstarch
2 tablespoons water
½ cup chopped California walnuts
¼ cup chopped green onion

In skillet over medium heat, brown chicken in salad oil. Stir in orange juice, poultry seasoning, salt, and ½ cup water. Reduce heat to low, cover, and simmer for 30–35 minutes, or until chicken is tender, basting occasionally with liquid in skillet. Remove chicken to heated platter and keep warm.

Combine cornstarch and the 2 tablespoons water until smooth; gradually stir into hot liquid in skillet. Cook, stirring constantly, until sauce thickens.

Stir in walnuts and onion; cook until onion is limp. Pour over chicken. Serve with rice.

YIELD: 6 SERVINGS

Cincinnati Celebrates
THE JUNIOR LEAGUE OF CINCINNATI, OHIO

Yummy Chicken

3 pounds chicken parts

MARINADE:
⅓ cup soy sauce
3 tablespoons sugar
3 tablespoons brown sugar
3 tablespoons vinegar
1 tablespoon ground ginger
2 cloves garlic, minced
½ cup strong chicken broth
Monosodium glutamate
Freshly ground pepper

Place chicken in glass bowl. Combine marinade ingredients, pour over chicken, and marinate 2–3 hours.

Bake chicken in a 350° oven, uncovered, for an hour or more.

Marinade is also good for whole chicken or cubes of beef or pork on skewers.

YIELD: 4–6 SERVINGS

THE JUNIOR LEAGUE OF EVANSVILLE, INDIANA

•   •   •   •   •   •   •   •   •   •   •   •   •   •   •   •   •   •   •

Quick Chicken Paprika

¼ cup chopped onion
½ stick butter
1 teaspoon paprika
1½–2 cups boiling water
2 chicken bouillon cubes
1 3-pound frying chicken, cut into serving pieces
1 tablespoon flour mixed with ¼ cup water
½ cup sour cream

Sauté onion in butter. Add paprika, water, bouillon cubes, and chicken. Cook, covered, over low heat for 45 minutes to 1 hour, or until tender.

Stir flour mixture into liquid to make gravy. Add sour cream and cook, stirring, for 3 more minutes.

Serve over rice or noodles.

YIELD: 4 SERVINGS

Bluff City Cooks
THE JUNIOR LEAGUE OF GREATER ALTON, ILLINOIS

·   ·   ·   ·   ·   ·   ·   ·   ·   ·   ·   ·   ·   ·   ·   ·   ·   ·

Tarragon Baked Chicken

3 3½-pound frying chickens, cut into serving pieces (or any other
assortment of pieces, such as boned breasts for a party)
2 cups buttermilk
1½ cups melted butter
¾ teaspoon tarragon
4½ tablespoons lemon juice
¼ cup minced parsley
½ cup sesame seeds
3 teaspoons seasoned salt
4 cups cornflake crumbs

A day in advance, put chicken in shallow dish. Pour buttermilk over it, cover tightly, and refrigerate overnight. Next day pour off buttermilk and pat chicken dry with paper towels.

Mix butter with tarragon and add lemon juice. Combine parsley, sesame seeds, seasoned salt, and cornflake crumbs and mix well. Dip chicken pieces in butter, then roll in crumbs to coat thoroughly. Arrange on 9 x 13-inch baking pan. Spoon remaining butter over chicken. Cover tightly and refrigerate until 1½ hours before serving.

Recipe continues . . .

Bake at 350° without turning for about 1½ hours, or until chicken is golden and fork-tender. Baste occasionally with pan drippings.

YIELD: 12 SERVINGS

Cookbook
THE JUNIOR LEAGUE OF GRAND RAPIDS, MICHIGAN

· · · · · · · · · · · · · · · · · · · ·

Apricot Chicken and Wine

1 2½–3-pound broiler-fryer, cut into serving pieces
3 tablespoons butter
Dash pepper and salt
1 cup finely chopped celery
1 6-ounce can water chestnuts, drained and sliced
½ teaspoon salt
½ teaspoon crushed dried rosemary
2–3 cups cooked rice
½ cup Chablis or Rhine wine
1 16-ounce can apricot halves
4 teaspoons cornstarch
¼ cup Sauterne or vermouth

Brown chicken in butter; remove and salt and pepper to taste. Set aside.

In same skillet, cook celery, water chestnuts, half the salt, and the rosemary until celery is tender. Remove from heat and stir in rice and the ½ cup wine. Empty rice mixture into 9 x 13-inch dish and lay chicken on top. Cover with foil and bake in preheated 375° oven for 45 minutes.

While the chicken is baking, drain apricots, reserving syrup. Combine cornstarch, remaining ¼ teaspoon salt, and apricot syrup in a small saucepan. Cook until thickened. Then add the ¼ cup of wine.

Arrange apricot halves around chicken on top of rice and pour thickened glaze over all.

Bake, uncovered, for another 10 minutes.

YIELD: 6 SERVINGS

Discover Dayton
THE JUNIOR LEAGUE OF DAYTON, OHIO

. . . .

Skillet Chicken in Orange Sauce

1 3-pound broiler-fryer, cut in serving pieces
½ cup butter or margarine
¼ cup flour
2 tablespoons brown sugar
1 teaspoon salt
½ teaspoon ground ginger
⅛ teaspoon pepper
½ cup water
1½ cups orange juice
2 oranges, pared and sectioned

Slowly brown chicken in butter or margarine in a large skillet; remove from pan and set aside.

Blend flour, brown sugar, salt, ginger, and pepper into drippings in pan. Cook, stirring constantly, until mixture bubbles. Stir in water and orange juice slowly. Continue cooking and stirring until sauce thickens and boils.

Return the chicken to pan. Simmer, covered, for 30 minutes. Arrange orange sections around chicken; continue cooking 15 minutes longer, or until chicken is tender.

Serve with fluffy hot rice seasoned with parsley.

YIELD: 4 SERVINGS

THE JUNIOR LEAGUE OF INDIANAPOLIS, INDIANA

. . . .

Oven-Fried Chicken in Honey-Butter Sauce

1 frying chicken, cut into serving pieces
1 cup flour
2 teaspoons salt
¼ teaspoon pepper
2 teaspoons paprika
¾ cup butter
¼ cup honey
¼ cup lemon juice

Dip chicken pieces into a mixture of flour, salt, pepper, and paprika. Melt ½ cup butter in a shallow baking pan in a hot oven. Remove pan from oven. Arrange chicken in single layer in pan, turning to coat with butter.

Bake skin side down in a hot 400° oven for 30 minutes. Turn chicken. Pour over chicken a honey-butter sauce made by melting the remaining ¼ cup butter in a saucepan and adding honey and lemon juice.

Bake chicken another 30 minutes. After 15 minutes, baste with honey-butter sauce in pan.

YIELD: 4 SERVINGS

Tested, Tried, and True
THE JUNIOR LEAGUE OF FLINT, MICHIGAN

· · · · · · · · · · · · · · · · · ·

Libby's Baked Chicken

6 large whole chicken breasts, split
3–4 cups fresh bread crumbs
¼ teaspoon garlic powder
1 cup Parmesan cheese
½ teaspoon poultry seasoning
Salt, pepper, and parsley flakes
½ cup melted butter
Juice of 1 orange

Wash and dry chicken breasts. Mix bread crumbs, garlic, cheese, and seasonings and spread in flat pan. Dip chicken into melted butter, then into bread crumb mixture. Coat thoroughly in crumbs. Place in shallow pan and let stand 1 or 2 hours.

Preheat oven to 325°. Bake chicken slowly until an attractive color, basting with remaining melted butter mixed with orange juice. When browned, cover with heavy foil and bake for 30 minutes longer on each side or until very tender.

YIELD: 12 SERVINGS

THE JUNIOR LEAGUE OF YOUNGSTOWN, OHIO

Chicken Dijon

2 tablespoons butter
2½–3-pound chicken, cut into quarters or parts
2 cups dry white wine
¼ teaspoon dried tarragon
¼ teaspoon thyme
1 bay leaf
½ teaspoon salt
¼ teaspoon coarsely ground pepper
2 egg yolks
2 tablespoons sour cream
1–2 tablespoons Dijon mustard

Heat butter in a heavy skillet. Brown chicken well on all sides. Add wine, tarragon, thyme, bay leaf, salt, and pepper. Bring to a boil, cover, and simmer until chicken is tender, about 45 minutes to 1 hour.

Remove chicken and keep warm in a heated serving dish. Discard bay leaf. Add egg yolks to the sauce in the skillet and blend well. Add the

Recipe continues . . .

sour cream and mustard. Heat, stirring briskly and constantly, but do not boil. Pour sauce over chicken.

YIELD: 4 SERVINGS

Marigolds to Munch On
THE JUNIOR LEAGUE OF PEORIA, ILLINOIS

· · · · · · · · · · · · · · · · · · ·

Barbecued Chicken with Honey-Mustard Glaze

2 whole chicken breasts, split
4 chicken legs, including thighs
1 8-ounce can tomato sauce
½ cup olive oil
½ cup orange juice
¼ cup vinegar
1½ teaspoons dried crushed oregano
1 teaspoon salt
6 peppercorns
1 clove garlic, minced

Arrange chicken breasts and legs in shallow glass baking dish. In a large screw-top jar, combine remaining ingredients. Cover and shake vigorously to blend. Pour tomato sauce mixture over chicken, cover, and marinate for 2 hours at room temperature or overnight in refrigerator, turning occasionally. Drain, reserving marinade.

Grill chicken over medium coals for 30 minutes, or until cooked, brushing with marinade and turning several times. Just before serving, brush with Honey-Mustard Glaze.

YIELD: 6 SERVINGS

HONEY-MUSTARD GLAZE:
¼ cup honey
½ teaspoon dry mustard

Combine honey and dry mustard.

THE JUNIOR LEAGUE OF SOUTH BEND, INDIANA

Chicken with Avocado

3-pound broiler-fryer, cut into serving pieces
6 tablespoons butter
2 small onions, chopped
1 chicken bouillon cube
½ teaspoon chili powder
Dash cinnamon
3 tablespoons flour
1 cup orange juice or ½ cup juice and ½ cup dry white wine
1 avocado, sliced
Grated orange rind

Brown chicken in 3 tablespoons butter in a heavy skillet. Remove chicken and arrange in large baking dish.

Sauté onions lightly in same skillet. Stir in bouillon cube, chili powder, and cinnamon. Spread over chicken; cover casserole and bake for 20 minutes in 350° oven.

Heat remaining butter in same skillet; stir in flour and cook until smooth and lightly browned. Blend in orange juice or mixture of juice and wine. When somewhat thickened, pour over chicken, cover, and bake 25 minutes longer.

Recipe continues . . .

Check seasoning, cover entire top with avocado slices, and salt very lightly. Bake 10 minutes more, uncovered. Sprinkle top with grated orange rind before serving.

YIELD: 4 SERVINGS

Peacock Pie and Other Perfections
THE JUNIOR LEAGUE OF BATTLE CREEK, MICHIGAN

. . . .

Chicken Supreme

6 broiler-fryer breasts
6 chicken legs and thighs
2 cups sour cream
¼ cup lemon juice (or to taste)
4 teaspoons Worcestershire sauce
4 teaspoons celery salt
2 teaspoons paprika
4 teaspoons freshly ground salt
4 cloves garlic, finely chopped
½ teaspoon freshly ground pepper
2 cups dry bread crumbs
1 cup half butter and half shortening
Parsley for garnish

A day in advance, bone chicken breasts and thighs but not legs; separate breasts, legs and thighs. Wash and layer between paper towels to dry.

In a very large bowl, combine sour cream, lemon juice, Worcestershire sauce, celery salt, paprika, salt, garlic and pepper; mix thoroughly. Add chicken, making sure each piece is well coated. Cover and refrigerate for 12–24 hours.

When ready to bake, preheat oven to 350°. Take out each piece of chicken individually and roll in bread crumbs, coating well. Place side by side in large greased roasting pan.

Melt butter and shortening, pour half over poultry, and bake, uncovered, for 45 minutes. Drizzle the rest of butter mixture over chicken and bake another 15 minutes.

Arrange on platter and garnish with lots of parsley.

YIELD: 12 SERVINGS

THE JUNIOR LEAGUE OF COLUMBUS, OHIO

.   .   .   .

Chicken Helene

3-pound chicken, cut into serving pieces
Flour seasoned with seasoned salt and lemon pepper
½ cup butter
½ pound fresh mushrooms, sliced
2 tablespoons flour
¾ cup chicken broth
½ cup dry white wine
½ cup thinly sliced green onion
1 10-ounce package frozen artichoke hearts, cooked, drained,
and cut into bite-size pieces

Dust chicken with seasoned flour. Melt 4 tablespoons butter in shallow baking pan. Place chicken in pan skin side down. Bake, uncovered, at 350° for 45 minutes.

Meanwhile, sauté mushrooms in 2 tablespoons butter until wilted. Put remaining butter in saucepan, melt, and stir in flour. Cook for 2 minutes and add broth and wine. Cook, stirring constantly, until sauce is thick and smooth.

Remove chicken from oven. Turn pieces over, sprinkle with onion and artichokes. Pour sauce over top. Return to oven; reduce heat to 325° and bake 25 minutes longer.

Serve with rice.

YIELD: 6 SERVINGS

THE JUNIOR LEAGUE OF COLUMBUS, OHIO

.   .   .   .

Corn 'n' Chicken Scallop

1 1-pound can cream-style corn
1 cup milk
1 egg, lightly beaten
1 tablespoon flour
4 green onions and tops, chopped
6–8 chicken drumsticks
Paprika
Salt and pepper
30 saltines
2 tablespoons butter
1 3-ounce can broiled sliced mushrooms, drained

In a 9 x 13 x 2-inch casserole, combine corn, milk, egg, flour, and green onions.

Sprinkle drumsticks with paprika and arrange over the corn. Season with a little salt and pepper. Crumble the saltines over all and dot with butter. Bake at 350° for 1 hour, or until chicken is tender.

Empty mushrooms into the center of casserole. Return to oven for a few minutes to heat through.

YIELD: 6–8 SERVINGS

THE JUNIOR LEAGUE OF FARGO-MOORHEAD, NORTH DAKOTA/MINNESOTA

South American Chicken

1 red Spanish or white sweet onion, coarsely chopped
½ cup butter or ½ cup olive oil
2 or 3 garlic cloves, minced
3 3-pound frying chickens, cut into serving pieces
½ teaspoon paprika
½ teaspoon Tabasco
1 teaspoon Worcestershire sauce
2 medium sweet potatoes, peeled and diced
1 tablespoon oregano
2 bay leaves
1 tablespoon chopped parsley
½ teaspoon pepper
1 1-pound can tomatoes
½ cup tomato purée
1 cup dry white wine
1 pound zucchini, diced
1 small eggplant, diced
1 pound mushrooms, sliced
1 cup chopped green onion
1 green pepper, chopped
1 cup chopped celery
1 10-ounce package frozen peas
½ cup chopped pimento
½ cup chopped parsley

Sauté onion in butter or olive oil in a large pan until brown. Add garlic, then chicken, paprika, Tabasco, and Worcestershire. Add sweet potatoes, oregano, bay leaves, 1 tablespoon parsley, pepper, tomatoes, purée, and wine; bring to a boil, lower heat and simmer, covered, for 25 minutes. Add zucchini, eggplant, mushrooms, green onion, green pepper, and celery; cook, covered, about 10 minutes or until mixture reaches boiling point. Remove cover and simmer 25 minutes. Add peas; when almost cooked check sauce for seasonings and stir in pimento and ½ cup parsley.

Recipe continues . . .

Thicken sauce, if necessary, with cornstarch stirred with water until smooth.

YIELD: 10–12 SERVINGS

Cincinnati Celebrates
THE JUNIOR LEAGUE OF CINCINNATI, OHIO

· · · · · · · · · · · · · · · · · · · ·

Glazed Chicken Strips

5–6 whole chicken breasts, split and boned
¼ cup flour
1½ teaspoons garlic salt
½ teaspoon seasoned salt
1 teaspoon paprika
½ teaspoon dried dill
¼ cup vegetable oil
1 cup white wine
⅓ cup wine vinegar
⅓ cup catsup
⅓ cup brown sugar, packed
1 teaspoon dry mustard
2 round, unsliced loaves French bread
Garlic butter

Skin chicken and cut each breast into three or four finger-size strips.

Combine flour, garlic salt, seasoned salt, paprika, and dill in paper bag. Rinse chicken and drain; shake in paper bag.

Brown chicken in heated oil; don't crowd. Remove strips as they brown and put in shallow pan (13 x 9-inch), arranged in a single layer.

Blend wine, vinegar, catsup, brown sugar, and mustard. Spoon over chicken. Bake at 375° until glazed, approximately 20 minutes.

Cut lid off bread, hollow out to a ½-inch shell. Brush inside loaf with garlic butter. Toast in the hot oven for 10 minutes.

Serve chicken strips in the toasted bread loaves. Have guests take pieces of bread with the chicken.

YIELD: 12 SERVINGS

Sunflower Sampler
THE JUNIOR LEAGUE OF WICHITA, KANSAS

· ·

Sweet and Sour Chicken Wings

1 cup sugar
½ cup vinegar
1 cup chicken stock
3–4 tablespoons catsup
1 teaspoon monosodium glutamate
Dash salt
1 tablespoon soy sauce
3 pounds chicken wings
Garlic salt
Cornstarch
1 egg
1 tablespoon water
Oil for frying

In saucepan, combine sugar, vinegar, chicken stock, catsup, glutamate, salt, and soy sauce. Heat, stirring occasionally, until sugar is melted. Set aside.

Cut off and discard wing tips. Sprinkle wings on both sides with garlic salt and let stand for 1 hour. Coat wings with cornstarch, dip in egg beaten with the water, and brown in hot oil.

Place browned wings on jelly-roll pan and cover with sauce. Bake at 325° for 1 hour, basting occasionally.

YIELD: 6–8 SERVINGS

The Discovery Shop Cookbook
THE JUNIOR LEAGUE OF SIOUX CITY, IOWA

· ·

Poulet à la Campagne

½ cup butter
⅓ cup flour
2 cups rich chicken stock
1 cup dry white wine
½ cup dry sherry
1 cup light cream
Salt and white pepper
½ cup chopped parsley
2 4½-pound roasting chickens, poached or roasted,
meat removed from bones
1 cup cooked carrots
1 cup cooked peas
1 cup cooked white turnips
1 pound small fresh mushrooms
2 15-ounce cans artichoke hearts
Pastry for single crust
1 egg, beaten

Melt butter; stir in flour. Stirring constantly, add stock, wine, sherry, and cream and cook until thickened. Add salt and white pepper to taste; stir in parsley.

Arrange alternating layers of chicken and vegetables in 3-quart casserole; pour sauce over all and cover casserole with pastry. Cut slits in top, brush with beaten egg, and bake at 350° for 1 hour, or until top is well browned.

YIELD: 10–12 SERVINGS

Cincinnati Celebrates
THE JUNIOR LEAGUE OF CINCINNATI, OHIO

. . . .

Chicken Strata with Water Chestnuts

9 slices white bread, crust removed and buttered
4 cups diced cooked chicken
½ pound mushrooms, sliced and sautéed in butter
1 small can water chestnuts, diced
8 slices sharp cheese
½ cup mayonnaise
4 eggs, well beaten
2 cups milk
1 10¾-ounce can cream of mushroom soup
1 10¾-ounce can cream of celery soup
1½ cups bread crumbs

Line a large buttered pan with bread. Cover with chicken, mushrooms, water chestnuts, and cheese. Mix all liquids together and pour over bread. Cover with foil and let stand overnight in the refrigerator.

Bake at 350° for 30 minutes. Remove foil, sprinkle with crumbs and bake for 30 minutes longer.

YIELD: 6–8 SERVINGS

THE JUNIOR LEAGUE OF YOUNGSTOWN, OHIO

. . . .

Baked Chicken Sandwiches

8 slices white bread
4 slices American cheese
2 whole cooked chicken breasts, cooled, boned, skinned, and sliced
3 eggs
1¾ cups milk
Salt, pepper, and garlic salt to taste
1 cup crushed cornflakes
1 tablespoon melted butter
1 10¾-ounce can cream of mushroom soup
½ can milk

Recipe continues . . .

Arrange four slices of bread in well-greased 9 x 9-inch shallow baking dish. Top each slice with one slice cheese, a quarter of the chicken, and another slice of bread.

Beat eggs, add milk, salt, pepper, and garlic salt and pour over sandwiches. Mix cornflakes with melted butter and sprinkle over top.

Bake in 350° oven for 1 hour, or until set and golden brown.

Mix together soup and milk; heat and serve as sauce.

YIELD: 4 SERVINGS

THE JUNIOR LEAGUE OF SAGINAW, MICHIGAN

·   ·   ·   ·   ·   ·   ·   ·   ·   ·   ·   ·   ·   ·   ·   ·   ·

Indian Curry

4 slices bacon, diced
¼ cup thinly sliced celery
¼ cup thinly sliced onion
½ garlic clove, minced
2 tablespoons vegetable oil
¼ cup flour
½ cup applesauce
¼ cup curry powder
3 tablespoons tomato paste
1 tablespoon sugar
1 tablespoon lemon juice
2 bouillon cubes
1¼ cups water
Salt to taste
Milk or light cream
3 cups cooked and cubed chicken meat

In saucepan, sauté bacon, celery, onion, and garlic in vegetable oil for 10 minutes. Sprinkle in flour and cook mixture over low heat, stirring frequently, for 5 minutes.

Add applesauce, curry powder, tomato paste, sugar, lemon juice, bouillon cubes, water, and salt to taste. Cook, covered, over low heat for 45 minutes. If sauce is not used at once, cool and refrigerate or freeze.

To serve the curry, combine 1 cup of sauce with 1 cup of milk or light cream, add chicken and heat through.

Serve over steamed rice with the usual condiments—peanuts, shredded coconut, and chutney.

YIELD: 6 SERVINGS

VARIATION:

Cooked diced shrimp or meat may be substituted for the chicken.

Sunflower Sampler
THE JUNIOR LEAGUE OF WICHITA, KANSAS

· ·

Curried Chicken and Broccoli Bake

2 10-ounce packages frozen, chopped broccoli, thawed
1 cup diced cooked chicken breast
¼ cup toasted slivered almonds
1 10¾-ounce can cream of chicken soup
½ cup milk
½ cup mayonnaise
2 teaspoons lemon juice
1½ teaspoons curry powder
1 4-ounce can mushrooms
1 cup buttered croutons

Toss together all ingredients but the croutons. Spoon into 9 x 9-inch baking dish; top with the buttered croutons.

Bake in 350° oven for 40–45 minutes.

YIELD: 6 SERVINGS

THE JUNIOR LEAGUE OF DES MOINES, IOWA

· ·

Swiss Chicken Casserole

4 cups diced cooked chicken
2 cups diced celery
2 cups toasted bread crumbs
1 cup mayonnaise
Dash of pepper
½ cup milk
¼ cup chopped onion
1 teaspoon salt
1 8-ounce package Swiss cheese, cut into thin strips
¼ cup slivered almonds

Combine all ingredients except almonds. Spoon into a greased 2-quart casserole; sprinkle with almonds. Cover and bake at 350° for 30–40 minutes.

To make a day ahead, omit baking and refrigerate overnight. Then bake, covered, at 350° for 50 minutes and uncovered for 10 minutes more.

YIELD: 6 SERVINGS

The Discovery Shop Cookbook
THE JUNIOR LEAGUE OF SIOUX CITY, IOWA

.   .   .   .

Easy Chicken Divan

2 10-ounce packages frozen broccoli, cooked and drained
2 cups sliced cooked chicken breasts
2 10¾-ounce cans cream of chicken soup
1 cup mayonnaise
1 teaspoon lemon juice
½ teaspoon curry powder
½ cup shredded sharp cheddar cheese
½ cup bread crumbs
1 tablespoon melted butter

Arrange broccoli, then chicken in buttered oblong or round casserole. Combine soup, mayonnaise, lemon juice, and curry powder and pour over chicken. Sprinkle cheese on top. Combine bread crumbs with butter and sprinkle on top of cheese. Bake at 350° for 25–30 minutes.

Can be made ahead and refrigerated, but add 20 minutes to cooking time if it is cold.

YIELD: 6 SERVINGS

THE JUNIOR LEAGUE OF TOLEDO, OHIO

·   ·   ·   ·   ·   ·   ·   ·   ·   ·   ·   ·   ·   ·   ·   ·   ·   ·   ·

Turkey Mornay

2 10-ounce packages frozen broccoli spears, cooked until tender-crisp
¼ pound prosciutto, thinly sliced
1 pound sliced cooked breast of turkey
¼ cup butter
¼ cup flour
1 cup rich chicken broth
1 cup light cream
2 tablespoons grated Parmesan cheese
2 tablespoons shredded Swiss cheese
2 tablespoons sherry
Salt to taste
Dash cayenne
¼ cup grated Parmesan cheese

Drain broccoli and arrange it in a baking dish. Cover with the prosciutto, then with the turkey.

In separate saucepan melt butter and blend in flour. Stir in the chicken stock and cream; cook, stirring constantly, until sauce is smooth and thick. Stir in 2 tablespoons each Parmesan and Swiss cheese, sherry, salt, and cayenne. Heat just until cheese is melted.

Recipe continues . . .

Pour sauce over turkey; sprinkle with the ¼ cup grated Parmesan. Bake at 350° until the sauce is hot and the cheese brown and bubbly, about 30 minutes.

YIELD: 6 SERVINGS

Soupçon
THE JUNIOR LEAGUE OF CHICAGO, ILLINOIS

·   ·   ·   ·   ·   ·   ·   ·   ·   ·   ·   ·   ·   ·   ·   ·   ·   ·   ·

Cornish Hens with Ham-Rice Stuffing

6 Cornish hens

HAM-RICE STUFFING:
1 cup sliced celery
½ pound mushrooms, chopped
½ cup chopped onion
½ cup butter
3 cups cooked brown rice
1 cup finely chopped cooked ham
½ teaspoon salt
⅛ teaspoon thyme
⅛ teaspoon crumbled rosemary

BASTING SAUCE:
½ cup melted butter
¼ cup dry white wine
½ teaspoon garlic salt
Dash pepper
⅛ teaspoon thyme
⅛ teaspoon crumbled rosemary

Wash hens and pat dry. To make stuffing, sauté celery, mushrooms, and onion in butter until tender. Add remaining stuffing ingredients and mix well. Lightly stuff hens. Close openings with skewers.

Combine basting sauce ingredients and baste hens. Bake at 400° for 1 hour, or until tender, basting occasionally.

YIELD: 6 SERVINGS

Cookbook
THE JUNIOR LEAGUE OF GRAND RAPIDS, MICHIGAN

· · · · · · · · · · · · · · · ·

Cornish Hens with Cherry Sauce

2 Cornish hens

CHERRY SAUCE:
1½ tablespoons cornstarch
4 tablespoons sugar
¼ tablespoon salt
¼ tablespoon dry mustard
¼ tablespoon ginger
1 1-pound can water-packed, pitted sour red cherries
1 tablespoon slivered orange rind
½ cup orange juice
¼ cup currant jelly
2 tablespoons dry sherry

Roast hens at 425° for 1 hour, or until tender.

In saucepan, combine cornstarch, sugar, salt, dry mustard, and ginger. Drain the can of cherries. Add liquid to the cornstarch mixture; add orange rind, orange juice, and currant jelly. Cook, stirring constantly, until mixture thickens.

Add drained cherries and sherry just before serving.

YIELD: 2–4 SERVINGS

Soupçon
THE JUNIOR LEAGUE OF CHICAGO, ILLINOIS

· · · · · · · · · · · · · · · ·

Hoosier Rock Cornish Hens

1 stick margarine
½ cup flour
1 teaspoon ground sage
1 teaspoon poultry seasoning
½ teaspoon thyme
½ teaspoon ground ginger
Salt and pepper to taste
4 1-pound Cornish hens, split lengthwise

Melt margarine in saucepan; add flour and all seasonings and stir to make a paste. Brush paste all over hens.

Place hens skin side up in a baking dish and bake for 30–40 minutes at 375°, or until very tender. If necessary, place hens under broiler for about 4 minutes to brown.

YIELD: 8 SERVINGS

THE JUNIOR LEAGUE OF INDIANAPOLIS, INDIANA

• • • • • • • • • • • • • • • • • • • •

Roast Cornish Hens

2 Cornish hens
Salt
Ginger
Butter
1 slice bacon

GRAVY:

1 tablespoon butter
2 tablespoons flour
¾ cup milk
¼ cup heavy cream
2 tablespoons sherry
½ teaspoon salt
½ teaspoon parsley flakes
¼ teaspoon pepper

Clean birds. Sprinkle cavities with salt and ginger. Secure wings and legs to body with skewers or string. Rub birds with butter; place in shallow roasting pan. Cover each breast with ½ slice of bacon. Roast at 375° for 1 hour.

Pour hen drippings into a skillet. Add 1 tablespoon butter; melt. Blend in flour over low heat. Gradually stir in remaining ingredients. Simmer gently about 3 minutes, stirring constantly. Serve with hens.

YIELD: 4 SERVINGS

Be Our Guest
THE JUNIOR LEAGUE OF MILWAUKEE, WISCONSIN

Potted Duck

Flour
5-pound ready-to-cook duck
2 tablespoons oil
½ onion, chopped
1 large carrot, sliced
1 stalk celery, sliced
½ cup red wine
1½ cups water
1 teaspoon parsley flakes
6 leaves fresh sweet basil, minced, or 1 teaspoon dry
1 teaspoon thyme leaves
Salt and ground pepper to taste
4–5 ounces egg noodles

Lightly flour duck and brown in oil on all sides in a large pot. Remove duck and cook chopped onion in drippings in pot. Add remaining vegetables, wine, water, herbs, salt, and pepper. Return duck to pot, cover, and simmer for 1½ hours.

Remove duck to heated platter, carve, and keep warm.

Add noodles to pot and cook for 10 minutes, or until tender.

Serve duck and noodles with red wine and a green salad.

YIELD: 3–4 SERVINGS

THE JUNIOR LEAGUE OF FARGO-MOORHEAD, NORTH DAKOTA/MINNESOTA

Roast Goose with Apple Stuffing

10-pound ready-to-cook goose
½ cup gin
1 13½-ounce can chicken broth

APPLE STUFFING:
8–10 apples, peeled and chopped
1 loaf stale bread, broken into small pieces
3 medium onions, finely chopped
4 tablespoons melted butter
Poultry seasoning
2 eggs, well beaten
¼ cup gin
Salt and pepper to taste

Stuff the goose with a mixture of all stuffing ingredients; truss. Place breast side up on a rack in roasting pan and prick skin in fat layer around legs and wings. Pour the gin and chicken broth over goose. Place in 500° oven for about 30 minutes, or until skin browns.

Turn breast side down; reduce heat to 325°, and roast for 2 hours, basting frequently and removing fat from pan.

Turn breast up again and roast for about 2 hours longer, or for a total roasting time of 25 minutes per pound.

YIELD: 8 SERVINGS

THE JUNIOR LEAGUE OF SAGINAW, MICHIGAN

Chicken à la Roma

1 cup chopped onion
⅓ cup butter
1 28-ounce can tomatoes, sliced
1 pound mushrooms, sliced and cooked
1 teaspoon tarragon
1 teaspoon basil
1 teaspoon sugar
1½ teaspoons salt
8 cooked chicken breast halves, cut in large chunks
3 tablespoons flour
2 cups half and half
¾ cup Chablis
2 cups shredded Swiss cheese
2 cups shredded mozzarella cheese
½ cup grated Parmesan cheese
6 ounces lasagna noodles, cooked and drained

Sauté onion in 2 tablespoons of the butter until tender. Add tomatoes, mushrooms, tarragon, basil, sugar, and ½ teaspoon salt. Simmer until sauce thickens. Stir in chicken.

In a separate pan melt remaining butter; blend in flour and remaining salt. Add half and half and cook, stirring constantly, until thickened. Stir in wine.

Pour one-third of tomato mixture into a 3-quart casserole. Spoon one-third of the wine sauce over it and top with one-third of each cheese. Top with layer of half the noodles. Repeat. Top with third layer of tomato mixture, wine sauce, and cheese. Bake in 350° oven for 45 minutes, or until hot and bubbly.

YIELD: 8–10 SERVINGS

THE JUNIOR LEAGUE OF COLUMBUS, OHIO

Chicken-Macaroni Bake

2 cups diced cooked chicken
1 7-ounce package uncooked elbow macaroni
½ pound cheddar cheese, shredded
2 10¾-ounce cans cream of mushroom soup
2 cups milk
½ green pepper, chopped
1 2-ounce jar pimento, diced
4 hard-boiled eggs, chopped
1 teaspoon salt
Dash pepper
1 3-ounce can water chestnuts, sliced
1 small onion, chopped

Combine and mix all ingredients in a large bowl. Refrigerate overnight. Turn into an 8½ x 13-inch glass baking dish.

Bake at 350° for 1¼ hours.

Tuna, shrimp, or crabmeat may be substituted for the chicken.

YIELD: 8–10 SERVINGS

THE JUNIOR LEAGUE OF CHAMPAIGN-URBANA, ILLINOIS

Turkey (or Chicken) Tetrazzini

2½ cups broken raw spaghetti
½ stick butter
3 tablespoons chopped onion
1 4-ounce can mushrooms with liquid
1 10¾-ounce can cream of chicken soup
1 13-ounce can evaporated milk
¼ teaspoon marjoram
2 tablespoons chopped pimento
2 cups cubed cooked turkey or chicken meat
½ cup cubed sharp cheddar cheese
½ teaspoon salt
½ teaspoon celery salt
½ cup grated Parmesan cheese

Cook spaghetti in 1½ quarts of water until tender. Drain and rinse. In skillet, melt butter and sauté onion until onion is transparent. Add liquid from can of mushrooms and stir in chicken soup, evaporated milk, mushrooms, marjoram, pimento, meat, and cheddar cheese cut in chunks. Season sauce to taste with salt and celery salt.

Put spaghetti into buttered oblong casserole and pour sauce over top. Sprinkle with Parmesan cheese.

Bake at 325° for 30 minutes.

Can be prepared ahead and kept in refrigerator until baking.

YIELD: 6–8 SERVINGS

Bluff City Cooks
THE JUNIOR LEAGUE OF GREATER ALTON, ILLINOIS

Fish and Seafood

Stuffed Sole

6 sole filets
1 6-ounce can large shrimp
1 10¾-ounce can cream of mushroom soup
½ cup Sauterne
1 4-ounce can sliced mushrooms
1 cup shredded Swiss cheese
¼ teaspoon salt
Dash pepper
1 teaspoon dried parsley flakes

Wash and dry filets.

Chop shrimp coarsely, reserving 6 whole shrimp. Add ¼ cup soup, ¼ cup Sauterne, and remaining ingredients to chopped shrimp and mix well.

Spoon shrimp stuffing evenly across center of each filet. Roll filets and place seam side down in casserole.

Blend remaining soup and Sauterne together and spoon over stuffed fish rolls. Top with reserved shrimp. Bake for 30 minutes at 350°.

YIELD: 6 SERVINGS

Cincinnati Celebrates
THE JUNIOR LEAGUE OF CINCINNATI, OHIO

. . . .

Filet of Sole Florentine

2 10-ounce packages frozen chopped spinach, cooked and drained
12–16 ounces fresh sole filets
Salt and pepper to taste
½ cup minced mushrooms
2 tablespoons butter
1 cup white sauce (see Index)
3 tablespoons Parmesan cheese

Spread cooked and drained spinach over bottom of shallow baking dish. Place filets on top of spinach. Salt and pepper to taste.

Sauté mushrooms in butter and pour over sole.

Add 2 tablespoons Parmesan cheese to cream sauce, pour over fish, and sprinkle with remaining Parmesan cheese.

Bake at 375° for ½ hour.

YIELD: 4 SERVINGS

Gourmet Gab
THE JUNIOR LEAGUE OF SAGINAW, MICHIGAN

·   ·   ·   ·   ·   ·   ·   ·   ·   ·   ·   ·   ·   ·   ·   ·   ·   ·

Fish and Broccoli Roll-Ups with Cream Sauce

1–1½ pounds thin fish filets (sole or flounder, fresh or frozen)
2 10-ounce packages frozen broccoli, cooked, or
one bunch fresh broccoli, cooked
Juice and grated peel of 1 lemon
Salt and pepper
3 tablespoons butter
3 tablespoons flour
½ teaspoon salt
2 cups milk or half and half
2 tablespoons sherry
Slivered almonds (optional)
Lemon wedges

Wrap each filet around a cooked broccoli branch and arrange seam side down in a 12 x 8 x 2-inch glass baking dish. Sprinkle with lemon juice and salt and pepper to taste.

In a saucepan, melt butter and gradually stir in flour and salt until smooth. Gradually add the milk or half and half and cook, stirring, over medium heat until the sauce boils. Stir in the lemon peel and sherry.

Pour sauce over the filets and sprinkle with slivered almonds. Bake

Recipe continues . . .

in a preheated oven at 350° for 20–25 minutes, or until the fish flakes easily with a fork. Serve with lemon wedge for garnish.

YIELD: 4–6 SERVINGS

THE JUNIOR LEAGUE OF SOUTH BEND, INDIANA

· · · · · · · · · · · · · · · · · ·

Filet of Sole with Shrimp Sauce

3 pounds sole filets
Butter for sautéeing
Salt, pepper, and paprika
1½ pounds mushrooms, sliced
5 tablespoons flour
6 tablespoons butter
2 cups milk
¼ cup sherry
1 tablespoon grated onion
1 teaspoon sweet basil
1 teaspoon chopped parsley
⅛ teaspoon cayenne
1½ teaspoons monosodium glutamate
1 pound cooked shrimp, diced
½ pound Parmesan cheese, grated
Salt to taste
Dash Tabasco

Wash and dry sole. Sauté each side in hot butter for 1 minute. Put in shallow baking dish and sprinkle with salt, pepper, and paprika.

Sauté mushrooms in butter and spread mushrooms over sole. In the same skillet, make sauce of flour, butter, milk, sherry, grated onion, sweet basil, parsley, cayenne, and gourmet powder. Transfer sauce to a double boiler; add shrimp and all but ½ cup cheese. Cook until cheese is melted. Stir in salt to taste and Tabasco.

Spoon sauce over sole and mushrooms. Sprinkle with remaining cheese and bake for ½ hour at 350°. Brown under broiler if desired.

YIELD: 6 SERVINGS

Peacock Pie and Other Perfections
THE JUNIOR LEAGUE OF BATTLE CREEK, MICHIGAN

·   ·   ·   ·   ·   ·   ·   ·   ·   ·   ·   ·   ·   ·   ·   ·   ·   ·

Sole Baked in White Wine, Hungarian-Style

½ pound mushrooms
4 cold cooked medium potatoes, thinly sliced
2 tablespoons butter
1½ teaspoons salt
½ teaspoon pepper
1 teaspoon paprika
⅔ cup white wine
1 cup sour cream
2 pounds fresh sole filets
Snipped parsley or chives

About 1½ hours before serving, preheat oven to 375°.

Wash mushrooms, trim off stem ends, then slice lengthwise.

In buttered 8 x 12-inch baking dish, arrange potatoes, top with mushrooms, dot with butter, and sprinkle with half the salt, pepper, and paprika. Pour wine over all. Spread with half the sour cream.

Arrange pieces of fish on sour cream and sprinkle with the rest of the salt, pepper, and paprika. Top with the rest of the sour cream.

Bake for 30–40 minutes, or until fish is done. Sprinkle with parsley or chives and serve.

YIELD: 6–8 SERVINGS

THE JUNIOR LEAGUE OF FARGO-MOORHEAD, NORTH DAKOTA/MINNESOTA

·   ·   ·   ·   ·   ·   ·   ·   ·   ·   ·   ·   ·   ·   ·   ·   ·   ·

Asparagus and Fish Bake

2 pounds fresh asparagus
½ cup water
¾ teaspoon salt
4 fresh or frozen flounder filets (1 pound)
2 tablespoons butter
¼ cup chopped onion
2 tablespoons flour
1¾ cups milk
¼ cup dry white wine
2 teaspoons lemon juice
¼ teaspoon dried dill weed
⅛ teaspoon pepper
2 tablespoons chopped fresh parsley

Wash asparagus and break off each spear as far down as it snaps easily. Place in large skillet; add water and ¼ teaspoon salt. Bring to boil. Reduce heat and simmer, covered, until just tender. Drain and divide into four portions.

Wrap 1 fish filet around each bundle of asparagus and fasten with wooden pick. Arrange in large baking dish.

Melt butter in medium saucepan. Add onion and cook over medium heat until tender. Blend in flour. Remove from heat; stir in milk. Return to heat and cook, stirring constantly, until mixture thickens and comes to a boil. Stir in wine, lemon juice, remaining ½ teaspoon salt, dill, pepper, and parsley. Spoon sauce over fish.

Cover and bake at 350° for 30 minutes.

YIELD: 4 SERVINGS

THE JUNIOR LEAGUE OF KANSAS CITY, KANSAS

Halibut and Blue Cheese Casserole

6 halibut steaks
3 tablespoons butter
1 small onion, chopped
¼ cup flour
½ teaspoon salt
½ teaspoon pepper
½ teaspoon celery seed
2 tablespoons steak sauce
2 cups milk or light cream
¾ cup blue cheese, crumbled
¼ cup sliced stuffed green olives

Place steaks in buttered baking dish.

Melt butter in skillet, add onion and cook until tender. Stir in flour, add seasonings and milk, and stir until sauce is thickened. Remove from heat. Add cheese and olives and stir.

Pour sauce over fish and bake at 350° for 30 minutes.

Use leftovers to create fish chowder with some canned tomato soup, boiled cubed potatoes, and any leftover vegetables.

YIELD: 6 SERVINGS

Marigolds to Munch On
THE JUNIOR LEAGUE OF PEORIA, ILLINOIS

Baked Stuffed Pike

1 small onion, finely chopped
½ cup chopped mushrooms
½ stick butter
1 cup soft bread crumbs
1 cup crabmeat
2 eggs, beaten
1 tablespoon chopped parsley
Dash cayenne
3 tablespoons sherry
3–4 pounds ready-to-cook whole pike or any firm-fleshed fish
Butter

Sauté onion and mushrooms in butter for 5 minutes. Add rest of stuffing ingredients and mix. Stuff into cleaned fish and close opening with skewers. Bake in buttered baking dish for 1 hour at 350°, brushing fish with butter during baking. Serve with Mushroom-Crabmeat Cream Sauce.

YIELD: 6 SERVINGS

MUSHROOM-CRABMEAT CREAM SAUCE:
1 small onion, finely chopped
½ cup chopped mushrooms
½ stick butter
2 tablespoons flour
2 cups light cream
¼ cup mashed crabmeat
Dash nutmeg
Dash thyme
½ teaspoon basil
1 teaspoon chopped parsley
1 tablespoon sherry

Sauté onion and mushrooms in butter for 5 minutes. Add flour and stir. Add cream and cook, stirring constantly, until thickened. Add remaining ingredients. Pour some over fish to serve; serve the rest in a sauceboat.

The Discovery Shop Cookbook
THE JUNIOR LEAGUE OF SIOUX CITY, IOWA

· · · · · · · · · · · · · · · · · · · ·

Salmon Steaks

¾ cup butter
2 teaspoons grated lemon rind
3 tablespoons lemon juice
2 tablespoons chopped parsley
¾ pound fresh mushrooms, finely chopped
6 tablespoons sliced almonds
8–10 salmon steaks

Melt butter; add lemon rind and juice. Blend in parsley and mushrooms; mix well. Stir in almonds. Set aside.

Cover broiler pan with aluminum foil; pierce holes in foil. Arrange steaks on foil. Broil 3–5 inches from heat for 12–15 minutes, or until fish is flaky and golden; do not turn. Spoon sauce on salmon; return to broiler for 3 minutes.

Serve immediately with additional warm sauce.

YIELD: 8–10 SERVINGS

Be Our Guest
THE JUNIOR LEAGUE OF MILWAUKEE, WISCONSIN

· · · · · · · · · · · · · · · · · ·

Hot Salmon Mousse

1 1-pound can red salmon
1 envelope unflavored gelatin
½ cup diced celery
1 tablespoon sugar
1 teaspoon salt
½ tablespoon flour
½ teaspoon dry mustard
½ teaspoon pepper
2 egg yolks
1½ tablespoons melted butter
¾ cup half and half
¼ cup vinegar

Drain salmon, reserving liquid. Soften gelatin in reserved liquid; add celery and salmon and mix.

Combine remaining ingredients in top of a double boiler. Stir over hot water until smooth.

Combine salmon mixture and egg mixture. Spoon into 3-cup ring mold and refrigerate for several hours, or until set. Unmold on chilled platter and serve with Sour Cream Sauce.

YIELD: 4 SERVINGS

SOUR CREAM SAUCE:
1 cup sour cream
1 tablespoon vinegar
1½ tablespoons lemon juice
½ teaspoon sugar
½ teaspoon grated onion

Combine all ingredients.

THE JUNIOR LEAGUE OF SAGINAW, MICHIGAN

· · · · · · · · · · · · · · · ·

Salmon Roulade with Lemon Sauce

5 tablespoons butter
5 tablespoons flour
1 teaspoon salt
1 ¼ cups milk
½ cup shredded cheddar cheese
½ cup grated Parmesan cheese
6 eggs, separated
¼ teaspoon cream of tartar
Grated Parmesan cheese
Salmon filling
Lemon parsley sauce

Melt butter and blend in flour and salt. Gradually add milk and cook, stirring constantly, until sauce is thick and smooth. Add cheeses and heat, stirring, until cheese is melted.

Beat egg yolks. Gradually beat in cheese sauce. Beat egg whites with cream of tartar until stiff peaks form. Fold one half of beaten egg whites into cheese mixture. Carefully fold in remaining egg whites.

Turn into oiled 15 x 10 x 1-inch jelly-roll pan lined with wax paper and bake at 350° for 12 minutes, or until firm. Turn out on towel sprinkled with Parmesan cheese. Carefully remove paper. Roll up from long side, rolling soufflé and towel together. Cool. Unroll. Spread with Salmon Filling. Roll up.

Place seam side down on baking sheet. Bake at 350° for 15–20 minutes, or until heated through. Slice and serve with Lemon Sauce. This may be prepared beforehand to the point of the final baking.

YIELD: 6 SERVINGS

Recipe continues . . .

SALMON FILLING:

1 15½-ounce can salmon
¾ cup chopped fresh mushrooms
½ cup diced celery
¼ cup minced onion
1½ tablespoons butter
¼ teaspoon salt
⅛ teaspoon pepper
⅓ cup sour cream

Drain and flake salmon; save liquid for the sauce. Sauté mushrooms, celery, and onion in butter. Cool slightly. Combine with salmon, seasonings, and sour cream.

LEMON SAUCE:

2 tablespoons butter
2 tablespoons flour
1¼ cups chicken broth
Reserved salmon liquid
¼ teaspoon salt
2 egg yolks, beaten
1 tablespoon finely minced parsley
2 tablespoons lemon juice

In heavy saucepan, melt butter and blend in flour. Gradually stir in chicken broth and salmon liquid. Add salt. Cook, stirring constantly, until sauce is thick and smooth.

Add a small amount of sauce to egg yolks. Add egg yolks to sauce. Cook over low heat, stirring rapidly, for 2–3 minutes. Blend in the parsley and lemon juice.

YIELD: ABOUT 2 CUPS

THE JUNIOR LEAGUE OF SOUTH BEND, INDIANA

· · · · · · · · · · · · · · · · · · ·

Jim's Favorite Baked Walleye or Northern Pike

Butter
2–3 pounds fresh or frozen fish
Salt and pepper
1 cup white sauce (see Index)
¼ cup cooking sherry or white wine
1 6½-ounce can tiny shrimp
¼ cup shredded Swiss cheese

Generously butter a glass casserole before placing fish in it. Salt and pepper fish and cover tightly with buttered aluminum foil. Cook at 350° for 45 minutes.

While fish is baking, make a medium white sauce, substituting ¼ cup of sherry or white wine for milk. Add tiny shrimp and Swiss cheese.

When fish is cooked, remove foil, add cheese sauce, and broil until bubbly and lightly browned.

YIELD: 4–6 SERVINGS

THE JUNIOR LEAGUE OF SOUTH BEND, INDIANA

·   ·   ·   ·   ·   ·   ·   ·   ·   ·   ·   ·   ·   ·   ·   ·   ·   ·

Cold Salmon Mousse

3 tablespoons flour
3 tablespoons powdered sugar
2 teaspoons Dijon mustard
2 teaspoons salt
Few grains cayenne
4 eggs
1½ cups milk
½ cup tarragon vinegar
3 tablespoons melted butter
2 envelopes unflavored gelatin
¼ cup cold water
3 cups flaked cooked salmon
1 cup heavy cream, whipped

Recipe continues . . .

Mix flour, sugar, mustard, salt, and cayenne in top of a double boiler. Add eggs and whisk until smooth. Add milk. Stir in vinegar (slowly, or sauce will curdle); mix well. Cook over hot water until thickened, stirring constantly. Add butter.

Soften gelatin in cold water; add to hot mixture. Stir until gelatin is completely dissolved. Add salmon. Chill, stirring occasionally.

When slightly thickened, fold in whipped cream.

Turn into a 2-quart mold that has been rinsed with cold water. Chill until firm.

Unmold on lettuce. Serve with Cucumber-Dill Sauce.

This can be made the day before and covered with plastic wrap. It is especially delectable in a fish-shaped mold with slices of pimento, olive, and thin slices of radish set in appropriate places for eyes, scales, etc.

YIELD: 6–8 SERVINGS

CUCUMBER-DILL SAUCE:
1 cucumber, peeled and seeded
Salt
1 cup sour cream
1 tablespoon lemon juice or tarragon vinegar
1 teaspoon dill weed
1 teaspoon chopped chives
¼ teaspoon white pepper

Shred cucumber with coarse grater. Sprinkle with salt; let stand at room temperature for 1 hour.

Drain thoroughly. Combine with remaining ingredients. Chill.

YIELD: 1¾ CUPS

Soupçon
THE JUNIOR LEAGUE OF CHICAGO, ILLINOIS

Salmon Turbot

2 tablespoons butter
2 heaping tablespoons flour
Salt and pepper to taste
2 cups milk
2 eggs, well beaten
1 15-ounce can Alaska red salmon
2 slices white bread, trimmed and cubed
Additional butter

Melt butter and blend in flour, salt, and pepper. Stir in milk and cook, stirring, until thickened. Remove from heat and stir in the eggs.

In a buttered baking dish, place a layer of salmon, then a layer of sauce alternately. Cover with bread cubes and dot with butter.

Bake at 350° for 45 minutes. Serve immediately.

This is excellent served with broccoli, whole brown potatoes, and a slaw salad.

YIELD: 6 SERVINGS

Discover Dayton
THE JUNIOR LEAGUE OF DAYTON, OHIO

. . . .

Baked Coho Salmon with Sour Cream Stuffing

3–4-pound dressed Coho salmon
2½ teaspoons salt
¾ cup chopped celery
½ cup chopped onion
¼ cup melted fat
1 quart toasted bread crumbs (commercial herb may be used)
½ cup sour cream
¼ cup diced peeled lemon
2 teaspoons grated lemon rind
1 teaspoon paprika
2 tablespoons cooking oil

Recipe continues ...

Wash and dry fish. Sprinkle inside with 1½ teaspoons salt.

To prepare stuffing, cook celery and onion in fat until tender. Combine all ingredients except cooking oil, and mix thoroughly. (Makes 1 quart stuffing.)

Place fish on a well-greased bake-and-serve platter. Stuff fish loosely.

Brush fish with cooking oil. Bake at 350°, basting occasionally, for 45–60 minutes, or until fish flakes easily when tested with fork.

Coho salmon has recently become very plentiful in Lake Michigan, but any large whole fish of similar size may be used.

YIELD: 6 SERVINGS

Soupçon
THE JUNIOR LEAGUE OF CHICAGO, ILLINOIS

. . . .

Stuffed Lake Trout

3 cups herbed bread cubes
1 cup chopped tomato
1 cup chopped zucchini
1 cup sliced fresh mushrooms, sautéed
½ teaspoon salt
1 dash each savory and basil
2 tablespoons chopped onion
½ cup chopped celery
2 tablespoons lemon juice
⅓ cup butter
3-pounds whole, ready-to-cook fish
Lemon wedges and parsley for garnish

Mix all ingredients except fish, lemon wedges, and parsley with half the butter. Stuff inside fish. Place fish on greased foil on cookie sheet. Brush remaining butter over all.

Bake at 350° for 30–40 minutes. Remove to heated platter and garnish with lemon wedges and lots of parsley or leafy foliage.

YIELD: 6 SERVINGS

Cookbook
THE JUNIOR LEAGUE OF GRAND RAPIDS, MICHIGAN

· · · · · · · · · · · · · · · ·

Baked Trout

1 small trout
Dash fresh dill
1 shallot or green onion, chopped
1 teaspoon olive oil
1 teaspoon sherry
1 tablespoon fish stock or bottled clam juice
1–2 slices lemon

Sprinkle cavity of fish with fresh dill. Place fish in an aluminum foil boat. Sprinkle with shallot, olive oil, sherry, and stock or clam juice. Top with 1 or 2 slices of lemon.

Close foil boat and bake in preheated 425° oven for 15–20 minutes, depending on the size of the fish.

Serve in the foil boat.

YIELD: 1 SERVING

Discover Dayton
THE JUNIOR LEAGUE OF DAYTON, OHIO

· · · · · · · · · · · · · · · ·

Terrific Tuna Pie

1 10¾-ounce can cream-style mushroom soup
¼ cup milk
2 tablespoons flour
2 tablespoons onion flakes
1 10-ounce package frozen peas, thawed and drained
2 6½-ounce cans tuna
1 4-ounce can pimento, chopped
1 9-inch baked pie shell
1 cup shredded cheddar cheese
¼ cup buttered crumbs

In saucepan, combine soup, milk, flour, and onion flakes. Cook, stirring, until sauce is thickened.

Add peas, tuna, and pimento and bring to a boil. Turn into baked pie shell and sprinkle with cheese and crumbs.

Bake at 425° for 12–15 minutes.

YIELD: 4–6 SERVINGS

THE JUNIOR LEAGUE OF DES MOINES, IOWA

•   •   •   •   •   •   •   •   •   •   •   •   •   •   •   •   •   •

Tuna Soufflé Roulade

CRUST:
¼ cup butter
½ cup flour
2 cups half and half
3 eggs, separated
½ teaspoon baking powder

Melt butter, stir in flour, then half and half, and simmer 3 minutes. Remove from heat and stir in the egg yolks; cool. Beat the egg whites until stiff. Add the baking powder to the yolk mixture and then carefully fold in the egg whites.

Pour batter into a well-buttered, wax-paper-lined jelly-roll pan and bake at 450° for 20 minutes. Cool a little, then turn out onto wax paper. Cover with filling and roll lengthwise, jelly-roll fashion. Slice vertically to serve.

YIELD: 6 SERVINGS

FILLING:

1 6½-ounce can tuna
½ cup chopped green onion
½ teaspoon grated horseradish
1 cup mayonnaise

Mix all ingredients together. Chopped green or ripe olives and mushrooms may be added as a variation.

This makes an attractive luncheon dish.

THE JUNIOR LEAGUE OF INDIANAPOLIS, INDIANA

.   .   .   .

Baked Tuna Loaf

2 6½-ounce cans tuna, drained and flaked
3 cups fresh bread crumbs
1 egg
1 tablespoon minced parsley
1 teaspoon salt
¼ teaspoon pepper
½ cup chopped celery
1 small onion, chopped
1 10¾-ounce can cream of chicken or cream of mushroom soup
1 4-ounce can chopped mushrooms, drained

Recipe continues . . .

Mix all ingredients except soup and mushrooms. Shape into loaf and place in baking dish. Mix soup with mushrooms and pour over top of loaf.

Bake at 375° for 30 minutes.

YIELD: 6 SERVINGS

THE JUNIOR LEAGUE OF KANSAS CITY, KANSAS

Tuna Delight Casserole

8 ounces green noodles
1 medium onion, chopped
5 stalks celery, chopped
2 tablespoons butter
1 10-ounce can tuna, drained and flaked
1 10¾-ounce can cream of mushroom soup
½ cup milk
1 cup sour cream
Salt and pepper
Grated Parmesan cheese

Cook noodles according to package directions; drain. Empty into greased 2½-quart casserole.

Sauté onion and celery in butter. Add, with remaining ingredients except cheese, to noodles; mix well. Sprinkle with Parmesan cheese.

Cover and bake at 350° for 20 minutes.

YIELD: 4–6 SERVINGS

Be Our Guest
THE JUNIOR LEAGUE OF MILWAUKEE, WISCONSIN

Creamy Baked Whitefish

1 pound fresh whitefish filets
4 tablespoons butter
½ teaspoon salt
Dash pepper
1 tablespoon lemon juice
½ cup mayonnaise
¼ teaspoon paprika
1 tablespoon parsley

Line flat pan with enough foil to wrap fish. Place fish, skin side down, on foil. Dot with butter. Add salt, pepper, and lemon juice. Spread mayonnaise over fish. Sprinkle paprika and parsley over mayonnaise. Wrap fish with foil.

Bake in a 350° oven for 25–30 minutes, or until fish flakes easily.

YIELD: 4 SERVINGS

Cookbook
THE JUNIOR LEAGUE OF GRAND RAPIDS, MICHIGAN

· · · · · · · · · · · · · · · · ·

Easy Whitefish

2–2½ pounds fresh whitefish filets
Salt and pepper
1 large white onion, sliced
1–2 lemons, sliced
1 stick butter or margarine
Minced garlic

Wash filets; drain. Arrange in a greased, ovenproof dish. Season to taste with salt and pepper. Place onion and lemon over fish. Slice butter into tablespoons and place on fish. Sprinkle with garlic (watch it!).

Recipe continues . . .

Cover with aluminum foil and seal edges. Bake at 350° for 30 minutes.

YIELD: 4 SERVINGS

VARIATION:

Place fish and other ingredients on heavy-duty aluminum foil. Cover tightly; seal edges. Charcoal grill for 20–25 minutes. Test doneness by opening foil and flaking with fork.

Be Our Guest
THE JUNIOR LEAGUE OF MILWAUKEE, WISCONSIN

Baked Stuffed Whitefish

1 stick butter
2 cups bread cubes
¼ cup chopped fresh parsley
¼ cup minced fresh onion
2–3-pound whole whitefish, boned and ready to cook

Melt butter and pour half over bread cubes mixed with parsley and onions. Blend until all bread is moist.

Generously butter fish. Stuff with bread mixture; skewer and sew closed with kitchen thread and needle.

Place fish in 2-inch-deep baking pan. Pour remaining butter over fish and bake at 325° for 45 minutes.

Cut into 2-inch slices and serve.

YIELD: 4 SERVINGS

THE JUNIOR LEAGUE OF SAGINAW, MICHIGAN

Party Buffet Seafood au Gratin

9 pounds seafood
½ pound butter
1 cup flour
7 cups milk
1 cup tomato purée
1 tablespoon plus 2 teaspoons salt
½ teaspoon red pepper
1½ teaspoons paprika
2 cloves garlic, freshly crushed
2 tablespoons monosodium glutamate
5 ounces Gruyère cheese, cut into small pieces
¼ pound American cheese, finely diced
½–1 cup sherry

Use a combination of shrimp, lobster, and crabmeat in any proportion you choose. Cook the seafood before you make the sauce.

In a large, heavy kettle, melt butter over low heat; add flour and stir for 1 minute.

Stirring constantly, add milk, tomato purée, salt, red pepper, paprika, garlic, glutamate, Gruyère cheese, and American cheese; stir and cook until sauce is thick and bubbling.

Correct seasoning. Add sherry and seafood and cook over low heat until seafood is heated through.

Serve on biscuits, toast, or in patty shells.

If desired, keep warm on the buffet table in large chafing dish set over hot water. Refill chafing dish as needed.

YIELD: 30 SERVINGS

Peacock Pie and Other Perfections
THE JUNIOR LEAGUE OF BATTLE CREEK, MICHIGAN

Quick Crabmeat with Sherry in Shells

2 cups crabmeat
2 hard-boiled eggs, chopped
1 cup mayonnaise
1 teaspoon grated onion
1 teaspoon chopped parsley
2 teaspoons lemon juice
½ teaspoon Worcestershire sauce
½ teaspoon prepared mustard
3 tablespoons sherry
Buttered bread crumbs

Mix all ingredients except crumbs together and put in ceramic shells. Sprinkle crumbs on top. Bake at 400° for 15 minutes.

YIELD: 6 SERVINGS

Peacock Pie and Other Perfections
THE JUNIOR LEAGUE OF BATTLE CREEK, MICHIGAN

. . . .

Crab Fritters

¾ cup flour
1½ teaspoons baking powder
½ teaspoon salt
About ¼ cup milk
1 egg
1 7-ounce can crabmeat
¼ cup mayonnaise-type salad dressing
1 teaspoon Worcestershire sauce
Cooking oil

Combine dry ingredients and stir in milk beaten lightly with the egg. Stir in remaining ingredients to make a thick batter.

Drop batter from a teaspoon in hot oil, about 380°. Cook until golden brown; drain on paper.

Serve with tartar or hot sauce. May be frozen and reheated in 300° oven on paper towels.

YIELD: 25 FRITTERS

The Discovery Shop Cookbook
THE JUNIOR LEAGUE OF SIOUX CITY, IOWA

· · · · · · · · · · · · · · · · · ·

Seafood-Stuffed Crepes

12 crepes (see Index)
1 cup shredded Swiss cheese
Butter

FILLING:
1 stick butter
½ cup minced green onion
2 pounds fresh or canned crabmeat
Salt and white pepper to taste
⅛ teaspoon garlic powder
½ cup dry vermouth

SAUCE:
⅔ cup dry vermouth
¼ cup cornstarch
¼ cup milk
4 cups heavy cream or half and half
Salt and white pepper to taste
1½ cups shredded Swiss cheese

For filling, melt butter in a large skillet. Stir in green onion, then the crabmeat. Toss lightly and cook for a few minutes. Add seasonings and ver-

Recipe continues . . .

mouth and boil rapidly until liquid is almost evaporated. Scrape into a bowl and set aside.

To make the sauce, pour vermouth into the same skillet and boil rapidly until reduced to 2 tablespoons. Remove from heat and stir in cornstarch mixed with milk. Return to low heat and stir in cream slowly with salt and pepper. Cook several minutes until slightly thickened. Stir in Swiss cheese and cook, stirring, until melted and well blended.

To fill crepes, blend half the sauce with the crabmeat. Put a large spoonful of filling on each crepe and roll. Place seam side down in a buttered dish. Repeat until all crepes are filled. Spoon remaining sauce over crepes and sprinkle with Swiss cheese. Dot with butter and refrigerate.

Remove from refrigerator 30 minutes before baking. Bake at 400° for 20 minutes.

YIELD: 6 SERVINGS FOR ENTREE; 12 FOR APPETIZER

THE JUNIOR LEAGUE OF KANSAS CITY, KANSAS

· · · · · · · · · · · · · · · ·

Sherried Crabmeat

2 6½-ounce cans crabmeat
¼ cup butter or margarine
3 teaspoons flour
½ teaspoon salt
Dash pepper
Dash cayenne
¾ cup bottled clam juice
½ cup heavy cream
1½ tablespoons dry sherry
1 hard-boiled egg, finely chopped

TOPPING:

2 tablespoons butter
1 tablespoon finely chopped onion
½ cup sliced fresh mushrooms
1 tablespoon chopped parsley
1 tablespoon chopped chives
¼ cup dry bread crumbs

Drain crabmeat and remove cartilage.

Melt the ¼ cup butter over medium heat. Add flour, salt, and peppers. Cook, stirring constantly, until mixture becomes smooth and bubbly. Add clam juice and cream. Heat to just below boiling. Add sherry, egg, and crabmeat.

Melt the 2 tablespoons butter in small skillet. Sauté onion, mushrooms, parsley, and chives until vegetables are tender. Stir in bread crumbs.

To serve, divide crabmeat mixture into 6 puff pastry shells and sprinkle with topping.

YIELD: 6 SERVINGS

THE JUNIOR LEAGUE OF CHAMPAIGN-URBANA, ILLINOIS

·　·　·　·　·　·　·　·　·　·　·　·　·　·　·　·　·

Puffin' Crab

2 tablespoons butter
2 tablespoons flour
1 cup hot milk
3 egg yolks
½ cup mayonnaise plus 1 teaspoon creamy salad dressing
1 6½-ounce can crabmeat, flaked
Salt and pepper
Dash cayenne
3 egg whites
1 teaspoon paprika

Recipe continues . . .

Make a thick white sauce by melting the butter, stirring in the flour, and gradually adding the hot milk. Cook, stirring, for 5 minutes.

Cool mixture. Beat in the egg yolks, fold in the mayonnaise, and add the crabmeat. Season to taste, add cayenne.

Beat the egg whites until stiff. Fold into the crabmeat mixture and empty into a greased casserole. Dust with paprika and bake in a 400° oven until brown and puffed, about 25 minutes.

This is really a soufflé, but a very reliable one; it does not "collapse," making it easier to serve for company. Great with cold beer and a cucumber salad.

YIELD: 4 SERVINGS

Marigolds to Munch On
THE JUNIOR LEAGUE OF PEORIA, ILLINOIS

·   ·   ·   ·   ·   ·   ·   ·   ·   ·   ·   ·   ·   ·   ·   ·   ·

Jiffy Crabmeat Casserole

1 pint light cream
2 cups mayonnaise
1 1-pound can crabmeat
2 tablespoons chopped parsley
2 tablespoons chopped onion
3 hard-boiled eggs, chopped
½ cup sherry
1 8-ounce package prepared stuffing mix

Mix cream and mayonnaise. Add remaining ingredients, reserving a little stuffing for topping.

Place in a greased 2-quart casserole and bake at 375° for 45 minutes.

YIELD: 10–12 SERVINGS

Cincinnati Celebrates
THE JUNIOR LEAGUE OF CINCINNATI, OHIO

·   ·   ·   ·   ·   ·   ·   ·   ·   ·   ·   ·   ·   ·   ·   ·   ·

Clams Florentine

1 pound fresh spinach, washed well, or 1 10-ounce package frozen
Salt
¾ cup chopped green onion
1 clove garlic, minced
6 tablespoons butter
3 tablespoons dry white wine
½ cup chopped parsley
2 7-ounce cans minced clams, drained and chopped
½ cup bread crumbs
2 egg yolks
½ teaspoon Worcestershire sauce
4 drops Tabasco
Salt and pepper to taste
½ cup bread crumbs
3 tablespoons butter
¼ cup grated Parmesan cheese

Cook spinach in a minimum of water. Add a little salt, cover, and cook about 8–10 minutes, or until spinach is tender; stir occasionally. Drain and squeeze out as much moisture as possible. Chop.

Sauté green onion and garlic in butter until limp. Add wine and cook until it evaporates. Add parsley and spinach and sauté for 1–2 minutes. Add clams, bread crumbs, egg yolks, and seasonings. Mix well and taste for seasoning.

Butter 8 scallop shells or a casserole and distribute mixture. Sauté bread crumbs in butter until nicely browned and sprinkle over tops. Sprinkle with Parmesan cheese.

Bake at 425° for about 10 minutes, or until hot and brown.

YIELD: 8 SERVINGS

Cookbook
THE JUNIOR LEAGUE OF GRAND RAPIDS, MICHIGAN

Oysters Baked in Wine Sauce

1½ cups dry white wine
3 dozen oysters, drained
4 tablespoons butter
3 tablespoons flour
¾ cup heavy cream
Salt and pepper
Dash cayenne
3 tablespoons buttered crumbs
Grated Parmesan cheese (optional)
Additional butter (optional)

Heat wine in heavy skillet. When just under boiling add oysters and poach for 1 minute. Lift out with slotted spoon and arrange in shallow casserole.

Strain wine through fine sieve. Reserve.

Melt butter in saucepan; stir in flour and cook briefly. Gradually blend in wine in which oysters were poached. Stir until smooth and thick. Add cream. Season to taste with salt, pepper, and cayenne. Pour over oysters and top with crumbs.

Bake in 450° oven for 10 minutes, or until golden brown.

You may sprinkle Parmesan cheese on top and dot with butter if desired.

YIELD: 5–6 SERVINGS

Peacock Pie and Other Perfections
THE JUNIOR LEAGUE OF BATTLE CREEK, MICHIGAN

Scalloped Oyster Puff

Butter
3 individual packets saltines from a 16-ounce box
1 pint fresh oysters, drained
Salt
Pepper
Nutmeg
Milk

Butter a deep 2-quart casserole. Break crackers into bite-size pieces and cover bottom of casserole. Place slivers of butter evenly over crackers. Then arrange oysters on top of crackers. Sprinkle with salt, pepper, and nutmeg. Cover with another layer of broken crackers, another layer of oysters, etc., until casserole is filled. Next, pour milk over mixture to ¼ inch from top of dish.

Let mixture sit for 30 minutes; cover and bake at 350° for 1 hour. When done, mixture will puff up soufflé-style.

YIELD: 8 SERVINGS

THE JUNIOR LEAGUE OF DES MOINES, IOWA

. . . .

Escalloped Oysters

½ package herb-seasoned stuffing
1 teaspoon powdered sage
1 teaspoon salt
1 teaspoon paprika
¼ teaspoon black pepper
½ cup melted butter
2 pints raw oysters, drained
1 cup milk

Recipe continues . . .

Mix together first five ingredients with butter to make crumb mixture.

In a buttered baking dish, layer crumbs and oysters alternately until all are used. Pour in milk and bake at 350°, uncovered, for 45 minutes.

Terrific as a side dish with turkey or roast beef.

YIELD: 6 SERVINGS

THE JUNIOR LEAGUE OF YOUNGSTOWN, OHIO

. . . .

Shrimp and Lobster Curry

CURRY SAUCE:
¼ cup butter
¼ cup chopped onion
1 clove garlic, minced
1 stalk celery, chopped
1 tart apple, diced
1 bay leaf
⅓ cup flour
2 teaspoons curry powder (or to taste)
½ teaspoon salt
½ teaspoon dry mustard
3 cups chicken stock
¼–½ cup light cream or milk (optional)

SEAFOOD:
¾ pound cooked peeled shrimp
½ pound cooked lobster meat

Heat butter. Sauté onion, garlic, celery, apple, and bay leaf until cooked but not brown. Sprinkle with flour, curry powder, salt, and dry mustard. Gradually stir in stock. Cook, stirring constantly, until thickened. Add cream, if desired, and simmer 10–15 minutes.

Add seafood; heat.

Serve with rice and desired condiments.

Turkey or chicken may be used instead of seafood.

YIELD: 6 SERVINGS

Soupçon
THE JUNIOR LEAGUE OF CHICAGO, ILLINOIS

· · · · · · · · · · · · · · · · · · ·

Lemon-Shrimp Skewers

½ cup chili sauce
2 tablespoons corn syrup
2 tablespoons red wine vinegar
¼ cup salad oil
½ teaspoon salt
¼ teaspoon pepper
2 lemons, cut in wedges
2 pounds large uncooked shrimp, shelled and deveined

Combine chili sauce, corn syrup, vinegar, oil, salt, and pepper. Beat until sauce is smooth.

Thread lemon wedges and shrimp alternately on skewers. Brush with sauce. Broil 3–4 minutes on each side.

Serve hot, squeezing the hot lemon juice over shrimp.

YIELD: 4 SERVINGS

THE JUNIOR LEAGUE OF CHAMPAIGN-URBANA, ILLINOIS

· · · · · · · · · · · · · · · · · · ·

Hurried Curried Shrimp

1½ tablespoons butter
½ cup chopped onion
1 small apple, diced
½ teaspoon curry powder (or to taste)
1 10½-ounce can cream of shrimp soup
1 cup cooked shrimp
1 cup sour cream
Parsley sprigs
Paprika

Melt butter in the top of a double boiler over direct heat. Add onion, apple, and curry powder and sauté until onion is soft and transparent but not browned. Add soup. Set pan over hot water and stir until smooth.

Add shrimp and sour cream and heat until hot. Garnish with parsley and a sprinkle of paprika.

Serve over hot rice with choice of condiments: chutney, sliced bananas, coconut, chopped peanuts, chopped dates, raisins, chopped chives, or green onion tops. Recipe can be doubled or tripled for company buffets.

YIELD: 4 SERVINGS

Cookbook
THE JUNIOR LEAGUE OF GRAND RAPIDS, MICHIGAN

Shrimp Creole

1 cup diced celery
½ cup chopped onion
¼ cup chopped green pepper
1 clove garlic, minced
¼ cup butter
3½ cups fresh or canned tomatoes
1 teaspoon salt
1 teaspoon sugar
⅛ teaspoon pepper
1 bay leaf
Few drops Tabasco sauce
1–1½ pounds shrimp, cleaned and cooked

Cook celery, onion, green pepper, and garlic in butter until vegetables are tender. Add tomatoes, salt, sugar, pepper, and bay leaf and Tabasco sauce. Cover and simmer 45–60 minutes. Discard bay leaf.

Add shrimp and heat through. Serve over cooked rice.

YIELD: 6–8 SERVINGS

THE JUNIOR LEAGUE OF COLUMBUS, OHIO

· · · · · · · · · · · · · · · · · · · ·

Skillet de Jonghe

¼ cup butter
2 cloves garlic, minced
½ cup fine bread crumbs
1 pound fresh shrimp, cleaned

Recipe continues . . .

In saucepan, melt butter and add garlic, bread crumbs, and shrimp. Cook about 5 minutes, or just until shrimp are tender, stirring constantly.

YIELD: 3 SERVINGS

The Cook's Book
THE JUNIOR LEAGUE OF CEDAR RAPIDS, IOWA

Shrimp-Scallop Creole

3 large onions, sliced
½ cup chopped celery
½ pound margarine or butter
2 28-ounce cans whole tomatoes
2 whole cloves
2 bay leaves
Salt and pepper to taste
1 teaspoon sugar
1 12-ounce can tomato paste
1½ pounds cooked shrimp
1 pound raw scallops, sliced

Sauté onions and celery in butter or margarine until onions are golden in color. Add canned tomatoes and bring to a boil. Add cloves, bay leaves, salt, pepper, sugar, and tomato paste. Cook until mixture thickens, about 45 minutes on medium heat.

Remove cloves and bay leaves. Add shrimp and scallops and simmer for another 6–10 minutes.

Serve hot over rice.

YIELD: 6–8 SERVINGS

Discover Dayton
THE JUNIOR LEAGUE OF DAYTON, OHIO

Lemon-Shrimp Oriental

2 cups sliced fresh mushrooms
1 medium green pepper, cut into strips
1½ cups sliced celery
¼ cup sliced onion
2 tablespoons cooking oil
1 pound shrimp, shelled and deveined
1 6-ounce package pea pods
2 tablespoons cornstarch
1 teaspoon sugar
1 teaspoon salt
1 cup water
1 teaspoon chicken bouillon granules
1½ teaspoons grated lemon peel
3 tablespoons lemon juice

Sauté vegetables for about 10 minutes in oil. Add shrimp and cook, stirring and tossing shrimp, for 3–5 minutes longer. Combine cornstarch, sugar, salt, water, bouillon, and lemon, add to vegetables, and cook, stirring, until liquid is hot and thickened.

Serve over rice.

YIELD: 4 SERVINGS

THE JUNIOR LEAGUE OF ST. PAUL, MINNESOTA

Shrimp-Broccoli au Gratin

1 12-ounce bag frozen, peeled, deveined shrimp
2 10-ounce packages frozen broccoli
2 cups shredded sharp cheddar cheese
1½ sticks butter
4 tablespoons chopped onion
4 tablespoons flour
¼ teaspoon curry powder
1 teaspoon salt
2 cups milk or half and half
2 tablespoons lemon juice
1½ cups soft bread crumbs

Defrost shrimp; cook broccoli. Arrange broccoli in bottom of a 2-quart baking dish. Sprinkle with shredded cheese.

Melt 1 stick (½ cup) butter and in it sauté onion until transparent. Stir in flour, curry powder, and salt. Gradually stir in milk. Cook, stirring constantly, over low heat until sauce is thickened.

Stir in lemon juice; add shrimp and pour over broccoli. Melt ½ stick butter, mix with crumbs, and sprinkle on top. Bake for 30 minutes at 350°.

YIELD: 8 SERVINGS

THE JUNIOR LEAGUE OF ST. PAUL, MINNESOTA

Riverside Seafood

1 small onion, chopped
1 4-ounce can mushrooms
3 tablespoons butter
1 10¾-ounce can cream of chicken soup
Pepper and dash Tabasco
1 teaspoon Worcestershire sauce
½ cup cream
½ cup sliced ripe olives
½ pound shrimp, cooked
1 7½-ounce can crabmeat
Sherry (optional)
Toasted slivered almonds for garnish

Sauté onion and mushrooms in butter until onion is tender. Add soup and seasonings and simmer for a few minutes. Then add cream, olives, and seafood. Mix well. Add sherry to taste, if desired.

Top with toasted slivered almonds and serve over Chinese noodles or toast.

YIELD: 4 SERVINGS

The Cook's Book
THE JUNIOR LEAGUE OF CEDAR RAPIDS, IOWA

Milwaukee Stir-Fried Shrimp and Vegetables

2 tablespoons oil
1 teaspoon finely chopped fresh ginger
¾ pound shrimp, shelled and deveined
2 tablespoons butter
1 8-ounce can water chestnuts, drained and sliced
1 pound fresh pea pods
1 tablespoon sliced green onion
2 tablespoons chicken stock
1 tablespoon soy sauce
1 tablespoon dry sherry
¼ teaspoon monosodium glutamate
Salt
1½ teaspoons sugar
1 tomato, peeled and cut in wedges

Heat oil in wok or large skillet. Stir-fry ginger for 10 seconds. Add shrimp and cook about 1½ minutes, or until shrimp changes color. Add butter, water chestnuts, pea pods, and green onion; stir-fry for 2 minutes.

Blend in remaining ingredients except tomato wedges. Add tomatoes; stir-fry for 2 minutes.

Serve immediately on hot cooked rice.

YIELD: 3–4 SERVINGS

Be Our Guest
THE JUNIOR LEAGUE OF MILWAUKEE, WISCONSIN

Quick Seafood Supper

1 12-ounce package frozen macaroni and cheese
1 7½-ounce can king crab or 1 6¾-ounce package frozen crabmeat
6 tablespoons sherry
1 10¾-ounce can condensed cream of shrimp soup
Buttered bread crumbs

Thaw macaroni and cheese.

Blend macaroni and cheese, crabmeat, sherry, and soup and put into a buttered casserole. Sprinkle buttered bread crumbs on top.

Bake at 350° for 20 minutes or until hot and bubbly.

This casserole is especially good served in patty shells.

YIELD: 3 SERVINGS

THE JUNIOR LEAGUE OF ST. PAUL, MINNESOTA

Deluxe Crabmeat (or Salmon) Casserole

3 cups shell macaroni
2 cups flaked crabmeat or salmon
1 cup shrimp
2 10½-ounce cans mushroom soup
1½ cups evaporated milk
1 teaspoon Worcestershire sauce
½ cup slivered almonds
4 tablespoons minced parsley
1 green pepper, seeded and chopped
½ cup sherry
4 tablespoons butter
4 tablespoons grated Parmesan cheese

Recipe continues . . .

Cook and drain macaroni. Mix all ingredients together except butter and cheese in baking dish. Melt butter, pour over top, and sprinkle with cheese.
Bake for 45 minutes at 350°.

YIELD: 12 SERVINGS

THE JUNIOR LEAGUE OF TOLEDO, OHIO

Game

Fried Partridge

1 partridge, cut into serving pieces
½ cup flour
Salt and pepper
Shortening
Water

Roll partridge pieces in the flour seasoned with salt and pepper. Brown in shortening until crispy. Add small amount of water; cover and cook over medium-low heat for about 30 minutes, or until tender.

YIELD: 2 SERVINGS

THE JUNIOR LEAGUE OF SAGINAW, MICHIGAN

· · · · · · · · · · · · · · · · · · ·

Gourmet Delight Pheasant or Partridge

4 pheasants or partridges, quartered
½ stick butter
1 cup brandy
2 cups chicken stock
1 onion, chopped
1 clove garlic, minced
Salt and pepper to taste
1 quart heavy cream
1 10-ounce bottle horseradish
½ pound mushrooms, sautéed in butter

Brown quartered birds well in butter. Place in baking dish and pour the brandy over. Light brandy and let flame burn out. Add chicken stock, onion, and garlic. Season with salt and pepper.

Bake in 350° oven for ½ hour, basting several times.

Remove dish from oven and pour over the heavy cream mixed with horseradish. Replace in oven and bake 1½ hours.

Just before serving, add the mushrooms. Serve over wild rice.

YIELD: 6–8 SERVINGS

The Discovery Shop Cookbook
THE JUNIOR LEAGUE OF SIOUX CITY, IOWA

.   .   .   .

Pheasant Supreme

2 pheasants
Salt and pepper
2 apples, peeled and quartered
1 cup dry vermouth mixed with 1 cup water
2 tablespoons butter
2 tablespoons flour
¼ cup currant jelly
1 teaspoon garlic powder
Pinch curry powder
1 cup heavy cream
½ cup dry vermouth

Sprinkle birds with salt and pepper; stuff with apples. Roast on rack at 450° for 45 minutes. Baste every 15 minutes with pan drippings and watered vermouth. (This prevents bird from drying out.)

For sauce, melt butter; stir in flour. Add jelly, garlic powder, curry, cream, and vermouth. Cook and stir until thickened. Stir in drippings from roasting pan. Add salt and pepper to taste.

Cut pheasants into serving pieces and pass the sauce.

YIELD: 4 SERVINGS

Soupçon
THE JUNIOR LEAGUE OF CHICAGO, ILLINOIS

.   .   .   .

Amana Pheasant

Flour
Salt and pepper
Breasts and legs of 2 pheasants
Shortening
2 cups milk
1 10½-ounce can mushroom soup
1 cup dry white wine
1 heaping teaspoon curry powder

Flour, salt, and pepper pheasant and brown in shortening. Transfer pheasant pieces to casserole and pour pan drippings over them.

Combine remaining ingredients. Pour over pheasant and bake, covered, in 300° oven for 3 or more hours. Baste frequently. If necessary, add more milk.

Meat should be moist and fall off bone when done.

YIELD: 4 SERVINGS

The Cook's Book
THE JUNIOR LEAGUE OF CEDAR RAPIDS, IOWA

·   ·   ·   ·   ·   ·   ·   ·   ·   ·   ·   ·   ·   ·   ·   ·   ·

Brandied Pheasant

4 pheasants, halved or quartered
1 stick butter
1 cup brandy
2 cups chicken stock
1 onion, chopped
1 clove garlic, crushed
Salt and pepper to taste
1 quart heavy cream, whipped
2 5-ounce jars horseradish
2 pounds fresh mushrooms

Brown pheasants on all sides in half the butter and place in roasting pan. Pour brandy over game, ignite, and let flame burn out.

Add chicken stock, onion, garlic, and seasonings and bake 30 minutes at 350°, basting several times. Next add whipped cream combined with horseradish. Bake an additional 1½ hours, basting and turning every 15 minutes.

Sauté mushrooms in remaining butter and add to thickened gravy. Serve the pheasant with the mushroom and cream sauce and wild rice.

YIELD: 8 SERVINGS

The Cook's Book
THE JUNIOR LEAGUE OF CEDAR RAPIDS, IOWA

. . . .

Marinated Pheasant

1 cup vegetable oil
1 clove garlic, minced
¾ teaspoon pepper
2 teaspoons salt
2 teaspoons ginger
1 7-ounce bottle 7-Up
1 pheasant, quartered, or fileted breasts
Flour and shortening

Combine first six ingredients and add pheasant. Let marinate for 2–8 hours. Drain, reserving marinade.

Dip pheasant in flour and fry in shortening until browned. Place in baking dish with marinade, cover, and bake for 1¼ hours at 350°.

YIELD: 2 SERVINGS

The Discovery Shop Cookbook
THE JUNIOR LEAGUE OF SIOUX CITY, IOWA

. . . .

Roast Quail with Port Wine

12 ready-to-cook quail
½ teaspoon salt
¼ cup chopped green onion
1 teaspoon dried tarragon
Butter
12 slices bacon, simmered in water for 10 minutes and drained
2 tablespoons cooking oil

SAUCE:
1 tablespoon minced green onion
1 tablespoon butter
1 tablespoon drippings
1½ cups beef bouillon
¼ cup port

Season cavities of the quail with salt, green onion, and tarragon. Truss birds, rub with butter, and tie a slice of bacon around each breast.

Place birds on a rack in roasting pan and cook at 400° for 30–40 minutes, basting every 10 minutes with a mixture of ¼ cup melted butter and the oil.

For the sauce, sauté onion in butter and drippings from roasting pan. Add bouillon and port. Bring to a boil and boil rapidly for several minutes.

Correct seasoning and spoon the sauce over the birds.

YIELD: 6 SERVINGS, 2 BIRDS EACH

Soupçon
THE JUNIOR LEAGUE OF CHICAGO, ILLINOIS

Wild Ducks in Honey

2 mallard or other wild ducks
Salt and pepper

GAME MARINADE:
2 onions, sliced
2 carrots, sliced
2 cloves
4 crushed peppercorns
1 bay leaf
2 cloves garlic, crushed
4 sprigs parsley
2 juniper berries
3 cups red wine
1 cup olive oil
1 cup vinegar

STUFFING AND BASTING SAUCE:
4 tablespoons salt
2 tablespoons ground ginger
2 tablespoons basil
1 tablespoon freshly ground pepper
2 cups honey
½ cup butter
¼ cup orange juice
3 tablespoons lemon juice
2 tablespoons grated orange rind
¼ tablespoon dry mustard
2 oranges, sliced into 6 wedges
2 tablespoons potato flour
Water
¼ cup cognac

Season ducks with salt and pepper and place in ceramic casseroles. Scatter the marinade vegetables and spices over them. Combine the wine, oil, and

Recipe continues . . .

vinegar; pour over ducks. Cover; place in refrigerator for 5 days, turning ducks occasionally.

Remove ducks from marinade; pat dry inside and out.

For the stuffing and sauce, combine salt, ginger, basil, and pepper. Rub half of this mixture inside the ducks. Combine honey, butter, orange juice, lemon juice, orange rind, and mustard in top of double boiler; heat thoroughly. Rub 3 tablespoons honey mixture inside each duck. Stuff ducks with as many orange wedges as possible. Spoon 4 tablespoons more of the honey mixture into each duck. Truss. Rub remaining basil mixture outside ducks.

Place each duck on a large sheet of aluminum foil. Pour remaining honey mixture over each; wrap securely. Bake for 2 hours at 325°. Unwrap ducks and continue baking ½ hour longer, basting frequently.

Pour drippings into a saucepan. Combine potato flour with a little water; stir into drippings. Bring to a boil, stirring.

Pour cognac over ducks and ignite. Serve with sauce.

YIELD: 4 SERVINGS

Soupçon
THE JUNIOR LEAGUE OF CHICAGO, ILLINOIS

· · · · · · · · · · · · · · · · ·

Minnesota Mallard Duck

Breasts of 4 mallard ducks
Salt, pepper, and paprika
½ pound mushrooms, sliced
1 medium onion, diced
2 tablespoons butter
2 tablespoons vermouth
2 10¾-ounce cans mushroom soup
¼ cup dry sherry
2 tablespoons flour
1 teaspoon oregano
1 teaspoon tarragon
¼ cup chives
1 cup sour cream

Season ducks lightly with salt, pepper, and paprika.

Stew mushrooms and onion in butter and vermouth until onion is transparent.

Mix soup and sherry together in a casserole. Stir in flour, herbs, and the stewed onion and mushrooms.

Place duck breasts in casserole in the soup mixture, cover and bake at 325° for 2 hours. Stir in the sour cream and bake for 10–15 minutes longer.

The sauce is wonderful served over wild rice.

YIELD: 4 SERVINGS

THE JUNIOR LEAGUE OF ST. PAUL, MINNESOTA

Roast Wild Duck

1 wild duck
Bacon drippings
Salt, pepper, and paprika
Small onion
1 cup milk
½ cup sherry

Rub duck with bacon drippings and sprinkle generously inside and out with salt, pepper, and paprika. Place small onion in cavity.

Place duck in roaster, add 1 cup milk to roaster, cover, and cook at 325° for 2 hours. Cook breast side down for half the cooking time, breast side up for last half. Add ½ cup sherry and cook for 30 minutes longer.

Serve with Wine Sauce.

YIELD: 2 SERVINGS

WINE SAUCE:
1 cup currant jelly
¼ cup butter
¼ cup sherry

Slowly melt jelly with the butter. Add sherry and heat.

THE JUNIOR LEAGUE OF SAGINAW, MICHIGAN

· · · · · · · · · · · · · · · · · ·

Venison with Lingonberry Sauce

1 7-pound leg of venison
1 teaspoon salt
½ teaspoon ground ginger
¼ teaspoon pepper
1 cup beef stock
½ cup melted butter

SAUCE:

1 cup fresh lingonberries or jarred if fresh are not available
2 tablespoons water
6 tablespoons sugar
1 tablespoon cornstarch
Water

Rub venison with a mixture of salt, ginger, and pepper. Place on a rack in a roasting pan; cover with foil. Bake at 325° for 2½–3 hours, or until tender. Baste occasionally with stock mixed with butter. Let venison rest while you make sauce. Reserve drippings.

Combine lingonberries and water; simmer, covered, 15 minutes. Stir in sugar.

Remove excess fat from pan drippings, blend in cornstarch mixed with a little water. Cook, stirring constantly, until thickened. Add water, if needed. Stir in the lingonberries and check seasonings.

Spoon some sauce over venison, pass the rest.

YIELD: 14 SERVINGS

Soupçon
THE JUNIOR LEAGUE OF CHICAGO, ILLINOIS

· ·

. . . .

Condiments and Preserves

. . . .

Mustard

1 cup vinegar
1 4-ounce can dry mustard
3 eggs
1 cup sugar

Combine vinegar and mustard and let stand overnight.

Next day, beat eggs and sugar together. Stir into mustard-vinegar mixture and cook in double boiler over boiling water, stirring constantly, until thickened.

Fill jars and let cool. Store in the refrigerator.

YIELD: APPROXIMATELY 2½ CUPS

Soupçon
THE JUNIOR LEAGUE OF CHICAGO, ILLINOIS

. . . .

Red Cinnamon Apples

1 cup sugar
½ cup water
¼ cup red hot cinnamon candies
8–10 apples

In large skillet, mix sugar, water, and candies. Let simmer while peeling and coring 8–10 apples (leave apples whole).

Put apples in liquid and simmer until just tender, turning apples occasionally. Remove to platter. Pour liquid over apples. Chill.

These are beautiful, bright red apples with a jelled glaze. Liquid may have to be boiled a bit after apples are removed to make sure it jells.

YIELD: 10–12 SERVINGS

Bluff City Cooks
THE JUNIOR LEAGUE OF GREATER ALTON, ILLINOIS

. . . .

Indiana Apple Butter

Approximately 10 pounds apples
Water
½ cup cinnamon candies
5 cups sugar
1 tablespoon ground cinnamon
2 teaspoons whole cloves

Pare apples and quarter. Cook until very tender with a little water in a Dutch oven or preserving kettle. Purée the cooked apples through a food mill. Measure 10 cups of the purée into a 9 x 13-inch shallow glass baking dish. *Never use an aluminum pan.* While still warm, stir in the cinnamon candies, sugar, ground cinnamon, and whole cloves. Mix well.

Bake the purée in a 350° oven for ½ hour, then turn the oven down to 325°. Cook for 3½–5 hours longer, depending on the type of apples and how fast the mixture thickens. Stir often as the apple butter has a tendency to cook faster around the edges of the dish.

When the apple butter is of a medium-thick consistency, *put directly into hot sterilized glass jars.* Seal jars immediately. Store in a cool, dry place.

Terrific all year round on homemade breads and rolls.

YIELD: 6–8 PINTS

THE JUNIOR LEAGUE OF SOUTH BEND, INDIANA

* * * * * * * * * * * * * * * * *

Illinois Apple Butter

2 pounds apples
¾ cup apple juice
¼ cup vinegar
Brown sugar
Cinnamon
Ground clove

Recipe continues . . .

Wash the apples, quarter them, and remove the core, blossom, and stem ends. Put the apples in a kettle with the apple juice and vinegar. Cook the apples, covered, over low heat until they are tender. Force the pulp through a colander or food mill and measure the purée.

For each quart of purée, add 2 cups dark brown sugar, 1 teaspoon cinnamon, and ¼ teaspoon cloves. Cook over medium heat, stirring constantly, until the butter is thick enough to spread.

Pour the boiling butter into hot sterilized jars and seal at once.

YIELD: 3–4 CUPS

THE JUNIOR LEAGUE OF ROCKFORD, ILLINOIS

· · · · · · · · · · · · · · · · · · ·

Raw Cranberry Relish

1 1-pound package raw cranberries
1 orange
1 1-pound can crushed pineapple
1 10-ounce package shelled walnuts
1 cup diced celery
1 cup sugar

Clean cranberries; squeeze orange and reserve juice. Discard membrane from the inside of the orange hull. Grind cranberries and orange hull in meat grinder, using medium or large wheel.

Drain pineapple; save juice. Chop nuts. Combine cranberries, orange, celery, pineapple, and nuts. Pour reserved orange juice and small amount of pineapple juice over mixture of ingredients.

Stir in sugar and let the relish ripen for several hours or overnight. Can be frozen.

Great with poultry and beef.

YIELD: ABOUT 1 QUART

Bluff City Cooks
THE JUNIOR LEAGUE OF GREATER ALTON, ILLINOIS

· · · · · · · · · · · · · · · · · · ·

Spiced Cranberries

2 quarts fresh cranberries
1⅓ cups cider vinegar
⅔ cup water
6 cups sugar
2 tablespoons ground cinnamon
1 tablespoon ground cloves
1 tablespoon ground allspice

Wash and inspect cranberries and discard any bruised fruit. Put good cranberries in large kettle and add remaining ingredients. Cook slowly over low heat for 45 minutes.

Pour into hot sterilized glasses and seal.

YIELD: 6–8 HALF PINTS

Soupçon
THE JUNIOR LEAGUE OF CHICAGO, ILLINOIS

· · · · · · · · · · · · · · · · ·

Cranberry-Tangerine Chutney

4 tangerines
2 cups fresh cranberries
1 medium apple, peeled and diced
½ cup golden raisins
½ cup orange marmalade
½ cup vinegar
1½ cups water
1¼ cups sugar
1 tablespoon curry powder
¾ teaspoon cinnamon
½ teaspoon ginger
¼ teaspoon ground cloves
Dash allspice

Recipe continues . . .

Peel tangerines; remove all membranes and seeds. Cut sections in half.

Combine all ingredients, including tangerine sections, in a saucepan; bring to a boil over medium heat. Reduce heat, cover, and simmer for 30 minutes, stirring occasionally to prevent sticking.

Pour into hot sterilized jars and seal or store in refrigerator in covered containers.

Nice to serve with meats or poultry.

YIELD: ABOUT 3 PINTS

Soupçon
THE JUNIOR LEAGUE OF CHICAGO, ILLINOIS

· · · · · · · · · · · · · · · · · · ·

Pear Chutney

½ teaspoon whole allspice
½ teaspoon whole cloves
4–5 pounds pears, pared and sliced about ¼ inch thick (15 pears)
1½ cups seedless raisins
½ cup finely chopped green pepper
4 cups sugar
½ cup crystallized ginger
3 cups cider vinegar
½ teaspoon salt
2 2-inch sticks cinnamon

Tie allspice and cloves in double thickness of cheesecloth.

Combine all ingredients in large saucepan; leave uncovered. Bring to a boil; reduce heat. Simmer slowly for 1 hour, or until thick.

Discard spices. Spoon into hot sterilized jars and seal.

YIELD: 8 HALF PINTS

Soupçon
THE JUNIOR LEAGUE OF CHICAGO, ILLINOIS

· · · · · · · · · · · · · · · · · · ·

Curried Fruit Casserole

1 29-ounce can pears
1 29-ounce can peach halves
1 16-ounce can apricot halves
1 20-ounce can pineapple chunks
10 maraschino cherries
⅓ cup melted butter
¾ cup brown sugar, packed
4 teaspoons curry powder

Drain fruit well. Mix butter, brown sugar, and curry powder.

Arrange fruit in a shallow baking dish, hollow side of fruit up. Dot all over with butter and sugar mixture. Bake for 1 hour at 325°, basting frequently.

YIELD: 10 SERVINGS

THE JUNIOR LEAGUE OF COLUMBUS, OHIO

· · · · · · · · · · · · · · · · · · ·

Pineapple for Ham

1 28-ounce can crushed pineapple
¼–½ pound cheddar cheese, shredded
¾ cup sugar
2 tablespoons flour
Salt
Buttered bread crumbs

Combine crushed pineapple with juice, cheddar cheese, sugar, flour, and a pinch of salt. Top with buttered crumbs and bake in 350° oven for 40 minutes.

Recipe continues . . .

Serve as an accompaniment for baked ham or roast pork.

YIELD: APPROXIMATELY 4 CUPS

The Cook's Book
THE JUNIOR LEAGUE OF CEDAR RAPIDS, IOWA

·   ·   ·   ·   ·   ·   ·   ·   ·   ·   ·   ·   ·   ·   ·   ·   ·   ·   ·

Crème de Menthe Jelly

2½ cups sugar
1 cup green crème de menthe
1 cup water
Half a 6-ounce bottle of liquid pectin
Fresh mint sprigs

In double boiler, over rapidly boiling water, combine sugar, crème de menthe, and water. Stir until sugar is dissolved.

Remove from heat and stir in pectin. Skim if necessary.

Dip mint sprigs into boiling water for 30 seconds and put 1 sprig of mint into each hot sterilized jar. Pour in jelly and seal.

YIELD: 4 CUPS

THE JUNIOR LEAGUE OF SAGINAW, MICHIGAN

·   ·   ·   ·   ·   ·   ·   ·   ·   ·   ·   ·   ·   ·   ·   ·   ·   ·   ·

Gram's Currant Jelly

Place a few quarts of currants in a large kettle. Add water until you can just see it—not covering all the berries. Cook on stove at low to medium heat until berries shrivel. Strain overnight through a dish towel or a colander. Do not push or press berries, as this clouds the jelly.

2 cups currant juice
About 1½ cups sugar

Bring juice to a rolling boil in large pan for 5 minutes. Skim white foam off while it's cooking. Add sugar, stirring constantly. Bring to a boil and cook until it jells on a spoon.

Pour into warm jelly jars immediately. Let cool and set, then seal.

YIELD: 1 PINT JELLY FOR EACH PINT OF JUICE

THE JUNIOR LEAGUE OF ROCKFORD, ILLINOIS

Indiana State Fair Prize-Winning Peach Jam

6 pounds fully ripe peaches
1¼ cups lemon juice
15 cups sugar
1 6-ounce bottle fruit pectin

Pit fruit, but do not peel. Cut into small pieces or put into blender or processor and mash coarsely.

Measure 8 cups mashed fruit into large saucepan. Add lemon juice and sugar. Mix well. Place over high heat, bring to a full rolling boil, and boil hard for 1½ minutes, stirring constantly.

Remove from heat and stir in pectin. Let cool slightly, then pour into jars and cover with hot paraffin.

YIELD: ABOUT 17 CUPS

THE JUNIOR LEAGUE OF INDIANAPOLIS, INDIANA

Mincemeat

This recipe is over 100 years old.

6 pounds boneless stewing beef
5 pounds apples, peeled, cored, and chopped
2 pounds currants
2 tablespoons cloves
2 tablespoons cinnamon
1 tablespoon pepper
½ cup molasses
½ pound butter
1 pound preserves, any kind
1 orange, including rind, ground
1 pound suet, chopped
2 pounds raisins
½ pound citron, chopped
2 tablespoons allspice
1 tablespoon salt
3 pounds brown sugar
1 quart cider, boiled
Juice, rind, and pulp of 2 lemons
1 pint brandy

Combine all ingredients in large preserving kettle and bring to a boil. Cook slowly for 2 hours, stirring often.

Seal in jars while boiling hot.

YIELD: ABOUT 18 PINTS

Peacock Pie and Other Perfections
THE JUNIOR LEAGUE OF BATTLE CREEK, MICHIGAN

· · · · · · · · · · · · · · · · · · · ·

Green Tomato Mincemeat

This mincemeat does not contain meat!

3–4 cups peeled and chopped cooking apples
4 cups chopped and peeled green tomatoes
2 cups white sugar
1 pound raisins
¼ cup vinegar
½ cup butter
1 teaspoon each salt, cloves, and allspice
2 teaspoons cinnamon

Simmer all ingredients in a large kettle until thickened, about 2½ hours. Stir occasionally.

While still boiling hot, spoon into sterilized jars to ⅛ inch from top. Using two-piece lids, seal the jars. Invert the jars until all are filled. Turn right side up to cool.

YIELD: 1 QUART

Discover Dayton
THE JUNIOR LEAGUE OF DAYTON, OHIO

. . . .

Beet Pickles

2 1-pound cans whole beets
1 cup liquid from canned beets
1 cup vinegar
¾ cup sugar
1 tablespoon salt
Dash pepper

Recipe continues . . .

Cut beets into thirds and pack into a 1-quart jar. Combine remaining ingredients, bring to a boil, and pour over beets in jar. Let stand about 24 hours.

Store in refrigerator.

YIELD: 1 QUART

THE JUNIOR LEAGUE OF ST. PAUL, MINNESOTA

· ·

Aristocratic Ginger Pickles

4 pounds small pickling cucumbers
½ cup salt
3 tablespoons alum
1 tablespoon ginger
¼–½ cup mixed celery seed, whole cloves, and stick cinnamon
2 cups cider vinegar
1 pint water
6 cups sugar

Thinly slice the pickling cucumbers and cover with brine made with the ½ cup salt and ½ gallon water. Let stand for 4 days. Drain and rinse.

Cover cucumbers with fresh water, add the alum, and simmer for ½ hour. Drain.

Cover with fresh water again. Add the ginger and simmer for ½ hour. Drain.

Tie the spices in a cheesecloth bag. Cover pickles and spices with the vinegar, 1 pint water, and the sugar. Boil pickles with spices in the syrup until pickles are clear, about 35–40 minutes.

Pack a few of the cloves in each jar before sealing. Process in boiling water bath for 5 minutes.

YIELD: 6 CUPS

THE JUNIOR LEAGUE OF ROCKFORD, ILLINOIS

· ·

Bread and Butter Pickles

25 medium cucumbers
10 medium onions
½ cup kosher coarse salt
½ pint water
2 cups sugar
2 teaspoons mustard seed
2 teaspoons celery seed
½ teaspoon turmeric
1 pint cider vinegar

Cut cucumbers and onions into ¼-inch slices or smaller. Place in crock layered with salt. Let stand 3 hours, then drain well.

Mix water, sugar, mustard seed, celery seed, turmeric, and vinegar. Bring to a boil. Slowly add cucumbers and onions and heat through.

Pack in hot sterilized jars and seal.

YIELD: 5 QUARTS

THE JUNIOR LEAGUE OF TOLEDO, OHIO

· · · · · · · · · · · · · · · · · · · ·

Cousin Carol's Dill Pickles

1 bushel pickling cucumbers
Dill weed
Garlic cloves, sliced
Hot peppers
3 quarts water
1 quart white vinegar
1 cup salt

Put cucumbers in washing machine on a cold-water setting and agitate for a few minutes only.

Recipe continues . . .

Pack cucumbers into jars with a piece of dill, garlic slice, and hot pepper on both top and bottom.

In large saucepan, combine water, vinegar and salt. Bring to a boil and boil for 5 minutes. Pour boiling liquid into jars; tighten lids. Let sit for 4 or 5 days, until taste suits you, then store in refrigerator.

YIELD: ABOUT 12 PINTS

THE JUNIOR LEAGUE OF SPRINGFIELD, ILLINOIS

· ·

Sioux City Chow Chow

12 green peppers
3–6 red peppers
4 cups cabbage
4 cups onions, coarsely chopped
4 cups green tomatoes, coarsely chopped
½ cup salt
4 cups vinegar
6 cups sugar
2 cups water
1 tablespoon celery salt
1 tablespoon mustard seed
1½ teaspoons turmeric

With coarse blade in meat grinder, grind all vegetables. Sprinkle with ½ cup salt and let stand overnight.

Next day, drain and rinse with cold water. Add remaining ingredients. Bring to a boil and cook for 5 minutes. Place in hot sterilized jars, wipe lids, and seal.

Makes a good condiment for meat.

YIELD: 11 PINTS

The Discovery Shop Cookbook
THE JUNIOR LEAGUE OF SIOUX CITY, IOWA

· ·

Dilled Green Beans

2 pounds fresh green beans
4 cloves garlic
4 heads of dill
½ teaspoon cayenne
¼ cup salt
2½ cups water
2½ cups vinegar

Pack beans lengthwise into hot sterilized jars, leaving ¼-inch head space. To each jar, add 1 clove garlic and 1 head of dill.

Combine remaining ingredients and bring to a boil. Pour over beans, leaving ¼-inch head space. Adjust caps. Process for 10 minutes in boiling water bath.

YIELD: 4 PINTS

THE JUNIOR LEAGUE OF KANSAS CITY, KANSAS

·   ·   ·   ·   ·   ·   ·   ·   ·   ·   ·   ·   ·   ·   ·   ·   ·   ·

Dill Tomatoes

12 cloves garlic
24 sprigs fresh dill
6 quarts green tomatoes, washed and quartered
4 quarts water
2 quarts cider vinegar
1 cup salt

In each of 12 sterilized jars, place 1 clove garlic, sliced, and 1 sprig of dill. Pack jars with tomatoes, and cover with another sprig of dill.

Boil water, vinegar, and salt for 5 minutes. Fill jars with this mixture; seal.

Recipe continues . . .

Store in a cool dark place for 3 months for fermentation to take place before using.

YIELD: 12 PINTS

Bluff City Cooks
THE JUNIOR LEAGUE OF GREATER ALTON, ILLINOIS

· · · · · · · · · · · · · · · · · ·

Corn Relish

4 10-ounce packages frozen corn, thawed, or 12 ears cooked fresh corn
1 medium head cabbage, finely chopped
4 large onions, chopped
2 red peppers, seeded and chopped
4 green peppers, seeded and chopped
2 quarts vinegar
3 cups sugar
½ cup salt
¼ cup dry mustard
1 teaspoon turmeric
¾ cup flour

If fresh corn is used, cut kernels off cobs and combine in large kettle with the cabbage, onions, red peppers, green peppers, and 1 quart of the vinegar. Bring to a boil.

Mix together the sugar, salt, mustard, turmeric, flour, and remaining quart of vinegar. Stir into the boiling relish and let boil ½ hour.

Seal in hot sterilized jars.

YIELD: ABOUT 6 PINTS

THE JUNIOR LEAGUE OF KANSAS CITY, KANSAS

· · · · · · · · · · · · · · · · · ·

Edith's Zucchini Pickles

2 pounds small to medium zucchini
2 onions
¼ cup salt
2 cups white vinegar
2 cups sugar
1 teaspoon celery seed
1 teaspoon turmeric
2 teaspoons mustard seed

Wash zucchini; cut into thin slices. Peel and quarter onions; slice thinly. Cover all with water and add salt. Let stand 2 hours. Drain thoroughly.

Bring remaining ingredients to a boil and pour over vegetables. Let stand 2 hours.

Put all in a kettle and bring to a boil. Boil for 5 minutes.

Pack in hot sterilized jars and seal.

YIELD: 4–5 HALF PINTS

Soupçon
THE JUNIOR LEAGUE OF CHICAGO, ILLINOIS

·   ·   ·   ·   ·   ·   ·   ·   ·   ·   ·   ·   ·   ·   ·   ·   ·

Zucchini Relish

10 cups peeled and ground zucchini
4 cups grated onion
5 tablespoons salt
2¼ cups cider vinegar
5 cups sugar
1 teaspoon pepper
1 red pepper, finely chopped
1 green pepper, finely chopped
1 tablespoon dry mustard
1 tablespoon turmeric
1 tablespoon cornstarch

Recipe continues . . .

Mix zucchini, onion, and salt and let stand overnight. Drain and rinse in cold water. Drain well. Add remaining ingredients. Bring to a boil and cook slowly for 30 minutes.

Put in sterilized jars and seal.

YIELD: 6½ PINTS

THE JUNIOR LEAGUE OF SAGINAW, MICHIGAN

Chili Sauce

8 quarts tomatoes, peeled
2 cups chopped onion
3 cups chopped red or green peppers, or both (about 12 peppers)
½ cup salt
1½ quarts wine or cider vinegar
3 cups sugar
1 tablespoon celery seed
1 tablespoon cinnamon
2 teaspoons ground clove
2 teaspoons ginger
2 teaspoons nutmeg

Grind tomatoes, onion, and peppers. Combine all ingredients in a large kettle and simmer for 3 hours, or until sauce is as thick as a meat sauce.

YIELD: 6–8 QUARTS

THE JUNIOR LEAGUE OF YOUNGSTOWN, OHIO

Sweet Piccalilli

5 pounds green tomatoes
2 pounds onions
3 pounds green peppers
½ cup salt
2 tablespoons celery seed
2 tablespoons white mustard seed
1 teaspoon whole cloves
1 teaspoon whole allspice
1 tablespoon horseradish (optional)
1 quart cider vinegar
2½ cups sugar

Coarsely shred or grind tomatoes, onions, and peppers. Add salt and let stand overnight. Drain.

Tie spices in cheesecloth and boil for 10 minutes in vinegar mixed with the sugar and horseradish if desired. Add drained vegetables and bring to a rolling boil. Pour hot mixture into sterilized jars and seal immediately.

If desired, add some of the spices out of the bag before sealing.

YIELD: ABOUT 6 PINTS

Bluff City Cooks
THE JUNIOR LEAGUE OF GREATER ALTON, ILLINOIS

· · · · · · · · · · · · · · · · · ·

Strawberry-Lime Jam

4½ cups very ripe strawberries
2 teaspoons grated lime rind
¼ cup lime juice
1 1¾-ounce box powdered fruit pectin
7 cups sugar

Recipe continues . . .

Stem and crush berries. Measure 4½ cups into large kettle. Add lime rind and juice. Mix in fruit pectin. Place over high heat and stir until mixture comes to a rolling boil. Immediately stir in sugar. Bring to a rolling boil; boil rapidly for 1 minute, stirring constantly.

Remove from heat and skim off foam with metal spoon. Stir and skim for 5–10 minutes while cooling to prevent floating fruit.

Ladle into sterilized glasses. Cover with ¼ inch paraffin.

YIELD: 6 8-OUNCE GLASSES

Soupçon
THE JUNIOR LEAGUE OF CHICAGO, ILLINOIS

· · · · · · · · · · · · · · · · · ·

Spiced Pear Jam with Pineapple

3 pounds firm cooking pears
1 orange, seeded
1 lemon, seeded
2 cups crushed pineapple
4–5 cups sugar
3 or 5 whole cloves
1 6-inch cinnamon stick
1 1-inch piece ginger
1 cup chopped walnuts

Peel and core pears. Wash orange and lemon well. Put fruit except pineapple through a food grinder, using a coarse blade. Save juices.

Add juices to fruit pulp along with pineapple, sugar, cloves, cinnamon stick, ginger, and walnuts. Stir the mixture while heating it. Boil for 45 minutes.

Pour into hot sterilized jars and seal.

YIELD: 5 HALF PINTS

Soupçon
THE JUNIOR LEAGUE OF CHICAGO, ILLINOIS

· · · · · · · · · · · · · · · · · ·

Christmas Jam

1 12-ounce package dried apricots, chopped
1 1-pound 14-ounce can crushed pineapple
3½ cups water
1 8-ounce jar maraschino cherries, quartered
6 cups sugar

In large saucepan, combine apricots, pineapple and juice, water, and cherry liquid; let stand 1 hour. Cook slowly until apricots are tender.

Add sugar; cook slowly, stirring often, until thick and clear. Add cherries; cook a few minutes longer.

Pour into hot sterilized jars; seal.

YIELD: 6–8 HALF PINTS

Soupçon
THE JUNIOR LEAGUE OF CHICAGO, ILLINOIS

Egg and Cheese Dishes

Fresh Noodles

2 whole eggs and 2 egg yolks
½ egg shell of cold water
About 4 cups flour

Beat eggs and water until very light and add enough flour to make a very stiff dough. Knead on flowered board for a few minutes, or until smooth. Roll out *very thinly* on floured board. Let dry for about 1 hour, then cut into strips from ¼–1½ inches as desired. Dust lightly with flour. Cook in boiling salted water for about 5 minutes, or until tender.

Can be frozen and used as needed.

YIELD: 1 POUND NOODLES

THE JUNIOR LEAGUE OF ROCKFORD, ILLINOIS

Green Square Noodles

1 8-ounce package egg or green vegetable noodles
1 16-ounce carton cream-style cottage cheese
¾ cup sour cream
2 tablespoons melted butter
1 egg, beaten
½ cup each chopped parsley and green onion

Cook and drain noodles. Combine remaining ingredients and combine with noodles.

Spoon into a well-buttered casserole and bake for 45 minutes at 350°.

YIELD: 8 SERVINGS

The Cook's Book
THE JUNIOR LEAGUE OF CEDAR RAPIDS, IOWA

Curried Eggs in Shrimp Sauce

8 hard-boiled eggs
⅓ cup mayonnaise
½ teaspoon salt
¼–½ teaspoon curry powder
¼ teaspoon dry mustard
2 tablespoons butter
2 tablespoons flour
1 10¾-ounce can shrimp soup
1 soup can milk
½ cup shredded cheddar cheese
Few drops Tabasco
1 cup soft bread crumbs
1 tablespoon melted butter
Parsley for garnish

Halve eggs; crumble yolks, mix with mayonnaise and seasonings, and fill whites. Arrange eggs in 10 x 6 x 1½-inch baking dish.

Melt 2 tablespoons butter. Stir in flour, then soup and milk and cook, stirring, until sauce thickens. Add cheese and stir until melted, then stir in Tabasco.

Cover eggs with sauce. Mix crumbs with melted butter and arrange around edge of baking dish. Bake at 350° for 15–20 minutes, or until bubbly. Garnish with parsley.

Can be made early in the day. Great for luncheon with spinach salad and Parmesan toast strips.

YIELD: 5–6 SERVINGS

Cincinnati Celebrates
THE JUNIOR LEAGUE OF CINCINNATI, OHIO

Scalloped Eggs and Bacon

¼ cup chopped onion
2 tablespoons butter
2 tablespoons flour
1½ cups milk
1 cup shredded cheddar cheese
6 hard-boiled eggs, sliced
1½ cups crushed potato chips
12 slices bacon, crisply fried and crumbled

Cook onion in butter until transparent. Blend in flour, add milk and cheese, and cook, stirring, until cheese is melted and mixture is slightly thickened.

Put a layer of egg slices in bottom of 7 x 11-inch glass baking dish. Pour half the cheese mixture over eggs, then half the chips, then half the bacon. Repeat layers. Bake for 30 minutes at 350°. A double recipe fits into a 9 x 13-inch casserole.

This dish may be made one day ahead and refrigerated.

YIELD: 4 SERVINGS

THE JUNIOR LEAGUE OF SOUTH BEND, INDIANA

. . . .

Quiche Florentine

2 unbaked 9-inch pastry shells
1 pound fresh spinach
16 slices bacon, crisply fried and crumbled
12 ounces Swiss cheese, shredded
6 eggs
3 cups minus 3 tablespoons half and half
1 teaspoon dry mustard
¼ teaspoon salt
⅛ teaspoon red pepper
3 tablespoons dry white wine

Line two deep pie dishes with pastry and flute edge.

Wash spinach and cut off stems. Without drying spinach, put in a large pot over medium heat and cook 5–10 minutes, or until tender (do not add more water), stirring and turning leaves often. Drain well; use paper towels to squeeze out as much moisture as possible. Chop spinach into very small pieces and set aside.

Toss together bacon and cheese and sprinkle into the pastry-lined pans. Spread spinach on top.

Beat together all remaining ingredients and pour over the cheese, bacon, and spinach to just below the rim of each pie shell. Bake in preheated 450° oven for 10 minutes. Reduce temperature to 300° and bake for 45–50 minutes, or until the custard is set and the top is light brown.

Perfect for luncheon or supper with a green salad and a slice of melon for dessert.

YIELD: 2 9-INCH PIES, 6–8 SERVINGS

Discover Dayton
THE JUNIOR LEAGUE OF DAYTON, OHIO

·   ·   ·   ·   ·   ·   ·   ·   ·   ·   ·   ·   ·   ·   ·   ·   ·   ·   ·

Tomato Quiche

2 medium fresh tomatoes
1 unbaked 9-inch pastry shell
4 eggs
1½ cups milk
2 cups shredded Swiss cheese
½ cup chopped onion
1¼ teaspoon salt
¼ teaspoon black pepper

Finely chop one tomato. Slice the other and set both aside.

Line 9-inch pie plate with pastry and flute edge. Prick bottom and sides. Refrigerate 10 minutes, then bake at 450° until golden, about 8 minutes. Remove from oven.

Recipe continues . . .

Reduce oven to 325°. Lightly beat eggs. Stir in milk, cheese, onion, salt, pepper, and the reserved chopped tomato. Pour into baked pie shell. Bake at 325° for 30 minutes. Top with reserved sliced tomato. Bake until a knife inserted in center comes out clean, or about 25 minutes more. Let stand at room temperature 10 minutes before cutting. Serve with salad, rolls, and dessert.

YIELD: 6 SERVINGS

THE JUNIOR LEAGUE OF SOUTH BEND, INDIANA

. . . .

Quiche aux Champignons
(Quiche with bacon and mushrooms)

1 stick pie crust mix
8 slices bacon, diced
5 tablespoons butter
2 tablespoons minced shallot
½ pound fresh mushrooms, sliced
1½ teaspoons salt
2 tablespoons Madeira
3 eggs
2 cups heavy cream or 1 cup heavy cream and 1 cup half and half
Dash nutmeg
Dash black pepper
½ cup shredded Swiss cheese

Line a 9-inch pie plate with pastry and bake according to package directions for a partially baked shell. To keep pastry from puffing, slightly prick shell and cover with aluminum foil weighted down with ¼ cup dry beans. Cool. Discard beans and foil.

Cook bacon until crisp; drain on paper towels and sprinkle on bottom of the cooled pie crust.

In heavy skillet, melt 3 tablespoons butter and in it sauté shallot for 1–2 minutes. Stir in mushrooms, 1 teaspoon salt, and the wine; cover and simmer for 5 minutes. Uncover and boil until most of the moisture evaporates. Spread in pie crust with bacon.

Meanwhile, beat together eggs, cream, remaining ½ teaspoon salt, nutmeg, and pepper. Pour over bacon and mushrooms. Sprinkle top with shredded cheese. Dab top with remaining 2 tablespoons butter cut in large pea-size pieces. Bake in upper half of 375° preheated oven for 30–35 minutes, or until top is browned and puffy.

Cool slightly before serving.

YIELD: 6 SERVINGS

THE JUNIOR LEAGUE OF COLUMBUS, OHIO

· · · · · · · · · · · · · · · · · · · ·

Mushroom Quiche

4 tablespoons butter
2 tablespoons minced shallot
1 pound fresh mushrooms, thinly sliced
1½ teaspoons salt
1 teaspoon lemon juice
1 baked 10-inch pastry shell—do not puncture
4 eggs
1 cup heavy cream
⅛ teaspoon pepper
⅛ teaspoon nutmeg
½ cup shredded Swiss cheese

Melt 3 tablespoons butter in a skillet, add shallot, and cook for a few minutes, stirring constantly. Add mushrooms, 1 teaspoon salt, and lemon juice. Cover skillet and simmer over low heat for 10 minutes. Uncover, increase heat, and boil for 5–10 minutes, until liquid is completely evaporated and mushrooms have begun to sauté in the butter. Stir to prevent scorching. Put mushroom mixture in pie shell.

Beat the eggs and cream together, add the remaining ½ teaspoon

Recipe continues . . .

salt, pepper, and nutmeg. Pour the custard over mushrooms. Sprinkle the top with cheese.

Bake in a 350° oven for 35 minutes, or until the quiche is puffy, brown, and a knife inserted in it comes out clean.

YIELD: 8 SERVINGS

Sunflower Sampler
THE JUNIOR LEAGUE OF WICHITA, KANSAS

· ·

Quiche Lorraine with Ham

4 slices bacon, crisply fried and crumbled
¼ medium onion, diced and sautéed until soft
1 baked 9-inch pastry shell—do not puncture
8 slices of ham, shredded
8 paper-thin slices of Swiss cheese
3 eggs
¼ teaspoon dry mustard
1 cup light cream, heated
Nutmeg

Sprinkle bacon and onion over bottom of pie crust. Add half of the ham. Put 4 slices of cheese over ham. Add rest of ham and cheese on top.

Beat eggs and mustard, add hot cream, and continue beating. Pour over ham and cheese. Let stand 10 minutes. Sprinkle a tiny bit of nutmeg on top and bake in a 350° oven for 30–35 minutes, or until custard is set.

YIELD: 6 SERVINGS

Sunflower Sampler
THE JUNIOR LEAGUE OF WICHITA, KANSAS

· ·

Creamed Eggs in Chive Biscuit Ring

BISCUIT RING:
¼ cup chopped chives
½ cup melted butter
2 packages refrigerated biscuits

CREAMED EGGS:
¼ cup butter
¼ cup flour
2 cups milk
½ teaspoon salt
2 tablespoons prepared mustard
6 hard-boiled eggs, shelled and quartered

To make biscuit ring: Add chives to melted butter. Dip biscuit rounds into butter and chive mixture and stand them upright in an ungreased 8-inch ring mold. Bake in a 375° oven for 20 minutes. Turn out onto a warm serving dish.

Melt butter in saucepan. Add flour and blend until smooth. Add milk gradually and cook until thickened, stirring occasionally. Add salt and mustard. Gently fold in eggs and continue to heat for a few minutes.

Fill center of biscuit ring and serve immediately.

YIELD: 4–6 SERVINGS

THE JUNIOR LEAGUE OF SOUTH BEND, INDIANA

Bacon, Beef, and Eggs for Brunch

SAUCE:
3 slices bacon, diced
¼ pound chipped beef, coarsely shredded
2 tablespoons butter
¾ cup sliced mushrooms
¼ cup flour
2 cups milk
Pepper to taste

EGGS:
8 eggs
¾ teaspoon salt
½ cup evaporated milk
2 tablespoons melted butter

Fry bacon until crisp. Remove pan from heat and add the chipped beef, butter, and mushrooms and mix well.

Sprinkle the flour over bacon and mushroom mixture. Gradually stir in milk and cook, stirring, until thickened. Season sauce with pepper and set aside.

Combine eggs, salt, evaporated milk, and melted butter and scramble in a large skillet. Keep eggs moist.

In a baking dish, alternate layers of eggs and sauce.

At this point the dish may be covered and refrigerated for a day or so. To serve, heat in a 275° oven for 45 minutes.

YIELD: 5 SERVINGS

Bluff City Cooks
THE JUNIOR LEAGUE OF GREATER ALTON, ILLINOIS

. . . .

Chili Cheese Soufflé

MEAT LAYER:
¼ cup chopped onion
¾ pound lean ground beef
3 tablespoons shortening
1 teaspoon salt
1 teaspoon chili powder
3 tablespoons flour

SOUFFLÉ LAYER:
⅓ cup shortening
⅓ cup flour
1 teaspoon salt
⅛ teaspoon paprika
1 teaspoon chili powder (optional)
1½ cups milk
2 cups shredded American cheese
4 egg yolks
4 egg whites

Brown onion and ground beef in the shortening. Sprinkle with salt, chili powder, and flour. Reduce heat and cook 5 minutes. Turn into ungreased 2-quart casserole or soufflé dish.

In saucepan, melt shortening. Stir in flour, salt, paprika, and chili powder. Add milk and cook until thick, stirring constantly. Add cheese and stir until melted. Remove from heat. Beat in egg yolks, one at a time.

Beat egg whites until stiff, but not dry, and fold into cheese mixture. Pour over meat in dish. Set dish in a pan of hot water and bake at 350° for 55–60 minutes or until a knife inserted in soufflé comes out clean. Serve immediately.

YIELD: 4–6 SERVINGS

THE JUNIOR LEAGUE OF ST. PAUL, MINNESOTA

Green Egg Omelet

2 tablespoons butter
⅓–½ cup chopped onion
¼ cup chopped green pepper
4 eggs
¼ cup milk
Salt and pepper to taste

Melt butter in 9-inch skillet and in it cook onion and pepper until tender.

Lightly beat eggs with milk, salt, and pepper. Pour into skillet and stir only enough to mix eggs with vegetables. Cook over medium heat until firm around the edges and no longer runny on top. Turn with large spatula and continue cooking until dry.

YIELD: 4 SERVINGS

THE JUNIOR LEAGUE OF KANSAS CITY, KANSAS

. . . .

Jim's Favorite Scrambled Eggs

¼ pound mushrooms, sliced
3 teaspoons butter or margarine
8 link sausages
6 eggs
⅓ cup milk
1 teaspoon seasoned salt
1 cup shredded cheddar cheese

Sauté mushrooms in 2 teaspoons butter until cooked. Set aside.

Cook sausages until brown, drain, and cut into bite-size pieces.

In blender, blend eggs, milk, and seasoned salt.

Melt remaining butter in a skillet. Add egg mixture and cook, stirring, over low heat until eggs become somewhat firm. Add cheese, mushrooms, and sausages and mix well.

Cover and cook at a very low temperature until eggs are cooked and cheese is melted, stirring frequently.

YIELD: 4 SERVINGS

THE JUNIOR LEAGUE OF ROCKFORD, ILLINOIS

Curried Eggs

4 teaspoons butter
2 heaping tablespoons flour
2 cups milk
3 tablespoons sherry
1 scant teaspoon curry powder
5–6 hard-boiled eggs

Melt butter and stir in flour. Gradually stir in milk and cook, stirring, until sauce is smooth and thickened. Stir in sherry and curry powder.

Slice eggs into baking dish and pour sauce over. Heat in 300° oven until warmed through.

Serve on toast points.

YIELD: 4 SERVINGS

THE JUNIOR LEAGUE OF DES MOINES, IOWA

Eggs Egg-cellent

1 28-ounce can Chinese vegetables or bean sprouts
2 tablespoons grated onion
8 eggs
Salt to taste
1 4-ounce can mushrooms, sautéed (optional)
5 water chestnuts, sliced (optional)
½ cup leftover cooked ham, chicken, etc. (optional)

Rinse and drain vegetables or bean sprouts and mix with onion. If time permits, chill and drain again.

Beat eggs with fork and add salt and any of the optional ingredients. Cook in lightly buttered small skillet as for pancakes. Serve with Chinese Brown Sauce.

YIELD: 8 SERVINGS

CHINESE BROWN SAUCE:
2 tablespoons cornstarch
2 teaspoons chicken bouillon granules
Water
2 tablespoons soy sauce
1 teaspoon bead molasses (optional)
2 cups water

Mix cornstarch and chicken bouillon with a little water and add other ingredients. Bring to a boil and simmer until thickened, stirring constantly.

Reheat when ready to serve.

Peacock Pie and Other Perfections
THE JUNIOR LEAGUE OF BATTLE CREEK, MICHIGAN

Breakfast Pudding

1 pound mild bulk sausage
6 eggs
2 cups milk
1 teaspoon salt
1 teaspoon dry mustard
Crusts from 6 slices bread
8 ounces shredded cheddar cheese

Brown sausage and set aside to cool.

Beat eggs; add milk, salt, and mustard and beat again. Add crumbled sausage and bread crusts torn into bite-size pieces; stir. Put into greased 1-quart baking dish and refrigerate overnight.

Add cheese and bake at 350° for 40–45 minutes, or until brown around edges.

YIELD: 6–8 SERVINGS

THE JUNIOR LEAGUE OF TOLEDO, OHIO

. . . .

Marvelous Eggs

3 dozen eggs
½ cup milk
1 stick butter
2 10¾-ounce cans cream of mushroom soup
½ cup sherry
½ pound cheddar cheese, shredded

Mix together eggs and milk and scramble in butter in a large skillet. Empty scrambled eggs into a greased 9 x 13-inch pan. Combine soup with sherry and pour over the eggs. Sprinkle with cheddar cheese.

Recipe continues . . .

Let stand overnight in the refrigerator. Remove 1 hour before baking, then bake at 250° for 50 minutes. Do not overcook.

Ideal for brunches.

YIELD: 16 SERVINGS

THE JUNIOR LEAGUE OF YOUNGSTOWN, OHIO

·   ·   ·   ·   ·   ·   ·   ·   ·   ·   ·   ·   ·   ·   ·   ·   ·

Do-Ahead Brunch Casserole

16 eggs
2 teaspoons salt
1 cup evaporated milk
¼ cup melted butter
½ teaspoon pepper

Combine all ingredients and scramble until set but still soft. Fill 11 x 13-inch dish with alternate layers of the scrambled eggs and Mushroom-Beef Sauce.

After dish is assembled, cover and refrigerate overnight.

To serve, bake, covered, at 275° for 1½ hours. If not made a day ahead, cover and bake at 275° for 1 hour.

YIELD: 12 SERVINGS

MUSHROOM-BEEF SAUCE:
½ pound chipped beef, shredded
½ pound mushrooms, sliced
¼ cup butter
¼ cup flour
4 slices bacon, cooked and crumbled
1 quart hot milk
½ teaspoon salt
¼ teaspoon pepper

Sauté beef and mushrooms in butter until mushrooms are tender. Stir in flour and bacon. Add milk, salt, and pepper. Stir and cook until sauce is slightly thickened.

THE JUNIOR LEAGUE OF EVANSVILLE, INDIANA

· · · · · · · · · · · · · · · · · · · ·

Cheese Brunch

10 slices white bread
Softened butter
¾ pound shredded cheddar cheese
¾ pound shredded Monterey Jack cheese
8 eggs, lightly beaten
3–4 cups light cream or milk
1 teaspoon brown sugar
¼ teaspoon paprika
1½ teaspoons salt
½ teaspoon onion powder
¼ teaspoon pepper
⅛ teaspoon cayenne
1 teaspoon Worcestershire sauce
1 teaspoon dry mustard

Butter bread on one side, then cube. Butter a large shallow baking dish. Put in half the bread cubes, sprinkle with half the cheeses, then repeat both layers. Combine remaining ingredients and pour over bread and cheese. Refrigerate 8–24 hours before baking.

Bake at 325° for 1 hour.

Serve hot as entree or cold for lunch.

Can be baked and reheated. Can be frozen after baking.

YIELD: 10–12 SERVINGS

Tested, Tried, and True
THE JUNIOR LEAGUE OF FLINT, MICHIGAN

· · · · · · · · · · · · · · · · · · · ·

Stuffed Eggs Mornay

MORNAY SAUCE:

¼ cup soft butter

1 teaspoon salt

4 tablespoons flour

¼ teaspoon white pepper

2 cups hot milk

4 tablespoons shredded Swiss cheese

4 tablespoons grated Parmesan cheese

EGGS:

8 hard-boiled eggs

Fresh mushrooms, cooked and finely chopped

4 tablespoons soft butter

4 tablespoons Mornay sauce

Grated Parmesan cheese

Put all sauce ingredients in an electric blender, cover container, and turn to low speed. When blades have reached full speed, turn to high for 30 seconds.

Pour in top of a double boiler and cook over simmering water for 15 minutes, stirring occasionally.

Halve the eggs lengthwise. Remove yolks and reserve whites. Mash yolks until smooth and mix with an equal amount of cooked and chopped mushrooms, the butter and the 4 tablespoons Mornay sauce.

Fill egg whites with mixture, mounding it high.

Spread layer of Mornay sauce in a shallow dish, arrange eggs in sauce, and coat with more sauce. Sprinkle with Parmesan cheese and brown under broiler.

This can be made ahead of time, covered, and refrigerated.

YIELD: 12–16 SERVINGS

Sunflower Sampler
THE JUNIOR LEAGUE OF WICHITA, KANSAS

Simple Fondue

1 clove garlic
2 cups dry white wine
1 pound Swiss cheese, shredded
1 large loaf crusted bread, torn into bite-size pieces
1 teaspoon cornstarch
3 tablespoons gin
Dash Tabasco

Rub fondue pot with garlic.

Heat wine in pot or in saucepan over low heat. When air bubbles rise to surface, add cheese gradually and stir constantly with wooden spoon until cheese is melted.

Mix cornstarch with gin and stir into cheese mixture. Add Tabasco.

Spear bread with fondue forks and dip into fondue. Keep pot faintly bubbling.

YIELD: 4 SERVINGS

THE JUNIOR LEAGUE OF SPRINGFIELD, ILLINOIS

. . . .

Shiela's Eggs

Butter
4 slices bread
¼ pound cheddar cheese, shredded
4 eggs, well beaten
2 cups milk
½ teaspoon salt
⅛ teaspoon pepper
½ teaspoon dry mustard

Recipe continues . . .

Butter bread and place buttered side down in a jelly-roll pan. Sprinkle cheese over the bread. Combine remaining ingredients and pour over the bread and cheese. Bake for 30 minutes in a 350° oven, or until puffy.

Cooked diced mushrooms, ham, or broccoli may be added.

YIELD: 4–6 SERVINGS

THE JUNIOR LEAGUE OF FARGO-MOORHEAD, NORTH DAKOTA/MINNESOTA

Cottage Cheese Pancakes

1 cup cottage cheese
6 eggs
½ cup flour
¼ teaspoon salt
¼ cup oil
¼ cup milk
½ teaspoon vanilla

Put all ingredients in blender and blend at high speed for 1 minute, stopping to stir down once. Cook on hot, greased griddle, using ¼ cup batter for each pancake, until brown on both sides.

Batter can be made 12 hours ahead. Cooked pancakes can be frozen. Serve hot with syrup.

YIELD: 4–6 SERVINGS

Cookbook
THE JUNIOR LEAGUE OF GRAND RAPIDS, MICHIGAN

Spaghetti Carbonara

1 pound spaghetti
Olive oil
6 eggs
1 cup grated Parmesan cheese
Salt and pepper to taste
½ pint light cream
1 pound bacon, fried and diced

Boil spaghetti with a little olive oil in plenty of lightly salted water until done. Drain and rinse with cold water.

Mix eggs, cheese, salt, and pepper and beat until frothy. Stir in cream.

Pour egg mixture in heavy pan; add spaghetti, bacon, and a little olive oil. Stir over low heat until the sauce adheres to the spaghetti. Serve immediately.

YIELD: 8 SERVINGS

THE JUNIOR LEAGUE OF SAGINAW, MICHIGAN

·   ·   ·   ·   ·   ·   ·   ·   ·   ·   ·   ·   ·   ·   ·   ·   ·

Macaroni Loaf

½ cup scalded milk
1 cup soft bread crumbs
3 eggs, well beaten
1 cup macaroni, broken into small pieces and cooked
¼ cup melted butter
1 pimento, chopped
1 tablespoon chopped parsley
1 tablespoon chopped onion
1 6-ounce package American cheese with pimento, shredded
Dash salt
½ teaspoon pepper
Dash paprika

Recipe continues . . .

Pour hot milk over bread crumbs. Add beaten eggs, then stir in all remaining ingredients. Empty into loaf pan, set pan in shallow pan of hot water, and bake for 50 minutes in a slow (325°) oven.

This dish is excellent topped with creamed tuna, shrimp, crabmeat, chicken, or peas.

YIELD: 4 SERVINGS

Gourmet Gab
THE JUNIOR LEAGUE OF SAGINAW, MICHIGAN

Beans, Rice, and Other Grains

Lamb-Rice Casserole

2 cups tomato sauce
2 bay leaves
2 stalks celery with leaves
½ teaspoon salt
1 teaspoon paprika
1 tablespoon brown sugar
4 cups cooked rice
2 cups diced cooked lamb
½ cup grated Parmesan cheese

Combine first six ingredients in a saucepan and simmer over low heat for 45 minutes. Remove bay leaves and celery stalks.

Mix sauce with the rice and lamb and spoon into a greased 2-quart casserole. Sprinkle the cheese over the top and bake for 25 minutes at 350°.

YIELD: 6 SERVINGS

THE JUNIOR LEAGUE OF SOUTH BEND, INDIANA

Old Settler Baked Beans

½ pound bacon
½ pound ground beef
1 large onion, chopped
½ cup sugar
½ cup brown sugar
¼ cup catsup
¼ cup barbecue sauce
2 tablespoons prepared mustard
2 tablespoons molasses
½ teaspoon chili powder
1 teaspoon salt
½ teaspoon pepper
1 16-ounce can kidney beans
1 16-ounce can lima beans
1 28-ounce can pork and beans

In skillet, brown the bacon, beef, and onion. Drain off excess fat and mix with other ingredients in a large casserole.

Bake at 350° for 1 hour.

YIELD: 8 SERVINGS

THE JUNIOR LEAGUE OF KANSAS CITY, KANSAS

Baked Kidney Beans

1 1-pound can kidney beans
1 cup chopped celery
⅓ cup chopped sweet pickle
¼ cup chopped onion
1 cup finely cubed sharp cheddar cheese
½ teaspoon salt
½ teaspoon chili powder
½ teaspoon Worcestershire sauce
Dash Tabasco
½ cup mayonnaise
1 cup coarsely crushed corn chips

Drain beans and rinse in cold water. Combine with celery, pickle, onion, and cheese. Blend seasonings with mayonnaise and toss with bean mixture.

Spoon into shallow buttered baking dish. Sprinkle corn chips on top and bake at 450° for 10 minutes.

YIELD: 6 SERVINGS

THE JUNIOR LEAGUE OF CHAMPAIGN-URBANA, ILLINOIS

· · · · · · · · · · · · · · · · ·

Easy Baked Beans

1 onion, chopped
12 slices bacon, diced
¾ cup catsup
1 1-pound 12-ounce can beans with molasses
1 15-ounce can butter beans
1 15-ounce can kidney beans
2 tablespoons vinegar
4 tablespoons brown sugar
Dash garlic salt

Cook onion and bacon until onion is transparent and bacon is crisp. Combine with all other ingredients.

Empty into bean pot or casserole and bake in oven for 45 minutes at 350°.

YIELD: 16–18 SERVINGS

THE JUNIOR LEAGUE OF CHAMPAIGN-URBANA, ILLINOIS

. . . .

Baked Limas with Sour Cream

1 pound dried baby lima beans
3 teaspoons salt
¾ cup butter or margarine
¾ cup brown sugar
1 tablespoon dry mustard
1 tablespoon molasses
1 cup sour cream

Like all good bean dishes, this fabulous Pennsylvania Dutch recipe needs a little foresight.

Soak dried limas overnight in water. The next day drain off the water, cover with fresh water, add 1 teaspoon salt, and cook until tender, about 30–40 minutes. Drain again, rinse under hot water, and put in a medium-size casserole. Dab butter or margarine over the hot beans.

Mix the brown sugar, dry mustard, and remaining salt together in a bowl and sprinkle over the beans. Stir in molasses. Pour over the sour cream and mix carefully.

Bake in a 350° oven for 1 hour.

This dish can be prepared ahead of time, then tucked in the oven for final cooking.

YIELD: 8 SERVINGS

Bestir Yourself
THE JUNIOR LEAGUE OF TOLEDO, OHIO

. . . .

Kansas City Barley Casserole

1 cup quick barley
1 cup chopped celery
1 medium onion, chopped
1 stick butter
1 tablespoon basil
2 cups chicken stock
1 8-ounce can mushrooms
1½ tablespoons chopped parsley
1 tablespoon Worcestershire sauce
Salt and pepper to taste

Sauté barley, celery, and onion in butter. Add remaining ingredients and empty into a 2-quart casserole. Bake at 325° for 1½ hours.

Very good when served with quail.

YIELD: 6 SERVINGS

THE JUNIOR LEAGUE OF KANSAS CITY, KANSAS

· · · · · · · · · · · · · · · · · · · ·

St. Paul's Basic Barley Casserole

4–5 tablespoons butter
1 large onion, chopped
½ pound fresh mushrooms, sliced
1 cup pearl barley
2 cups chicken broth

Melt butter and sauté onion and mushrooms in it until onion is transparent. Add barley and brown lightly. Place in buttered casserole. Pour in 1 cup of the broth, cover, and bake at 350° for 30 minutes. Uncover and add second cup of broth. Cook until liquid is absorbed and barley is tender, about 1–1¼ hours.

YIELD: 4 SERVINGS

THE JUNIOR LEAGUE OF ST. PAUL, MINNESOTA

· · · · · · · · · · · · · · ·

Midwest Scrapple

¼ cup minced onion
1 pound ground beef
½ pound ground pork
1½ teaspoons ground sage
⅛ teaspoon cayenne
1½ teaspoons salt
½ teaspoon black pepper
3½ cups water
1 cup corn meal

Combine all ingredients except corn meal in a saucepan. Bring to a boil and boil gently for 20 minutes. Gradually stir in cornmeal and cook, stirring, until thickened.

Pour into a 5 x 9-inch loaf pan and chill.

Cut into slices about ½ inch thick. Dust with flour and fry in oil until lightly browned.

YIELD: 12 SERVINGS

Discover Dayton
THE JUNIOR LEAGUE OF DAYTON, OHIO

· · · · · · · · · · · · · ·

Corn Bread Dressing

1 quart day-old bread cubes
1 quart crumbled corn bread
1 quart crumbled biscuits
¾ cup chopped onion
¼ cup chopped green onion and tops
1 cup chopped celery
¼ cup finely chopped parsley
1½ teaspoons sage
1 teaspoon salt
¼ teaspoon pepper
1 cup turkey or chicken broth
½ cup melted butter
2 eggs, lightly beaten

Combine all ingredients except broth, butter, and eggs. Toss well. Add broth, butter, and eggs. Mix lightly but well.

Either stuff neck cavity and body of turkey or cook separately in a well-greased baking dish or casserole during the last 45 minutes of turkey roasting time.

YIELD: 11–12 CUPS

THE JUNIOR LEAGUE OF SAGINAW, MICHIGAN

"Corn Belt" Corn and Rice

½ pound cheddar cheese, cut into ½-inch cubes
1 1-pound can whole kernel corn, drained
2 cups cooked rice
1 cup finely diced celery
1 cup milk
2 tablespoons finely chopped onions
1 teaspoon salt
½ teaspoon pepper
½ teaspoon paprika
2 tablespoons butter

Combine all ingredients except butter in a baking dish. Dot the top with the butter.

Bake, uncovered, in a 350° oven for 30 minutes, or until slightly brown on top.

YIELD: 10 SERVINGS

THE JUNIOR LEAGUE OF SPRINGFIELD, ILLINOIS

. . . .

Beef with Rice and Eggplant

1 medium eggplant, peeled and cut into 1-inch cubes
1 pound ground beef
5 tablespoons butter or salad oil
½ cup minced onion
¼ cup chopped green pepper
1 tablespoon minced parsley
1 teaspoon salt
½ teaspoon pepper
2 cups cooked rice
½ cup bread crumbs
2 tablespoons grated Parmesan cheese

Recipe continues ...

Cook eggplant in boiling water until tender; drain and mash.

Brown beef in 3 tablespoons butter. Add onion and green pepper and simmer until tender. Mix eggplant, meat mixture, parsley, salt, pepper, and rice; spoon into baking dish.

Heat remaining butter; stir in crumbs and spread on top of meat mixture. Sprinkle with cheese and bake at 375° for 20–25 minutes, or until brown.

YIELD: 5–6 SERVINGS

THE JUNIOR LEAGUE OF ROCKFORD, ILLINOIS

Preston Mann's Hunter's Creek Rice Casserole

1 cup uncooked brown rice
1 tablespoon butter
2 stalks celery, chopped
1 medium onion, chopped
½ cup chopped green and red peppers (pimento may be substituted)
1 6-ounce can mushrooms, drained
3 cups chicken broth, or 3 cups water and 3 chicken bouillon cubes

Fry rice in butter until brown. Add other ingredients and bake in a covered casserole for 2 hours at 300°, or until liquid is absorbed.

YIELD: 8 SERVINGS

Tested, Tried, and True
THE JUNIOR LEAGUE OF FLINT, MICHIGAN

Rice Pouri

2½ cups converted rice, cooked just until done
½ cup salad oil
½ cup dehydrated onion flakes
½ teaspoon garlic powder
1 cup dry white wine
2 chicken bouillon cubes, dissolved in 1 cup hot water
1 cup evaporated milk
2 teaspoons salt
½ teaspoon pepper
¼ cup margarine
½ teaspoon basil
½ teaspoon ground rosemary
1⅓ cups sliced almonds, toasted and salted
Chopped parsley

Mix everything but parsley in a 2–2½-quart casserole; bake at 350° for 1 hour.

Garnish with parsley before serving.

YIELD: 10–12 SERVINGS

Cincinnati Celebrates
THE JUNIOR LEAGUE OF CINCINNATI, OHIO

Easy Paella

4 pounds chicken pieces
⅓ cup olive oil (no substitute)
⅓ cup water
1 small onion, finely chopped
1 clove garlic, sliced
¼ cup butter
2 cups uncooked rice
¼ teaspoon saffron
1 quart chicken broth
2 teaspoons oregano
1 4-ounce jar pimento, sliced
1 10-ounce package frozen peas, cooked
½ pound mushrooms, sliced
1 pound cooked shrimp
1 pound Italian sausage, cooked and sliced about ¾ inch thick
1 dozen cherrystone clams in the shell

Brown the chicken parts in olive oil. Add water, cover, and cook chicken for 30 minutes, or until tender. Remove chicken pieces and add the onion and garlic to the pan. Cook about 5–10 minutes and set aside.

In a large casserole or paella pan, melt butter. Add rice and saffron. Stir over medium heat for 5–10 minutes and add chicken broth. Bring to a boil and cook for 20 minutes. Remove from heat and add chicken parts, pan juices with onion and garlic, oregano, pimento, peas, mushrooms, shrimp, sausage, and clams. Bake at 350° for about 30–45 minutes.

YIELD: 6–8 SERVINGS

THE JUNIOR LEAGUE OF COLUMBUS, OHIO

Wild Rice Casserole with Fowl

1 cup uncooked wild rice
½–1 pound bulk pork sausage
1 4-ounce can sliced mushrooms, undrained
2 10¾-ounce cans mushroom soup
½ teaspoon Worcestershire sauce
12 slices or chunks of cooked turkey, chicken, or pheasant
1½ cups dry bread crumbs
¼ cup melted butter

Cook rice as directed on package. While rice is cooking, sauté sausage meat in skillet at medium heat until browned. Pour off excess fat; stir and break the sausage into bits.

Add mushrooms and liquid, mushroom soup, and Worcestershire sauce. Toss mixture lightly with cooked rice.

Spoon half the rice into a greased 2-quart casserole, add cooked meat, and top with remaining rice mixture. Cover with bread crumbs mixed with butter and bake for 30 minutes at 375°.

If made the day before and stored in refrigerator, bake for 45 minutes at 375°.

YIELD: 8 SERVINGS

THE JUNIOR LEAGUE OF CHAMPAIGN-URBANA, ILLINOIS

. . . .

Wild Rice with Almonds

1 12-ounce package uncooked wild rice, soaked in water overnight
½ cup butter
1 large onion, chopped
1 cup slivered almonds
2 10½-ounce cans consommé
1 can water
1 10¾-ounce can cream of chicken soup
½ teaspoon salt and pepper

Recipe continues ...

Mix rice with other ingredients and bake, covered, for 3–4 hours at 300°. Stir occasionally and add more water if necessary.

YIELD: 18 SERVINGS

Peacock Pie and Other Perfections
THE JUNIOR LEAGUE OF BATTLE CREEK, MICHIGAN

. . . .

Wild Rice with Cheese

1 cup cubed American cheese
1 cup chopped ripe olives
1 cup chopped fresh mushrooms
1 1-pound can tomatoes
½ cup chopped onion
1 cup uncooked wild rice, soaked in water overnight
½ cup olive oil
1½ cups boiling water
1½ teaspoons salt
¼ teaspoon pepper

Mix all ingredients in a large baking dish and cook, uncovered, for 1½ hours at 350°. Stir occasionally during the first hour to mix rice throughout.

YIELD: 8–12 SERVINGS

Peacock Pie and Other Perfections
THE JUNIOR LEAGUE OF BATTLE CREEK, MICHIGAN

. . . .

Wild Rice and Turkey Casserole

1 cup uncooked wild rice, soaked in water overnight
1 pound mushrooms, sliced
1 onion, chopped
6 tablespoons butter
2 teaspoons salt
¼ teaspoon freshly ground pepper
3 cups diced cooked turkey
½ cup blanched sliced almonds
3 cups turkey or chicken broth
1½ cups heavy cream
3 tablespoons grated Parmesan cheese

Cover rice with boiling water and soak for 1 hour. Drain well.

Sauté mushrooms and onion in 1 tablespoon butter until onion is transparent.

In buttered casserole, combine rice, vegetables, salt, pepper, turkey, and almonds. Mix broth and cream. Add to casserole, cover and bake at 350° for 1½ hours. Sprinkle with cheese and dot with remaining 5 tablespoons butter. Bake at 450° for 5 minutes.

Note: Packaged converted half-and-half rice may be substituted for the wild rice. If so, use only 1 cup cream and 2 cups broth.

YIELD: 6 SERVINGS

THE JUNIOR LEAGUE OF ROCKFORD, ILLINOIS

Superb Wild Rice

5 slices bacon
½ cup chopped onion
¼ cup chopped green pepper
1 4-ounce can mushrooms
2 tablespoons butter
1 10¾-ounce can cream of mushroom soup
1 cup crushed canned tomatoes
1 teaspoon beau monde seasoning
1 cup wild rice soaked in water overnight
½ cup sherry

Fry bacon crisp, remove from pan, and drain on paper toweling. Add the onion, green pepper, and mushrooms with liquid to the bacon drippings and sauté for about 5 minutes. Add the butter, mushroom soup, tomatoes, and the seasoning and heat until well blended.

Wash and drain the wild rice; add to the soup mixture. Stir in the sherry. Empty into a 2-quart well-buttered casserole and crumble bacon on top. Cover casserole and bake for 2 hours at 325°.

YIELD: 10–12 SERVINGS

THE JUNIOR LEAGUE OF FARGO-MOORHEAD, NORTH DAKOTA/MINNESOTA

Vegetables

Artichoke Hearts Casserole

1 14-ounce can artichoke hearts or 10-ounce package frozen hearts
3 ounces cream cheese, softened
1 cup bottled blue cheese dressing
¼ cup vermouth
½ teaspoon lemon juice
Parmesan cheese

Rinse and drain artichoke hearts (or cook and drain frozen artichoke hearts).

Combine cream cheese, blue cheese dressing, vermouth, and lemon juice. Add artichoke hearts.

Pour into baking dish and bake at 350° for 35–40 minutes. During the last 5–10 minutes of baking, sprinkle top of the casserole with Parmesan cheese.

YIELD: 4–6 SERVINGS

THE JUNIOR LEAGUE OF DES MOINES, IOWA

. . . .

Asparagus Parmesan

2 pounds fresh asparagus spears or 2 10-ounce packages frozen asparagus
4 tablespoons butter
1 cup mayonnaise
½ teaspoon salt
¼ teaspoon pepper
¼ teaspoon dry mustard
Juice of 1 lemon
1 cup well-buttered bread crumbs
⅔–1 cup grated Parmesan cheese

Cook asparagus until tender. Drain and arrange in casserole.

Melt butter and heat until it turns golden brown. Blend in mayonnaise, seasonings, and lemon juice and pour over asparagus. Sprinkle bread crumbs over top, then cheese.

Bake in 375° oven for 10–15 minutes, or until brown.

YIELD: 6 SERVINGS

The Cook's Book
THE JUNIOR LEAGUE OF CEDAR RAPIDS, IOWA

·   ·   ·   ·   ·   ·   ·   ·   ·   ·   ·   ·   ·   ·   ·   ·   ·   ·   ·

Asparagus-Cheese Bake

1 1-pound can asparagus spears
Milk
6 hard-boiled eggs, sliced
½ pound fresh mushrooms, sliced
Sliced almonds
2 tablespoons butter
2 tablespoons flour
½ pound cheddar cheese, shredded
Dash cayenne
Salt and pepper to taste

Drain liquid from asparagus into a measuring cup and add milk enough to make 1 cup liquid. Set aside.

In a 9 x 12-inch baking dish, layer asparagus, eggs, mushrooms, and almonds. Repeat layers.

For sauce, melt butter, add flour, and blend. Add asparagus liquid with milk. Stir until thickened. Add cheese and stir until melted. Add seasonings.

Pour sauce over the layers in baking dish and bake at 350° for ½ hour.

YIELD: 4 SERVINGS

Bluff City Cooks
THE JUNIOR LEAGUE OF GREATER ALTON, ILLINOIS

·   ·   ·   ·   ·   ·   ·   ·   ·   ·   ·   ·   ·   ·   ·   ·   ·   ·   ·

Swiss Green Beans

4 tablespoons butter
2 tablespoons flour
1 teaspoon salt
1 teaspoon pepper
1 teaspoon sugar
½ teaspoon grated onion
1 cup sour cream
4 cups cooked French-style green beans
½ pound Swiss cheese, shredded
2 cups crushed cornflakes

Melt half the butter and stir in flour, salt, pepper, sugar, and onion. Stir in sour cream and cook, stirring, until sauce is hot and thickened. Fold in beans and cheese. Empty into baking dish.

Melt remaining butter and stir in cornflakes. Sprinkle on top of casserole and bake at 400° for 20 minutes.

YIELD: 6 SERVINGS

THE JUNIOR LEAGUE OF ROCKFORD, ILLINOIS

.   .   .   .

Crunchy Bean Casserole

2 10-ounce packages frozen French-style green beans, cooked
1 16-ounce can water chestnuts, sliced
1 20-ounce can bean sprouts
1 pound fresh mushrooms, sautéed in butter
1 10¾-ounce can condensed mushroom soup
¼ cup shredded sharp cheddar cheese
1 3-ounce can French fried onions

Drain beans and canned vegetables well. Arrange layers of beans, water chestnuts, sprouts, mushrooms, and soup in baking dish; repeat. Top with cheese.

Bake at 400° for 20 minutes. Sprinkle onions on top and bake 10 minutes more.

YIELD: 10 SERVINGS

Tested, Tried, and True
THE JUNIOR LEAGUE OF FLINT, MICHIGAN

· · · · · · · · · · · · · · · · · · ·

Broccoli Parmesan

1 small onion, chopped
3 tablespoons butter
2 tablespoons flour
1 cup milk
1 egg yolk, beaten
1 10-ounce package frozen broccoli, cooked
¼ cup grated Parmesan cheese
Cracker crumbs

Sauté onion in butter until onion is tender but not brown. Stir in flour and gradually stir in milk. Cook, stirring, until sauce is smooth and thickened. Remove sauce from heat, cool a little, then stir in egg yolk, broccoli, and cheese.

Empty into small casserole and sprinkle with cracker crumbs. Bake in a 350° oven for 30 minutes.

YIELD: 4 SERVINGS

THE JUNIOR LEAGUE OF CHAMPAIGN-URBANA, ILLINOIS

· · · · · · · · · · · · · · · · · · ·

Cheesy Broccoli Casserole

¼ cup chopped onion
6 tablespoons butter
2 tablespoons flour
½ cup water
8 ounces processed yellow cheese, cubed
1 10-ounce package frozen chopped broccoli, thawed
3 eggs, well beaten
Buttered bread crumbs

Sauté onion in 4 tablespoons butter until onion is soft. Stir in flour and water. Cook over low heat, stirring, until sauce is thick and comes to a boil. Blend in cheese.

Combine sauce and broccoli, add eggs, and mix gently. Empty mixture into a greased 9 x 13-inch pan and sprinkle with buttered bread crumbs. Bake at 325° for 45 minutes to 1 hour.

YIELD: 6–8 SERVINGS

THE JUNIOR LEAGUE OF DES MOINES, IOWA

· · · · · · · · · · · · · · · · · · ·

Broccoli and Corn Scallop

2 tablespoons chopped onion
2 tablespoons margarine
1 tablespoon flour
1¼ cups milk
1 8-ounce package Monterey Jack cheese, shredded
1 12-ounce can whole kernel corn, drained
½ cup salted cracker crumbs
2 10-ounce packages frozen broccoli spears, cooked and drained

Sauté onion in 1 tablespoon margarine; blend in flour. Gradually stir in milk and cook, stirring constantly, until sauce is thickened. Add cheese and stir until cheese is melted. Stir in corn and half the cracker crumbs.

Arrange broccoli in a 7 x 11-inch baking dish. Pour cheese sauce over broccoli. Toss remaining crumbs and margarine and sprinkle on top. Bake at 350° for 30 minutes.

May be made ahead. Cover and refrigerate overnight, then bake, uncovered, at 350° for 45 minutes.

YIELD: 8 SERVINGS

THE JUNIOR LEAGUE OF DES MOINES, IOWA

· · · · · · · · · · · · · · · ·

Broccoli Casserole

2 10-ounce packages frozen broccoli
Pepper to taste
1 teaspoon monosodium glutamate
1 10¾-ounce can cream of chicken soup
Juice of 1 lemon
½ cup mayonnaise
6 slices American cheese
½ cup fresh bread crumbs
2 tablespoons melted butter or margarine

Cook broccoli as package directs and drain well.

Arrange in buttered 2-quart baking dish. Sprinkle with pepper and glutamate.

Mix soup, lemon juice, and mayonnaise together. Pour over broccoli and lay cheese slices on top. Sprinkle with bread crumbs and pour melted butter over all.

Bake, uncovered, for 45 minutes at 350°.

YIELD: 6–8 SERVINGS

THE JUNIOR LEAGUE OF SPRINGFIELD, ILLINOIS

· · · · · · · · · · · · · · · ·

Broccoli with Cashew Nuts

2 tablespoons minced onion
2 tablespoons butter
1 cup sour cream
1 teaspoon sugar
1 teaspoon vinegar
½ teaspoon poppy seeds
¼ teaspoon salt
2 10-ounce packages frozen broccoli spears, cooked and drained
1 cup chopped cashew nuts

Cook onion in butter until brown and translucent. Remove from heat and stir in sour cream, sugar, vinegar, and seasonings. Pour over hot broccoli. Sprinkle chopped cashews on top.

YIELD: 8 SERVINGS

Cookbook
THE JUNIOR LEAGUE OF GRAND RAPIDS, MICHIGAN

. . . .

Deluxe Broccoli Bake

2 10-ounce packages frozen broccoli
2 cups small whole onions
4 tablespoons butter
2 teaspoons flour
¼ teaspoon salt
¼ teaspoon pepper
1 cup milk
1 3-ounce package cream cheese, cubed
1 cup soft bread crumbs
¼ cup grated Parmesan cheese

Cook broccoli and drain. Cook onions in boiling salted water until tender, about 10 minutes; drain.

In saucepan, melt 2 tablespoons butter, blend in flour, and add salt and pepper. Add milk all at once; cook and stir until sauce is thick and bubbly. Reduce heat and blend in cream cheese until smooth. Stir in vegetables. Empty into 1½-quart casserole and sprinkle with bread crumbs mixed with the cheese. Bake at 350° for 40 minutes.

YIELD: 6 SERVINGS

Bluff City Cooks
THE JUNIOR LEAGUE OF GREATER ALTON, ILLINOIS

· · · · · · · · · · · · · · · · · · · ·

Red Cabbage Casserole

1 medium head red cabbage, shredded
2 apples, peeled, cored, and chopped
Large handful washed fresh cranberries
⅓–½ cup light brown sugar
Pinch cloves (optional)
Pinch salt
½–¾ cup cider or apple juice

Mix all ingredients in buttered casserole. Cover and bake about 45 minutes at 350°.

Good with turkey.

YIELD: 6 SERVINGS

THE JUNIOR LEAGUE OF COLUMBUS, OHIO

· · · · · · · · · · · · · · · · · ·

Buffet Carrots

2½ pounds fresh carrots, cut into narrow strips
½ cup mayonnaise or ¼ cup mayonnaise and
¼ cup sour cream
2 tablespoons minced onion
1 tablespoon prepared horseradish
Salt and pepper to taste
¼ cup fine cracker crumbs
2 tablespoons butter
Paprika
Chopped parsley (optional)

Cook carrots in salted water until just tender. Drain, saving ¼ cup of cooking liquid. Arrange strips in shallow pan for baking.

Combine ¼ cup of the cooking liquid with mayonnaise, onion, horseradish, salt, and pepper. Pour sauce over carrots, top with cracker crumbs, and dot with butter. Sprinkle with paprika and parsley if desired.

Bake, uncovered, at 375° until brown, approximately 15–20 minutes.

YIELD: 6 SERVINGS

Cookbook
THE JUNIOR LEAGUE OF GRAND RAPIDS, MICHIGAN

. . . .

Glazed Carrots

2 pounds carrots, peeled and sliced
½ teaspoon salt
½ cup honey
4 tablespoons sugar
4 tablespoons vegetable oil
1 teaspoon grated lemon rind
¼ teaspoon ground ginger

Cook carrots in boiling salted water to cover in a large skillet for 10 minutes. Drain.

Add honey, sugar, and oil. Cook, covered, over low heat until carrots are tender, about 20 minutes. Stir in lemon rind and ginger.

YIELD: 6 SERVINGS

The Discovery Shop Cookbook
THE JUNIOR LEAGUE OF SIOUX CITY, IOWA

Cauliflower Suisse

2 medium heads cauliflower
½ cup shredded Swiss cheese
¼ cup mayonnaise
½ cup sour cream
Crumbled bacon
Well-buttered bread crumbs

Divide cauliflower into flowerets, cook, and drain.

Melt cheese and mayonnaise in a double boiler and stir in sour cream. Put cauliflower in casserole and pour sauce over. Top liberally with both the crumbled bacon and the bread crumbs.

Bake in 350° oven until heated through, about 30 minutes.

Sauce may also be used on broccoli.

YIELD: 6 SERVINGS

The Cook's Book
THE JUNIOR LEAGUE OF CEDAR RAPIDS, IOWA

Green Cauliflower

1 whole cauliflower
1 10-ounce package frozen peas
1 medium onion, chopped
1 tablespoon butter
½ cup light cream
Salt and pepper
Croutons or cherry tomatoes for garnish

Cook whole a perfect head of cauliflower for 25–40 minutes. (Lemon slices will help keep it white).

While cauliflower is cooking, cook peas with the onion. Drain, blend in blender with the butter and cream, adding salt and freshly ground pepper to taste.

Drain cauliflower completely and cover with purée of peas. Garnish with butter-browned croutons or cherry tomatoes warmed in butter.

YIELD: 4 SERVINGS

Marigolds to Munch On
THE JUNIOR LEAGUE OF PEORIA, ILLINOIS

. . . .

Celery Casserole

4 cups 1-inch slices celery
1 5-ounce can water chestnuts, sliced
1 10¾-ounce can cream of chicken soup
¼ cup diced pimento
½ cup soft bread crumbs
¼ cup toasted slivered almonds
2 tablespoons melted butter
Salt and pepper to taste

Cook celery in salted water for 8 minutes; drain. Mix water chestnuts, soup, and pimento with celery and empty into casserole. Mix bread crumbs, almonds, butter, salt and pepper and toss over top.

Bake at 350° for 35 minutes.

YIELD: 6 SERVINGS

Marigolds to Munch On
THE JUNIOR LEAGUE OF PEORIA, ILLINOIS

. . . .

Des Moines Corn Pudding

2 12-ounce cans whole kernel corn, drained
2 tablespoons flour
2 tablespoons sugar
2 tablespoons butter or margarine
2 eggs
1 teaspoon salt
½ large green pepper, chopped
½ 2-ounce can pimento, chopped
¼ pound cheddar cheese, shredded
¼ cup milk

Mix all ingredients together in baking dish and bake at 350° for 35 minutes.

YIELD: 6–8 SERVINGS

THE JUNIOR LEAGUE OF DES MOINES, IOWA

. . . .

Columbus Corn Pudding

3 eggs, beaten
⅓ stick butter, melted
½ cup white sugar
1 tablespoon flour
½ teaspoon onion salt
½ teaspoon salt
2–3 cups fresh corn

Blend all ingredients except corn. Empty corn into an 8-inch-square casserole and pour egg mixture over corn.

Bake at 350° for 45 minutes.

YIELD: 6 SERVINGS

THE JUNIOR LEAGUE OF COLUMBUS, OHIO

· · · · · · · · · · · · · · · · · · ·

Evansville Corn Pudding

¼ cup corn meal
3 tablespoons brown sugar
¾ teaspoon salt
1 egg
¾ cup scalded milk
3 tablespoons butter
1 1-pound can creamed corn

Mix all ingredients in large bowl. Transfer to casserole.

Bake at 325° for 1 hour, stirring several times during the first 25 minutes of baking.

This recipe can successfully be doubled.

YIELD: 6 SERVINGS

THE JUNIOR LEAGUE OF EVANSVILLE, INDIANA

· · · · · · · · · · · · · · · · · · ·

Baked Corn

2 1-pound cans whole kernel corn, drained
2 cups milk
3 eggs, beaten
1 cup crushed cracker crumbs
½ cup chopped onion
¼ cup chopped pimento
2 teaspoons salt
Green pepper rings

Heat corn and milk to simmering.

To beaten eggs add crumbs, onion, pimento, and salt. Stir in corn and milk mixture. Pour into a 2-quart buttered casserole and top with green pepper rings. Bake at 350° for 50–60 minutes.

YIELD: 12 SERVINGS

THE JUNIOR LEAGUE OF FARGO-MOORHEAD, NORTH DAKOTA/MINNESOTA

Milwaukee Moussaka

2 medium eggplants
Salt
¼ pound bacon, diced
2 medium onions, sliced
½ green pepper, chopped
1 28-ounce can tomatoes, drained
½ teaspoon sage
¼ teaspoon thyme
¼ teaspoon marjoram
¼ teaspoon salt
⅛ teaspoon ground black pepper
Dash garlic powder
Olive oil
½ pound Swiss cheese, shredded
Grated Parmesan cheese

Peel eggplants. Cut lengthwise into ½-inch slices. Sprinkle with salt and set aside.

Cook bacon until crisp and drain off excess drippings. Add onions and green pepper and cook until tender. Stir in tomatoes, herbs, and seasonings. Simmer for 10–15 minutes.

Press moisture from eggplant slices and sauté in olive oil until lightly browned, adding additional olive oil as necessary.

Arrange half the eggplant in greased 1½-quart baking dish. Add half the tomato mixture and half the Swiss cheese; sprinkle with Parmesan cheese. Repeat layers. Bake at 350° for 35–45 minutes, or until done. Let stand 15 minutes before serving.

YIELD: 8 SERVINGS

VARIATION:
Substitute ½ pound bulk Italian sausage for bacon.

Be Our Guest
THE JUNIOR LEAGUE OF MILWAUKEE, WISCONSIN

Scalloped Eggplant

1 medium eggplant, peeled and diced
½ cup boiling water
2 tablespoons chopped parsley
1 small onion, finely chopped
1 tablespoon butter
3 tablespoons melted butter
¾ cup cracker crumbs
½ cup milk
Shredded cheddar cheese

Cook eggplant in boiling water until tender, about 15 minutes. Drain well and sprinkle parsley.

Sauté the onion in 1 tablespoon butter and add to eggplant.

Combine melted butter and cracker crumbs.

Place layers of eggplant and layers of crumbs in a baking dish, ending with crumbs. Pour milk over casserole and sprinkle with cheese.

Bake for ½ hour at 375°.

YIELD: 4 SERVINGS

Bluff City Cooks
THE JUNIOR LEAGUE OF GREATER ALTON, ILLINOIS

•   •   •   •   •   •   •   •   •   •   •   •   •   •   •   •   •

Baked Eggplant, Tomato and Cheese

1 medium eggplant
3 teaspoons salt
½ cup flour
¼ cup olive oil
1½ pounds tomatoes, peeled and sliced
½ teaspoon freshly ground pepper
½ pound mozzarella cheese, thinly sliced
½ cup grated Parmesan cheese
2 tablespoons butter

Recipe continues . . .

Peel eggplant and cut into slices ½ inch thick. Sprinkle with 2 teaspoons salt; let stand 1 hour, then rinse, drain, and dry thoroughly. Coat with flour and brown in 2 tablespoons oil.

Put half the slices in the bottom of a 12 x 8 x 2-inch baking dish. Cover with half the tomato slices; sprinkle with pepper and remaining 1 teaspoon salt. Add slices of cheese and grated cheese. Repeat layers. Dot with butter and drizzle remaining oil over casserole.

Bake at 350° for 30 minutes.

This is an excellent meatless main dish.

YIELD: 4–6 SERVINGS

Cincinnati Celebrates
THE JUNIOR LEAGUE OF CINCINNATI, OHIO

Toledo Mushroom Casserole

8 slices buttered bread, crust removed and cut into 1-inch cubes
½ cup chopped onion
½ cup chopped celery
½ cup chopped green pepper
½ cup mayonnaise
¾ teaspoon salt
Dash pepper
1–1½ pounds fresh mushrooms, washed, cut into large pieces,
and sautéed in a little butter
2 eggs, lightly beaten
1½ cups half and half
1 10¾-ounce can cream of mushroom soup
½–¾ cup shredded cheddar cheese

Put half the bread cubes in the bottom of buttered 7½ x 12-inch oblong casserole. Combine onion, celery, green pepper, mayonnaise, salt, and pepper and pour over bread in casserole. Distribute mushrooms over the top, then remaining bread. Combine eggs and half and half and pour over all.

Store overnight, tightly covered, in the refrigerator. Before baking, spread mushroom soup over the top. Bake at 325° for 55–60 minutes. Remove from oven 10 minutes before end of baking time and sprinkle cheese on top. Bake until cheese is melted and browned.

Makes a wonderful accompaniment to any meat.

YIELD: 8 SERVINGS

THE JUNIOR LEAGUE OF TOLEDO, OHIO

·   ·   ·   ·   ·   ·   ·   ·   ·   ·   ·   ·   ·   ·   ·   ·   ·   ·

Quiche Stuffed Mushrooms

2 pounds large fresh mushrooms
5 slices bacon
6 tablespoons butter
2 tablespoons minced onion
2 eggs, lightly beaten
1 cup heavy cream
2¾ cups shredded Swiss cheese
¾ teaspoon salt

Rinse mushrooms, pat dry, and remove stems. Chop stems (makes about 1½ cups) and set stems aside.

In a large skillet, sauté bacon until crisp, drain on paper towels, crumble, and set aside. Pour bacon drippings from skillet.

In same skillet, melt butter. Use about 4 tablespoons of the butter to brush the outside of the mushroom caps and place caps in a large shallow baking pan. To butter remaining in skillet, add onion and sauté for 2 minutes. Add reserved mushroom stems; sauté 2 minutes longer. Remove from heat.

Recipe continues . . .

In a bowl, combine eggs, cream, cheese, and salt. Stir in bacon and mushroom mixture. Fill caps.

Bake for 30 minutes at 350°.

YIELD: 24 SERVINGS

THE JUNIOR LEAGUE OF COLUMBUS, OHIO

Peoria Mushroom Casserole

⅓ cup soft butter or margarine
1 tablespoon chopped parsley
1 tablespoon prepared mustard
1 tablespoon grated onion
⅛ teaspoon cayenne
1 teaspoon salt
2½ tablespoons flour
⅛ teaspoon nutmeg
1 pound washed fresh mushrooms
1 cup heavy cream

Blend together all ingredients except mushrooms and cream.

Slice the mushrooms in half lengthwise. Arrange a layer in the bottom of a buttered 1½-quart casserole. Dot with half of butter mixture. Top with rest of the mushrooms, then rest of the butter mixture. Pour the heavy cream over all and bake, uncovered, for about 55 minutes at 325°.

May be completely prepared the day before, refrigerated, then reheated at serving time at 350°.

YIELD: 4 SERVINGS

Marigolds to Munch On
THE JUNIOR LEAGUE OF PEORIA, ILLINOIS

Apple-Onion Casserole

3 large mild onions, sliced
½ cup brown sugar (or to taste)
Salt and pepper
¼ cup butter
4–6 cooking apples, peeled and sliced
Buttered bread crumbs

Lightly butter a casserole. Add a layer of onions; sprinkle with half the brown sugar. Season with salt and pepper and dab on half the butter. Add a layer of apples and top with remaining sugar. Season again with salt and pepper and dab on more butter. Top with buttered bread crumbs.

Bake at 300° for 2 hours.

Marvelous with pork, duck, or pheasant.

YIELD: 6 SERVINGS

THE JUNIOR LEAGUE OF INDIANAPOLIS, INDIANA

· · · · · · · · · · · · · · · · · ·

Fried Onion Rings

1–2 Bermuda onions
1 egg
1 cup milk
1–2 cups self-rising flour
Oil for frying

Slice onions and separate into rings.

Beat egg lightly in a medium-size mixing bowl; stir in milk. Place flour in a separate bowl. Dip rings first in liquid, then in flour, then liquid, then flour.

Recipe continues ...

Fry in hot shallow oil until lightly browned. Drain on absorbent paper and keep warm in a low oven.

YIELD: 4 SERVINGS

THE JUNIOR LEAGUE OF EVANSVILLE, INDIANA

Baked Stuffed Onions

6 medium onions
1½ cups prepared dry stuffing mix
1½ cups shredded sharp cheddar cheese
¾ cup melted butter
⅓ cup hot water

Peel and cut onions crosswise in three or four thick slices.

Combine all other ingredients. Spread mixture evenly between onion slices. Put each onion back together and wrap securely in a double thickness of aluminum foil.

Bake at 375° about 1 hour, or until tender.

YIELD: 3–6 SERVINGS

Peacock Pie and Other Perfections
THE JUNIOR LEAGUE OF BATTLE CREEK, MICHIGAN

Cedar Rapids Onion Pie

1 uncooked 9-inch pastry shell
½ pound bacon
3 pounds sweet onions, thinly sliced
Butter
3 eggs, beaten
1 cup sour cream
4 tablespoons sherry
½ teaspoon salt
¼ teaspoon ground black pepper
2 tablespoons minced parsley

Bake pastry for 12 minutes in 475° oven. Remove and cool.

Cook bacon until crisp, then crumble. Sauté onions in butter until transparent. Combine eggs, sour cream, sherry, and seasonings. Add bacon and onions and pour into baked pastry shell.

Bake for 30 minutes at 350°.

Serve cut into wedges with steak or roast beef.

YIELD: 6 SERVINGS

The Cook's Book
THE JUNIOR LEAGUE OF CEDAR RAPIDS, IOWA

. . . .

Youngstown Onion Pie

1 cup finely crushed cracker crumbs
¼ cup melted butter
3 cups thinly sliced onion
2 tablespoons butter
2 eggs, lightly beaten
¾ cup milk
¾ teaspoon salt
Dash pepper
¼ cup shredded cheddar cheese
Paprika

Mix together cracker crumbs and melted butter. Using back of a large spoon, press the mixture into the bottom and sides of an 8-inch pie plate.

In a skillet, sauté onion in butter until transparent. Spread carefully into the crumb-lined pie plate and pour over a mixture of the eggs, milk, salt, and pepper. Sprinkle top with cheese and paprika.

Bake at 350° for 30 minutes, or until knife comes out dry. Serve hot. Delicious with roast beef or steak.

YIELD: 4 SERVINGS

THE JUNIOR LEAGUE OF YOUNGSTOWN, OHIO

. . . .

Scalloped Onions

2 pounds onions
1 teaspoon salt
Pepper
1 teaspoon paprika
1 teaspoon celery salt
3 teaspoons margarine
¼ cup water
½ cup dry bread crumbs
1 tablespoon melted margarine

Peel onions and slice ¼ inch thick. Combine seasonings and sprinkle between layers of onions arranged in a buttered casserole. Dot with margarine, add water, cover, and bake at 400° for 1 hour.

Uncover, sprinkle top with bread crumbs mixed with margarine. Bake an additional 15 minutes.

YIELD: 6–8 SERVINGS

THE JUNIOR LEAGUE OF DES MOINES, IOWA

· · · · · · · · · · · · · · · · · ·

Petits Pois à la Française
(Little Peas with Lettuce)

3½ tablespoons butter
2 pounds young green peas, shelled or frozen
1 head lettuce, shredded
10 small white onions
2 sprigs fresh thyme
4 sprigs parsley
1 teaspoon sugar
½ teaspoon salt
⅛ teaspoon pepper

Melt 2 tablespoons of the butter in a heavy saucepan with a tight cover. Add all remaining ingredients and stir to mix well. Cover pan tightly and simmer on low heat, stirring occasionally. Moisture from the lettuce should be sufficient, but you can add a spoonful of water if necessary.

Cook for about 45 minutes, or until peas are tender. Add the remaining butter, mix well, and serve.

YIELD: 6–8 SERVINGS

The Discovery Shop Cookbook
THE JUNIOR LEAGUE OF SIOUX CITY, IOWA

· · · · · · · · · · · · · · · · · ·

Potato Soufflé

4 large Idaho potatoes, unpeeled
3 eggs, separated
1 teaspoon salt
1 teaspoon grated onion
Dash Tabasco and pepper
2 tablespoons melted butter
Almonds, whole or slivered

Bake and mash potatoes; add egg yolks and seasonings, beating well. Beat egg whites until stiff and fold into mixture. Spoon carefully into 1½-quart buttered round soufflé or casserole dish. Brush with butter and sprinkle with almonds.

Bake at 350° for about 30 minutes.

Soufflé may be frozen before baking.

YIELD: 4–6 SERVINGS

The Cook's Book
THE JUNIOR LEAGUE OF CEDAR RAPIDS, IOWA

Creamy New Potatoes

2 tablespoons chopped chives
2 medium cloves garlic, minced
1 tablespoon butter
1 11-ounce can cheddar cheese soup
¼ cup sour cream
2 tablespoons water
2 pounds small new potatoes, peeled and cooked

In saucepan, cook chives and garlic in butter for a few minutes. Stir in soup until smooth. Blend in sour cream and water. Add potatoes. Heat, stirring occasionally.

Can be prepared ahead and heated in 250°–300° oven.

YIELD: 6–8 SERVINGS

Bluff City Cooks
THE JUNIOR LEAGUE OF GREATER ALTON, ILLINOIS

· · · · · · · · · · · · · · · · · · · ·

Potatoes au Gratin

3 pounds frozen hash brown potatoes
1 pint half and half
½ pound butter
1 pound soft processed cheese
8 ounces sharp cheddar cheese, shredded

Pour frozen hash brown potatoes in a 9 x 13-inch baking dish. Mix and melt the remaining ingredients in a saucepan, pour over potatoes, and let stand for about 1 hour.

Bake in preheated 350° oven for 1 hour.

May be frozen after baking. Try the rich cheesy sauce as a base for macaroni and cheese.

YIELD: 12 LARGE SERVINGS

Discover Dayton
THE JUNIOR LEAGUE OF DAYTON, OHIO

· · · · · · · · · · · · · · · · ·

Crispy Potatoes

4 Idaho potatoes, unpeeled
Salt to taste
½ cup melted butter
1 cup grated Parmesan cheese

Cut Idaho potatoes in ⅛-inch slices. Arrange in single layer on cookie sheets. Season to taste with salt. Pour melted butter over potatoes and top with the Parmesan cheese.

Bake at 350° for 45 minutes, or until crisp. Drain on paper toweling.

YIELD: 6 SERVINGS

Be Our Guest
THE JUNIOR LEAGUE OF MILWAUKEE, WISCONSIN

· · · · · · · · · · · · · · · · · ·

Parmesan Potatoes

1 medium onion, chopped
6 tablespoons butter
3 cups half and half
1 24-ounce package frozen hash brown potatoes
Salt and pepper to taste
⅔ cup grated Parmesan cheese
2 tablespoons melted butter

Sauté onion in butter in large saucepan. Add half and half and heat almost to boiling. Stir in frozen hash brown potatoes. Heat until mixture thickens slightly. Season with salt and pepper to taste.

Pour into a greased 9 x 13-inch baking dish and sprinkle with Parmesan cheese. Top with melted butter and bake at 325° for 1 hour, or until brown.

YIELD: 6–8 SERVINGS

Be Our Guest
THE JUNIOR LEAGUE OF MILWAUKEE, WISCONSIN

· ·

Potato Gnocchi

4–5 medium Idaho potatoes, peeled and quartered
1 cup water
6 tablespoons butter
Salt and pepper to taste
⅛ teaspoon nutmeg
1 cup flour
3 eggs
½ cup grated Parmesan cheese
6 tablespoons spinach purée or baby food strained spinach
Additional Parmesan cheese and butter for baking

Boil potatoes until tender; drain well. Rice the potatoes and set aside.

In a saucepan, mix water, butter, salt, pepper, and nutmeg; bring to a boil. Remove from heat, quickly stir in flour, and stir until mixture leaves sides of pan and forms a ball. Then, with electric mixer, add eggs, one at a time, beating well after each addition. Add Parmesan cheese. Beat in potatoes and spinach purée.

On lightly floured board, drop 1 tablespoon at a time and roll into a ball. Drop dumplings into simmering water and cook, uncovered, for 15 minutes. Remove and drain.

Recipe continues . . .

Place gnocchi in shallow buttered baking dish, brush with additional butter and sprinkle with Parmesan cheese. Just before serving, place under broiler until gnocchi are browned.

YIELD: 4 SERVINGS

Tested, Tried, and True
THE JUNIOR LEAGUE OF FLINT, MICHIGAN

. . . .

Herbed Potato Latkes

2 eggs
3 cups grated potatoes
⅓ cup grated onion
3 tablespoons flour
1½ teaspoons salt
½ teaspoon parsley flakes
½ teaspoon rosemary
¼ teaspoon ground sage
¼ teaspoon pepper
Peanut oil

Beat eggs until light and foamy. Stir in grated potatoes, onion, flour, seasonings, and herbs until thoroughly blended.

Heat peanut oil to a depth of ⅛–¼ inch in large heavy skillet. Drop ¼ cup potato mixture at a time into the hot oil. Fry on both sides until golden brown. Add oil to pan as needed to keep proper depth. Drain latkes.

Serve hot with applesauce or sour cream.

YIELD: 16 LATKES

THE JUNIOR LEAGUE OF KANSAS CITY, KANSAS

. . . .

Potatoes Supreme

1 cup sour cream
2 cups cottage cheese
2 teaspoons salt
2 tablespoons grated onion
1 small clove garlic, minced
6 medium potatoes, cooked and diced
½ cup shredded American cheese
Dash paprika

Combine sour cream, cottage cheese, salt, onion, and garlic. Gently fold in diced potatoes and pour into buttered 1½-quart casserole. Top with shredded cheese and paprika.

Bake at 350° for 40–45 minutes, or until thoroughly heated and browned lightly.

YIELD: 6 SERVINGS

THE JUNIOR LEAGUE OF TOLEDO, OHIO

. . . .

Swiss Cheese Potatoes

4–5 medium potatoes, peeled
¼ teaspoon salt
¼ teaspoon pepper
1½ pounds fresh mushrooms, sliced
1 clove garlic
1 cup shredded Swiss cheese
1 small onion, minced
Parsley (optional)
2 cups heavy cream
½ cup butter or margarine

Recipe continues ...

Slice potatoes into thin rounds. Wash and dry. Sprinkle with salt and pepper. Wash and dry mushroom slices.

Rub a 2-quart casserole with garlic and butter well. Put in a layer of potatoes and a layer of mushrooms; sprinkle with cheese, onion, and parsley. Repeat layers, ending with cheese. Top with cream, dot with butter and bake at 375° for 1–1½ hours.

Serve very hot.

YIELD: 10–12 SERVINGS

Tested, Tried, and True
THE JUNIOR LEAGUE OF FLINT, MICHIGAN

· · · · · · · · · · · · · · · ·

German Potato Pancakes

What makes this recipe authentic is that it doesn't use any flour.

4 large Idaho potatoes, peeled
3–4 large eggs, lightly beaten
1 teaspoon salt
¾ teaspoon nutmeg (or to taste)
Shortening

Grate potatoes into the eggs and add salt and nutmeg. *Be sure to grate, not shred.* Fry one pancake at a time, in enough shortening to just cover the bottom of a skillet. Cook until edges are lacy and pancake is brown. Flip only once.

Serve with syrup and butter.

YIELD: 5 SERVINGS

THE JUNIOR LEAGUE OF ST. PAUL, MINNESOTA

· · · · · · · · · · · · · · · ·

Scalloped Potatoes

4 medium potatoes, peeled and sliced
1 small onion, sliced
1 cup heavy cream
1½ cups water
¾ teaspoon salt
2 tablespoons butter

Arrange potato and onion slices in layers in buttered 1½-quart casserole.

Mix cream, water, and salt. Pour over potatoes and onion.

Place butter on top of casserole in chunks. Bake in a 300° oven for 1½–2 hours.

The cream does not make a thick sauce but much of it cooks into the potatoes.

YIELD: 4–5 SERVINGS

THE JUNIOR LEAGUE OF FARGO-MOORHEAD, NORTH DAKOTA/MINNESOTA

•   •   •   •   •   •   •   •   •   •   •   •   •   •   •   •   •   •   •

Sweet Potato Casserole

2 16-ounce cans sweet potatoes
¼ cup butter
1 cup sugar
½ teaspoon salt
2 eggs
½ cup milk
½ teaspoon vanilla
1 cup brown sugar
¼ cup butter
⅓ cup flour
2 teaspoons cinnamon
1 cup chopped nuts

Recipe continues . . .

Heat sweet potatoes to boiling and drain. Mash potatoes with butter. Add sugar, salt, eggs, milk, and vanilla and mix well. Pour into ungreased 9-inch-square glass baking pan.

Mix brown sugar, butter, flour, and cinnamon with fingertips until mixture is crumbly. Stir in nuts. Spread on top of sweet potato mixture and bake at 350° for 40 minutes.

This dish may be made the day before and refrigerated before baking. It's very rich, but everyone loves it!

YIELD: 10–12 SERVINGS

THE JUNIOR LEAGUE OF SOUTH BEND, INDIANA

Orange Sweet Potatoes

6 medium-size cooked or canned sweet potatoes
1 cup orange juice
1 tablespoon cornstarch
2 teaspoons grated orange rind
4 tablespoons melted butter
½ cup brown sugar, packed
½ cup sugar

Arrange potatoes in baking pan. Combine remaining ingredients in saucepan and cook over moderate heat, stirring, until thickened. Pour over potatoes and bake at 350° for 1 hour.

YIELD: 6 SERVINGS

THE JUNIOR LEAGUE OF FARGO-MOORHEAD, NORTH DAKOTA/MINNESOTA

Savory Chopped Spinach

1 10-ounce package frozen chopped spinach
½ cup sour cream
3 ounces cream cheese, softened
1 tablespoon dried minced green onion
1 tablespoon horseradish
Salt to taste
3 slices bacon

Cook spinach according to package directions. Drain thoroughly. Add sour cream and stir until blended. Add cream cheese, onion, horseradish, and salt.

Cook bacon until crisp. Drain on paper towels and crumble.

Butter a 1½-pint casserole. Spoon spinach mixture into casserole, top with crumbled bacon and bake at 350° for 20–30 minutes.

YIELD: 3 SERVINGS

Tested, Tried, and True
THE JUNIOR LEAGUE OF FLINT, MICHIGAN

· · · · · · · · · · · · · · · · · · ·

Spinach and Artichokes

2 10-ounce packages frozen artichoke hearts
2 10-ounce packages frozen chopped spinach
1 stick butter
8 ounces cream cheese
Grated Parmesan cheese

Cook artichokes and spinach separately and drain. Put artichokes in buttered casserole.

Recipe continues . . .

Cream butter and cream cheese together. Mix spinach with creamed butter and cheese and pour over artichokes. Top with Parmesan cheese and bake for 30–40 minutes at 350°.

YIELD: 6–8 SERVINGS

The Discovery Shop Cookbook
THE JUNIOR LEAGUE OF SIOUX CITY, IOWA

· · · · · · · · · · · · · · · · · ·

Herb Spinach Bake

1 10-ounce package frozen chopped spinach
1 cup cooked rice
1 cup shredded American cheese
2 eggs, lightly beaten
2 tablespoons soft butter or margarine
⅓ cup milk
2 tablespoons chopped onion
½ teaspoon Worcestershire sauce
1 teaspoon salt
¼ teaspoon crushed rosemary or crushed thyme leaves

Cook and drain spinach. Mix with cooked rice, cheese, eggs, butter, milk, onion, and seasonings. Pour mixture into 10 x 6 x 1½ -inch baking dish. Bake in moderate oven, 350°, for 20–25 minutes, or until knife inserted halfway comes out clean.

Cut in squares to serve.
Can be fixed ahead and baked just before serving.

YIELD: 6 SERVINGS

Marigolds to Munch On
THE JUNIOR LEAGUE OF PEORIA, ILLINOIS

· · · · · · · · · · · · · · · · · ·

Molded Spaghetti and Spinach

8 ounces spaghetti
2 10-ounce packages frozen chopped spinach
½ cup finely chopped onion
½ cup grated Parmesan cheese
4 tablespoons softened butter
2 eggs, lightly beaten
3 cups fresh mushrooms, quartered or sliced if large
4 tablespoons butter
2 16-ounce jars meatless spaghetti sauce

Cook spaghetti according to package directions and drain. Meanwhile, cook frozen spinach according to package directions with the onion; drain. Combine the hot spaghetti with the spinach, cheese, the softened butter, and the eggs. Mix well. Turn into a greased and wax-paper-lined 6½-cup ring mold.

Cover and bake in a 375° oven for 25 minutes.

Meanwhile, in saucepan, cook mushrooms in remaining butter until tender. Add spaghetti sauce and heat through.

Cool the ring mold for 5 minutes, then unmold onto serving platter and fill the center with the mushroom sauce. Serve as an accompaniment to meat, fish, or poultry.

This dish can be made ahead and reheated in a 250° oven.

YIELD: 8 SERVINGS

THE JUNIOR LEAGUE OF SOUTH BEND, INDIANA

16th Avenue Spinach

2 10-ounce packages frozen chopped spinach, thawed
3 tablespoons butter
Dash garlic powder
1 scant tablespoon flour
½ cup light cream
Dash nutmeg, salt, and pepper
½ cup slivered almonds
½ cup seedless raisins

Cook spinach according to package directions. Drain spinach well and combine with 2 tablespoons of butter, garlic powder, flour, and cream and season with nutmeg, salt, and freshly ground black pepper.

Sauté nuts lightly in remaining butter. Soak raisins in cold water for 10 or 15 minutes and carefully drain. Add raisins to nuts.

Just prior to serving, combine nut-raisin mixture with spinach.

YIELD: 6 SERVINGS

The Cook's Book
THE JUNIOR LEAGUE OF CEDAR RAPIDS, IOWA

. . . .

Baked Squash

1 pound yellow crookneck squash, diced
½ cup chopped green pepper
½ cup chopped onion
¼ stick butter or margarine
½ cup shredded cheddar cheese
1 egg
½ cup mayonnaise
1 teaspoon sugar
Salt and pepper
1 2-ounce jar pimento
Buttered bread crumbs

Simmer squash, pepper, and onion in water until tender. Drain well and stir in butter or margarine. Mix with remaining ingredients except crumbs in casserole. Top with crumbs and bake at 350° for 20–30 minutes.

YIELD: 4 SERVINGS

Bluff City Cooks
THE JUNIOR LEAGUE OF GREATER ALTON, ILLINOIS

Squash with Almonds

1 pound yellow summer squash
¼ cup butter
Salt and pepper to taste
¼ teaspoon basil
½ cup heavy cream
⅛ teaspoon ginger
¼ cup brown sugar
½ cup finely sliced almonds

Split squash in half lengthwise, and slice in ½-inch slices crosswise. In skillet, melt butter; add squash and brown lightly. Sprinkle with salt, pepper, and basil.

Empty all into a casserole; add cream, dust with ginger, sprinkle on brown sugar, and top with sliced almonds. Bake at 350° for about 20 minutes, or until the top is brown.

YIELD: 4–6 SERVINGS

Marigolds to Munch On
THE JUNIOR LEAGUE OF PEORIA, ILLINOIS

Gingered Acorn Squash

4 acorn squash
1 tablespoon butter
1 tablespoon light cream
½ teaspoon powdered ginger
1 cup brown sugar
Salt and pepper to taste

Split squash, remove seeds, and put cut side down in pan. Add a bit of water and bake at 325° for about 1 hour, or until tender.

Scoop out pulp and mix with the rest of the ingredients. Fill the four best shells.

When ready to serve, put under broiler 1 inch below medium heat to warm and brown.

YIELD: 4 SERVINGS

Marigolds to Munch On
THE JUNIOR LEAGUE OF PEORIA, ILLINOIS

·   ·   ·   ·   ·   ·   ·   ·   ·   ·   ·   ·   ·   ·   ·   ·   ·

Squash à l'Orange

1 5–6 pound buttercup squash
1 medium orange
⅓ cup brown sugar
⅓–½ stick butter or margarine

Buttercup squash is a dark green winter squash with light green stripes and a button on top. Place it whole on a baking sheet and bake until soft to the touch on the outside, about 45 minutes at 400°

Remove squash from oven and cut out a circle on top. Reserve the circle.

Remove squash seeds and membranes with a spoon and scoop some of the squash from sides into the center of the vegetable.

Grate the rind of the orange and squeeze the juice into a small sauce-pan. Add the brown sugar and butter and heat, stirring, until butter is melted and sugar is dissolved. Pour the hot mixture into the squash and mix it lightly with the cooked squash inside the shell, being careful not to puncture the shell.

Return reserved circle of squash to top of squash and return all to a 300° oven to stay warm.

When ready to serve, place the whole squash in a serving dish, remove top, and scoop out the servings.

YIELD: 6–8 SERVINGS

THE JUNIOR LEAGUE OF ST. PAUL, MINNESOTA

·   ·   ·   ·   ·   ·   ·   ·   ·   ·   ·   ·   ·   ·   ·   ·

Summer Tomatoes

6 large tomatoes, halved
Salt and pepper
Bread crumbs
4–5 tablespoons melted butter
2 hard-boiled eggs
6 tablespoons butter
1½ teaspoons prepared mustard
Dash Tabasco
3 teaspoons finely minced chives
2 teaspoons finely minced parsley
2 tablespoons Worcestershire sauce
2 teaspoons sugar
4 tablespoons red wine vinegar
2 raw eggs

Season tomato halves with salt and pepper, mound top with bread crumbs, and drizzle with the melted butter. Set aside.

Recipe continues . . .

For deviled topping, mash cooked eggs and add next eight ingredients, seasoning with salt and pepper. Stir in raw eggs and cook in double boiler until thick. Remove from heat and let stand at least 15 minutes.

Broil tomatoes 6–8 inches from heat until crumbs brown. Before serving, top each tomato half with a heaping spoonful of the sauce.

Serve with steak, roasts, or fried chicken.

YIELD: 6 SERVINGS

The Cook's Book
THE JUNIOR LEAGUE OF CEDAR RAPIDS, IOWA

·   ·   ·   ·   ·   ·   ·   ·   ·   ·   ·   ·   ·   ·   ·   ·

Tomato Soufflé

3 large ripe tomatoes (1½ pounds)
4 tablespoons butter
1 chicken bouillon cube
½ tablespoon tomato paste
Dash sugar
4 tablespoons flour
1 cup milk
Salt and cayenne
6 egg yolks
8 egg whites

Peel and seed tomatoes and chop very finely. Melt butter in a skillet and add bouillon cube and tomatoes. Cook over medium-low heat until juices are evaporated. Stir in tomato paste and sugar.

Remove from the heat. Stir in flour and then milk. Return to the heat and cook over medium heat, stirring, until the mixture starts to thicken. Season with salt and cayenne to taste. Remove from the heat again and beat in the egg yolks, one at a time.

In another bowl, beat the egg whites until they are stiff but not dry. In a separate bowl, carefully fold egg whites into tomato mixture.

Pour into buttered 2-quart soufflé dish and bake in preheated 375° oven for 17–20 minutes, or until browned on top and well risen.

Serve immediately.

YIELD: 8 SERVINGS

Discover Dayton
THE JUNIOR LEAGUE OF DAYTON, OHIO

Tomato-Onion-Zucchini Casserole

4–6 large tomatoes, peeled and sliced
6 zucchini, peeled and sliced
2–3 onions, peeled and sliced
Butter
Grated Parmesan cheese
Salt and pepper to taste
½ 8-ounce package seasoned stuffing

Layer vegetables in a casserole, dotting each layer with butter. Sprinkle with cheese mixed with salt and pepper and cover the top with stuffing. Dot with butter.

Bake for 1 hour at 300°.

YIELD: 8 SERVINGS

Marigolds to Munch On
THE JUNIOR LEAGUE OF PEORIA, ILLINOIS

Zucchini and Cheese Casserole

8–10 small zucchini
½ cup butter
1 cup shredded cheddar cheese
½ cup shredded Gruyère cheese
1 cup sour cream
1 teaspoon salt
½ teaspoon paprika
¼ cup chopped fresh chives
1 cup bread crumbs
¼ cup grated Parmesan cheese
Butter

Wash and boil whole zucchini until almost tender, about 10 minutes. Cut off ends and cut in half lengthwise. Arrange in shallow buttered 13 x 9 x 2-inch casserole.

Melt butter; add cheddar and Gruyère cheeses, sour cream, salt, paprika, and chives. Spoon over zucchini and sprinkle with bread crumbs and Parmesan cheese. Dot with butter and bake at 350° for 30–45 minutes, or until bubbly.

YIELD: 6 SERVINGS

Cincinnati Celebrates
THE JUNIOR LEAGUE OF CINCINNATI, OHIO

Zucchini Soufflé

1 medium zucchini, sliced
1 large onion, chopped
Salt, pepper, and celery salt
1 cup cracker crumbs
1½ tablespoons butter
½ cup grated Parmesan cheese
½ cup milk
2 eggs
1½ cups shredded cheddar cheese

Cook zucchini and onion until tender; drain and mash. Season with salt, pepper, and celery salt to taste. Add cracker crumbs, butter, Parmesan cheese, milk, and eggs.

Place in greased 2-quart casserole. Top with cheddar cheese. Bake at 350° for 40–45 minutes.

YIELD: 12 SERVINGS

THE JUNIOR LEAGUE OF YOUNGSTOWN, OHIO

. . . .

Leolo's Zucchini

1 onion, sliced
1 clove garlic, minced
¼ cup oil
2 pounds zucchini, sliced
4 cups diced peeled tomatoes
1 green pepper, seeded and chopped
Salt and pepper
Minced parsley
Grated Parmesan cheese

Recipe continues . . .

Sauté onion and garlic in the oil. Add zucchini, tomatoes, green pepper, and salt and pepper to taste. Cook until vegetables are tender.

Sprinkle with minced parsley and Parmesan cheese and serve hot.

YIELD: 8 SERVINGS

THE JUNIOR LEAGUE OF FARGO-MOORHEAD, NORTH DAKOTA/MINNESOTA

Poppy Seed Zucchini

¼ cup butter
4 cups sliced zucchini
⅓ cup chopped onion
½ cup sour cream
1 teaspoon salt
2 teaspoons paprika
2 teaspoons poppy seeds

Melt butter; add zucchini and onion. Cover and cook until tender.

Mix remaining ingredients. Stir gently into zucchini mixture and heat through. Do not boil.

YIELD: 4 SERVINGS

Cookbook
THE JUNIOR LEAGUE OF GRAND RAPIDS, MICHIGAN

Zucchini Chinese-Style

¼ cup bacon drippings
1 pound zucchini, thinly sliced
1 clove garlic
¼ cup water
1 small onion, sliced
2 tablespoons soy sauce

Combine all ingredients except soy sauce and stir-fry in skillet for 10 minutes. Remove garlic. Add soy sauce and cook 5 more minutes.

YIELD: 3–4 SERVINGS

Bestir Yourself
THE JUNIOR LEAGUE OF TOLEDO, OHIO

Zucchini Crepes

1 cup sifted all-purpose flour
1 teaspoon salt
¾ teaspoon baking powder
¾ teaspoon garlic powder
¼ teaspoon pepper
5 eggs
⅔ cup milk
2 cups finely shredded zucchini
¼ cup olive oil
2 cups sour cream
2 cups grated Parmesan cheese
Chopped parsley for garnish

Sift flour, salt, baking powder, garlic powder, and pepper into a bowl. Beat eggs; add milk and beat until blended. Add to the dry ingredients and blend. Add zucchini.

Recipe continues . . .

Heat 2 tablespoons olive oil on a griddle. Use ¼ cup batter for each crepe, spreading it into a 6-inch circle. Fry until golden brown on both sides, turning once.

Spread each crepe with 2 tablespoons sour cream and sprinkle with 2 tablespoons grated Parmesan cheese. Roll and arrange side by side in buttered shallow baking dish. Garnish with additional cheese and chopped parsley and reheat to serving temperature in 250° oven before serving.

YIELD: 14–16 CREPES

THE JUNIOR LEAGUE OF SOUTH BEND, INDIANA

. . . .

Stuffed Zucchini

6 zucchini
½ cup chopped raw spinach
2 tablespoons minced onion
Grated Parmesan cheese
2 tablespoons butter
1 cup bread crumbs
Salt and pepper
Crisply cooked bacon, crumbled

Cook zucchini in boiling salt water for 10 minutes. Cut zucchini in half lengthwise and scoop out centers. Mix pulp with raw spinach, minced onion, Parmesan cheese, and remaining ingredients except bacon. Fill zucchini shells with mixture and bake in 350° oven for 15 minutes.

Sprinkle with crumbled bacon pieces before serving.

YIELD: 6 SERVINGS

Marigolds to Munch On
THE JUNIOR LEAGUE OF PEORIA, ILLINOIS

. . . .

Vegetable Potpourri

1½ cups thinly sliced onion
2 cups julienne-sliced celery
1½ cups julienne-sliced carrot
2 cups French-style canned or fresh green beans
¾ cup thinly sliced green pepper
2 cups tomato wedges
1 6-ounce can sliced mushrooms with liquid
4 tablespoons butter
1 tablespoon sugar
2 teaspoons salt
1 teaspoon pepper
3 tablespoons quick-cooking tapioca

Combine all ingredients in large mixing bowl and mix well. Empty into a 3-quart casserole, cover, and bake at 325° for 1¼ hours.

YIELD: 12 SERVINGS

THE JUNIOR LEAGUE OF DES MOINES, IOWA

. . . .

Vegetable Collage

1 10-ounce package frozen French-style green beans
1 10-ounce package frozen baby lima beans or corn
1 10-ounce package frozen English peas
1 green pepper, thinly sliced
Salt and pepper
1 cup heavy cream, whipped
1 cup mayonnaise
Grated Parmesan cheese

Recipe continues . . .

Cook frozen vegetables separately. Parboil green pepper. Drain all vegetables; combine, and season to taste with salt and pepper.

Arrange vegetables in greased 2-quart casserole. Mix whipped cream and mayonnaise together and spoon over vegetables. Top with cheese. Bake at 300° for 30–40 minutes, or until brown on top.

YIELD: 8–10 SERVINGS

Sunflower Sampler
THE JUNIOR LEAGUE OF WICHITA, KANSAS

Salads and Salad Dressings

Antipasto Salad

1 4-ounce can chick peas, drained
1 6-ounce jar marinated artichoke hearts, quartered
1 2-ounce can anchovy filets, drained and diced
1 4-ounce jar pimentos, drained and diced
½ pound salami, cut into ¼-inch cubes
8 ounces mozzarella cheese, cut into ¼-inch cubes
12 pitted ripe olives
½ head iceberg lettuce, cut into bite-size pieces
1 celery heart, thinly sliced

DRESSING:
6 tablespoons olive oil
5 tablespoons wine vinegar
1 teaspoon salt
¼ teaspoon pepper

Combine chick peas, artichokes and liquid, anchovies, pimentos, salami, mozzarella, olives, lettuce, and celery in a large bowl.

Combine oil, vinegar, salt, and pepper in a jar. Shake well.

When ready to serve, pour dressing over salad and toss lightly.

Great with any meal.

YIELD: 12 SERVINGS

THE JUNIOR LEAGUE OF ROCKFORD, ILLINOIS

·   ·   ·   ·   ·   ·   ·   ·   ·   ·   ·   ·   ·   ·   ·   ·   ·   ·   ·

Marinated Artichokes and Brussels Sprouts

2 10-ounce packages frozen brussels sprouts, cooked
1–2 10-ounce packages artichoke hearts, cooked
1 small onion, chopped
4–6 ounces bottled Italian salad dressing

Combine all ingredients and marinate for 4–24 hours.

Serve on salad greens.

YIELD: 4 SERVINGS AS SALAD; 6–8 AS HORS D'OEUVRE

VARIATION:

Add canned button mushrooms, sliced green olives, or sliced black olives.

THE JUNIOR LEAGUE OF SPRINGFIELD, ILLINOIS

·　·　·　·　·　·　·　·　·　·　·　·　·　·　·　·

Marinated Asparagus

2 pounds fresh asparagus
½ cup olive oil
½ cup vegetable oil
1 clove garlic
1 teaspoon seasoned salt
½ teaspoon monosodium glutamate
1 teaspoon sugar
1 teaspoon fresh parsley

Cook asparagus in salted water until just fork-tender; drain. Combine remaining ingredients and pour over asparagus while it is still warm. Marinate at least 6 hours.

Serve at room temperature.

YIELD: 6–8 SERVINGS

THE JUNIOR LEAGUE OF EVANSVILLE, INDIANA

·　·　·　·　·　·　·　·　·　·　·　·　·　·

Avocado Tossed Salad

1 head lettuce
2 tomatoes, peeled and diced
½ cup chopped ripe olives
2 green onions, chopped
½ cup shredded cheese
1 cup crushed corn chips

DRESSING:
½ cup mashed avocado
1 tablespoon lemon juice
½ cup sour cream
⅓ cup vegetable oil
½ teaspoon seasoned salt
½ teaspoon sugar
¼ teaspoon salt
¼ teaspoon Tabasco
½ teaspoon chili powder

Mix dressing ingredients and chill.

Tear lettuce into bite-size pieces and combine with tomatoes, olives, onions, and cheese in a salad bowl.

When ready to serve, toss with the dressing. Add crushed corn chips just before serving.

YIELD: 4 SERVINGS

Sunflower Sampler
THE JUNIOR LEAGUE OF WICHITA, KANSAS

Beans, Beans, Beans

1 1-pound can cut green beans
1 1-pound can dark red kidney beans
1 1-pound can garbanzo beans
1 8-ounce can pitted ripe olives
1 red onion, thinly sliced
1 cup sweet pickle relish
½ cup minced green pepper
½ cup salad oil
⅓ cup red wine vinegar with garlic
¼ cup Burgundy
½ cup sugar
¼ teaspoon Italian seasoning
¼ teaspoon garlic salt

Drain beans and combine with olives, onion, pickle relish, and green pepper. Combine remaining ingredients and pour over bean-olive-relish mixture. Cover and refrigerate overnight.

YIELD: 8–10 SERVINGS

Tested, Tried, and True
THE JUNIOR LEAGUE OF FLINT, MICHIGAN

·   ·   ·   ·   ·   ·   ·   ·   ·   ·   ·   ·   ·   ·   ·   ·

Serbian Beet Salad

2 pounds young beets
2 tablespoons vinegar
2 tablespoons water
Salt to taste
1 teaspoon caraway seeds
2 teaspoons grated horseradish

Recipe continues . . .

Boil beets until tender, between 30–60 minutes. Peel and slice thinly. Dilute vinegar with water and pour over still-warm beets. Season with salt and caraway seeds and stir in grated horseradish.

Let stand 3–4 hours in refrigerator before serving.

YIELD: 4–5 SERVINGS

THE JUNIOR LEAGUE OF KANSAS CITY, KANSAS

Jellied Beet Salad

1 3-ounce package lemon gelatin
1 cup hot water
⅞ cup juice from beets
2 tablespoons lemon juice or vinegar
¼ teaspoon salt
½ teaspoon minced onion
1 tablespoon grated horseradish
½ cup chopped celery
2 tablespoons chopped green pepper
1 cup julienne-sliced beets
⅓ cup nuts

Dissolve gelatin in hot water. Add beet liquid, lemon or vinegar, and spices. Let mixture thicken and then fold in vegetables and nuts.

Pour into 1-quart ring mold and chill until firm.

YIELD: 5–6 SERVINGS

Peacock Pie and Other Perfections
THE JUNIOR LEAGUE OF BATTLE CREEK, MICHIGAN

Many-Color Relish

1½ cups coarsely shredded carrot
2 cups shredded cabbage
1 cup slivered red onion
1 cup diced celery
1 large green pepper, slivered
½ cup olive oil
5 tablespoons lemon juice
2 teaspoons salt
½ teaspoon sugar
Dash dry mustard
1 tablespoon dill weed

In large salad bowl, combine all the vegetables. Mix the olive oil, lemon juice, salt, sugar, mustard, and dill weed. Toss the oil dressing with the mixed vegetables and chill.

YIELD: 6 SERVINGS

THE JUNIOR LEAGUE OF TOLEDO, OHIO

.   .   .   .

Cabbage Crock Salad

1 large cabbage
2 onions
2 green peppers
2 carrots
2 cups sugar
2 cups vinegar
2 tablespoons celery seed
2 tablespoons mustard seed

Shred vegetables and soak for several hours in salted water (1 tablespoon salt to a quart of water). Drain, press out liquid, and dry with towel.

Recipe continues . . .

Heat sugar, vinegar, and celery and mustard seed, stirring until sugar is dissolved. Cool, mix with vegetables, and chill.

This salad is ready to eat when cold, but will remain crisp and fresh in refrigerator a long time if stored in covered glass container.

YIELD: 8 SERVINGS

The Discovery Shop Cookbook
THE JUNIOR LEAGUE OF SIOUX CITY, IOWA

. . . .

Old-Fashioned Sweet and Sour Cole Slaw

1½ pounds green cabbage, shredded
1 teaspoon salt
⅔ cup sugar
1 cup heavy cream or cultured sour cream
⅓ cup vinegar
1 cup slivered buttered toasted almonds (optional)

Place shredded cabbage in covered dish and refrigerate for several hours.

Mix ingredients in order given 30 minutes before serving. Chill and serve.

There is nothing better with fried or barbecued chicken.

YIELD: 8 SERVINGS

Sunflower Sampler
THE JUNIOR LEAGUE OF WICHITA, KANSAS

. . . .

Italian Carrot and Zucchini Salad

2 large carrots, sliced
2 medium zucchini, sliced
½ cup salad oil
¼ cup white wine vinegar
1 teaspoon salt
¼ teaspoon pepper
¼ teaspoon dry tarragon or ¾ teaspoon fresh
¼ teaspoon dry basil leaves or ¾ teaspoon fresh
¼ teaspoon oregano
Lettuce

Cook carrots for 3 minutes in 1 cup boiling salted water. Add zucchini and cook 2 minutes. (This is actually just steaming the zucchini.) Drain.

Mix oil, vinegar, salt, pepper, and herbs. Pour over hot vegetables. Cover and chill for several hours or overnight. Serve on lettuce.

The use of fresh herbs from your garden enhances the appearance and flavor. Vary the taste, if desired, by using an herbed vinegar or omitting one or more of the herbs and using some you have on hand. For instance, dilled vinegar and fresh dill with the basil and oregano are good.

YIELD: 2 SERVINGS

Bluff City Cooks
THE JUNIOR LEAGUE OF GREATER ALTON, ILLINOIS

. . . .

Cauliflower Salad

1 head cauliflower
1 head lettuce
1 onion, chopped
1 pound bacon, crisply fried and crumbled
1½ cups mayonnaise-type salad dressing
¼ cup sugar
⅓ cup grated Parmesan cheese

Recipe continues . . .

Chop cauliflower and lettuce quite fine and mix with onion and bacon.

Mix salad dressing, sugar, and Parmesan cheese and pour over the salad. Allow to stand several hours before serving (salad will shrink after it is mixed).

YIELD: 6–8 SERVINGS

THE JUNIOR LEAGUE OF FARGO-MOORHEAD, NORTH DAKOTA/MINNESOTA

. . . .

Japanese Chicken Salad

3–4 cooked chicken breasts, slivered
1½ heads lettuce, washed and torn
3 green onions, thinly sliced
1 3-ounce can chow mein noodles
1 4-ounce package slivered almonds
¼ cup poppy seeds or toasted sesame seeds

Mix first three ingredients. Add noodles, almonds, and poppy seeds to chicken mixture just before tossing with the dressing.

DRESSING:
4 tablespoons sugar
2 teaspoons salt
½ teaspoon pepper
4 tablespoons vinegar
½ cup salad oil

Combine dressing ingredients in container and shake to blend.

YIELD: 6 SERVINGS

THE JUNIOR LEAGUE OF YOUNGSTOWN, OHIO

. . . .

Chicken Salad Pie

2 cups cooked chicken, diced
¾ cup shredded cheddar cheese
½ cup diced celery
½ cup drained crushed pineapple
⅓ cup blanched slivered almonds or walnuts
½ teaspoon paprika
½ teaspoon salt
¾ cup mayonnaise
1 9-inch baked pastry shell
½ cup heavy cream, whipped
½ cup shredded carrot for garnish

Combine chicken with cheese, celery, pineapple, nuts, paprika, salt, and ½ cup of the mayonnaise; spread in baked pie shell.

Carefully fold together the whipped cream and remaining mayonnaise. Spread over salad in pie shell leaving 1 inch of salad around edge uncovered. Garnish with carrot. Chill until serving time, but at least 1 hour.

YIELD: 6 SERVINGS

THE JUNIOR LEAGUE OF SPRINGFIELD, ILLINOIS

· · · · · · · · · · · · · · · · · ·

Crabmeat Salad

2 cups canned crabmeat
¾ cup sliced celery
4 green onions, chopped
2 tablespoons toasted slivered almonds
¼ cup minced parsley
¼ cup mayonnaise
1 tablespoon prepared mustard
¼ cup heavy cream, whipped
Salt
Salad greens and lemon wedges for garnish

Recipe continues . . .

Combine crab, celery, onions, almonds, and parsley. Chill.

Fold mayonnaise and mustard into whipped cream. Add to crab mixture and mix lightly. Add salt to taste.

Mound in center of Cucumber Ring and garnish with greens and lemon wedges.

CUCUMBER RING:
1 3-ounce package lime gelatin
1¼ cups boiling water
1–2 tablespoons vinegar (or to taste)
1 tablespoon grated onion
¾ teaspoon salt
Dash pepper
1½ cups thinly sliced cucumbers

Dissolve gelatin in boiling water. Add vinegar, onion, salt, and pepper and chill until partially thickened. Stir in cucumber. Pour into ring mold and chill until firm.

YIELD: 8 SERVINGS

Tested, Tried, and True
THE JUNIOR LEAGUE OF FLINT, MICHIGAN

. . . .

Ring of Eggs

10 hard-boiled eggs
1½ tablespoons unflavored gelatin
⅓ cup cold water
1 cup boiling water
1½ cups mayonnaise
½ teaspoon salt
White pepper to taste
2 tablespoons catsup
3 tablespoons lemon juice
Tomato wedges and cucumber slices for garnish

Put eggs through ricer.

Add cold water to gelatin and let stand 5 minutes, then add boiling water and stir until gelatin is dissolved. Cool; add eggs. Combine remaining ingredients and stir. Empty mixture into a 9-inch ring mold and refrigerate at least overnight.

Unmold just before serving and garnish with tomato wedges and cucumber slices. Center may be filled with chicken or shrimp salad.

Egg ring may be prepared several days ahead.

YIELD: 1 9-INCH RING

The Cook's Book
THE JUNIOR LEAGUE OF CEDAR RAPIDS, IOWA

. . . .

Italian Salad

1 small head cauliflower, cut into flowerets
2 carrots, cut into 2-inch strips
1 green pepper, cut into 2-inch strips
1 3-ounce jar pimento-stuffed olives
¾ cup wine vinegar
½ cup salad oil
1 teaspoon salt
½ teaspoon pepper
½ cup water

Mix all ingredients and cook in covered saucepan for 5 minutes. Refrigerate, covered, at least 24 hours.

Drain and serve.

YIELD: 4–6 SERVINGS

THE JUNIOR LEAGUE OF YOUNGSTOWN, OHIO

. . . .

German Green Bean Salad

1 1-pound can whole green beans, drained
1 onion, cut into rings
1 1-pound can julienne-sliced beets, drained
1 bunch radishes, thinly sliced
¼ cup vinegar
2 tablespoons salad oil
½ teaspoon salt
1 tablespoon sugar
Dash pepper
Lettuce
Crisply fried bacon, crumbled

Combine beans, onion, beets, and radishes. Mix vinegar, salad oil, salt, sugar, and pepper. Pour over green bean mixture. Chill for several hours. Serve on lettuce. Top with crisp bacon.

YIELD: 8 SERVINGS

THE JUNIOR LEAGUE OF EVANSVILLE, INDIANA

. . . .

Green Bean Salad Mediterranean

1 9-ounce package frozen French-style green beans, thawed
1 medium onion, thinly sliced and separated into rings
1 3–4-ounce can sliced mushrooms, drained
⅓ cup Italian salad dressing
¼ teaspoon salt
Dash freshly ground pepper
2 medium tomatoes, cut into wedges, or cherry tomatoes

Drain thawed beans thoroughly. Place in salad bowl with onion rings and mushrooms.

Combine salad dressing, salt, and pepper. Add to vegetables and toss. Marinate in refrigerator at least 2 hours, tossing occasionally.

Just before serving, arrange tomatoes on salad.

YIELD: 4–6 SERVINGS

THE JUNIOR LEAGUE OF SAGINAW, MICHIGAN

Herring Luncheon Salad

1 16-ounce jar herring in wine sauce
1 large sweet onion, sliced
1 can seeded white grapes
1 3-ounce package blanched almonds
1 tablespoon sugar
2 medium apples, sliced
2 tablespoons fresh lemon juice
1 pint sour cream, whipped to soft peaks

Wash herring well in cold water, squeeze, and pat dry. Cut each herring in half. Mix with onion, grapes, almonds, sugar, apples, and lemon juice, then fold in sour cream. Refrigerate.

Serve on lettuce leaves with rye rounds for luncheon.

YIELD: 4 SERVINGS

Discover Dayton
THE JUNIOR LEAGUE OF DAYTON, OHIO

Seafood Macaroni Salad

2 cups shell macaroni, cooked and drained
2 tablespoons minced onion
2 teaspoons salt
¼ cup French salad dressing
1 teaspoon sweet basil
¼ teaspoon garlic powder
¼ teaspoon pepper
1 teaspoon lemon juice
1 cup cooked and diced shrimp
3 stalks celery, chopped
1 green pepper, diced
¼ cup mayonnaise
Bibb lettuce

Combine the first eight ingredients. Refrigerate for at least 1 hour. Add shrimp, celery, green pepper, and mayonnaise. Refrigerate for 20 hours. Serve on Bibb lettuce.

YIELD: 6 SERVINGS

THE JUNIOR LEAGUE OF TOLEDO, OHIO

· · · · · · · · · · · · · · · · · · · ·

Fresh Mushroom Salad

1 pound fresh mushrooms
3 green onions and tops, chopped
¼ cup fresh lemon juice
⅔ cup salad oil
½ teaspoon salt
½ teaspoon dry mustard
1 tablespoon Worcestershire sauce
Shredded lettuce
10 slices bacon, crisply fried and crumbled

Wash mushrooms and dry well. Cut off stems and use for some other purpose. Slice caps ⅛ inch thick. Combine mushrooms, onions, lemon juice, salad oil, salt, mustard, and Worcestershire sauce. Marinate in the refrigerator at least 4 hours.

Serve on bed of lettuce and sprinkle bacon on top.

YIELD: 10 SERVINGS

THE JUNIOR LEAGUE OF CHAMPAIGN-URBANA, ILLINOIS

· · · · · · · · · · · · · · · · · · ·

Toss Me Fancy

½ pound whole fresh mushrooms, trimmed
1 pound asparagus spears, cooked
1 pint cherry tomatoes, peeled
1 small onion, thinly sliced
1¼ cups olive oil
½ cup red wine vinegar
1 teaspoon cracked black pepper
2 teaspoons salt
1 clove garlic, minced
Salad greens

Cook mushrooms for 5 minutes in salted boiling water. Drain, cool, and mix with asparagus, tomatoes, and onion.

Combine olive oil, vinegar, and seasonings. Heat and pour over vegetables. Marinate at least overnight.

Serve on bed of crisp salad greens.

YIELD: 4–6 SERVINGS

The Cook's Book
THE JUNIOR LEAGUE OF CEDAR RAPIDS, IOWA

· · · · · · · · · · · · · · · · · · ·

Marinated Mushroom Salad

1 pound fresh mushrooms
1 tablespoon Dijon mustard (or to taste)
4 tablespoons red wine vinegar
½ teaspoon dried tarragon
½ teaspoon salt
½ teaspoon dried oregano (optional)
¼ teaspoon pepper
¾ cup olive oil
1 head lettuce, separated into leaves
1 avocado, peeled and thinly sliced
½ cup pitted black olives, sliced
3 tablespoons chopped parsley

Slice mushrooms evenly and set aside.

In a separate bowl, combine mustard and vinegar. Add tarragon, salt, oregano, pepper, and olive oil and blend thoroughly with whisk. Pour dressing over mushrooms, making sure each slice is thoroughly coated. Let stand for 2–3 hours.

Serve on bed of lettuce and garnish with avocado slices, black olives, and parsley.

YIELD: 6–8 SERVINGS

THE JUNIOR LEAGUE OF FARGO-MOORHEAD, NORTH DAKOTA/MINNESOTA

Mustard Ring

4 eggs
1 cup water
½ cup cider vinegar
¾ cup sugar
1 envelope unflavored gelatin
1½ tablespoons dry mustard
½ teaspoon turmeric
¼ teaspoon salt
½ pint heavy cream
2 tablespoons capers
⅔ cup finely chopped celery
Parsley for garnish

Beat eggs in top of double boiler. Add water and vinegar. Mix together sugar and unflavored gelatin plus mustard, turmeric, and salt; stir into egg mixture. Cook over boiling water until slightly thickened, stirring constantly.

Cool mixture until thick. Whip cream and fold in. Add capers and celery. Turn into a 1½-quart ring mold. Chill.

When firm, unmold. Garnish with parsley.

YIELD: 8 SERVINGS

THE JUNIOR LEAGUE OF DES MOINES, IOWA

Dilled Tossed Salad

½ head lettuce
½ bunch curly endive
¼ head red cabbage
1 medium onion, sliced
½ cup sliced radishes
2–4 ounces blue cheese, crumbled
¾ cup vegetable oil
½ teaspoon salt
¼ teaspoon garlic salt
¼ teaspoon onion salt
¼ teaspoon celery salt
½ teaspoon dry mustard
⅛ teaspoon pepper
½ teaspoon dill weed
1 tablespoon minced onion
¼ cup wine vinegar
1 tablespoon lemon juice
Salad greens

Tear lettuce and endive into bite-size pieces. Thinly slice cabbage across the grain to make ribbons. Separate sliced onions into rings. Toss lettuce, endive, cabbage, onion, radishes, and blue cheese together and chill.

Combine remaining ingredients except salad greens and mix well.

Just before serving, toss with greens.

YIELD: 6–8 SERVINGS

THE JUNIOR LEAGUE OF SAGINAW, MICHIGAN

Green on Green Salad

1 head iceberg lettuce
1 head romaine
1 head red leaf lettuce
1 package fresh spinach
1 head cauliflower, shredded

DRESSING:
1½ cups sour cream
1 cup mayonnaise
¾ teaspoon garlic powder
1 cup grated Parmesan cheese

Tear salad greens into bite-size pieces and toss with spinach in a salad bowl. Put cauliflower on top.

Combine all ingredients for salad dressing. When ready to serve, add dressing and toss.

YIELD: 15–20 SERVINGS

Sunflower Sampler
THE JUNIOR LEAGUE OF WICHITA, KANSAS

Michigan Caesar Salad

½ cup salad oil
¼ cup red wine vinegar
1 tablespoon lemon juice
1 large clove garlic, finely minced
2 teaspoons Worcestershire sauce
¼ teaspoon salt
Freshly ground pepper to taste
½ cup grated Parmesan cheese
½ cup (2 ounces) crumbled blue cheese
1 head lettuce, torn into bite-size pieces
1 cup croutons
1 egg

To make dressing, shake together first seven ingredients in screw-top jar. Chill in refrigerator a few hours or overnight to blend flavors.

Sprinkle cheeses over lettuce in salad bowl and top with croutons.

Before serving, add egg to dressing; shake until well blended. Pour dressing on salad and toss.

YIELD: 6–8 SERVINGS

THE JUNIOR LEAGUE OF SAGINAW, MICHIGAN

Fresh Garden Salad

¾ cup vinegar
¼ cup water
4½ teaspoons sugar
1½ teaspoons mustard seed
1½ teaspoons celery salt
¾ teaspoon salt
⅛ teaspoon pepper
6 ripe tomatoes, cut into eighths
1 large red onion, sliced
1 green pepper, sliced
1 large cucumber, peeled

In saucepan, combine vinegar, water, sugar, and seasonings. Bring to a boil and boil for 1 minute.

In a salad bowl, combine tomatoes, onion, and green pepper. Pour hot dressing over, cool, then refrigerate for 4 hours.

Slice in the cucumber just before serving.

YIELD: 6–8 SERVINGS

The Discovery Shop Cookbook
THE JUNIOR LEAGUE OF SIOUX CITY, IOWA

· · · · · · · · · · · · · · · · · · ·

Spinach Mushroom Salad

1 pound fresh spinach, washed and trimmed
2 hard-boiled eggs, chopped
¼ pound fresh mushrooms, trimmed and sliced
10 slices bacon, crisply fried and crumbled

Recipe continues . . .

DRESSING:
1 cup salad oil
½ cup sugar
⅓ cup catsup
¼ cup red wine vinegar
1 teaspoon Worcestershire sauce
1 teaspoon salt
½ small onion, minced

In salad bowl, combine spinach, eggs, and mushrooms. Mix dressing ingredients; toss with salad ingredients and top with crumbled bacon.

YIELD: 6 SERVINGS

THE JUNIOR LEAGUE OF DES MOINES, IOWA

. . . .

Susan's Spinach Salad

1 pound spinach, washed and well drained
1 cup white seedless grapes, halved
1 cup broken pecans

DRESSING:
1 pound small curd cottage cheese
½ tablespoon yellow mustard
1 teaspoon salt
2 tablespoons horseradish
½ cup sour cream
¼ cup sugar
3 tablespoons vinegar

The day before serving, gently mix together dressing ingredients and refrigerate.

To assemble salad, place spinach in bowl, add grapes and pecans, and toss with dressing.

YIELD: 6–8 SERVINGS

THE JUNIOR LEAGUE OF INDIANAPOLIS, INDIANA

Fresh Spinach Salad

1 pound spinach, washed and chilled
Chopped green onion
Green pepper, chopped
8 slices bacon
3 tablespoons brown sugar
2 tablespoons red wine vinegar
1 tablespoon lemon juice
1 tablespoon Worcestershire sauce
Garlic salt to taste
2 hard-boiled eggs, chopped

Fill salad bowl with spinach, green onion, and green pepper.

Fry bacon until crisp and set aside. Stir remaining ingredients except eggs into bacon drippings and pour over salad greens. Crumble bacon on top and sprinkle with chopped eggs.

YIELD: 6 SERVINGS

The Discovery Shop Cookbook
THE JUNIOR LEAGUE OF SIOUX CITY, IOWA

Spinach-Bacon Salad

1 cup olive or salad oil
¼ cup tarragon vinegar
1 teaspoon salt
1 teaspoon sugar
1 teaspoon paprika
1 teaspoon dry mustard
1 teaspoon Worcestershire sauce
1 teaspoon grated onion
¼ teaspoon dry basil
1 pound spinach, washed and trimmed
½ pound bacon, crisply fried and crumbled

Mix dressing ingredients and toss with spinach and bacon.

YIELD: 4 SERVINGS

Peacock Pie and Other Perfections
THE JUNIOR LEAGUE OF BATTLE CREEK, MICHIGAN

Spinach and Fruit Salads

Two different party salads with a flavorful dressing that complements both.

SPINACH SALAD:
1 pound fresh spinach, washed
2 heads Boston lettuce
2 avocados, peeled and cut in wedges
1 11-ounce can mandarin oranges, drained
1 Bermuda onion, thinly sliced

FRUIT SALAD:
1 pound fresh spinach, washed
2 heads Boston lettuce
1 pound purple grapes, halved and seeded
½ cup chopped walnuts
2 grapefruit, peeled and sectioned
3 oranges, peeled and sectioned

DRESSING:
1 cup oil
½ cup sugar
⅓ cup vinegar
1 tablespoon dry mustard
1 tablespoon celery seed
1 teaspoon salt
2 green onions, sliced

Salads: Tear greens into bite-size pieces into salad bowl. Add remaining ingredients.

Dressing: Combine all ingredients except onions in blender; blend thoroughly. Stir in onions and chill for several hours.

Add enough dressing to salads to moisten and toss lightly.

YIELD: 10–12 SERVINGS

Be Our Guest
THE JUNIOR LEAGUE OF MILWAUKEE, WISCONSIN

Junior League Gourmet Salad

½ cup vinegar
1 tablespoon celery seed
½ cup sugar
1 medium onion, chopped
1 teaspoon dry mustard
1 teaspoon salt
1 cup salad oil
2 heads lettuce or the equivalent in mixed greens
½ pound bacon, cooked and crumbled
1 4-ounce can sliced mushrooms, drained
1 2½–4-ounce jar salted pepitas
1 cup sour cream

In a saucepan, bring vinegar and celery seed to a boil; cool. In a blender or processor, blend sugar, chopped onion, mustard, and salt. Add vinegar and celery seed mixture and blend again. Add salad oil and blend again. Dressing may be prepared ahead and refrigerated.

To assemble salad, place greens in a bowl, top with bacon, mushrooms, and pepitas. Toss with dressing. Put small dabs of sour cream on top of salad and toss if desired.

YIELD: 8 SERVINGS

THE JUNIOR LEAGUE OF INDIANAPOLIS, INDIANA

Wilted Lettuce Salad

1 large head lettuce
2 stalks celery, chopped
6 slices red onion
5 slices bacon
1 tablespoon flour
½ cup vinegar
½ cup water
1 teaspoon dry mustard
½ cup sugar
1 teaspoon salt

Tear lettuce into large salad bowl. Add celery and onion.

Dice bacon and cook until browned. Add the rest of the ingredients and cook over low heat, stirring, until mixture thickens. Toss with salad while mixture is still warm.

YIELD: 6 SERVINGS

THE JUNIOR LEAGUE OF ROCKFORD, ILLINOIS

. . . .

Wilted Spinach Salad

2 pounds fresh spinach or mixed greens
½ pound fresh mushrooms, thinly sliced
½ pound bacon
½ cup sliced green onion
3 eggs
¼ cup sugar
¼ cup red wine vinegar
Salt and pepper to taste
2 hard-boiled eggs, sliced (optional)

Recipe continues . . .

Tear greens into salad bowl. Add mushrooms.

Cook bacon until crisp, remove from pan, crumble, and set aside. Sauté onion in bacon drippings until limp. Remove onion and drain on paper toweling. Combine eggs, sugar, vinegar, and salt and pepper and pour into warm bacon drippings. Cook, stirring constantly, until thickened. Add onion.

Pour dressing over greens, tossing lightly until well coated. Garnish with bacon and egg slices, if desired. Serve at once.

YIELD: 8 SERVINGS

THE JUNIOR LEAGUE OF INDIANAPOLIS, INDIANA

• • • • • • • • • • • • • • • • • • • •

Spring Salad

1 1-pound can tiny peas
1 1-pound can white corn
1 1-pound can French-style green beans
1 4-ounce jar pimentos, diced
1 cup finely chopped celery
1 cup finely chopped green pepper
½ cup finely chopped onion

DRESSING:
2 tablespoons water
¾ cup sugar
¾ cup cider vinegar
½ cup salad oil
½ teaspoon salt
¼ teaspoon pepper

Drain canned vegetables and mix with fresh vegetables.

Heat dressing ingredients until sugar is dissolved. Cool and pour over vegetables.

Refrigerate for 5 or 6 hours before serving.

YIELD: 8 GENEROUS SERVINGS

THE JUNIOR LEAGUE OF SPRINGFIELD, ILLINOIS

Mexican Chili Salad

4 large tomatoes, peeled and chopped
1 large red onion, chopped
2 heads lettuce, chopped
1 pound longhorn or cheddar cheese, shredded
1 15-ounce can kidney beans, drained
1 pound ground beef, cooked, drained, and crumbled
1 avocado, peeled and diced
1 cup broken corn chips
French salad dressing

Combine vegetables, cheese, beans, beef, avocado, and corn chips. Toss with enough French dressing to moisten.

YIELD: 12 SERVINGS

THE JUNIOR LEAGUE OF ST. PAUL, MINNESOTA

Potato Salad

2 pounds small white potatoes
Vinegar
2 cups chopped celery
1 hard-boiled egg, chopped
½ cup grated onion or green onion
¼ cup chopped cucumber
Mayonnaise to taste
Salt and pepper

Boil potatoes with jackets until barely done. Cool slightly. Peel and slice while hot. Sprinkle vinegar over potatoes and let stand several hours.
Add other ingredients and chill.

YIELD: 6 SERVINGS

Peacock Pie and Other Perfections
THE JUNIOR LEAGUE OF BATTLE CREEK, MICHIGAN

. . . .

Hot German Potato Salad

5–6 medium red potatoes
½ pound bacon
½ cup chopped onion
½ cup chopped celery
1 tablespoon flour
3 tablespoons sugar
1½ teaspoons salt
½ teaspoon celery seed
¼ teaspoon pepper
½ cup water
⅓ cup vinegar
¼ cup chopped pimento
¼ cup chopped green pepper
Parsley for garnish

Cook and cube potatoes into a 2-quart heat-resistant bowl or casserole.

Fry bacon until crisp; crumble and set aside. Sauté onion and celery in bacon drippings for 5 minutes. Remove from heat. Blend flour, sugar, salt, celery seed, and pepper. Stir into onion mixture with water and vinegar. Return to heat and boil for 1 minute. Pour over potatoes.

Add crumbled bacon, pimento, and green pepper. Cover and let stand for 1 hour.

Uncover and bake in 350° oven for 20 minutes, or until heated through. Garnish with parsley.

YIELD: 6 SERVINGS

THE JUNIOR LEAGUE OF ROCKFORD, ILLINOIS

·　·　·　·　·　·　·　·　·　·　·　·　·　·　·　·　·

Peas Vinaigrette

2 10-ounce packages frozen tiny peas, thawed
½ cup salad oil
3 tablespoons vinegar
2 tablespoons finely chopped green onion
2 tablespoons finely chopped sweet pickle
1 tablespoon minced parsley
1 tablespoon diced pimento
1 teaspoon salt
⅛ teaspoon pepper

Cook frozen peas by pouring 1–2 kettles of boiling water over them. Drain well and chill.

Combine remaining ingredients for dressing and put into small jar. Shake well. Pour dressing over chilled peas and let stand in refrigerator for 2 hours.

Before serving, toss lightly with a fork.

Recipe continues . . .

This is super served as a cold vegetable for a dinner party. Men really seemed to like it.

YIELD: 8 SERVINGS

THE JUNIOR LEAGUE OF KANSAS CITY, KANSAS

·   ·   ·   ·   ·   ·   ·   ·   ·   ·   ·   ·   ·   ·   ·

Rice Salad

4 cups cooked rice
½ cup chopped green onion
½ cup finely chopped celery
½ cup finely chopped, seeded, cucumber
¼ cup finely chopped green pepper
Fresh parsley, chopped
Fresh tarragon, chopped

VINAIGRETTE SAUCE:
12 tablespoons vegetable oil
4 tablespoons wine vinegar
1 teaspoon salt
24 grinds of the pepper mill

Blend the sauce ingredients together, then combine with the rice and vegetables. Pile on a platter or put into a salad bowl. Sprinkle the tarragon and parsley on top.

Refrigerate and serve cold.

YIELD: 8 SERVINGS

THE JUNIOR LEAGUE OF KANSAS CITY, KANSAS

·   ·   ·   ·   ·   ·   ·   ·   ·   ·   ·   ·   ·   ·   ·

Kraut Salad

1 1-pound 13-ounce can sauerkraut, drained, squeezed,
and chopped a bit
1 16-ounce can bean sprouts, sliced
1 cup celery, finely chopped
1 large green pepper, finely chopped
1 medium onion, finely chopped
1 2-ounce can pimento, chopped, or ½ cup chopped radishes
¾ cup vinegar
1½ cups sugar

Combine all vegetables. Heat vinegar and sugar; bring to a boil, cool, and pour over vegetables. Marinate for 24 hours.

This will keep a long time refrigerated. It can be used either as a salad or a relish.

YIELD: 8 SERVINGS

Marigolds to Munch On
THE JUNIOR LEAGUE OF PEORIA, ILLINOIS

Super Salad

1 head iceberg lettuce
1 head romaine
1 bunch spinach
2 small zucchini, sliced
1 small Bermuda onion, sliced
1 cup cubed feta cheese
½ cup fresh peas
½ cup sliced asparagus tips
2 cups olive oil
½ cup cider vinegar
1 clove garlic, mashed
1 cup sliced mushrooms
12 cherry tomatoes, halved
Salt
Freshly ground black pepper

Tear greens in bite-size pieces into salad bowl. Add zucchini, onion, cheese, peas, and asparagus. Chill until serving time.

Combine olive oil, vinegar, and garlic in a jar; shake vigorously. Just before serving, arrange mushrooms and tomatoes on salad. Pour dressing on top and toss lightly. Season to taste with salt and pepper.

YIELD: 10–12 SERVINGS

Be Our Guest
THE JUNIOR LEAGUE OF MILWAUKEE, WISCONSIN

Herbed Tomatoes

6 ripe tomatoes
1 teaspoon salt
¼ teaspoon coarse black pepper
½ teaspoon each thyme and marjoram
¼ cup finely chopped parsley
¼ cup chopped chives
⅔ cup salad oil
¼ cup tarragon vinegar

Peel tomatoes and place in bowl; sprinkle with seasonings and herbs. Combine oil and vinegar and pour over; cover and chill at least 1 hour, occasionally spooning the dressing over tomatoes.

At serving time, drain off dressing to pass in separate bowl.

YIELD: 6 SERVINGS

Peacock Pie and Other Perfections
THE JUNIOR LEAGUE OF BATTLE CREEK, MICHIGAN

· · · · · · · · · · · · · · · · · · ·

Soufflé Salad with Herbed Green Peas

2 3-ounce packages lemon gelatin
2 cups hot water
½ cup cold water
2 tablespoons lemon juice
1½ cups mayonnaise
1 teaspoon salt
¼ teaspoon celery salt
Dash Tabasco
1 tablespoon minced onion
1 cup coarsely shredded cucumber, drained
½ cup finely chopped celery
2 cups shredded cheddar cheese (about ½ pound)

Recipe continues . . .

Dissolve gelatin in hot water; add cold water, lemon juice, mayonnaise, salt, celery salt, Tabasco, and minced onion. Stir until well blended, then chill until firm around edges of dish. Remove from refrigerator and beat with electric or hand mixer until light and fluffy.

Fold in cucumber, celery, and cheese; mix well and pour into well-oiled 6-cup ring mold. Chill until firm.

Unmold on serving plate and fill center with Herbed Green Peas.

YIELD: 6–8 SERVINGS

HERBED GREEN PEAS:
2 10-ounce packages frozen green peas
⅔ cup finely sliced pickled onions
⅓ cup garlic or French salad dressing
½ teaspoon dried dill weed

Cook peas according to package directions until just tender; drain and chill. Combine peas with pickled onions, dressing, and dill; toss well to blend and turn into center of molded salad.

Peacock Pie and Other Perfections
THE JUNIOR LEAGUE OF BATTLE CREEK, MICHIGAN

· · · · · · · · · · · · · · · · · · ·

Hattie's Cucumber Salad

1 3-ounce package lime gelatin
¾ cup hot water
¼ cup lemon juice (or to taste)
1 teaspoon onion juice
1 cup sour cream or mayonnaise
1 cup chopped cucumber
Chopped pimento

Dissolve gelatin in water and lemon juice and chill until partially set. Fold in remaining ingredients and pour into 3-cup ring mold.

Chill until set. Unmold and garnish as desired.

YIELD: 5–6 SERVINGS

Peacock Pie and Other Perfections
THE JUNIOR LEAGUE OF BATTLE CREEK, MICHIGAN

· · · · · · · · · · · · · · · · · · · ·

Frozen Fruit Cups

6 ripe bananas, cut into small pieces
1 1-pound 4-ounce can crushed pineapple
2 1-pound 13-ounce cans apricots, coarsely chopped
2 tablespoons lemon juice
1 cup sugar
1 6-ounce can frozen orange juice
1 6-ounce can water

Combine all ingredients. Spoon into paper-lined muffin tins. Freeze.

Remove from freezer a few minutes before serving.

Keeps well in frozen bags. Can be served as salad or dessert. Children like this particularly.

YIELD: 30–40 CUPS

Cincinnati Celebrates
THE JUNIOR LEAGUE OF CINCINNATI, OHIO

· · · · · · · · · · · · · · · · · · · ·

Frozen Cranberry Salad

1 16-ounce can crushed pineapple, drained
1 1-pound can whole cranberry sauce
1 cup sour cream
½ cup chopped pecans
½ 2-ounce can shredded coconut

Combine all ingredients and spoon into a metal pan or ice cube trays. Freeze.

Cut in squares and serve.

YIELD: 12 SERVINGS

THE JUNIOR LEAGUE OF EVANSVILLE, INDIANA

. . . .

Molded Cranberry Salad

1 pound fresh cranberries
1 orange
1½ cups sugar
1 cup finely chopped English walnuts
1 pint boiling water
2 3-ounce packages lemon gelatin
1 cup chopped celery
Mayonnaise

Grind cranberries and orange; add sugar. Let stand 1 hour. Mix water and gelatin and let cool. Mix all the ingredients except mayonnaise together and chill overnight in an 8 x 10-inch pan. Serve with mayonnaise.

Particularly good with turkey.

YIELD: 12 SERVINGS

Bestir Yourself
THE JUNIOR LEAGUE OF TOLEDO, OHIO

. . . .

Raspberry–Bing Cherry Salad

1 16-ounce jar bing cherries
2 3-ounce packages raspberry gelatin
¼ cup lemon juice
1 10-ounce package frozen red raspberries
½ cup cream sherry
½ cup currant jelly
½ cup water

Drain juice from cherries into a pint measuring cup and add enough water to make 2 cups liquid. Heat to boiling. Dissolve gelatin in the boiling liquid. Cool to room temperature or until just warm. Add cherries, lemon juice, raspberries, cream sherry, and currant jelly which has been melted in ½ cup water.

Pour into a 1½-quart mold or 9-inch-square pan and chill until set. Makes a beautiful salad, especially for the holidays.

YIELD: 8 SERVINGS

THE JUNIOR LEAGUE OF TOLEDO, OHIO

. . . .

Strawberry Gelatin Mold

2 1-pound packages frozen strawberries
1 6-ounce package strawberry gelatin
1 13¼-ounce can crushed pineapple, drained
2 bananas, sliced
8 ounces cream cheese
½ cup sour cream
½ teaspoon salt

Thaw and drain strawberries, reserving juice. Add enough water to juice to make 2 cups liquid. Heat liquid to boiling and pour over gelatin. Cool. Add strawberries, pineapple, and bananas. Divide into two portions.

Recipe continues . . .

Pour half the gelatin mixture into a 6½-cup mold or pan. Chill until firm. Mix cream cheese, sour cream, and salt until smooth. Spread cheese mixture carefully over the firm gelatin mixture. Chill a short time, then add remaining gelatin mixture. Chill until firm.

YIELD: 12 SERVINGS

Tested, Tried, and True
THE JUNIOR LEAGUE OF FLINT, MICHIGAN

· · · · · · · · · · · · · · · · · · · ·

Emerald Salad Ring

1 3-ounce package lime or lemon gelatin
¾ cup hot water
1 cup creamed cottage cheese
1 cup mayonnaise
¾ cup unpeeled, shredded, and drained cucumber
2 tablespoons grated onion
½ cup slivered almonds

Dissolve gelatin in hot water. Cool until slightly set.
   Blend cottage cheese and mayonnaise in blender, then add cucumber, onion, and almonds. Fold into gelatin and empty into a 5-cup ring mold. Chill until set.

YIELD: 8–10 SERVINGS

THE JUNIOR LEAGUE OF YOUNGSTOWN, OHIO

· · · · · · · · · · · · · · · · · ·

Thanksgiving Molded Salad

¾ cup sugar
1 3-ounce package strawberry gelatin
1 3-ounce package pineapple gelatin
1¾ cups boiling water
1 15-ounce can pineapple chunks
1 cup orange juice
2 cups sliced cranberries
2 cups chopped unpeeled apple
1 cup halved and seeded Tokay grapes
½ cup chopped walnuts
½ cup chopped celery (optional)

Dissolve sugar and gelatins in boiling water; drain pineapple chunks, reserving syrup. Add pineapple syrup and orange juice to sugar and gelatin water and chill until partly set. Add cranberries, apple, grape halves, pineapple chunks, nuts, and chopped celery; mix to distribute evenly in gelatin.

Pour into individual molds or one rectangular cake pan and chill until firm.

Serve on crisp lettuce leaves. Pass favorite salad dressing, sour cream, or yogurt dressing.

YIELD: 12 SERVINGS

THE JUNIOR LEAGUE OF ST. PAUL, MINNESOTA

Pear Avocado Salad

1 16-ounce can pear halves
1 tablespoon vinegar
¼ teaspoon salt
1 3-ounce package lime gelatin
3 ounces cream cheese, softened
1 medium avocado, pitted, peeled, and diced
Salad greens

Drain and dice pears, reserving syrup; set aside. Add enough water to syrup to make 1¾ cups liquid. Bring the syrup, vinegar, and salt to a boil. Add lime gelatin and stir until dissolved. Gradually add ⅓ cup of the hot gelatin to the cream cheese; beat until smooth. Pour into a 4-cup mold and chill until almost firm.

Chill remaining gelatin until partially set; fold in pears and avocado. Spoon gently over cream cheese layer and chill until firm.

To serve, unmold on salad greens.

YIELD: 6 SERVINGS

THE JUNIOR LEAGUE OF SOUTH BEND, INDIANA

· ·

Schomer's Salad Dressing

¼ cup catsup
¾ cup vinegar
1½ cups sugar
1 teaspoon paprika
1 teaspoon salt
1 cup salad oil

Mix all ingredients except oil in mixer. Add oil and mix again.

Excellent on both fruit and green salads.

YIELD: 2 CUPS

THE JUNIOR LEAGUE OF YOUNGSTOWN, OHIO

· ·

Bacon Dressing

6 slices bacon
½ cup mayonnaise
¼ cup French salad dressing
2 tablespoons vinegar
2 tablespoons chopped onion
2 tablespoons finely chopped parsley
2 tablespoons chopped capers

Cook bacon until crisp. Drain and crumble.

Mix together mayonnaise, French dressing, vinegar, onion, parsley, and capers. Chill.

Serve over green salads. Sprinkle bacon on top.

YIELD: 1 CUP

Peacock Pie and Other Perfections
THE JUNIOR LEAGUE OF BATTLE CREEK, MICHIGAN

· · · · · · · · · · · · · · · · · ·

Pineapple Salad Dressing

3 tablespoons sugar
4 tablespoons flour
1 cup pineapple juice
2 eggs, well beaten
2 tablespoons butter
1 cup heavy cream, whipped

Mix sugar and flour with a little pineapple juice to make a paste. Add the rest of the juice and cook over simmering water until thick.

When thick, add eggs and butter. Cook for 10 minutes longer, stirring. Cool and fold in whipped cream.

This is especially nice when dressing is placed in a scooped-out pineapple half. Dunk strawberries and pineapple chunks into dressing.

YIELD: ABOUT 2 CUPS

THE JUNIOR LEAGUE OF INDIANAPOLIS, INDIANA

Sour Cream Dressing

1½ cups sour cream
½ cup cider vinegar
¾ cup oil
2 tablespoons grated onion
2 tablespoons horseradish
2 tablespoons chopped capers
1 teaspoon each dill seed, paprika, and salt
Freshly ground black pepper

Combine all ingredients. Shake well before serving.

YIELD: ABOUT 3 CUPS

The Cook's Book
THE JUNIOR LEAGUE OF CEDAR RAPIDS, IOWA

· ·

Blue Cheese Salad Dressing

3 tablespoons chopped green onion
½ cup mayonnaise
1 clove garlic, minced
¼ cup minced parsley
1 tablespoon anchovy paste
1 cup sour cream
¼ cup wine vinegar
1 tablespoon lemon juice
¼ cup crumbled blue cheese
¼ teaspoon salt
Dash freshly ground pepper

Add the chopped onion to the mayonnaise. Add garlic and parsley. Mix anchovy paste with the sour cream and add this to the mayonnaise mixture. Thin with vinegar and lemon juice. Add crumbled blue cheese. Beat thoroughly and add salt and pepper to taste.

Best chilled overnight.

YIELD: ABOUT 2½ CUPS

Discover Dayton
THE JUNIOR LEAGUE OF DAYTON, OHIO

· ·

Annor's Dressing

1 cup sugar
1 tablespoon flour
1–3 teaspoons celery seed
½ teaspoon turmeric
½ teaspoon dry mustard
½ cup water
½ cup cider vinegar
1 egg, lightly beaten
About ½ cup mayonnaise

Combine dry ingredients in saucepan and add water, vinegar, and egg. Cook and stir until thickened. Cool. When cold, add about ½ cup mayonnaise, or the amount required to obtain the desired consistency of dressing.

Cover and refrigerate.

A wonderful cooked dressing for potato salad or cole slaw, or mixed with ground ham for a delicious and different ham salad. If making potato salad, pour the dressing on the potato chunks while they are still hot—the flavor permeates.

YIELD: 2 CUPS

Discover Dayton
THE JUNIOR LEAGUE OF DAYTON, OHIO

Tarragon Dressing

½ cup salad oil
¼ cup lemon juice
3 tablespoons tarragon vinegar
2 tablespoons sugar
2 tablespoons minced onion
1 clove garlic, minced
1 teaspoon salt
½ teaspoon dry mustard
Freshly ground black pepper

Combine all ingredients in jar.

Excellent served on salad greens with cooked, drained artichoke hearts, radishes, avocado, and crisp, warm croutons.

YIELD: SCANT CUP

Peacock Pie and Other Perfections
THE JUNIOR LEAGUE OF BATTLE CREEK, MICHIGAN

Golden Baehr Celery Seed Dressing

1 scant cup sugar
½ teaspoon salt
1 teaspoon dry mustard
1 tablespoon celery seed
1 cup salad oil
Juice and pulp of 2 lemons

Recipe continues . . .

Mix dry ingredients. Add oil and lemon, alternately, beating thoroughly between additions. Chill.

Great served on fruit salad.

YIELD: 1¼ CUPS

Discover Dayton
THE JUNIOR LEAGUE OF DAYTON, OHIO

· · · · · · · · · · · · · · · · · · · ·

Honey Dressing

⅔ cup sugar
⅓ cup honey
½ cup vinegar
1 teaspoon dry mustard
1 teaspoon paprika
1 teaspoon celery seed
¼ teaspoon salt
1 cup salad oil

Mix together all ingredients except the oil. Add the oil slowly while mixing vigorously.

Can be made in the blender very easily.

Goes well with grapefruit sections.

YIELD: ABOUT 2 CUPS

THE JUNIOR LEAGUE OF TOLEDO, OHIO

· · · · · · · · · · · · · · · · · · · ·

Breads and
Coffee Cakes

Talbot House Crackers

4 cups flour
2 tablespoons sugar
1 teaspoon salt
½ teaspoon baking powder
½ cup butter
About 1 cup milk

Sift together dry ingredients. Cut in butter with a pastry blender until mixture resembles meal. Stir in enough milk to make a stiff dough.

Roll out ⅛–¼ inch thick on a floured cloth. Cut with floured round cookie cutter. Prick entire surface with tines of a fork and brush lightly with milk.

Place on ungreased baking sheet. Bake in preheated 425° oven for 15–18 minutes, or until light golden.

YIELD: 3–4 DOZEN CRACKERS

Discover Dayton
THE JUNIOR LEAGUE OF DAYTON, OHIO

.   .   .   .

Quick Butter Sticks

¼ cup butter or margarine
1 10-biscuit package refrigerated biscuits
Poppy seeds or sesame seeds

Heat oven to 450°. Melt the butter and pour half into an 8-inch-square pan. Take unbaked biscuits from can, pull them, and twist to approximately 8-inch lengths. Place in pan and pour remaining butter over. Sprinkle with poppy seeds or sesame seeds.

Bake 8–10 minutes in the preheated oven. Let stand in pan a couple of minutes to absorb butter.

Recipe may easily be increased.

YIELD: 10 STICKS

Bluff City Cooks
THE JUNIOR LEAGUE OF GREATER ALTON, ILLINOIS

·   ·   ·   ·   ·   ·   ·   ·   ·   ·   ·   ·   ·   ·   ·   ·   ·   ·

Helen's Natural Bread

4½ cups warm water
4 envelopes active dry yeast
½ cup oil
½ cup honey
4 teaspoons salt
½ cup wheat germ
½ cup cracked wheat
½ cup rye flour
½ cup soy flour
4½ cups whole-wheat flour
6 cups unbleached all-purpose flour

Combine warm water and yeast. Set aside. In a large bowl, combine oil, honey, salt, and wheat germ. Stir in cracked wheat, rye flour, soy flour, and yeast mixture.

Beat in the whole-wheat flour, 1 cup at a time; then work in enough of the all-purpose flour, 1 cup at a time, to make a firm dough. Knead the dough on a floured board until smooth and elastic, usually 20–25 minutes. Let the bread rise in warm place (85°–89°) for about 1½–2 hours. Punch down, cut the dough into four pieces, and let rest for 10 minutes.

Shape dough into loaves, put into oiled 4 x 8-inch bread pans, and let

Recipe continues . . .

rise again for approximately 1 hour, or until dough is rounded nicely over edges of pans.

Bake at 350° for 45–60 minutes. Remove from pans to a rack to cool.

YIELD: 4 LOAVES

THE JUNIOR LEAGUE OF CHAMPAIGN-URBANA, ILLINOIS

Quick Bran Bread

1 cup 100 percent bran cereal
½ cup raisins
½ cup molasses
2 tablespoons shortening
¾ cup boiling water
1 egg
½ teaspoon salt
½ teaspoon cinnamon
½ teaspoon baking soda
1 cup flour

Combine bran, raisins, molasses, and shortening. Pour hot water over mixture and stir until shortening is melted. Add egg and beat until blended. Add remaining dry ingredients; stir until just blended.

Pour into greased 5 x 9-inch loaf pan. Bake at 350° for 35 minutes.

YIELD: 1 LOAF

Peacock Pie and Other Perfections
THE JUNIOR LEAGUE OF BATTLE CREEK, MICHIGAN

High-Fiber Whole-Wheat Bread

3 cups whole-wheat flour
¼ cup sugar
1 tablespoon salt
2 envelopes active dry yeast
2¼ cups milk
¼ cup cooking oil
1 egg
3–4 cups all-purpose flour

Combine 2 cups whole-wheat flour with the sugar, salt, and yeast in a large mixing bowl. Heat milk and oil in saucepan over low heat until warm but not hot (120°–130°). Add egg and warm milk to the flour mixture. Beat 30 seconds at low speed and 3 minutes at medium speed.

By hand, gradually stir in the remaining 1 cup whole-wheat flour and 3–4 cups all-purpose flour to form a soft dough. Knead about 1 minute on a floured surface until smooth and elastic.

Place dough in greased 2½-quart bowl, turning dough to grease all sides. Cover dough; let rise in a warm place until doubled in bulk, about 1 hour.

Punch down dough. Shape into two loaves and place in two greased 4 x 8-inch loaf pans. Cover and let rise in warm place for 30 minutes. Bake in 350° oven for 40 minutes. Remove from pans immediately and cool on rack.

Children who don't like whole-wheat bread seem to like this bread.

YIELD: 2 LOAVES

THE JUNIOR LEAGUE OF SOUTH BEND, INDIANA

Gang-Gang's Brown Bread

½ cup brown sugar
2 teaspoons salt
1 egg, beaten
6 tablespoons melted margarine
1½ cups scalded milk
1 compressed yeast cake or envelope active dry yeast
½ cup warm water
3 cups graham flour
3 cups white flour
Oil

Stir sugar, salt, egg, and margarine into scalded milk; cool until lukewarm.

In a large mixing bowl, crumble or sprinkle yeast into warm water. Stir until combined. Stir milk mixture into yeast. Add half of each of the flours and beat until smooth. Stir in remaining flour.

Turn dough out onto floured board and knead until elastic and smooth. Place in a greased bowl and brush with oil. Cover and let rise in a warm place for 1½–2 hours, or until double in bulk.

Punch down and put into two 9 x 5 x 2½-inch greased loaf pans. Let rise 30 minutes to 1 hour, or until double.

Bake in preheated 350° oven for 35–40 minutes.

YIELD: 2 LOAVES

Discover Dayton
THE JUNIOR LEAGUE OF DAYTON, OHIO

Amish Rye Bread

1 envelope active dry yeast
1 tablespoon sugar
¼ cup warm water
1 quart warm water
3 cups rye flour
2 tablespoons salt
3 tablespoons caraway seed
1 tablespoon melted shortening
9 cups all-purpose flour

Dissolve yeast and sugar in the ¼ cup warm water. Let stand in a warm place until mixture is frothy.

Pour the quart of warm water in a very large bowl, about 8–10 quarts. Add rye flour, salt, caraway seed, shortening, and yeast mixture. Mix well. The batter should be about the consistency of heavy pancake batter. This is called the "sponge."

Let rise in a warm place for about 1½ hours, or until bubbles start to form on top of the dough. Gradually mix in as much of the all-purpose flour as is needed to make a firm dough. Turn out on floured board and knead about 10 minutes. Place in greased bowl and let rise again until double in bulk, about 1½–2 hours. Knead again for 10 minutes.

Form into two loaves and put in greased and floured loaf pans. Let rise until double in bulk. Bake for 1 hour in a 375° oven.

Especially good for corned beef sandwiches.

YIELD: 2 LOAVES

THE JUNIOR LEAGUE OF SOUTH BEND, INDIANA

Herb Bread

6 cups all-purpose flour
2 envelopes active dry yeast
2 tablespoons sugar
1 teaspoon salt
½ cup oats
¼ cup bran
¼ cup dry milk
1–2 cups wheat germ
1–2 tablespoons dehydrated onion
¼ teaspoon sage
¼ teaspoon celery seed
1–2 tablespoons dried parsley
1–2 teaspoons each oregano, thyme, marjoram, and black pepper
¼ cup melted butter
2¼ cups hot water
1 egg

Mix 2 cups flour in mixer bowl with the other dry ingredients. Add butter and water and beat for 2 minutes at medium speed. Add 1 cup flour and the egg and beat for 1 minute at high speed. Add remaining 3 cups flour.

Knead dough until smooth, then let rest for 20 minutes. Punch dough down, shape into two loaves, and put into greased pans. Let rise for 1–2 hours, or until double in bulk, then bake in a 400° oven for 20–30 minutes.

YIELD: 2 LOAVES

THE JUNIOR LEAGUE OF ROCKFORD, ILLINOIS

Herbed Beer Bread

3 cups self-rising flour
3 tablespoons sugar
2 tablespoons dried parsley flakes
1½ teaspoons dill weed
½ teaspoon rubbed sage (optional)
12 ounces beer

In large bowl, combine the dry ingredients. Add beer and stir only until mixed. The beer will foam while stirring.

Spoon into a greased 9 x 5 x 2½-inch loaf pan. Bake in preheated 350° oven for 30–40 minutes, or until lightly browned. Cool before slicing.

YIELD: 1 LOAF

Discover Dayton
THE JUNIOR LEAGUE OF DAYTON, OHIO

· ·

Dilly Casserole Bread

1 envelope active dry yeast
¼ cup warm water
1 cup creamed cottage cheese, heated to lukewarm
2 tablespoons sugar
1 tablespoon instant minced onion
1 tablespoon butter
2 teaspoons dill seed
½ teaspoon sesame seed
1 teaspoon salt
¼ teaspoon baking soda
1 egg
2¼–2½ cups all-purpose flour
Softened butter
Coarse salt

Recipe continues . . .

Soften yeast in water. Combine the cottage cheese, sugar, onion, butter, dill seed, sesame seeds, salt, soda, egg, and softened yeast in mixer bowl. Add flour slowly to form a stiff dough, beating well after each addition. (For the first addition of flour, use mixer on low speed.) Cover. Let rise in warm place (90°–95°) until light and doubled in bulk, about 50–60 minutes.

Stir dough down. Turn into well-greased casserole. Let rise in warm place until light, about 30–40 minutes. Bake at 350° for 40–50 minutes, or until golden brown. Brush with soft butter and sprinkle with coarse salt.

YIELD: 1 ROUND LOAF

Tested, Tried, and True
THE JUNIOR LEAGUE OF FLINT, MICHIGAN

Challah

2 envelopes active dry yeast
1 teaspoon sugar
1¾ cups warm water
6 scant cups flour
⅓ cup sugar
1 teaspoon salt
3 eggs
⅓ cup oil
Poppy seeds

Combine yeast, the 1 teaspoon sugar, and ¾ cup warm water in a bowl. Stir and cover.

Mix flour, the ⅓ cup sugar, and salt.

Beat eggs. Spoon out 3 tablespoons and reserve. Combine remaining egg with the oil and 1 cup warm water. Pour yeast mixture and egg mixture into flour alternately and mix well. Let rest for 5 minutes.

Knead dough for 6–8 minutes, or until elastic. Put into oiled bowl and turn dough around so it is oiled on all sides. Let rise for 2 hours, or until doubled in bulk. Punch down, knead again, and cut in half.

Divide each half into three parts and shape each part into a long roll. Braid 3 rolls together and put into a greased loaf pan. Repeat with other half of dough. Let rise for 45–60 minutes.

Brush top of loaves with reserved egg and sprinkle with poppy seeds. Bake at 350° for 45–60 minutes. Remove from pans immediately to cool on wire rack.

YIELD: 2 LOAVES

THE JUNIOR LEAGUE OF KANSAS CITY, KANSAS

Molasses Soda Bread

2 cups whole-wheat flour
1 cup white flour
½ cup sugar
1 teaspoon salt
2 teaspoons baking soda
2 cups buttermilk
½ cup molasses
1 cup seeded raisins (optional)

Combine whole-wheat flour, white flour, sugar, and salt. Stir the baking soda into the buttermilk, then stir the buttermilk into dry ingredients along with the molasses. Fold in raisins if desired.

Pour into two 4 x 8-inch greased loaf pans and let sit at room temperature for 1 hour. Bake in preheated 250° oven for 1–1¼ hours.

Recipe continues . . .

This freezes well and is great sliced and spread with cream cheese. Nutritious, too!

YIELD: 2 LOAVES

THE JUNIOR LEAGUE OF CHAMPAIGN-URBANA, ILLINOIS

· · · · · · · · · · · · · · · · · ·

Irish Oatmeal Bread

3 cups sifted all-purpose flour
1¼ cups quick rolled oats
1½ tablespoons baking powder
1½ teaspoons salt
1 egg
¼ cup honey
1½ cups milk
1 tablespoon butter or margarine

Preheat oven to 350°. Grease well a 9 x 5 x 3-inch loaf pan; set aside.

In a large bowl, mix flour, oats, baking powder, and salt.

In a medium bowl, using rotary beater, beat egg with honey and milk to mix well. Pour egg mixture into oat mixture, stirring with a wooden spoon just until dry ingredients are moistened (mixture will not be smooth).

Spread batter in pan. Bake 1¼ hours or until crusty and cake tester inserted in the center comes out clean. Turn loaf out of pan on wire rack. While still warm, brush top with melted butter.

This bread is delicious toasted and spread with butter and honey.

YIELD: 1 LOAF

Gourmet Gab
THE JUNIOR LEAGUE OF SAGINAW, MICHIGAN

· · · · · · · · · · · · · · · · · ·

Agnes Daley's Irish Soda Bread

2 tablespoons shortening
1 cup sugar
1 egg
1 teaspoon vanilla
1½ cups buttermilk
½ cup seedless raisins
2 teaspoons caraway seeds
1 teaspoon salt
1 teaspoon baking soda
3 teaspoons baking powder
3½ cups all-purpose flour

Blend shortening and sugar. Beat the egg and add vanilla and buttermilk. Combine the above two mixtures and add the raisins and caraway seeds.

Gradually add and mix in the salt, soda, baking powder, and flour. Knead well with hands.

Bake in an iron skillet lined with brown paper for 1¼ hours at 325°, or until done.

YIELD: 1 LOAF

THE JUNIOR LEAGUE OF FARGO-MOORHEAD, NORTH DAKOTA/MINNESOTA

Limpa

1 envelope active dry yeast
¼ cup warm water
½ cup firmly packed brown sugar
⅓ cup molasses
2 tablespoons orange marmalade
1 tablespoon butter
1 tablespoon salt
2 teaspoons caraway seeds
½ teaspoon anise
1½ cups hot water
4–4½ cups flour
2 cups rye flour

Soften yeast in warm water. Let stand 5–10 minutes.

Put sugar, molasses, marmalade, butter, salt, caraway seeds, and anise in large mixing bowl. Add hot water and blend well. When lukewarm, beat in 1 cup flour. Blend in softened yeast. Add rye flour; beat until very smooth. Beat in enough remaining flour to make a soft dough.

Turn onto a lightly floured surface. Let rest 5–10 minutes. Knead until smooth and elastic, 7–10 minutes. Form dough into a large ball. Put in a deep buttered bowl. Turn to butter top. Cover with wax paper and a towel and let stand in warm place (80°) until doubled in bulk, about 1½ hours.

Punch down with fist; turn out on a lightly floured surface. Divide dough into two portions; shape into balls. Cover; let rest 5–10 minutes. Transfer to greased baking sheet. Cover and let rise until doubled in bulk.

Bake at 375° for 25–30 minutes, or until lightly browned. Cool on racks.

YIELD: 2 LOAVES

Soupçon
THE JUNIOR LEAGUE OF CHICAGO, ILLINOIS

· ·

Swedish Rye Bread

2 envelopes active dry yeast
1 teaspoon sugar
½ cup warm water
2 cups scalded milk
2 cups water
1 tablespoon salt
2 tablespoons shortening
3–4 cups medium rye flour
1 cup brown sugar
6–7 cups white flour

Dissolve yeast and sugar in the ½ cup warm water. Add milk, 2 cups water, salt, shortening, and rye flour. Let rise 1 hour.

Add the brown sugar and the white flour. Let rise in greased bowl until double in bulk. Knead until easy to handle. Knead again and shape into round loaves.

Place loaves on greased baking sheets. When they are double in bulk, bake at 350° for about 40 minutes.

YIELD: 5–6 LOAVES

Cookbook
THE JUNIOR LEAGUE OF GRAND RAPIDS, MICHIGAN

Sweet Saffron Bread

1 compressed yeast cake or envelope active dry yeast
¼ cup warm water
1 tablespoon sugar
¼ cup margarine
¾ cup sugar
1 teaspoon salt
1 cup very hot milk
¾ teaspoon saffron
¾ cup hot water
6 cups sifted all-purpose flour
½ cup seeded raisins, softened in warm water and drained
¼ cup currants, softened in water or red wine and drained

Soften yeast in lukewarm water with the 1 tablespoon sugar.

In large mixing bowl, combine margarine, the ¾ cup sugar, salt, and hot milk.

Soak the saffron in the hot water for 10 minutes. Strain and add to milk mixture. Cool to lukewarm, then stir in softened yeast.

Mix 4 cups flour with the fruit and add to yeast mixture. Blend until smooth. Work in enough of the remaining 2 cups flour to make a soft dough. Turn out on floured board and knead until smooth. Return to bowl, cover lightly, and put in warm place for 2 hours, or until double in bulk.

Punch dough down, cut in half, and shape each half into a loaf. Bake on greased baking sheet in 350° oven for 45 minutes.

YIELD: 2 LOAVES

THE JUNIOR LEAGUE OF ST. PAUL, MINNESOTA

Spicy Apple Quick Bread

3 cups sifted all-purpose flour
1½ teaspoons baking soda
1½ teaspoons salt
1½ teaspoons cinnamon
¾ teaspoon nutmeg
½ teaspoon allspice
¼ teaspoon ground cloves
¾ cup shortening
1 cup plus 2 tablespoons light brown sugar, packed
3 eggs
1½ teaspoons vanilla
1½ cups shredded peeled apple
3 tablespoons cider vinegar plus water to make ¾ cup
¾ cup chopped walnuts

Mix and sift flour, baking soda, salt, and spices.

Cream shortening and sugar. Add eggs one at a time, beating well after each addition. Add vanilla. Stir in flour mixture, alternating with apples and vinegar liquid. Stir in walnuts.

Turn into greased 11 x 4 x 2-inch loaf pan and bake at 350° for 1½ hours, or until done. Cool on wire rack.

YIELD: 1 LOAF

THE JUNIOR LEAGUE OF TOLEDO, OHIO

Apricot Bread

1 cup dried apricots
½ cup white raisins
2 cups water
2 cups sugar
Dash cinnamon (optional)
Dash cloves (optional)
Dash nutmeg (optional)
1 teaspoon salt
¾ cup butter
2 eggs, beaten
4 cups sifted flour
2 teaspoons baking soda

Cut apricots into four or five pieces each and cook with the raisins in the water for 5 minutes. Add the sugar, spices, salt, and butter; cool.

When cool, add the eggs, flour, and soda. Pour into three lightly greased 8 x 5 x 3-inch loaf pans and bake at 350° for 45–55 minutes.

YIELD: 3 LOAVES

THE JUNIOR LEAGUE OF TOLEDO, OHIO

. . . .

Molly's Lemon Bread

1 lemon
6 tablespoons butter or margarine
1⅓ cups sugar
2 eggs
1½ cups sifted flour
1 teaspoon baking powder
½ teaspoon salt
½ cup milk

Grate lemon rind and squeeze out juice. Set aside.

Cream shortening, add 1 cup sugar and eggs and cream well. Add dry ingredients alternately with milk. Add 1 teaspoon grated lemon rind.

Line 9 x 5 x 3-inch loaf pan with wax paper, being sure wax paper comes over the top edges of pan. Spoon batter into prepared pan and bake 15 minutes in 350° oven, then for another 45 minutes in 325° oven.

Meanwhile, add remaining lemon rind to juice. Add remaining ⅓ cup sugar and stir. Pour over bread immediately after baked, while still hot.

YIELD: 1 LOAF

THE JUNIOR LEAGUE OF YOUNGSTOWN, OHIO

· · · · · · · · · · · · · · · · · · ·

Shear's Orange Bread

An old family recipe.

1 or 2 large oranges
1 cup ground dates
1 teaspoon baking soda
½ cup sugar
2 tablespoons softened butter
1 teaspoon vanilla
1 egg, beaten
2 cups flour
1 teaspoon baking powder
¼ teaspoon salt
½ cup broken nut meats

Squeeze juice from 1 orange. Add enough orange juice from other fresh oranges or frozen orange juice to make 1 cup and set aside.

Peel thin outer rind from ½ orange and put it, with dates, through a food grinder. Mix juice with ground dates and rind. Stir in soda, sugar,

Recipe continues . . .

softened butter, and vanilla. Add beaten egg and dry ingredients. Mix thoroughly. Stir in nuts.

Spoon batter into an oiled 9 x 5 x 3-inch bread pan and bake for 1 hour in 350° oven.

Remove from oven and cool in inverted pan for 10 minutes. Run knife around edge and remove from pan; cool upright.

Serve cold with soft butter or softened cream cheese.

YIELD: 1 LOAF

THE JUNIOR LEAGUE OF SPRINGFIELD, ILLINOIS

Orange Banana Nut Bread

1 cup finely chopped candied orange slices
1 tablespoon sugar
¼ cup butter
½ cup sugar
1 egg, beaten
1 banana, mashed (½ cup)
2½ cups sifted flour
2 teaspoons baking powder
½ teaspoon baking soda
½ teaspoon salt
½ cup chopped nuts
1 cup milk

Sprinkle orange slices with the 1 tablespoon sugar to prevent pieces from sticking together.

Cream butter with the ½ cup sugar. Add egg and banana and mix well.

Sift dry ingredients together. Add nuts and orange slices. Add this mixture alternately with milk to banana mixture. Pour into 8 x 4 x 3-inch greased and floured loaf pan.

Bake at 350° for 60 minutes, or until done.

YIELD: 1 LOAF

THE JUNIOR LEAGUE OF FARGO-MOORHEAD, NORTH DAKOTA/MINNESOTA

· · · · · · · · · · · · · · · · · · ·

Butter Nut Coffee Cake

1 envelope active dry yeast
¼ cup warm water
1 cup milk
½ cup butter
⅓ cup sugar
½ teaspoon salt
1 egg, beaten
4½–5 cups flour
Butter icing and nuts for topping

Sprinkle yeast over warm water and set aside.

Scald milk in saucepan; pour into mixing bowl. Add butter, sugar, and salt and cool to lukewarm. Stir in dissolved yeast and beaten egg. Beat in 2 cups flour and gradually stir in enough of the remaining flour to make a soft dough. Knead until smooth. Let rise until double in bulk.

Divide coffee cake dough in half and roll half into a 9 x 18-inch rectangular pan. Spread with half the filling, cut lengthwise into three 18-inch-long strips, and roll each strip lengthwise, sealing edges well. Braid the three strips together, place on a buttered baking sheet, and pinch ends together securely. Repeat with second half of dough. Cover and let stand in warm place until doubled in size. Bake 30–35 minutes in a 375° oven. Decorate with butter icing and nuts.

YIELD: 2 LOAVES

Recipe continues . . .

FILLING:

½ cup butter
1 cup confectioners' sugar
1 teaspoon vanilla

Cream together butter and sugar and beat in vanilla.

THE JUNIOR LEAGUE OF FARGO-MOORHEAD, NORTH DAKOTA/MINNESOTA

· · · · · · · · · · · · · · · ·

"Refrigerated" Hungarian Coffee Cake

1 cup milk
½ cup vegetable oil
½ cup sugar
1 teaspoon salt
2 compressed yeast cakes or envelopes active dry yeast
2 eggs, lightly beaten
4¼–4½ cups flour
½ cup butter
¾ cup sugar
2 teaspoons cinnamon
½ cup chopped or ground nuts
1 cup raisins

Scald milk. Pour in a large mixing bowl, and add oil, ½ cup sugar, and salt. Stir to dissolve and then cool to lukewarm.

Crumble yeast cakes or pour dry yeast into milk mixture. Stir to blend, then let stand until yeast is softened. Add beaten eggs.

Stir in 3 cups flour with a wooden spoon. Stir in remaining flour until dough leaves the sides of the bowl. Turn out onto lightly floured board or pastry cloth. Knead 5–10 minutes, or until dough is smooth and elastic. Place in a greased bowl—not aluminum—and turn once to bring greased side up. Cover with a thin, damp cloth and let rise in a warm, draft-free place for 1½ hours, or until double in bulk. If cloth dries, dampen again.

Punch dough down, turn over, and grease top lightly. Cover with plastic wrap or wax paper. Tie securely around top of bowl with a rubber band. Store in refrigerator until needed, but no longer than 2 days.

Three hours before serving, melt butter in a saucepan and in a small bowl combine ¾ cup sugar, cinnamon, and nuts.

Shape dough into small balls, 1–1½ inches in diameter. Roll each ball first in melted butter, then in cinnamon-sugar mixture.

Place balls in the bottom of a greased 9-inch tube pan so they do not touch each other. Sprinkle bottom layer with half the raisins. Arrange next layer of balls and sprinkle with remaining raisins. Cover with last layer of balls.

Cover and let rise in a warm place for 1½–2 hours, or until double in bulk. Bake in a preheated 375° oven for 35–40 minutes. Turn upside down on a wire rack to let hot cinnamon-sugar syrup run over loaf as it cools.

Serve by breaking balls apart with two forks.

YIELD: 1 LARGE LOAF

Discover Dayton
THE JUNIOR LEAGUE OF DAYTON, OHIO

.　.　.　.　.　.　.　.　.　.　.　.　.　.　.　.

Chocolate Chip Cake

¾ cup scalded milk
½ cup butter or margarine
⅓ cup sugar
1 teaspoon salt
2 envelopes active dry yeast
¼ cup lukewarm water
3 eggs
3½ cups sifted all-purpose flour
½ cup chocolate chips

Recipe continues . . .

Pour hot milk over butter or margarine, sugar, and salt. Stir to melt butter.

Soften yeast in the lukewarm water. Stir into cooled milk mixture. Add eggs and 2 cups flour. Beat until smooth. Add remaining flour. Stir in chocolate chips.

Turn dough into a well-buttered 10-inch tube pan. Sprinkle Coffee Topping over dough, cover pan, and let dough rise in warm place until doubled in bulk, about 1 hour.

Bake in a 375° oven for 35–40 minutes. Turn out of pan immediately to cool on rack.

YIELD: 8 SERVINGS

COFFEE TOPPING:
½ *cup sifted flour*
½ *cup sugar*
½ *cup butter or margarine*
½ *cup chopped nuts*
½ *cup chocolate chips*
1 teaspoon instant coffee
Dash salt
1 teaspoon vanilla
1 teaspoon cinnamon

Blend the flour, sugar, and butter into coarse crumbs. Blend nuts, chips, instant coffee, salt, vanilla, and cinnamon into the crumb mix.

THE JUNIOR LEAGUE OF INDIANAPOLIS, INDIANA

Sour Cream Coffee Cake

¼ pound butter
1 cup sugar
2 eggs, well beaten
1 teaspoon vanilla
1 cup sour cream
2 cups sifted flour
1 teaspoon baking powder
1 teaspoon baking soda
½ teaspoon salt

Cream butter and sugar. Add thoroughly beaten eggs, vanilla, and sour cream. Mix well. Gradually add flour, baking powder, baking soda, and salt. Mix thoroughly. Reserve 2 tablespoons of this batter for topping.

Pour half of the remaining batter into a greased and floured 8 x 8 x 2-inch pan. Add filling, remaining batter, and topping. Bake in a 350° oven approximately 50 minutes.

YIELD: 12 SERVINGS

FILLING:
⅓ cup raisins
1 teaspoon sugar
1 teaspoon cinnamon
¼ cup chopped nuts

Mix ingredients well.

If desired, ½ square grated bitter chocolate or 1 peeled and cored apple, thinly sliced, may be added to this filling.

Recipe continues . . .

TOPPING:

2 tablespoons batter
1 tablespoon butter
½ cup sifted flour
¼ cup sugar
1 teaspoon cinnamon

Mix all ingredients until crumbly.

Peacock Pie and Other Perfections
THE JUNIOR LEAGUE OF BATTLE CREEK, MICHIGAN

· · · · · · · · · · · · · · · ·

Flat Bread

2 cups all-purpose flour
2 cups whole-wheat flour
1 teaspoon baking soda
¼ teaspoon salt
¼ cup sugar
¾ cup shortening
1½ cups buttermilk

Combine all dry ingredients. Cut in shortening with a pastry cutter or two knives. Stir in buttermilk with a fork to make a rough dough.

Pull off a medium-size lump of dough and roll as thinly as possible on a floured board. Bake on a large cookie sheet at 400° until flat bread begins to brown, then turn over and brown lightly on the other side.

Store in a wax-paper-lined box in a dry place until ready to slice.

YIELD: 24–30 ROUNDS

THE JUNIOR LEAGUE OF FARGO-MOORHEAD, NORTH DAKOTA/MINNESOTA

· · · · · · · · · · · · · · · ·

Poppy Seed Coffee Cake

¼ cup poppy seeds
1 cup buttermilk
1 teaspoon almond extract
1 cup butter
1½ cups sugar
4 eggs, separated
2½ cups flour
1 teaspoon baking powder
1 teaspoon baking soda
Dash salt
½ cup sugar
1 teaspoon cinnamon

Combine and set aside the poppy seeds, buttermilk, and almond extract.

Cream butter and sugar. Add egg yolks and beat. Sift together the flour, baking powder, soda, and salt. Add alternately with the buttermilk mixture. Fold in beaten egg whites.

Pour half of the batter into a greased tube or bundt pan. Sprinkle half the sugar and cinnamon on batter. Add remaining batter and the remaining sugar and cinnamon. Cut through the batter with a knife for a marble effect.

Bake in 350° oven for 1 hour.

This cake freezes well.

YIELD: 16 SERVINGS

Sunflower Sampler
THE JUNIOR LEAGUE OF WICHITA, KANSAS

Mom's Pumpkin Bread

4 eggs
3 cups sugar
1 cup oil
⅔ cup water
2 cups mashed pumpkin, fresh or canned
3½ cups flour
2 teaspoons baking soda
3 teaspoons cinnamon
2 scant teaspoons nutmeg
1½ teaspoons salt
2 cups raisins
1 cup broken walnuts
6 tablespoons butter

Beat eggs and add sugar gradually. Add oil, water, and pumpkin. Stir together dry ingredients and mix into liquid. Add raisins and nuts.

Grease well four 1-pound coffee cans. Fill each half full of batter. Bake at 350° for 1 hour. During the last 15 minutes of baking time, put 1½ tablespoons butter on top of each loaf.

These make marvelous last-minute Christmas gifts.

YIELD: 4 1-POUND LOAVES

THE JUNIOR LEAGUE OF TOLEDO, OHIO

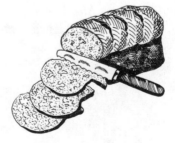

Rhubarb Bread

1 egg, beaten
1½ cups brown sugar
½ cup oil
1 cup sour milk
1 teaspoon vanilla
2½ cups flour
1 teaspoon salt
1 teaspoon baking soda
½ cup nuts
1½ cups diced rhubarb

Mix egg and brown sugar. Stir in oil, milk, and vanilla. Gradually stir in dry ingredients and mix well. Fold in nuts and rhubarb.

Empty into oiled loaf pans and bake for 40 minutes at 350°.

YIELD: 2 LOAVES

The Discovery Shop Cookbook
THE JUNIOR LEAGUE OF SIOUX CITY, IOWA

Pineapple Zucchini Bread

3 eggs
1 cup cooking oil
2 cups sugar
2 teaspoons vanilla
2 cups shredded, unpeeled zucchini
1 8¼-ounce can crushed pineapple, well drained
3 cups flour
2 teaspoons baking soda
2 teaspoons cinnamon
1 teaspoon salt
1 teaspoon nutmeg
¼ teaspoon baking powder
1 cup chopped dates
1 cup chopped pecans

Beat eggs, oil, sugar, and vanilla until thick. Stir in remaining ingredients; mix well.

Pour into two greased 5 x 9-inch loaf pans. Bake at 350° for about 1 hour.

YIELD: 2 LOAVES

THE JUNIOR LEAGUE OF SOUTH BEND, INDIANA

Zucchini Walnut Bread

1 cup raisins
3 cups flour
1 tablespoon cinnamon
1 teaspoon baking soda
1 teaspoon salt
¾ teaspoon baking powder
4 eggs
2 cups sugar
1 cup cooking oil
2 cups shredded, unpeeled zucchini
1 cup chopped walnuts
2 teaspoons grated lemon rind

Rinse raisins; drain. Mix with 2 tablespoons of the flour.

Sift remaining flour with the cinnamon, soda, salt, and baking powder. Beat eggs; gradually beat in sugar, then oil. With rubber spatula, blend in dry ingredients alternately with zucchini. Stir in raisins, nuts, and lemon rind.

Turn into two greased and floured 9 x 5 x 3-inch loaf pans and bake at 350° for about 55 minutes, or until top springs back when lightly touched. Cool in pans 10 minutes. Turn out on wire racks to cool.

YIELD: 2 LOAVES

THE JUNIOR LEAGUE OF CHAMPAIGN-URBANA, ILLINOIS

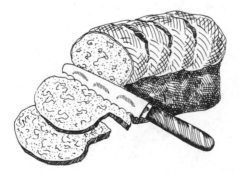

Brioche

A shortened version of French brioche.

1 envelope active dry yeast
¼ cup warm water
⅓ cup sugar
½ cup margarine
½ teaspoon salt
½ cup scalded milk, cooled
3¼ cups sifted flour
3 eggs plus 1 egg yolk, beaten
1 egg white

Dissolve yeast in warm water with sugar.

Cream margarine and salt together with wooden spoon. Add milk and 1 cup flour. Add yeast, eggs, and remaining flour. Beat 5–7 minutes by hand—this mixture will be sticky. Cover and let rise for about 2 hours. Stir down. Beat well; cover and refrigerate overnight.

Punch down the next day and divide into four sections. Make 24 large balls out of three sections and 24 small balls out of one section. Place large balls in well-greased muffin tins, make indentation on top, moisten small balls with water, and press into indentations. Cover and let rise about 1 hour.

Brush tops with egg white and bake at 375° for 15 minutes.

These brioche freeze well. Reheat in 250° oven before serving. If put into a "brown-in-bag," they will get hot without drying out.

YIELD: 2 DOZEN BRIOCHE

Cookbook
THE JUNIOR LEAGUE OF GRAND RAPIDS, MICHIGAN

Soft Pretzels

2 envelopes active dry yeast
2¼ cups warm water
⅓ cup sugar
2¼ teaspoons salt
5 tablespoons soft butter
1 egg
7–7½ cups flour
1 egg yolk
1 tablespoon water
Kosher salt

Soften yeast in water. Add sugar, salt, butter, egg, and 3 cups flour. Beat at medium speed until smooth. Add remaining flour to make a stiff dough. Cover and refrigerate 4–6 hours.

Turn cold dough out on lightly dusted bread board. Divide in half and each half into 15 pieces. Roll each piece to 18 inches in length. Form into pretzel shapes and place on lightly greased baking sheets.

Beat egg yolk and water and brush pretzels generously with mixture. Sprinkle generously with salt. Cover and let rise in warm place for 30 minutes.

Bake 15 minutes at 400°, or until golden. Cool on wire racks.

YIELD: 30 PRETZELS

Cookbook
THE JUNIOR LEAGUE OF GRAND RAPIDS, MICHIGAN

· ·

Bagels

¼ cup butter
1½ tablespoons sugar
½ teaspoon salt
1 cup scalded milk
1 compressed yeast cake or envelope active dry yeast
1 egg, separated
3¾ cups sifted flour
1 teaspoon cold water
Kosher salt or poppy seeds (optional)

Add butter, sugar, and salt to milk. When lukewarm, add yeast, well-beaten egg white, and flour. Knead. Let rise for about 1 hour. Punch dough down and divide into 24 pieces. Roll out each piece to about the width of a finger and twice the length, tapering the ends. Shape into rings, pinching ends together. Let stand on a floured board, to rise for about 10 minutes.

Drop bagels one at a time into very hot water that's just under the boiling point.

Turn each to cook the other side. The bagels must be light, keep their shape, and not break apart.

Place on a baking sheet. Beat egg yolk with the 1 teaspoon cold water and brush over the tops of the bagels. If desired, sprinkle the egg-brushed bagels with coarse salt or poppy seeds before baking. Bake in a 400° oven for 15 minutes, or until brown and crisp.

YIELD: 24 BAGELS

THE JUNIOR LEAGUE OF KANSAS CITY, KANSAS

Dakota Rolls

1 envelope active dry yeast
¼ cup warm water
1 cup scalded milk
3 tablespoons sugar
3 tablespoons shortening
1 teaspoon salt
1 egg, well beaten
3½ cups sifted all-purpose flour
¼ cup melted butter
¼ cup brown sugar

CARAMEL TOPPING:
1 cup brown sugar
2 tablespoons light corn syrup
1 tablespoon butter

Soften yeast in warm (110°) water. Stir and let stand for 5 minutes. Combine milk, sugar, shortening, and salt; cool. When lukewarm, add softened yeast and egg. Gradually stir in flour to form soft dough. Beat vigorously. Cover with greased wax paper and towel and let rise in a warm place (82°) for about 2 hours, or until double in bulk. Turn out on a flour-dusted canvas or board and roll out into an 8 x 16-inch oblong about ½ inch thick. Brush with melted butter and sprinkle with brown sugar. Roll up lengthwise like a jelly roll and cut in 1-inch slices.

Combine ingredients for Caramel Topping and heat slowly in a greased shallow pan or in muffin tins. Cool.

Place rolls, cut side down, over the mixture. Cover and let rise until double in bulk.

Bake in a 375° oven for 25 minutes. Remove from pan while hot and cool, bottom side up.

YIELD: 2 DOZEN ROLLS

THE JUNIOR LEAGUE OF FARGO-MOORHEAD, NORTH DAKOTA/MINNESOTA

· · · · · · · · · · · · · · · · · · · ·

Quick Yeast Dinner Rolls

1 envelope active dry yeast
2 cups warm water
¼ cup sugar
1 egg
¾ cup melted shortening
4 cups self-rising flour

Soften yeast in water and add sugar. Let stand 3–4 minutes. Add egg and shortening. Gradually mix in flour.

Grease 24 muffin tins. Fill half full. Bake at 425° for about 20 minutes, or until brown.

YIELD: 2 DOZEN ROLLS

THE JUNIOR LEAGUE OF EVANSVILLE, INDIANA

· · · · · · · · · · · · · · · · · · · ·

Sticky Buns

4½ cups flour
2 compressed yeast cakes or envelopes active dry yeast
½ cup warm milk
1½ teaspoons sugar
½ cup butter
⅓ cup sugar
2 eggs, beaten
½ cup milk
½ teaspoon salt
Soft butter
Cinnamon sugar
Raisins

TOPPING:

½ cup melted butter
½ cup light corn syrup
1 cup brown sugar, packed

Place ½ cup flour in bowl. Crumble yeast over top. Make a hollow; pour in warm milk and 1½ teaspoons sugar. Stir until well blended. Cover; let rise in warm place for 20 minutes.

Cream the ½ cup butter; gradually add ⅓ cup sugar, beating until light and fluffy. Stir in eggs, milk, and salt. Add 2 cups flour to butter mixture, then add yeast mixture and remaining 2 cups flour. Knead well. Cover and let rise 1½–2 hours, or until double in bulk.

Punch dough down; knead lightly. Roll out into large rectangle ½ inch thick. Spread with soft butter; sprinkle with cinnamon sugar and raisins. Roll up like a jelly roll and cut into 1½-inch slices.

In saucepan, combine topping ingredients. Heat slowly, stirring until blended. Spoon into bottom of two 9-inch-round cake pans. Place slices, cut side down, on topping mixture. Cover and let rise 30 minutes.

Bake at 350° for 25 minutes. Cool 3 minutes; invert on cooling racks.

YIELD: APPROXIMATELY 2 DOZEN BUNS

Be Our Guest
THE JUNIOR LEAGUE OF MILWAUKEE, WISCONSIN

Mary's Pecan Rolls

2 cups water
½ cup sugar
2 teaspoons salt
2 eggs, well beaten
2 envelopes active dry yeast, softened in ½ cup water with 1 teaspoon sugar
7–8 cups flour
½ cup softened shortening
1 stick butter, softened
2 teaspoons cinnamon
1 cup sugar

PECAN TOPPING:
1 cup softened butter
1 cup white corn syrup
2 cups brown sugar
Pecan halves (3–4 for each muffin tin)

Mix first four ingredients together. Add yeast mixture and stir well. Add 4 cups of the flour and beat well with a spoon. Add the shortening and mix well. Beat and knead in an additional 3–4 cups of flour to make a dough that is light but not sticky. Cover and let rise in a warm place for 1½–2 hours, or until doubled in size.

Punch down and roll dough out on floured surface into a large rectangle about ¼ inch thick. Spread softened butter over rectangle. Sprinkle with cinnamon and sugar. Roll up, starting with longest side. Cut into 4 dozen slices about ½ inch thick.

Combine first three ingredients for Pecan Topping and mix well. Put 1 tablespoon of topping into bottom of each muffin cup of muffin pan; place 3–4 pecan halves on top. Put one slice of the dough on top of the pecan halves in each muffin cup and let rise until doubled in bulk.

Bake in a 350° oven for 12–15 minutes. Remove from oven and allow to cool a few minutes, then turn pans upside down and cool a few minutes more before removing pans. Don't let the rolls cool too much or they will stick to the muffin pan.

These are absolutely delicious and worth the effort. They can be cooled and frozen for later use.

YIELD: 4–4½ DOZEN ROLLS

THE JUNIOR LEAGUE OF SPRINGFIELD, ILLINOIS

·   ·   ·   ·   ·   ·   ·   ·   ·   ·   ·   ·   ·   ·   ·   ·   ·   ·   ·

Croatian Pastry

3 cups flour
3 egg yolks
3 tablespoons evaporated milk
1 teaspoon vanilla
1 tablespoon bourbon or rum
⅛ teaspoon salt
2 cups confectioners' sugar
Oil for frying

Mix all ingredients together except the oil. Knead as for noodle dough, until firm and smooth.

Roll out the dough until paper-thin. Cut dough into 3-inch-wide strips. Then cut each strip diagonally at 3-inch intervals. Cut a slit in the middle of each strip and pull one end through the slit to form a bow-like design.

Deep-fry the dough in hot oil for 2–3 seconds on each side. It will balloon.

Before serving, and while still hot, sprinkle with additional confectioners' sugar.

YIELD: 6 DOZEN PASTRIES

THE JUNIOR LEAGUE OF KANSAS CITY, KANSAS

·   ·   ·   ·   ·   ·   ·   ·   ·   ·   ·   ·   ·   ·   ·   ·   ·   ·   ·

Aunt Bobby's Doughnuts

1 envelope active dry yeast
⅔ cup warm water
1½ tablespoons sugar
1½ cups warm milk
1 egg, beaten
½ cup melted shortening
⅓ teaspoon nutmeg
Flour
Confectioners' sugar
Milk
1 teaspoon vanilla
Oil for deep frying

To soften yeast, put in the warm water with the 1½ tablespoons sugar. Let stand 5 minutes. Combine warm milk, beaten egg, and melted shortening and cool to lukewarm. Stir in yeast mixture, nutmeg, and as much flour as needed to make a soft dough. Knead it a little, cover, and set in refrigerator overnight in greased bowl.

Next day, roll out to ¼–½ inch thick and cut with doughnut cutter. Let doughnuts stand until they rise to twice their size.

Fry in hot oil. Drain and glaze with confectioners' sugar mixed with a little milk and the vanilla.

Great with cider on a crisp fall day, especially Hallowe'en.

YIELD: 3–4 DOZEN DOUGHNUTS

THE JUNIOR LEAGUE OF CHAMPAIGN-URBANA, ILLINOIS

Quick Oat Cake

1¼ cups boiling water
1 cup quick oats
½ cup shortening
1 cup light brown sugar
1 cup white sugar
2 eggs
1½ cups flour
1 teaspoon cinnamon
½ teaspoon salt
1 teaspoon baking soda

Pour boiling water over oats and let stand 20 minutes. Cream shortening and sugars. Add eggs and beat well. Add oatmeal mixture, flour, cinnamon, salt, and soda. Pour into 9 x 12-inch greased cake pan and bake for 20 minutes in 350° oven.

Add topping and return cake to oven for about 10 minutes longer.

YIELD: 1 9 x 12-INCH CAKE

TOPPING:
6 tablespoons butter
1 cup light brown sugar
¼ cup heavy cream
1 teaspoon vanilla
1 cup shredded coconut

Melt butter and add sugar, cream, vanilla, and coconut. Spread over cake as soon as it comes from the oven.

Peacock Pie and Other Perfections
THE JUNIOR LEAGUE OF BATTLE CREEK, MICHIGAN

Bran Muffins

1 15-ounce package raisin bran
3 cups sugar
5 cups flour
5 teaspoons baking soda
2 teaspoons salt
1 cup salad oil
4 eggs, beaten
1 quart buttermilk

Mix all dry ingredients. Add oil, eggs, and buttermilk. Beat with a wooden spoon until well mixed.

Fill desired number of muffin tins two-thirds full and bake at 400° for 15–20 minutes.

This batter recipe may be kept indefinitely in the refrigerator for fresh hot muffins as needed.

YIELD: 60 MUFFINS

THE JUNIOR LEAGUE OF INDIANAPOLIS, INDIANA

Puffy French Toast

1 cup flour
1½ teaspoons baking powder
½ teaspoon salt
1 cup milk
2 eggs, well beaten
10 slices white bread
Oil for frying

Sift dry ingredients together. Stir in milk and eggs. Beat well.

Dip bread slices in batter and fry in ½ inch cooking oil in large skillet until lightly browned and fluffy on both sides. Drain on paper toweling and place in shallow pan in oven to keep warm until all are fried. Serve with Strawberry Cream Topping.

YIELD: 6–8 SERVINGS

STRAWBERRY CREAM TOPPING:
1 cup heavy cream
3 tablespoons sugar
¼ teaspoon vanilla
½ cup sliced strawberries

Whip cream and stir in remaining ingredients.

YIELD: 2 CUPS

THE JUNIOR LEAGUE OF EVANSVILLE, INDIANA

. . . .

Hearty Oatmeal Waffles

4 eggs
1¾ cups buttermilk
1 teaspoon baking soda
1½ cups sifted all-purpose flour
2 teaspoons baking powder
1 teaspoon salt
⅓ cup bacon drippings and/or vegetable oil
1 tablespoon honey
Dash cinnamon
1 cup quick-cooking oatmeal

Beat eggs until light. Add all other ingredients except oatmeal, beating until well blended. Stir in oatmeal.

Recipe continues . . .

Bake in preheated prepared waffle iron until steaming stops, or until done to your taste.

Serve steaming hot with butter and warm syrup.

A half cup of your favorite chopped nuts is a tasty addition. This batter may also be used for pancakes.

YIELD: 8–10 WAFFLES

Discover Dayton
THE JUNIOR LEAGUE OF DAYTON, OHIO

· · · · · · · · · · · · · · · · · ·

Dutch Babies

3 tablespoons butter
3 eggs
Pinch salt
½ cup flour
½ cup milk
Lemons
Confectioners' sugar
Cooked bacon and maple syrup or fresh fruit or berries

Coat a heavy 10-inch iron pan with butter. Beat together eggs, salt, flour, and milk. Pour into pan. Bake at 400° for 25–30 minutes, or until puffy and golden.

Cut in pie slices, squeeze a little lemon juice over, and shake on sugar.

Top with cooked slice of bacon and maple syrup, or with fresh fruits sprinkled with sugar.

YIELD: 4–6 SERVINGS

Cookbook
THE JUNIOR LEAGUE OF GRAND RAPIDS, MICHIGAN

· · · · · · · · · · · · · · · · · ·

Light and Fluffy 4-H Pancakes

2 eggs, separated
2 cups buttermilk
1¾ cups all-purpose flour
2 teaspoons sugar
2 teaspoons baking powder
½ teaspoon salt
1 teaspoon baking soda
2 tablespoons melted butter

Beat egg whites until stiff; set aside.

Beat egg yolks. Blend with buttermilk. Add sifted dry ingredients and beat until smooth. Stir in melted butter, then fold in beaten egg whites.

Bake on hot, greased griddle until bubbly on top and brown beneath. Turn to brown other side.

Serve hot with butter and maple syrup.

YIELD: 10–12 PANCAKES

THE JUNIOR LEAGUE OF FARGO-MOORHEAD, NORTH DAKOTA/MINNESOTA

. . . .

Giant Popovers

2 cups whole eggs (8 or 9)
2½ cups milk
½ cup melted butter
2½ cups sifted all-purpose flour
¾ teaspoon salt

Beat eggs slightly. Add milk and butter and beat until blended. Gradually beat flour and salt into egg mixture. Pour into ten well-buttered 5-ounce custard cups and place on cookie sheet.

Bake in preheated 375° oven for 1 hour. Remove from oven and cut a slit in the side of each; return to oven and bake 15 minutes longer.

Recipe continues . . .

Remove from custard cups immediately and serve with butter, preserves, or honey.

These get big; place on low rack in oven so they don't hit the top.

YIELD: 10 POPOVERS

Gourmet Gab
THE JUNIOR LEAGUE OF SAGINAW, MICHIGAN

· ·

Ephraim Pancakes

An old family recipe that makes thin, light, irresistible pancakes.

> *2 cups sifted all-purpose flour*
> *2 tablespoons sugar*
> *¾ teaspoon baking powder*
> *1 teaspoon salt*
> *2 eggs, well beaten*
> *2 cups buttermilk*
> *1 teaspoon baking soda*
> *½ cup hot water*
> *¼ cup melted butter*

Sift together flour, sugar, baking powder, and salt. Blend in eggs. Combine buttermilk and soda with water. Add to egg mixture and mix well. Stir in butter.

Cook on hot, greased griddle until lightly browned.

These are excellent with fresh blueberries added.

YIELD: 4–6 SERVINGS

Be Our Guest
THE JUNIOR LEAGUE OF MILWAUKEE, WISCONSIN

· ·

Desserts

FARM FRESH FRUIT

Chocolate Layer Cake

An old family recipe, handed down for three generations.

4 squares unsweetened chocolate (4 ounces)
⅔ cup butter
1 cup boiling water
½ cup buttermilk
2 cups sugar
2 cups cake flour
1½ teaspoons baking soda
1 teaspoon vanilla
2 eggs, beaten

Melt unsweetened chocolate in top of a double boiler. Cream butter, mix with chocolate in large mixing bowl, and *slowly* stir in boiling water. Add buttermilk.

Sift together sugar, cake flour, and baking soda. Slowly beat mixture into chocolate at medium speed in electric mixer. Fold in vanilla and eggs. Pour into two 9-inch cake pans that have been well greased and floured.

Bake in a 350° preheated oven for about 30 minutes, or until wooden pick comes out clean.

MOCHA FROSTING:
6 tablespoons cocoa
6 tablespoons hot black coffee
6 tablespoons butter
1 teaspoon vanilla
3 cups confectioners' sugar

Combine cocoa and coffee. Add butter and vanilla and beat until smooth. Gradually add sugar and beat until smooth.

Spread between and on top of cooled cake layers.

YIELD: 1 9-INCH LAYER CAKE

THE JUNIOR LEAGUE OF SPRINGFIELD, ILLINOIS

· · · · · · · · · · · · · · · · · ·

White Chocolate Cake

¼ pound white chocolate
½ cup boiling water
1 cup butter
2 cups sugar
4 eggs, separated
1 teaspoon vanilla
2½ cups sifted cake flour
½ teaspoon salt
1 teaspoon baking soda
1 cup buttermilk

CUSTARD CAKE FILLING:
3 eggs, well beaten
½ cup sugar
1 cup milk (scalded in double boiler)

CREAM CHEESE FROSTING:
8 ounces cream cheese
½ cup butter
1 1-pound box confectioners' sugar
1 teaspoon vanilla
Flaked coconut

Melt white chocolate in ½ cup boiling water; cool.

Meanwhile, cream together butter and sugar until fluffy. Add egg yolks one at a time and beat well after each addition. Add melted chocolate and vanilla; mix well.

Sift dry ingredients together and add alternately with buttermilk to the creamed mixture. Beat after each addition until smooth, but do not overbeat. Fold in stiffly beaten egg whites.

Divide batter into three 8- or 9-inch layer pans, greased, floured, and lined on the bottom with wax paper. Bake at 350° for 30 to 40 minutes. Cool.

Recipe continues . . .

Custard: Add eggs and sugar slowly to hot milk and cook over hot water, stirring constantly, until custard coats the spoon. Cool; spread between cake layers.

Frosting: Cream together all ingredients until fluffy and set in refrigerator to chill before icing cake. Press coconut into icing.

YIELD: 12–14 SERVINGS

Sunflower Sampler
THE JUNIOR LEAGUE OF WICHITA, KANSAS

· · · · · · · · · · · · · · · · ·

The Original Bourbon Cake

2 cups chopped candied cherries or half cherries and half dates
1½ cups light seedless raisins
2 cups bourbon
1½ cups butter or margarine
2⅓ cups white sugar
2⅓ cups firmly packed brown sugar
6 eggs, separated
5 cups sifted cake flour
4 cups chopped pecans (1 pound)
2 teaspoons nutmeg
1 teaspoon baking powder

Combine cherries, raisins, and bourbon. Cover and let stand overnight. Drain fruits. Reserve bourbon.

Cream butter and sugars together until light. Add egg yolks and beat well.

Combine ½ cup flour and pecans; set aside.

Sift together remaining 4½ cups flour, nutmeg, and baking powder. Add flour mixture and bourbon alternately to butter mixture, beating well after each addition.

Beat egg whites until stiff but not dry. Fold into batter. Fold soaked fruits and pecan-flour mixture into batter. Turn into greased 10-inch tube pan lined with greased wax paper.

Bake at 275° for 3½ hours. Cool.

Remove from pan and fill center of cake with cheesecloth which has been saturated with bourbon. Wrap in aluminum foil. Store in tightly covered container and keep in cool place, refrigerating if necessary.

This has been a Christmas tradition for many years.

YIELD: 1 10-INCH TUBE CAKE

Bluff City Cooks
THE JUNIOR LEAGUE OF GREATER ALTON, ILLINOIS

. . . .

Cherry Fruit Cake

1½ cups sifted all-purpose flour
1½ cups sugar
1 teaspoon salt
1 teaspoon baking powder
2 7¼-ounce packages pitted dates
1 pound diced candied pineapple
2 16-ounce jars maraschino cherries, drained
18 ounces pecan halves (about 5½ cups)
6 eggs
⅓ cup dark rum
½ cup light corn syrup

Grease two 5 x 9-inch loaf pans and line with foil, allowing 2-inch overhang; grease again.

Sift dry ingredients into very large mixing bowl; add fruits and pecans and toss until coated. Beat eggs and rum thoroughly, pour over fruit mixture and toss until combined. Turn mixture into loaf pans, pressing with a metal spatula to pack lightly.

Recipe continues . . .

Bake at 300° for 1¾ hours. Cool for 15 minutes. Remove from pans and tear off foil.

Brush cakes with corn syrup while warm. Cool thoroughly before serving or storing.

YIELD: 2 CAKES

Bluff City Cooks
THE JUNIOR LEAGUE OF GREATER ALTON, ILLINOIS

· · · · · · · · · · · · · ·

Susan's Whipped Cream Pound Cake

½ pound butter
3 cups sugar
6 eggs
3 cups flour
½ pint heavy cream
2 teaspoons vanilla

Cream butter and sugar. Add eggs one at a time and beat well after each addition. Beat some more—a lot more! Gradually stir in flour and heavy cream alternately. Stir in vanilla.

Pour mixture into a greased and floured bundt or tube pan. Place in cold oven, then turn heat to 325° and bake 1¼–1½ hours. Don't over-bake! Cool and enjoy.

Can be frozen. Excellent toasted.

YIELD: 8 SERVINGS

THE JUNIOR LEAGUE OF COLUMBUS, OHIO

· · · · · · · · · · · · · ·

Fresh Apple Cake with Vanilla Sauce

1 cup sugar
¼ cup shortening
1 egg, well beaten
3 medium apples, peeled and finely grated
1 teaspoon baking soda
¼ teaspoon salt
1 cup flour
½ teaspoon cinnamon
¼ cup chopped walnuts

Cream together sugar and shortening. Beat in egg and stir in apples.

Sift together dry ingredients and stir into apple mixture along with walnuts.

Pour into well-greased 8-inch-square pan and bake for 45 minutes at 350°. Serve warm with hot Vanilla Sauce.

YIELD: 9 SERVINGS

VANILLA SAUCE:
½ cup butter
½ cup light cream
1 cup sugar
1½ teaspoons vanilla

Combine all ingredients and cook in top of a double boiler until thick, stirring occasionally. Pour over individual serving of cake while both are warm.

THE JUNIOR LEAGUE OF DES MOINES, IOWA

Buttermilk Shortcake

2 cups self-rising flour
½ cup sugar
¾ cup shortening or lard
¾ cup buttermilk

Mix flour and sugar. Work in shortening with fingers or pastry blender. Stir in buttermilk to make a thick batter.

Press into a greased 8- or 9-inch pan and bake at 350° for 25 minutes.

YIELD: 6–8 SERVINGS

THE JUNIOR LEAGUE OF EVANSVILLE, INDIANA

* * * * * * * * * * * * * * * * *

Boiled Raisin Cake

3 cups water
8 ounces raisins
1 teaspoon baking soda
1½ cups sugar
2 tablespoons margarine
1 egg
¼ teaspoon salt
1 teaspoon cinnamon
½ teaspoon ground cloves
¼ teaspoon allspice
¼ teaspoon ginger
¼ teaspoon nutmeg
2 cups sifted flour

Pour the 3 cups of water over raisins and boil until liquid measures about 1 cup. Stir baking soda into liquid while hot.

Meanwhile, cream sugar, margarine, egg, salt, and spices. Add raisins and flour and mix well. Batter will appear thick. If desired, nuts may be added.

Spread batter into a 9 x 13-inch pan and bake in 375° oven for 30–35 minutes.

This is especially good frosted with your favorite vanilla frosting.

YIELD: 1 9 x 13-INCH CAKE

THE JUNIOR LEAGUE OF EVANSVILLE, INDIANA

Chocolate Intemperance

1 23-ounce package brownie mix
2 tablespoons water
3 eggs

Beat ingredients together.

Grease an 11 x 15-inch jelly-roll pan. Line with greased and floured wax paper. Spread batter in pan and bake 10–12 minutes in 350° oven. Turn onto a rack and peel off paper. Cool.

Lightly oil a 2-quart charlotte mold or casserole and line with cooled cake. (Cut rounds of cake to fit both top and bottom of mold and a strip for the sides. Place smaller round in bottom of mold.) Spoon the chilled Mocha Filling into mold. Chill 3–4 hours.

Unmold and cover with Chocolate Glaze. Spread glaze over top of cake and drizzle down sides.

Serve very thin slices—it's indecently opulent!

YIELD: 12–14 SERVINGS

Recipe continues . . .

MOCHA FILLING:
1½ pounds semisweet chocolate bars or chips
½ cup strong black coffee
3 eggs, separated
½ cup Tia Maria or Kahlúa
½ cup heavy cream
2 tablespoons sugar

Melt the chocolate with the coffee in the top of a double boiler. Remove from heat when chocolate is melted. Beat the egg yolks until pale yellow and stir gradually into the chocolate. Slowly add the Tia Maria or Kahlúa. Cool.

In a separate bowl, beat the egg whites, gradually adding sugar, until the whites are stiff. Whip the cream. Gently fold the whipped cream into the cooled chocolate mixture and then fold in the egg whites. Chill.

CHOCOLATE GLAZE:
½ pound semisweet chocolate
⅓ cup water

Melt the chocolate in the water and stir until smooth.

THE JUNIOR LEAGUE OF INDIANAPOLIS, INDIANA

Carrot Cake Cameron

2 cups sugar
1½ cups salad oil
2 cups flour
2 teaspoons baking powder
2 teaspoons cinnamon
1 teaspoon baking soda
1 teaspoon salt
4 eggs
3 cups shredded raw carrot
1 cup finely chopped pecans

Combine sugar and salad oil thoroughly. Sift together flour and baking powder, cinnamon, baking soda, and salt. Stir half the dry ingredients into sugar mixture. Mix remaining dry ingredients alternately with the eggs, beating well after each addition. Stir in carrot and pecans.

Pour the mixture into a lightly oiled 10-inch bundt or tube pan and bake at 350° for 1 hour and 10 minutes, or until it tests done. Let cake cool in upright position.

Remove from pan and let cool completely. Split cake in layers, spread with Orange Glaze, and reassemble cake.

YIELD: 1 10-INCH TUBE CAKE

ORANGE GLAZE:
1 cup sugar
¼ cup cornstarch
1 cup fresh orange juice
2 teaspoons butter
2 teaspoons grated orange rind
¼ teaspoon salt

Recipe continues . . .

In saucepan, mix together sugar and cornstarch. Gradually add orange juice and stir mixture until smooth. Add butter and orange rind along with salt. Cook mixture over low heat, stirring constantly, until thick and glossy. Let glaze cool completely.

Marigolds to Munch On
THE JUNIOR LEAGUE OF PEORIA, ILLINOIS

· · · · · · · · · · · · · · · · · ·

Italian Cream Cake

½ cup margarine
½ cup vegetable shortening
2 cups sugar
5 eggs, separated
2 cups flour
1 teaspoon soda
1 cup buttermilk
1 teaspoon vanilla
1 3½-ounce can flaked coconut
1 cup chopped pecans

CREAM CHEESE FROSTING:
8 ounces cream cheese, softened
¼ cup margarine, at room temperature
1 1-pound box confectioners' sugar
1 teaspoon vanilla
Chopped pecans (optional)

Cream margarine and shortening; add sugar and beat until mixture is smooth. Add egg yolks and beat well. Sift together flour and soda and add to creamed mixture alternately with buttermilk. Stir in vanilla. Add coconut and pecans. Fold in stiffly beaten egg whites.

Pour batter into three greased and floured 8-inch cake pans. Bake at 350° for 30–35 minutes, or until cake tests done. Cool.

Beat cream cheese and margarine until smooth; add sugar and mix well. Add vanilla and beat until smooth.

Divide frosting into approximately three parts and use one part for each layer. Top with pecans, if desired.

YIELD: 12 SERVINGS

Sunflower Sampler
THE JUNIOR LEAGUE OF WICHITA, KANSAS

Banana Cake

⅔ cup margarine
1⅔ cups sugar
3 eggs
1¼ cups mashed banana
2¼ cups flour
1¼ teaspoons baking powder
1¼ teaspoons baking soda
1 teaspoon salt
⅔ cup buttermilk
⅔ cup chopped nuts

Cream margarine and sugar. Blend in eggs. Add banana and mix well. Combine flour, baking powder, soda, and salt. Add to creamed mixture alternately with buttermilk. Stir in nuts.

Pour into greased and floured 9 x 13-inch baking pan and bake at 350° for 45–50 minutes. Cool.

Frost with Caramel Frosting.

YIELD: 1 9 X 13-INCH CAKE

Recipe continues . . .

CARAMEL FROSTING:
½ cup margarine
¼ cup milk
1 cup brown sugar, packed
3 cups sifted confectioners' sugar

Combine margarine, milk, and brown sugar in saucepan. Bring to a boil, stirring constantly. Cool for 10 minutes. Gradually stir in confectioners' sugar and beat until well blended.

THE JUNIOR LEAGUE OF TOLEDO, OHIO

· · · · · · · · · · · · · · · · · ·

Cranberry Cake

4 tablespoons butter
1⅓ cups sugar
2⅔ cups flour
4 teaspoons baking powder
¼ teaspoon salt
1¼ cups milk
1 pound fresh cranberries (4 cups)

Cream together butter and sugar. Add dry ingredients and milk and mix well. Fold in the cranberries.

Bake in 9 x 13-inch greased pan at 350° for 45 minutes.

Cut into squares and serve with hot or warm Vanilla Sauce.

YIELD: 12 SERVINGS

VANILLA SAUCE:
½ cup butter
1 cup sugar
¾ cup coffee cream
1 tablespoon cornstarch
1 teaspoon vanilla

Mix all ingredients in saucepan. Bring to a boil, stirring, and cook for 2 minutes.

YIELD: ABOUT 2 CUPS

THE JUNIOR LEAGUE OF ST. PAUL, MINNESOTA

· ·

Aunt Ella's Funny Cake

½ cup shortening
3 cups sugar
2 eggs
2 cups flour
2 teaspoons baking powder
1 cup milk
½ teaspoon vanilla
½ cup cocoa
1 cup water
2 9-inch unbaked pastry shells

Cream shortening; add 2 cups sugar and eggs. Stir in flour and baking powder. Stir in milk and vanilla.

In a saucepan, combine the remaining 1 cup sugar, cocoa, and water; heat until sugar is dissolved. Cool syrup slightly.

Pour syrup into the bottom of two 9-inch pie pans lined with unbaked pie crust. Carefully spoon batter over the syrup.

Bake at 350° for about 40–45 minutes.

YIELD: 12 SERVINGS

THE JUNIOR LEAGUE OF YOUNGSTOWN, OHIO

· ·

Pecan Torte

6 egg yolks
1½ cups sugar
2 tablespoons flour
2 teaspoons baking powder
¼ teaspoon salt
3 cups very finely chopped pecans
6 egg whites
Whipped cream
Chocolate curls, pecan halves, or strawberries for garnish

Beat egg yolks until thick and lemon colored. Gradually beat in half the sugar.

Mix together the flour, baking powder, and salt and stir in the pecans.

Beat egg whites until stiff and gradually beat in the remaining sugar. Carefully fold in egg yolk mixture, then the nut mixture.

Divide into two round 9-inch layer pans lined with greased wax paper. Bake at 350° for 25–30 minutes, or until no imprint remains when touched lightly with your finger. Cool.

Spread Whipped Cream Filling between layers and over top and sides of cake. Pipe decoratively with sweetened whipped cream and garnish with chocolate curls and pecan halves or strawberries.

YIELD: 16 SERVINGS

WHIPPED CREAM FILLING:
½ teaspoon gelatin
1 tablespoon milk
1 cup heavy cream
¼ cup sifted confectioners' sugar
1 teaspoon vanilla

Soften gelatin in the milk and dissolve over hot water. Whip cream until stiff and beat in the confectioners' sugar, the cooled gelatin, and vanilla.

THE JUNIOR LEAGUE OF ROCKFORD, ILLINOIS

Fudge Ribbon Torte

2 tablespoons butter
2 1-ounce squares unsweetened baking chocolate
1 cup sugar
1 6-ounce can evaporated milk (⅔ cup)
1 teaspoon vanilla
2 pints vanilla ice cream, softened
1 9-inch baked pastry shell
3 egg whites
3–4 tablespoons sugar
¼ cup crushed peppermint candy

In a saucepan, combine the butter, chocolate, 1 cup sugar, and evaporated milk. Cook, stirring, over low heat until thick. Remove from heat and add vanilla. Cool thoroughly before using in the torte.

Spread 1 pint softened ice cream in the pie shell and cover with half the fudge sauce. *Freeze until firm.* Again spread softened ice cream over first layer and top with remainder of fudge sauce. *Freeze until firm.*

Stiffly beat the egg whites with 3 or 4 tablespoons sugar. Reserve 2 teaspoons of the crushed candy and fold remainder into the meringue. Carefully spread meringue over frozen pie, being sure to seal edges. Sprinkle reserved candy on top.

Slide pie under broiler for 1 or 2 minutes, or until nicely brown. Don't take eyes off the pie while under the broiler!

The dessert may either be served at once or you may refreeze until needed.

YIELD: 8 SERVINGS

THE JUNIOR LEAGUE OF CHAMPAIGN-URBANA, ILLINOIS

Mocha Torte

1 6-ounce package chocolate bits
6 egg yolks, beaten
¼ cup water
2 tablespoons instant coffee
¼ cup sugar
⅓ pound very soft butter
3 Meringue Layers
1 cup heavy cream, whipped
Shaved chocolate

Melt chocolate bits over hot water. Add egg yolks, water, coffee, and sugar. Blend well and cool. Beat in soft butter.

Spread each Meringue Layer with chocolate filling and then whipped cream. Pile layers on top of each other and top with chocolate shavings.

Refrigerate until time to serve.

YIELD: 12 SERVINGS

MERINGUE LAYERS:
3 egg whites
1 cup sugar
1 teaspoon almond extract

Beat egg whites until very stiff, slowly adding the sugar and almond extract.

Line three buttered cake pans with brown paper. Spoon meringue into pans and bake at 250° until firm and pale in color. Cool before removing paper.

THE JUNIOR LEAGUE OF CHAMPAIGN-URBANA, ILLINOIS

Chocolate Ice Box Cake

12 ounces chocolate bits
8 egg yolks
4 egg whites, stiffly beaten
2 teaspoons vanilla
¼–½ teaspoon peppermint extract (optional)
2–3 cups heavy cream, whipped
2 cups graham cracker crumbs
½ cup melted butter or margarine
Shaved chocolate or peppermint candy

Melt chocolate bits in double boiler. Remove from heat. Beat in egg yolks and cool. Fold in egg whites and vanilla. Add the peppermint extract at this time if desired. Fold half the whipped cream into the custard.

Combine graham cracker crumbs with the melted butter or margarine. Press over bottom and sides of a 9-inch springform pan and bake in a preheated 375° oven for 8–10 minutes. Refrigerate.

Pour the custard into the graham cracker crust shell. Refrigerate until firm.

Spread the remaining cream over the top. Sprinkle with shaved chocolate or crushed peppermint candy. Chill for several hours before serving, or freeze and thaw in refrigerator one day before needed.

Remove from springform just before serving.

YIELD: 8 SERVINGS

THE JUNIOR LEAGUE OF CHAMPAIGN-URBANA, ILLINOIS

Praline Cheesecake

1 cup graham cracker crumbs
3 tablespoons granulated sugar
3 tablespoons melted butter
3 8-ounce packages cream cheese, softened
1¼ cups dark brown sugar
2 tablespoons flour
3 eggs
1½ teaspoons vanilla
½ cup finely chopped pecans
Maple syrup
Pecan halves

Combine crumbs, 3 tablespoons sugar, and butter; press onto bottom of 9-inch springform pan. Bake at 350° for 10 minutes.

Blend cream cheese, brown sugar, and flour at medium speed with a mixer. Add eggs, one at a time, beating well after each addition. Stir in vanilla and nuts.

Pour mixture over crumbs and bake at 350° for 50–55 minutes, or until set in middle.

Loosen cake from rim of pan but cool thoroughly before removing side of pan. Chill.

Brush with maple syrup and garnish with pecan halves, if desired.

YIELD: 10–12 SERVINGS

Cincinnati Celebrates
THE JUNIOR LEAGUE OF CINCINNATI, OHIO

Frozen Cheesecake

Margarine
1 cup vanilla wafer crumbs
2 8-ounce packages cream cheese
4 egg yolks
2 cups sugar
2 teaspoons vanilla
4 egg whites
1 cup heavy cream

Grease a 9-inch springform pan well with margarine and press wafer crumbs onto bottom and sides.

Soften cheese. Add egg yolks and beat until fluffy. Add sugar and vanilla and beat well.

In separate bowls, beat egg whites and whip cream. Fold into cheese and egg mixture.

Spoon mixture into prepared pan; freeze for 12–15 hours.

Garnish with cookie crumbs, crumbled chocolate bars, or fruit and serve frozen.

YIELD: 12 SERVINGS

THE JUNIOR LEAGUE OF EVANSVILLE, INDIANA

. . . .

Super Simple Cheesecake

1 cup graham cracker crumbs
½ stick margarine, softened
1 cup sugar
2 8-ounce packages cream cheese, softened
2 eggs
1¾ teaspoons vanilla
½ pint sour cream

Recipe continues . . .

Mix graham cracker crumbs with margarine and ¼ cup sugar. Press onto bottom and on sides of 9-inch pie plate.

Blend together cream cheese, ½ cup sugar, eggs, and ¾ teaspoon vanilla and spoon into prepared pie plate. Bake at 375° for 20 minutes. Remove from oven and cool.

Combine sour cream, the remaining ¼ cup sugar, and remaining teaspoon vanilla and spread on top of cake. Bake for 10 minutes at 475°

YIELD: 1 9-INCH CAKE

THE JUNIOR LEAGUE OF EVANSVILLE, INDIANA

Strawberry Shortcake—Circa 1900

2 cups sifted flour
2 teaspoons baking powder
½ teaspoon salt
2 tablespoons sugar
½ cup butter
½ cup light cream
Softened butter
Sliced sweetened strawberries

Sift together dry ingredients. Cut in butter until mixture is in coarse crumbs. Add cream, stirring just until dough follows fork around bowl.

On lightly floured surface, pat or roll dough to 1-inch thickness. Cut with cutter into eight individual servings. Bake on ungreased baking sheet 'in very hot (450°) oven 8–10 minutes.

Split cakes, spread layers, and top generously with soft butter. Spoon sweetened sliced berries between layers and on top.

Serve warm.

YIELD: 8 SERVINGS

The Cook's Book
THE JUNIOR LEAGUE OF CEDAR RAPIDS, IOWA

Paper Bag Apple Pie

6 large cooking apples
1 cup sugar
2 teaspoons flour
1 teaspoon lemon juice
Few dashes cinnamon
1 9-inch unbaked pastry shell
½ cup sugar
½ cup flour
½ cup butter

Peel, core, and slice the apples. Mix the apples with half the sugar, 2 teaspoons flour, lemon juice, and cinnamon. Empty into pie crust. Mix remaining sugar, the ½ cup flour, and the butter until mixture resembles coarse crumbs. Sprinkle on top of apples.

Place pie in a brown paper bag and tuck ends under pie. Bake at 425° for 50 minutes. Take out of bag and return to oven to brown for 5 minutes.

YIELD: 6–8 SERVINGS

THE JUNIOR LEAGUE OF SOUTH BEND, INDIANA

· · · · · · · · · · · · · · · · · ·

Wabash Valley Apple Pie

6–8 cooking apples, peeled, cored, and sliced
1 9-inch unbaked pastry shell
½ cup sugar
3 tablespoons flour
¾ teaspoon cinnamon
¼ teaspoon nutmeg

Place apples in pastry shell, filling it rather full as mixture will cook down.

Recipe continues . . .

Mix sugar, flour, cinnamon, and nutmeg and sprinkle on top of apples. Top with Crumb Crust. Bake pie at 400° for 15 minutes. Reduce heat to 325° and cook 35–40 minutes, or until apples are softened and mixture is bubbly.

CRUMB CRUST:

⅓ cup softened butter
⅔ cup sugar
1 cup flour

Cut butter into sugar and flour to a corn meal consistency. Sprinkle over apple mixture.

YIELD: 6–8 SERVINGS

THE JUNIOR LEAGUE OF INDIANAPOLIS, INDIANA

· · · · · · · · · · · · · · · · · · · ·

Apple-Peach Crumb Pie

5 cups sliced apples (about 8)
1 can sliced peaches, drained
¼ cup granulated sugar
¼ cup brown sugar
3½ tablespoons flour
1 teaspoon cinnamon
¼ teaspoon nutmeg
⅛ teaspoon salt
1 9-inch unbaked pastry shell

Mix all filling ingredients and spoon into the 9-inch pie shell. Cover with topping and bake at 400° for about 40 minutes.

YIELD: 1 9-INCH PIE

TOPPING:
⅓ cup softened butter
¾ cup flour
¼ cup sugar
¼ cup brown sugar
Cinnamon and nutmeg to taste

Mix all ingredients and sprinkle over top of pie.

THE JUNIOR LEAGUE OF COLUMBUS, OHIO

Mountain High Raspberry Pie

1 cup heavy cream
2 egg whites
1 10-ounce package frozen raspberries
1 cup sugar
1 tablespoon lemon juice
2 8-inch baked pastry shells or crumb crusts

Whip cream; set aside.

Beat egg whites until fluffy. Add berries, sugar, and lemon juice and beat at high speed for 15 minutes. Fold in whipped cream and spoon into pastry shells or crumb crusts. Freeze for several hours.

Cut and serve at once.

If fresh raspberries are available, use 1½ cups and increase sugar to 1¼ cups.

YIELD: 2 8-INCH PIES

Bluff City Cooks
THE JUNIOR LEAGUE OF GREATER ALTON, ILLINOIS

Cranberry Pie

2 cups raw cranberries
½ cup chopped nuts
1½ cups sugar
2 eggs
1 cup flour
½ cup melted butter

Butter a 9-inch pie plate and put into it the cranberries and nuts. Sprinkle with ½ cup sugar.

In small bowl, beat eggs with 1 cup sugar until light and fluffy. Stir in flour and melted butter. Pour batter over berries and bake at 325° for 1 hour.

Serve with vanilla ice cream, cranberry sherbet, or whipped cream for dessert or plain as coffee cake. Ideal for holiday menus.

YIELD: 6–8 SERVINGS

THE JUNIOR LEAGUE OF CHAMPAIGN-URBANA, ILLINOIS

Toasted Coconut Pie

3 eggs, beaten
1½ cups sugar
½ cup melted butter
4 teaspoons lemon juice
1 teaspoon vanilla
1 3½-ounce can flaked coconut
1 8-inch unbaked pastry shell

Combine filling ingredients. Pour into pie shell and bake at 350° for 40–45 minutes.

YIELD: 8 SERVINGS

THE JUNIOR LEAGUE OF CHAMPAIGN-URBANA, ILLINOIS

· · · · · · · · · · · · · · · · · ·

Chiffon Pumpkin Pie

3 eggs, separated
1 cup sugar
½ cup evaporated milk
½ teaspoon salt
1 teaspoon pumpkin pie spice
1¼ cups mashed pumpkin
1 envelope unflavored gelatin
¼ cup cold water
1 9-inch baked pastry shell

Beat egg yolks well and stir in sugar, milk, salt, and spice. Beat well. Add pumpkin and stir well. Cook over simmering water for 10–15 minutes, or until thick.

Soak gelatin in the cold water and add to the hot pumpkin mixture. Stir well. Cool.

Beat egg whites until stiff and fold in. Pour into pie shell and chill until set.

YIELD: 8 SERVINGS

THE JUNIOR LEAGUE OF YOUNGSTOWN, OHIO

· · · · · · · · · · · · · · · · · ·

Chewy Chess Pie

1 cup brown sugar
½ cup white sugar
1 teaspoon flour
2 eggs
2 tablespoons milk
1 teaspoon vanilla
½ cup melted butter
1 8- or 9-inch unbaked pastry shell

Mix sugars and flour; break eggs into mixture and mix. Stir in milk and vanilla; then add melted butter and mix.

Pour into pie shell and bake at 350° for 40 minutes.

YIELD: 1 8-INCH PIE

THE JUNIOR LEAGUE OF EVANSVILLE, INDIANA

· ·

Pecan Pie

3 eggs
1 cup dark corn syrup
⅓ teaspoon salt
⅔ cup sugar
1 cup pecans
2 tablespoons milk
2 9-inch frozen unbaked pie shells

Mix eggs, corn syrup, salt, and sugar until well blended. Stir in pecans and milk.

Pour into pie shells and bake for 45 minutes at 375°.

YIELD: 2 9-INCH PIES

THE JUNIOR LEAGUE OF EVANSVILLE, INDIANA

. . . .

Strawberry Schaum Pie

4 ounces cream cheese, softened
½ cup butter
1 cup flour
3 egg whites
1 cup sugar
1 pint strawberries, washed and hulled

Cut cream cheese and butter into flour with pastry blender. Pat into 8-inch pie plate and bake at 350° for 20 minutes.

Beat egg whites until soft peaks form; gradually beat in sugar until stiff peaks form. Fold strawberries into egg whites.

Spoon into baked pastry shell. Bake at 200° for 25 minutes.

YIELD: 8 SERVINGS

Be Our Guest
THE JUNIOR LEAGUE OF MILWAUKEE, WISCONSIN

. . . .

Blueberry Pie

Pastry for 2-crust pie
⅔ cup sugar
3 tablespoons flour
½ teaspoon grated lemon rind
1–2 teaspoons lemon juice
¼ teaspoon nutmeg
½ teaspoon cinnamon
¼ teaspoon salt
4 cups fresh or frozen blueberries (not in syrup)
1 tablespoon butter or margarine
Light cream and sugar for glaze

Line pie plate with pastry. Combine sugar, flour, lemon rind and juice, nutmeg, cinnamon and salt. Place half of berries in lined pie plate and sprinkle half of sugar mixture over berries. Repeat. Dot with butter.

Roll out top crust and place over pie. Cut 3–4 small slits near center. Glaze by brushing top crust with cream and sprinkling with sugar.

Bake at 425° for 40–50 minutes, or until crust is nicely browned.

YIELD: 1 9- OR 10-INCH PIE

Cookbook
THE JUNIOR LEAGUE OF GRAND RAPIDS, MICHIGAN

·   ·   ·   ·   ·   ·   ·   ·   ·   ·   ·   ·   ·   ·   ·   ·

Pat's Fresh Peach Pie

Pastry for 2-crust pie
3½ cups peeled and sliced fresh peaches
½ cup brown sugar
2 tablespoons flour
½ teaspoon salt
¼ cup butter
2 teaspoons lemon juice

Divide pastry in half; make a pie shell from one half, and cut the second half into lattice strips. Put peaches in pie shell.

Mix sugar, flour, salt, and butter in saucepan. Cook until thick and add lemon juice. Pour over peaches and cover with lattice top.

Bake 30 minutes at 425°.

YIELD: 6 SERVINGS

THE JUNIOR LEAGUE OF ROCKFORD, ILLINOIS

·   ·   ·   ·   ·   ·   ·   ·   ·   ·   ·   ·   ·   ·   ·   ·   ·   ·

Peach Chantilly Pie

4 cups puréed fresh peaches (6–8)
2 tablespoons fresh lemon juice
2 envelopes unflavored gelatin
2 tablespoons Curaçao or orange liqueur
4 tablespoons sugar
2 cups heavy cream
2 fresh peaches
A few green grapes
A few red raspberries

Mix puréed peaches with lemon juice; empty into sieve set into a bowl and drain off juices for 20 minutes, saving both purée and juice.

Stir gelatin and ½ cup juice over low heat until gelatin is dissolved. Mix purée with liqueur, sugar, and cooled gelatin.

Whip cream and fold into peach mixture. Spoon into baked shell and refrigerate for 4–6 hours. Just before serving, garnish with sliced peaches, a few green grapes, and some fresh raspberries.

This may be prepared a day ahead as it takes time to make, but do not garnish until ready to serve.

YIELD: 8 SERVINGS

Recipe continues . . .

RICH PIE CRUST:

⅓ cup butter
2 egg yolks
½ cup sugar
½ teaspoon grated lemon rind
2 teaspoons sherry
1 cup plus 2 tablespoons flour
⅛ teaspoon salt

Let butter reach room temperature. In electric mixer, blend egg yolks, sugar, butter, lemon rind, and sherry. Stir in 2 tablespoons flour and salt. Work in remaining flour.

Turn pastry out onto wax paper, flatten into an 8-inch circle, wrap, and chill for at least 1 hour or overnight.

Preheat oven to 350°. Pat dough evenly onto bottom and sides of a greased 11-inch pie plate or flan pan. Cut wax paper into the size of the dough and press onto crust. Cover with lima beans or rice to prevent pastry from puffing.

Bake for 15 minutes, or until lightly browned; reduce temperature to 300°, remove paper (save beans), and return to oven for 5 minutes longer.

THE JUNIOR LEAGUE OF SOUTH BEND, INDIANA

· · · · · · · · · · · · · · · · · ·

Sunny Silver Pie

1 envelope unflavored gelatin
¼ cup cold water
2 lemons
6 eggs, separated
2 cups sugar
2 baked pie shells
1 cup heavy cream, whipped

Soften gelatin in cold water. Set aside.

Grate lemon rinds and then squeeze juice from lemons. Combine egg yolks, 1½ cups of the sugar, rinds, and lemon juice in top of a double boiler. Beat over boiling water until light yellow, thick, and fluffy. Remove from heat and stir in gelatin while still hot.

Put egg whites in large bowl and beat until stiff but not dry. Stir one-third of the beaten egg whites into the egg yolk mixture, then fold egg yolk mixture gently into remaining egg whites. Divide into the baked pie shells and refrigerate for several hours.

Serve topped with whipped cream sweetened with remaining sugar. This is especially good after a dinner of ham or fish.

YIELD: 2 PIES

THE JUNIOR LEAGUE OF SOUTH BEND, INDIANA

· · · · · · · · · · · · · · · · · ·

Rum Pie

6 egg yolks
1 cup sugar
1 envelope unflavored gelatin
½ cup water
1 pint heavy cream
¼ cup dark rum
1 8-inch graham cracker pie crust
Grated bitter chocolate

Combine eggs and sugar. Beat until light. Soften gelatin in the ½ cup water and bring to boil. Add to egg mixture. Beat well and set aside to cool.

Beat cream until stiff and fold into egg mixture. Fold in rum. Spoon filling into pie shell and chill in refrigerator until set.

Grate chocolate over top before serving.

This may be frozen.

YIELD: 6 SERVINGS

THE JUNIOR LEAGUE OF TOLEDO, OHIO

· · · · · · · · · · · · · · · · · ·

Bananas Superb

6 ounces semisweet chocolate pieces
3 tablespoons rum
⅓ cup heavy cream
1 tablespoon butter
2 or 3 bananas, sliced
Vanilla or coffee ice cream

Melt chocolate with rum, cream, and butter; add sliced bananas, warm, and serve over ice cream.

If desired, flame with warm brandy before serving. This sauce is also good with crepes and ice cream.

YIELD: 2–4 SERVINGS

Cincinnati Celebrates
THE JUNIOR LEAGUE OF CINCINNATI, OHIO

·　·　·　·　·　·　·　·　·　·　·　·　·　·　·　·　·　·

Figs in Sour Cream

12–16 whole canned figs
1 pint sour cream
2 tablespoons brown sugar
2 tablespoons confectioners' sugar
1 to 2 tablespoons medium or dark rum
1 to 2 tablespoons crème de cacao

Drain figs in sieve for several hours and place on paper towels in refrigerator for further draining, occasionally patting figs dry and changing towels frequently.

Combine remaining ingredients and correct flavoring according to taste.

Combine fruit and sauce and serve in chilled bowl.
Sauce may also be used with seedless grapes or fresh peach halves.

YIELD: 4–6 SERVINGS

The Cook's Book
THE JUNIOR LEAGUE OF CEDAR RAPIDS, IOWA

· ·

Apple Crisp Dessert

7 medium tart apples, peeled
1 cup sugar
1 cup unsifted flour
1 teaspoon baking powder
¾ teaspoon salt
1 egg, well beaten
⅓ cup melted butter
Cinnamon

Dice the apples and put in a greased 8- or 9-inch baking dish.

Mix dry ingredients; add beaten egg and mix with fingers until crumbly. Pour crumbly mixture over apples, then sprinkle melted butter over the topping. Sprinkle with cinnamon.

Bake at 375° for 45 minutes.

If desired, serve with ice cream.

YIELD: 6 ½ -CUP SERVINGS

THE JUNIOR LEAGUE OF SOUTH BEND, INDIANA

· ·

Peach Cobbler

4 cups sliced fresh peaches or frozen unsugared peaches
1 cup sugar
3 tablespoons plus ¾ cup flour
2 tablespoons melted butter
¼ teaspoon salt
¼ cup shortening
2 tablespoons water

Preheat oven to 400°. Put peaches in bottom of an 8 x 8-inch pan. Bake in oven until peaches start to simmer. Mix together the sugar and the 3 tablespoons flour and sprinkle over the peaches. Add melted butter.

Put remaining flour into a bowl; add salt and shortening and work with fingertips until mixture resembles coarse oatmeal. Mix in water to form a stiff dough.

Roll out dough on lightly floured board into a square large enough to fit over the peaches. Prick pastry with fork and bake for 35–40 minutes.

YIELD: 8 SERVINGS

THE JUNIOR LEAGUE OF SPRINGFIELD, ILLINOIS

Hattie's Peach Luscious

¼ cup sugar
2 eggs, separated
3 tablespoons shortening
1 cup flour
3 teaspoons baking powder
½ teaspoon salt
Grated rind of 1 lemon
½ cup milk
8–10 large peaches, peeled and quartered
⅔ cup sugar
1 tablespoon lemon juice
¼ cup confectioners' sugar

Blend ¼ cup sugar, egg yolks, and shortening together in a few fast stirs. Combine flour, baking powder, salt, and lemon rind alternately with milk.

Rub sides of baking dish with shortening and fill with peaches. Sprinkle with the ⅔ cup sugar and the lemon juice. Pour batter over peaches. Bake at 350° for about 30 minutes. Remove from oven.

Cover with meringue made by beating 2 egg whites until stiff and gradually beating in the confectioners' sugar. Brown meringue in 325° oven for about 15 minutes.

YIELD: 6 SERVINGS

THE JUNIOR LEAGUE OF TOLEDO, OHIO

Strawberry Delight

¼ pound butter
2 eggs, beaten
1 pound confectioners' sugar
1 11-ounce box vanilla wafers
1 quart fresh strawberries, washed and hulled
1 pint heavy cream, whipped

Cream together butter, eggs, and sugar

Crumble vanilla wafers by rolling with a rolling pin. Spread half of the crumbs on the bottom of a buttered 8 x 12-inch pan. Spread creamed mixture over this. Layer strawberries on top. Whip cream stiff and spread over strawberries. Sprinkle with remaining crumbs.

Chill for at least 10 hours. Cut in squares to serve.

YIELD: **12** SERVINGS

Discover Dayton
THE JUNIOR LEAGUE OF DAYTON, OHIO

Strawberry Sublime

1 cup flour
¼ cup brown sugar
½ cup butter
½ cup chopped walnuts
1 cup granulated sugar
2 tablespoons lemon juice
2 egg whites
1 10-ounce package frozen strawberries, partially thawed
1 cup heavy cream, whipped
½ teaspoon vanilla

Mix flour, brown sugar, butter, and walnuts together and spread on cookie sheet. Toast at 375° for 10 minutes, stirring occasionally, until golden brown. Cool and crumble.

Beat sugar, lemon juice, egg whites, and strawberries at high speed for 15 minutes. Fold in whipped cream and vanilla.

Spread half the crumbs on bottom of 9 x 13-inch pan, cover with strawberry mixture, and top with remaining crumbs.

Freeze until ready to serve, at least 6 hours.

YIELD: 10–12 SERVINGS

Sunflower Sampler
THE JUNIOR LEAGUE OF WICHITA, KANSAS

· · · · · · · · · · · · · · · · · · ·

Heavenly Delight

2 eggs
4 tablespoons sugar
4 tablespoons lemon juice
1 17-ounce can Queen Anne pitted sweet cherries
1 20-ounce can pineapple chunks
1 11-ounce can mandarin oranges
18 large marshmallows
½ pint heavy cream, whipped

Beat eggs. Add sugar and lemon juice. Cook over low heat until thickened, stirring constantly. Set aside until cool.

Cut up fruit and marshmallows and combine in a 9 x 13-inch pan or serving bowl. Add lemon juice mixture, then fold in the whipped cream.

Chill overnight in refrigerator.

Delightful after a heavy meal.

YIELD: 10–12 SERVINGS

THE JUNIOR LEAGUE OF YOUNGSTOWN, OHIO

· · · · · · · · · · · · · · · · · · ·

"Instant" Trifle

2 4-ounce packages ladyfingers
Raspberry or apricot jam
¼ cup white wine or orange juice
1 6-ounce package instant French vanilla pudding
1 cup heavy cream, whipped
Toasted slivered almonds

Line bottom of an 8 x 8-inch pan with ladyfingers filled with jam. Sprinkle wine or juice over them. Refrigerate for 1½ hours.

Mix pudding according to package directions and pour on top of ladyfingers. Refrigerate until set.

Cover with sweetened whipped cream and sprinkle with toasted almonds.

YIELD: 8 SERVINGS

THE JUNIOR LEAGUE OF YOUNGSTOWN, OHIO

. . . .

Rich Custard

1¾ cups sugar
8 eggs
2 13-ounce cans evaporated milk
2 teaspoons vanilla
Rum or brandy

Put 1 cup of the sugar into a deep pan in which the custard is to be baked and place over heat, stirring constantly, until sugar melts and turns golden. Tip the pan around until it is entirely coated with the syrup. Cool.

To make custard, beat eggs, milk, vanilla, and the remaining ¾ cup sugar and mix well. Pour into the caramel-coated pan, cover, and place pan in a larger pan containing water.

Bake at 350° for almost 2 hours, or until a knife inserted in the center comes out clean. When done, chill, covered, overnight.

To serve, turn out on platter. Pour warmed rum or brandy over flan, light, and send to the table flaming.

YIELD: 8–10 SERVINGS

VARIATIONS:

Add ¼ cup blanched ground almonds or 2–3 tablespoons cocoa to basic recipe.

The Discovery Shop Cookbook
THE JUNIOR LEAGUE OF SIOUX CITY, IOWA

Southern Illinois Date Pudding

1 cup brown sugar
1 cup flour
2 teaspoons baking powder
1 cup pecans
¾ cup dates
⅓ cup milk

SYRUP:
1 cup brown sugar
2 cups boiling water
1 tablespoon butter

In electric mixer on low speed, mix brown sugar, flour, baking powder, pecans, dates, and milk.

In 9 x 13-inch pan, combine brown sugar, boiling water, and butter. Drop dough by spoonfuls onto syrup and bake for 20–25 minutes at 350°.

Syrup will be thick when pudding is done.

YIELD: 8 SERVINGS

THE JUNIOR LEAGUE OF SPRINGFIELD, ILLINOIS

Ozark Pudding

This recipe has been handed down through three generations. It originated somewhere in the hill country of the Ozarks in the late 1890s.

2 eggs
1 cup sugar
6 tablespoons flour
2½ teaspoons baking powder
2 teaspoons vanilla
Pinch salt
1 cup chopped pecans
1 cup diced unpeeled apples

Combine eggs, sugar, flour, baking powder, vanilla, and salt. Add nuts and apples and beat for about 5 minutes.

Pour into greased 8 x 8-inch pan and bake at 350° for 30–35 minutes. If desired, serve with heavy cream.

YIELD: 6 SERVINGS

THE JUNIOR LEAGUE OF SPRINGFIELD, ILLINOIS

· · · · · · · · · · · · · · ·

German Dessert Pancakes

An original German recipe handed down through three generations. It was originally cooked on a coal stove.

4 eggs
4 heaping tablespoons flour
1 cup milk
¾ teaspoon salt
1 tablespoon bacon drippings

Mix ingredients well in blender. Pour very thin layer of batter into very hot iron skillet. When done, the pancake should have a leopard pattern.

Serve with applesauce or jams. The German pancake should be as thin as a crepe and rolled with fillings in the center. May be flamed with rum or brandy, if desired, as well.

YIELD: 6 SERVINGS

THE JUNIOR LEAGUE OF EVANSVILLE, INDIANA

· ·

Hot Lemon Soufflé

¼ cup butter
½ cup sugar
6 tablespoons lemon juice
Grated rind of 2 lemons
4 eggs, separated, plus 1 egg white
Confectioners' sugar

Butter a 1-quart soufflé dish. In saucepan (not aluminum), heat butter with ¼ cup sugar, lemon juice and rind until butter is melted. Remove from heat and beat in egg yolks, one at a time. Heat, stirring constantly, until mixture thickens to about the consistency of heavy cream. Set aside.

Twenty to 30 minutes before serving, set oven to 425°. Stiffly whip 5 egg whites. Add remaining ¼ cup sugar and beat until glossy. Stir one-quarter of the egg whites into the lemon mixture. Add this mixture to remaining egg whites and fold together as lightly as possible.

Spoon into prepared dish and bake for 12–15 minutes, or until puffed and brown.

Sprinkle with confectioners' sugar and serve at once.

YIELD: 4–6 SERVINGS

THE JUNIOR LEAGUE OF COLUMBUS, OHIO

· ·

Cheese Blintz Soufflé

¼ pound butter
14 blintzes
1½ cups sour cream
¼ cup sugar
½ teaspoon salt
1 teaspoon vanilla
1 tablespoon orange juice
4 eggs, well beaten

Melt butter in casserole. Place blintzes in butter in one layer. Blend sour cream with sugar, salt, vanilla, orange juice, and eggs and pour over blintzes.

Bake at 350° for 45 minutes, or until top begins to brown.

Serve with sour cream, apple sauce, and cinnamon sugar.

YIELD: 6–7 SERVINGS

BLINTZ CREPE BATTER:
2 eggs
1 cup flour
½ teaspoon salt
1 cup water

Combine ingredients in blender jar; blend for about 1 minute. Scrape down sides with rubber spatula and blend for another 15 seconds, or until smooth. Refrigerate for 1 hour.

Cook in traditional crepe manner.

YIELD: ABOUT 14 CREPES

CHEESE BLINTZES:
2 cups cottage cheese
1 egg yolk
2 tablespoons sugar
1 tablespoon lemon juice
14 crepes

Drain cottage cheese in strainer or colander for at least ½ hour, then gently press out any excess liquid. In a bowl mix cottage cheese with egg yolk, sugar, and lemon juice.

Spoon some of the filling onto center of each cooked crepe. Fold over bottom, both sides, then the top, making little sealed packages. These may be frozen.

YIELD: 14 BLINTZES

THE JUNIOR LEAGUE OF CHAMPAIGN-URBANA, ILLINOIS

Chocolate Crème Custards

1 12-ounce package semisweet chocolate chips
4 tablespoons sugar
1 cup heavy cream
6 egg yolks, lightly beaten
1 cup heavy cream, whipped
Whipped cream for garnish

Melt chocolate in top of a double boiler over hot water. Add sugar and cream. Stir occasionally until mixture is smooth. Remove from heat to cool.

Add small amount of chocolate mixture to egg yolks, stirring constantly. Continue adding chocolate to eggs until all is smoothly blended. Refrigerate until completely cool, then fold in whipped cream. Chill 3 hours.

Serve in tall narrow glass dishes, such as Irish coffee cups, or in small, covered pots de crème. Top with whipped cream.

YIELD: 8 SERVINGS

THE JUNIOR LEAGUE OF COLUMBUS, OHIO

The Brandied Marshmallow

1 pound marshmallows
2 cups hot black coffee
1 cup finely chopped pecans
3 tablespoons rum or brandy
1 cup heavy cream, whipped
1 tablespoon sugar
1 teaspoon rum or brandy

In top of a double boiler, dissolve marshmallows in the hot coffee. Remove from heat and stir in the chopped pecans and 3 tablespoons rum or brandy.

Pour into ring mold; refrigerate.

To serve, unmold and fill center with whipped cream flavored with sugar and 1 teaspoon rum or brandy.

YIELD: 4–6 SERVINGS

The Cook's Book
THE JUNIOR LEAGUE OF CEDAR RAPIDS, IOWA

. . . .

Bittersweet Chocolate Crunch Bombe

¼ cup butter
¼ cup sugar
¾ cup graham cracker crumbs
½ cup coconut flakes
¼ cup chopped salted pecans
1 quart vanilla ice cream, softened
1 quart bittersweet chocolate ice cream, softened

Cream butter until fluffy; gradually add sugar and crumbs. Stir in coconut and pecan bits. Butter either a 7-cup bowl or bundt mold. Press mixture on sides and bottom.

Spread vanilla ice cream as evenly as possible to form about a 1-inch layer over crumb mixture, using back of large spoon or spatula. Immediately place in freezer to harden. (If ice cream is too soft to adhere to sides, set ice cream in freezer first to harden slightly; then mold.) Spoon chocolate ice cream in center to fill bowl. Freeze entire mold.

At serving time, unmold by dipping mold in sink of warm water and gently trying to loosen edges. Invert on chilled platter with slight bowl shape to it. Serve with your favorite fudge sauce to ladle over it

YIELD: 10–12 SERVINGS

THE JUNIOR LEAGUE OF COLUMBUS, OHIO

· · · · · · · · · · · · · · · · · · · ·

Chocolat Flambé d'Orange

2 tablespoons butter
4 tablespoons sugar
1½ ounces Jamaica rum
Grated rind and juice of 1 orange
2 cups chocolate sauce

Melt butter in hot chafing dish; add sugar and mix well. Stir in rum. Everything must be very hot. Tilt pan and flame rum. As it flames, again tilt pan in a circular motion to swirl all together. Grate the orange rind right into the hot mixture; then squeeze all the juice from the same orange. (It works best if the orange is very juicy!) Stir in the chocolate sauce and simmer 2–3 minutes.

Hot orange-flavored chocolate sauce is delicious on ice cream or plain cake. It can be put together at serving time with great flourish or done in advance and kept warm.

Keeps in covered jar in refrigerator for many months—if it lasts that long. Quantities can be multiplied easily.

YIELD: 6 SERVINGS

THE JUNIOR LEAGUE OF COLUMBUS, OHIO

· · · · · · · · · · · · · · · · · · · ·

Chocolate Soufflé with Mocha Sauce

¼ cup butter
2 squares unsweetened chocolate (2 ounces)
¼ cup flour
¼ teaspoon salt
1 cup milk
4 egg yolks
½ cup sugar
¼ teaspoon mace
1 teaspoon vanilla
6 egg whites
Pinch salt

Melt butter and chocolate in double boiler. Stir in flour and salt and blend thoroughly. Add milk, stirring constantly. Cook, stirring, until very thick.

Beat egg yolks. Add sugar gradually and beat until light. Add mace and vanilla. Mixture should be thick and lemon colored. Add chocolate mixture to yolk mixture.

Beat egg whites to soft peak stage with pinch of salt. Beat a bit more, then fold in chocolate mixture, using a large spatula or very large whisk.

Turn into buttered and sugared 2-quart soufflé dish.* Place in hot-water bath. Bake in 325° oven until well risen, lightly browned, and done, about 55–60 minutes. Serve at once with Mocha Sauce.

* Or spoon into buttered and sugared individual soufflé dishes and freeze immediately. Just before serving, place in hot-water bath while still frozen and bake at 325° until puffed and lightly browned, about 45–50 minutes.

YIELD: 4–6 SERVINGS

MOCHA SAUCE:
¼ cup softened butter
1 cup sifted confectioners' sugar
2 teaspoons cocoa
⅛ teaspoon salt
1 tablespoon strong cold coffee
1 teaspoon vanilla

Cream butter until light. Sift sugar with cocoa and salt and blend into softened butter. Blend in coffee and vanilla. Mix well.

YIELD: ABOUT 1 CUP

THE JUNIOR LEAGUE OF DES MOINES, IOWA

·　·　·　·　·　·　·　·　·　·　·　·　·　·　·

Cognac Toffee

½ cup butter
2 cups confectioners' sugar
2 tablespoons cocoa
2 eggs, separated
1 cup chopped pecans
1 teaspoon vanilla
2 tablespoons cognac
½ pound vanilla wafers, crushed
½ pint heavy cream, whipped and sweetened to taste
Strawberries

Cream butter. Blend in sugar and cocoa. Add beaten egg yolks, nuts, vanilla, and cognac. Fold in stiffly beaten egg whites.

Line a 9 x 9 x 2-inch pan with half the vanilla wafer crumbs. Spread cognac mixture over and top with remaining crumbs.

Refrigerate for at least 24 hours before serving.

Recipe continues . . .

About 4–6 hours before serving, spread with sweetened whipped cream. Serve topped with a few strawberries.

YIELD: 8 SERVINGS

Cincinnati Celebrates
THE JUNIOR LEAGUE OF CINCINNATI, OHIO

·   ·   ·   ·   ·   ·   ·   ·   ·   ·   ·   ·   ·   ·   ·   ·   ·   ·   ·

Frozen Frangos

1 cup butter
3 cups confectioners' sugar
4 ounces unsweetened chocolate, melted
1 cup chopped nuts
4 eggs
1 teaspoon vanilla
1 teaspoon peppermint extract

Cream butter and sugar until light and fluffy. Add chocolate, ¾ cup nuts, and remaining ingredients. Mix well.

Spoon into a double thickness of paper muffin liners. Sprinkle with remaining ¼ cup nuts.

Freeze. Serve directly from freezer.

YIELD: 25–30 SERVINGS

Be Our Guest
THE JUNIOR LEAGUE OF MILWAUKEE, WISCONSIN

·   ·   ·   ·   ·   ·   ·   ·   ·   ·   ·   ·   ·   ·   ·   ·   ·   ·   ·

Chocolate Mousse

2 cups semisweet chocolate chips
¾ cup milk
1 cup confectioners' sugar
2 cups heavy cream, whipped
3 tablespoons crème de cacao
1 teaspoon vanilla

In heavy saucepan, combine chocolate chips and milk; stir over low heat until well blended and smooth. Add confectioners' sugar and stir well. Cool. Fold whipped cream, crème de cacao, and vanilla into chocolate mixture.

Spoon into chocolate cups or paper baking cups placed in muffin pan. Freeze at least 1 hour. Peel off paper before serving.

YIELD: 10–12 SERVINGS

THE JUNIOR LEAGUE OF DES MOINES, IOWA

Mousse-in-a-Minute

1 6-ounce package chocolate bits
2 eggs
3 tablespoons very strong hot coffee
1–2 tablespoons rum or Cointreau (or to taste)
¾ cup scalded milk

In a blender container, combine the chocolate, eggs, coffee, rum or Cointreau, and milk. Blend the mixture at high speed for 2 minutes.

Pour into four dessert cups and chill.

To dress it up, if desired, line the serving containers with lady-

Recipe continues . . .

fingers, drizzle with Cointreau, and top with whipped cream flavored with Cointreau. Grate a little bitter chocolate over the cream.

YIELD: 4 SERVINGS

Marigolds to Munch On
THE JUNIOR LEAGUE OF PEORIA, ILLINOIS

· ·

Swedish Snow Pudding

2 cups milk
1 cup sugar
½ teaspoon salt
3 tablespoons cornstarch
1 tablespoon butter
1 teaspoon vanilla
2 large egg yolks, beaten
2 large egg whites
Orange segments from 5 oranges
Sugar
Orange juice

Heat milk in top of a double boiler until hot. Mix together sugar, salt, and cornstarch and stir into hot milk. Add butter and vanilla and cook until thick. Stir in beaten egg yolks. Remove from heat.

Beat egg whites until stiff and fold carefully into hot custard—some spots of white may remain. Cool and put in refrigerator.

Serve over orange segments, sugared to taste. Pour a little fresh or frozen orange juice over each serving.

YIELD: 5–6 SERVINGS

THE JUNIOR LEAGUE OF ROCKFORD, ILLINOIS

· ·

Frozen Lemon Dessert

3 egg yolks
½ cup sugar
3 teaspoons lemon juice
½ teaspoon lemon rind
1 cup crushed vanilla wafers
3 egg whites, stiffly beaten
1 cup heavy cream, whipped

Beat egg yolks with all but 2 tablespoons sugar. Add lemon juice and lemon rind and beat until light. Cook in double boiler, stirring constantly, until smooth and thickened. Cool.

Line bottom and sides of ice cube tray with wafer crumbs.

Beat remaining 2 tablespoons sugar into egg whites and fold into lemon mixture. Fold in whipped cream. Spoon into ice cube tray and sprinkle a few crumbs on the top.

Freeze for at least 4 hours before serving.

YIELD: 6 SERVINGS

THE JUNIOR LEAGUE OF TOLEDO, OHIO

· ·

Raspberry Mold

1 10-ounce package frozen raspberries
1 6-ounce package raspberry or strawberry gelatin
1½ cups boiling water
1 pint vanilla ice cream, softened
1 6-ounce can frozen pink lemonade concentrate

Drain raspberries; reserve syrup.

Dissolve gelatin in the hot water. Slowly add softened ice cream. Stir until well mixed. Stir in frozen lemonade, raspberry syrup, and raspberries.

Recipe continues . . .

Pour into 6-cup mold and chill until set.

YIELD: 8 SERVINGS

The Discovery Shop Cookbook
THE JUNIOR LEAGUE OF SIOUX CITY, IOWA

· ·

Coconut Chews

¾ cup shortening (half butter or margarine)
¾ cup confectioners' sugar
1½ cups flour
2 eggs
1 cup brown sugar, packed
2 tablespoons flour
½ teaspoon baking powder
½ teaspoon salt
1 tablespoon vanilla
½ cup chopped walnuts
½ cup flaked coconut

Cream shortening and sugar. Blend in flour. Press mixture in bottom of ungreased 9 x 13-inch pan. Bake at 350° for 12–15 minutes.

Mix remaining ingredients and spread over hot baked layer. Bake 20 minutes longer.

While warm, spread with Orange Lemon Icing. Cool and cut into small bars to serve.

ORANGE LEMON ICING:
1½ cups confectioners' sugar
2 tablespoons melted butter or margarine
3 tablespoons orange juice
1 teaspoon lemon juice

Mix all ingredients into a smooth icing.

YIELD: 16 BARS

THE JUNIOR LEAGUE OF SAGINAW, MICHIGAN

Cheesecake Bars

1 cup flour
⅓ cup brown sugar, packed
⅓ cup butter or margarine
8 ounces cream cheese, softened
¼ cup granulated sugar
1 egg
2 tablespoons milk
1 tablespoon lemon juice
1 tablespoon vanilla
2 tablespoons chopped walnuts

Mix together flour, brown sugar, and butter to fine crumbs. Reserve 1 cup of crumbs for topping. Press remainder into an ungreased 8-inch-square pan. Bake at 350° for 12 minutes, or until lightly browned.

In mixer bowl, cream together cream cheese and sugar. Add egg, milk, lemon juice, and vanilla. Beat well. Spread batter over baked crust. Combine walnuts with reserved crumb mixture and sprinkle over batter. Bake at 350° for 20–25 minutes.

Cool and cut into squares.

Do *not* double recipe; use single recipe only.

YIELD: 16 SQUARES

THE JUNIOR LEAGUE OF SAGINAW, MICHIGAN

Lemon Love Notes

½ cup soft butter or margarine
1 cup flour
¼ cup confectioners' sugar
2 tablespoons lemon juice
Grated rind of 1 lemon
2 eggs, well beaten
1 cup granulated sugar
2 tablespoons flour
½ teaspoon baking powder

Combine butter with the 1 cup flour and the confectioners' sugar and pat into a 9-inch-square pan. Bake at 350° for 15 minutes and cool.

Meanwhile, combine lemon juice and rind, eggs, sugar, the 2 table-spoons flour, and baking powder; spread on baked crust. Bake in 350° oven for 25 minutes (watch that it doesn't get too brown).

Cool. Spread with icing and cut into bars.

VANILLA ICING:
¾ cup confectioners' sugar
½ teaspoon vanilla
1 tablespoon butter
1½ teaspoons milk

Beat all ingredients into a smooth icing.

YIELD: 16 BARS

THE JUNIOR LEAGUE OF ST. PAUL, MINNESOTA

Spiced Sesame Bars

1 egg
¾ cup brown sugar
3 tablespoons melted butter
½ cup flour
¼ teaspoon salt
¼ teaspoon baking soda
¼ teaspoon allspice
¼ teaspoon mace
½ teaspoon cinnamon
¼ cup sesame seeds

Mix egg with brown sugar and melted butter. Stir in flour, salt, soda, and spices and mix well.

Grease an 8-inch-square pan and sprinkle half the sesame seeds on the bottom. Add egg mixture and sprinkle remaining sesame seeds on top.

Bake at 350° for 20 minutes. Cool and cut into bars.

YIELD: 12 BARS

THE JUNIOR LEAGUE OF ST. PAUL, MINNESOTA

·   ·   ·   ·   ·   ·   ·   ·   ·   ·   ·   ·   ·   ·   ·   ·   ·   ·

Nummy Butternut Bars

2 6-ounce packages chocolate chips
3 sticks margarine
2½ cups graham cracker crumbs
1 1-pound box confectioners' sugar
1 12-ounce jar peanut butter
1 cup pecans
1 cup flaked coconut

Recipe continues . . .

Line a 9 x 15-inch pan with foil. Melt 1 package chocolate chips and half a stick of margarine in a saucepan and spread evenly over foil.

Mix crumbs, sugar, and peanut butter with hands. Melt and stir in 2 sticks of remaining margarine, the pecans, and coconut. Mix well and press into pan.

Melt remaining package of chocolate chips with the last half stick of margarine. Pour over peanut butter layer.

Chill overnight and slice carefully into bars.

YIELD: 15 BARS

THE JUNIOR LEAGUE OF ST. PAUL, MINNESOTA

· · · · · · · · · · · · · · · · · · · ·

Toffee Bars

½ cup butter
½ cup confectioners' sugar
1 cup cake flour
2 eggs
1½ cups brown sugar
2 tablespoons flour
½ teaspoon baking powder
1 cup pecans and/or ½ cup coconut or a few chopped dates

Mix butter, confectioners' sugar, and cake flour and spread in 9 x 13-inch pan. Bake at 375° for 20–22 minutes.

Mix remaining ingredients, spread on top of baked base, and bake at 375° for 20–22 minutes.

Cool, then slice into bars to serve.

YIELD: 3 DOZEN BARS

Marigolds to Munch On
THE JUNIOR LEAGUE OF PEORIA, ILLINOIS

· · · · · · · · · · · · · · · · · · · ·

Chocolate Halfway Cookies

1 cup butter or shortening
½ cup granulated sugar
2 cups brown sugar
3 egg yolks, lightly beaten
1 tablespoon water
1 teaspoon vanilla
2 cups flour
¼ teaspoon salt
1 teaspoon baking powder
¼ teaspoon baking soda
1 6-ounce package chocolate bits
3 egg whites

Cream shortening, the granulated sugar, and ½ cup brown sugar. Add egg yolks, water, and vanilla. Sift dry ingredients and stir into sugar mixture to make a stiff dough.

Press dough into a 10 x 14 x 1-inch ungreased baking pan. Sprinkle chocolate bits on top and press slightly into dough.

Beat egg whites until stiff and gradually beat in remaining 1½ cups brown sugar. Beat well and spread over chocolate bits.

Bake at 350° for 25 minutes. Cool and cut into bars.

YIELD: 3–4 DOZEN COOKIES

THE JUNIOR LEAGUE OF EVANSVILLE, INDIANA

· · · · · · · · · · · · · · · · · · ·

Scottish Shortbread

1½ cups sweet butter (do not use margarine)
1¼ cups confectioners' sugar
3½ cups flour
½ cup cornstarch

Cream butter with sugar until light and fluffy. Sift flour with cornstarch and cut into butter until it resembles coarse meal. Mix as you would for pastry, adding just enough of the flour mixture to make a dough that can be gathered into a soft ball.

Knead on a lightly floured board for 1–2 minutes, or until smooth. Do not knead too long or dough will become greasy and the shortbread will be tough.

Divide dough in half. Press into 2 unbuttered 8-inch layer-cake pans. Using the back of a wooden spoon, press round indentations into the dough and prick entire surface with tines of a fork.

Bake at 350° for 45 minutes to 1 hour, or until an even pale brown. Do not overbake.

YIELD: 2 8-INCH CAKES

THE JUNIOR LEAGUE OF EVANSVILLE, INDIANA

·   ·   ·   ·   ·   ·   ·   ·   ·   ·   ·   ·   ·   ·   ·   ·   ·   ·

Refrigerator Cookies

1 cup butter
½ cup brown sugar
½ cup granulated sugar
1 egg, lightly beaten
2 cups flour
½ teaspoon baking soda
¼ teaspoon salt
½ teaspoon vanilla
½ cup broken nutmeats or ½ cup coconut

Cream butter and sugar. Add egg, flour, soda, salt, vanilla, and nuts. Form into a long roll and chill. When needed, slice thinly and bake at 400° for 8–10 minutes.

YIELD: 6 DOZEN COOKIES

THE JUNIOR LEAGUE OF EVANSVILLE, INDIANA

Rich Almond Cookies

1 cup butter
½ cup sugar
2½ cups sifted flour
½ cup chopped blanched almonds
Confectioners' sugar (optional)

Cream butter and sugar together. Add flour and mix. Add almonds and knead briefly.

Using hands, form into small balls. Place balls on cookie sheet and flatten slightly.

Bake at 375° for about 6 minutes—do not brown.

May be dusted with confectioners' sugar after baking.

YIELD: 4 DOZEN COOKIES

THE JUNIOR LEAGUE OF DES MOINES, IOWA

West Side Pecan Bars

1 cup sifted flour
½ teaspoon baking powder
¼ teaspoon salt
1½ cups brown sugar
½ cup melted and cooled butter
2 eggs, well beaten
1 teaspoon vanilla
2 tablespoons flour
¼ teaspoon salt
1½ cups chopped pecans

Sift first three ingredients into bowl. Add ½ cup brown sugar and butter and mix well. Pat into greased 9-inch-square pan. Bake at 350° for 10–15 minutes.

For pecan mixture, mix remaining ingredients, including remaining 1 cup brown sugar, and pour over baked base. Bake at 350° until browned, about 25–30 minutes.

Cool; cut into bars.

Freeze after baking.

YIELD: 16 BARS

The Cook's Book
THE JUNIOR LEAGUE OF CEDAR RAPIDS, IOWA

Cookie Monster Cookies

12 eggs
2 pounds brown sugar
1 tablespoon vanilla
1 tablespoon light corn syrup
8 teaspoons baking soda
1 pound butter (not margarine), softened
3 pounds chunky peanut butter
18 cups oatmeal (3 18-ounce boxes)
1 pound chocolate chips
1 pound M & M candies

Mix all ingredients in order given in a large pan. Drop by large table-spoonfuls or ice cream scoops, about six to a cookie sheet. Flatten and form slightly.

Bake for 12 minutes at 350°. Do not overbake. Let cool slightly before removing from cookie sheet.

This recipe does not call for flour. They freeze well.

YIELD: 8 DOZEN HUGE COOKIES

THE JUNIOR LEAGUE OF INDIANAPOLIS, INDIANA

Pumpkin Cookies

2 cups sifted flour
1 teaspoon baking powder
1 teaspoon baking soda
1 teaspoon cinnamon
½ teaspoon salt
1 cup sugar
1 cup shortening
1 egg
1 cup canned pumpkin
1 teaspoon vanilla
½ cup chopped nuts
½ cup dates (optional)

Mix dry ingredients. Cream sugar and shortening, add egg and pumpkin. Blend in flour mixture, then add vanilla, nuts, and dates. Drop from teaspoon on cookie sheet and bake 10–12 minutes in 350° oven. Cool and then frost.

ICING:
½ cup brown sugar
3 tablespoons butter
4 tablespoons milk
1 cup confectioners' sugar
¾ teaspoon vanilla

Boil brown sugar, butter, and milk for 2 minutes. Then pour into confectioners' sugar and vanilla. Stir to spreading consistency.

YIELD: ABOUT 4 DOZEN COOKIES

Marigolds to Munch On
THE JUNIOR LEAGUE OF PEORIA, ILLINOIS

Soft Oatmeal Cookies

1 cup sugar
½ cup shortening
½ cup butter
1 cup raisins, simmered 5 minutes and cooled
1 teaspoon cinnamon
½ teaspoon salt
2 eggs
1 cup chopped nuts
1 teaspoon baking soda, dissolved in ½ cup water from raisins
1 teaspoon vanilla
2 cups flour
2 cups oats

Combine and mix ingredients in order listed. Drop by spoonfuls onto greased baking sheet and bake in 375° oven for about 12–15 minutes.

YIELD: 5 DOZEN COOKIES

THE JUNIOR LEAGUE OF EVANSVILLE, INDIANA

. . . .

Date Cookies

2 10-ounce packages dates
Pecans
¼ cup shortening
¾ cup sugar
1 egg
1¼ cups sifted flour
½ teaspoon baking powder
½ teaspoon baking soda
½ teaspoon salt
½ cup sour cream

Recipe continues . . .

Slit dates and fill each with half a pecan.

Cream shortening and sugar, then beat in egg. Sift dry ingredients and add alternately with sour cream.

Drop dates into batter a few at a time and drop batter on greased baking sheet, spooning up one date per cookie.

Bake at 400° for 8–10 minutes. Spread with Brown Butter Icing.

YIELD: 4 DOZEN COOKIES

BROWN BUTTER ICING:
½ cup butter
3 cups sifted confectioners' sugar
¾ teaspoon vanilla
3 tablespoons water

Lightly brown the butter in saucepan. Remove from heat and gradually beat in confectioners' sugar, vanilla, and water.

THE JUNIOR LEAGUE OF TOLEDO, OHIO

·   ·   ·   (·   ·   ·   ·   ·   ·   ·   ·   ·   ·   ·   ·

Apple Spice Cookies

2 Jonathan or Winesap apples, peeled and chopped very fine
1 cup strong coffee or water
1 cup sugar
1 stick margarine
1 cup raisins
1 teaspoon cinnamon
¾ teaspoon cloves
¾ teaspoon nutmeg
1 teaspoon vanilla
2 cups flour
¼ teaspoon salt
1 teaspoon baking soda
1 cup chopped black walnuts or other nuts
Confectioners' sugar

Cook apples, coffee or water, sugar, margarine, raisins, cinnamon, cloves, and nutmeg in large saucepan until apples are tender. Cool and add vanilla. Stir in rest of ingredients except confectioners' sugar.

Drop by heaping spoonfuls onto baking sheet. Bake at 350° approximately 10 minutes.

Frost with confectioners' sugar.

YIELD: 1–2 DOZEN COOKIES

The Discovery Shop Cookbook
THE JUNIOR LEAGUE OF SIOUX CITY, IOWA

· ·

Forgotten Cookies

4 egg whites
¼ teaspoon salt
1½ cups sugar
2 teaspoons vanilla
12 ounces chocolate chips

Beat egg whites and salt until very stiff. Gradually beat in sugar. Stir in vanilla and chips.

Drop from teaspoon onto a greased cookie sheet; put into a preheated 375° oven. Turn oven off and leave cookies in the oven a minimum of 4 hours.

YIELD: 4–5 DOZEN COOKIES

THE JUNIOR LEAGUE OF CHAMPAIGN-URBANA, ILLINOIS

· ·

Chocolate Macaroon Cookies

2 cups sugar
½ cup salad oil
4 squares bitter chocolate, melted
4 eggs
2 teaspoons vanilla
2 cups flour
2 teaspoons baking powder
Confectioners' sugar

Cream sugar and oil. Add melted chocolate. Add eggs, one at a time, and beat well after each addition. Add vanilla. Blend in flour and baking powder. Chill.

Shape dough into small balls. Roll balls in confectioners' sugar and bake on a well-greased cookie sheet at 375° for 12–15 minutes. *Do not overbake.* Cookies should be soft when done.

Remove from sheet immediately.

These cookies freeze well.

YIELD: 6–8 DOZEN COOKIES

THE JUNIOR LEAGUE OF CHAMPAIGN-URBANA, ILLINOIS

· · · · · · · · · · · · · · · · · ·

Turtle Cookies

2 squares unsweetened chocolate
½ cup butter
2 eggs
¾ cup sugar
1 teaspoon vanilla
1 cup flour

Melt chocolate and butter. Cool. Beat eggs, sugar, and vanilla together. Add to chocolate mixture. Stir in flour.

Drop by the teaspoonful on a preheated waffle iron on medium setting. Close lid and cook for 1 minute. Remove with a fork.

Cool and frost with Chocolate Frosting.

CHOCOLATE FROSTING:
¼ cup brown sugar, firmly packed
¼ cup water
1 square unsweetened chocolate
2½ tablespoons butter
Confectioners' sugar

Bring all ingredients except confectioners' sugar to a full boil and boil for 3 minutes. Remove from heat and cool.

Stir in enough confectioners' sugar to achieve desired spreading consistency.

YIELD: 2–3 DOZEN COOKIES

THE JUNIOR LEAGUE OF CHAMPAIGN-URBANA, ILLINOIS

Illinois Brownies

4 squares bitter chocolate
½ pound butter or margarine
2 cups sugar
4 eggs
1 teaspoon vanilla
1¼ cups flour
Pinch salt

Melt chocolate and butter together and set aside to cool. Beat sugar and eggs in electric mixer until fluffy. Add cooled chocolate-butter mixture. Stir in vanilla, flour, and salt. Mix well.

Recipe continues . . .

Pour batter into a greased 9 x 13-inch metal baking pan. Bake at 325° for 35 minutes.

When cool, spread Bitter Chocolate Frosting over brownies and cut into squares.

YIELD: APPROXIMATELY 20 BROWNIES

BITTER CHOCOLATE FROSTING:
2 squares bitter chocolate
3 tablespoons butter or margarine
2 cups confectioners' sugar
1 teaspoon vanilla
Hot water

Melt chocolate and butter together. Blend with sugar and vanilla and add enough water to make frosting of spreading consistency.

YIELD: ABOUT 1 CUP

THE JUNIOR LEAGUE OF CHAMPAIGN-URBANA, ILLINOIS

· · · · · · · · · · · · · · · · · ·

East Side Coconut Bars

1½ cups brown sugar, firmly packed
½ cup butter
1 cup sifted flour
2 eggs, beaten
1 teaspoon vanilla
2 tablespoons flour
½ teaspoon baking powder
¼ teaspoon salt
1½ cups shredded moist coconut
1 cup chopped pecans or walnuts
Confectioners' sugar

Mix ½ cup brown sugar, butter, and 1 cup flour. Pack into buttered 8-inch-square pan and bake in 350° oven for 10 minutes.

Combine 1 cup brown sugar with remaining ingredients except confectioners' sugar. Pour over baked crust and bake 20 minutes at 325°.

While warm, sprinkle with confectioners' sugar. When cool, cut into bars.

YIELD: 12 BARS

The Cook's Book

THE JUNIOR LEAGUE OF CEDAR RAPIDS, IOWA

.   .   .   .

Downtown Apricot Squares

⅔ *cup dried apricots*
½ *cup softened butter*
¼ *cup granulated sugar*
1⅓ *cups sifted flour*
½ *teaspoon baking powder*
¼ *teaspoon salt*
1 *cup brown sugar, firmly packed*
2 *eggs, well beaten*
½ *teaspoon vanilla*
Confectioners' sugar

Rinse apricots. Cover with water and boil for 10 minutes; then drain, cool, and chop.

Mix until crumbly the butter, granulated sugar, and 1 cup of the flour. Pack into 8-inch-square pan and bake at 350° for 25 minutes.

Meanwhile, sift together remaining ⅓ cup flour, baking powder, and salt. Gradually beat brown sugar into well-beaten eggs. Add flour mixture and mix well. Stir in vanilla and apricots.

Recipe continues . . .

Spread apricot mixture over baked crumb layer and bake at 350° for 30 minutes, or until done.

Cool in pan. Cut into bars and roll in confectioners' sugar.

YIELD: 16 SQUARES

The Cook's Book
THE JUNIOR LEAGUE OF CEDAR RAPIDS, IOWA

Caramel Corn

2 cups unsalted popped popcorn
½ cup white corn syrup
2 cups brown sugar
2 sticks butter
½ teaspoon baking soda

Place popcorn in large pan or roaster.

Combine corn syrup, brown sugar, and butter and boil for 5 minutes. Remove from heat and add baking soda.

Pour mixture over corn, stir, and bake at 250° for 1 hour, stirring every 15 minutes.

YIELD: 2 CUPS

THE JUNIOR LEAGUE OF SPRINGFIELD, ILLINOIS

Buckeye Balls

1 stick butter
1½ cups peanut butter, smooth or crunchy
1 pound confectioners' sugar
1 tablespoon vanilla
1 12-ounce package chocolate chips
½ cake of paraffin

Cream butter and peanut butter together and beat in sugar and vanilla. Shape into small balls and refrigerate for ½ hour.

Melt chocolate and paraffin together in a double boiler. Dip peanut butter balls into chocolate with toothpick, covering all but a small circle.

Let cool on wax paper.

YIELD: 40 BALLS

THE JUNIOR LEAGUE OF TOLEDO, OHIO

Beverages

Strawberry Daiquiri

¾ 12-ounce can pink lemonade concentrate
½ 6-ounce can limeade concentrate
6 ounces rum
½ banana
8–10 strawberries
3 cups crushed ice
Strawberries for garnish

Put all ingredients in blender and blend to a soft mush.
Garnish each drink with a fresh strawberry.

YIELD: 6 DRINKS

THE JUNIOR LEAGUE OF COLUMBUS, OHIO

· · · · · · · · · · · · · · · · · ·

Peach Fuzz

2 fresh unpeeled peaches, sliced
1 6-ounce can frozen lemonade concentrate
6 ounces vodka (or light rum)
Crushed ice to fill blender

Blend all ingredients in blender until smooth.
Serve in small glasses.
Two cups frozen peaches may be substituted for fresh. Add sugar to taste if unsweetened.

YIELD: 5 CUPS

Bluff City Cooks
THE JUNIOR LEAGUE OF GREATER ALTON, ILLINOIS

· · · · · · · · · · · · · · · · · ·

Summer Slush

2½ cups bourbon
1 quart ginger ale
1 30-ounce can pineapple juice
1 6-ounce can frozen orange juice concentrate, thawed
1 6-ounce can frozen lemonade concentrate, thawed
3–4 cups 7-Up
Lime slices
Pineapple spears
Maraschino cherries

Mix first five ingredients and freeze to a slush.

To serve, mix ⅔ cup slush and ⅓ cup 7-Up in tall beverage glasses. Garnish each serving with a lime slice, pineapple spear, and cherry.

YIELD: 10–12 SERVINGS

THE JUNIOR LEAGUE OF ROCKFORD, ILLINOIS

Tumbleweeds

¼ cup light cream
¾ cup Kahlúa
1 quart French vanilla ice cream

Pour cream and Kahlúa in blender. Fill blender with ice cream and blend. Serve in champagne glasses.

YIELD: 6 SERVINGS

Recipe continues . . .

VARIATIONS:

May substitute chocolate chip or coffee ice cream. Top with fresh toasted coconut.

Sunflower Sampler
THE JUNIOR LEAGUE OF WICHITA, KANSAS

. . . .

Frozen Whiskey Sours

1 6-ounce can frozen lemonade concentrate, thawed
1 6-ounce can frozen orange juice concentrate, thawed
6 ounces water
10 ounces bourbon
1 quart 7-Up
Maraschino cherries

Combine all ingredients except cherries and freeze for 24 hours, or until "slushy."

Garnish with a cherry when serving.

This mixture may be kept frozen 3–4 months.

YIELD: 10 6-OUNCE SERVINGS

THE JUNIOR LEAGUE OF SPRINGFIELD, ILLINOIS

. . . .

Pat's Winter Warmer-Upper

1 tablespoon chocolate syrup
1 jigger dark crème de cacao (1½ ounces)
Strong hot black coffee
1 scoop vanilla ice cream
1 jigger green crème de menthe (1½ ounces)

For each serving, place syrup and crème de cacao in the bottom of a coffee mug. Fill cup three-quarters full with hot coffee. Add scoop of ice cream and pour crème de menthe over the ice cream.

YIELD: 1 SERVING

THE JUNIOR LEAGUE OF ST. PAUL, MINNESOTA

· · · · · · · · · · · · · · · · · · · ·

Ashleys

1 6-ounce can frozen limeade concentrate, thawed
6 ounces white rum
1 12-ounce bottle beer
Cherries or lime slices for garnish

Pour first three ingredients into a pitcher and mix. Pour over ice, either in glasses or punch bowl.

Garnish with cherries or lime slices.

Excellent as prelude to a ladies' luncheon.

Make the Ashleys as needed, as the beer can go flat if made ahead.

YIELD: 6–7 SMALL SERVINGS

THE JUNIOR LEAGUE OF YOUNGSTOWN, OHIO

· · · · · · · · · · · · · · · · · · ·

Rose Sparkler

½ bottle crème de cassis (black currant-flavored liqueur)
1 bottle champagne

Recipe continues ...

Mix and pour over ice.

Serve in champagne glasses.

Makes a wonderful drink before a luncheon.

YIELD: 8 SERVINGS

THE JUNIOR LEAGUE OF KANSAS CITY, KANSAS

· ·

Champagne Mist

2 ounces brandy
2 ounces juice from maraschino cherries
2 ounces Benedictine
1 teaspoon pulverized or fine sugar
1 quart carbonated water
Fruit for garnish (optional)

Put ice into a small punch bowl, add all ingredients and mix well. Or mix brandy, maraschino cherry juice, Benedictine, and sugar. Pour over crushed ice in champagne glasses and fill with carbonated water. Garnish with fruit if desired.

YIELD: ABOUT 6 SHORT DRINKS

THE JUNIOR LEAGUE OF TOLEDO, OHIO

· ·

Summertime Cooler

3½ cups freshly squeezed orange juice
2 cups dry white wine
½ cup orange-flavored liqueur
2 tablespoons lemon juice

Combine all ingredients except lemon juice in large pitcher. Stir to mix. Refrigerate until well chilled. Add lemon juice just before serving.

YIELD: 12 SERVINGS

THE JUNIOR LEAGUE OF ROCKFORD, ILLINOIS

. . . .

Ananasbowle

½ cup superfine sugar
2 cups chopped fresh pineapple
2 bottles Moselle wine
½ bottle chilled champagne or carbonated water

Add sugar to pineapple and let stand ½ hour. Add wine and chill 1–2 hours.

Before serving, add the champagne or carbonated water.

YIELD: 20 CUPS

THE JUNIOR LEAGUE OF KANSAS CITY, KANSAS

. . . .

Cranberry Punch

1 quart apple cider
6 ounces frozen apple juice concentrate
2 cups cranberry juice cocktail
1 bottle rosé wine
½ teaspoon bitters

Recipe continues . . .

Combine and chill all ingredients.

Pour over ice ring in punch bowl.

YIELD: 20 SERVINGS

THE JUNIOR LEAGUE OF ROCKFORD, ILLINOIS

Champagne Punch

3 fifths champagne (dry white preferred)
1 fifth gin
2 quarts ginger ale
1 quart carbonated water
1 12-ounce can frozen lemonade concentrate

Thoroughly chill champagne, gin, ginger ale, and carbonated water. Just before serving, pour all liquids into a large punch bowl. Slice the lemonade concentrate and add to the punch. Ice may be added last, if desired.

A fresh strawberry in the bottom of each cup is a festive touch.

If a sweeter punch is preferred, add powdered sugar, 1 tablespoon at a time, until desired sweetness is obtained.

This champagne punch is very smooth and very potent! Always serve with food accompaniment.

YIELD: 96 SERVINGS

Discover Dayton
THE JUNIOR LEAGUE OF DAYTON, OHIO

Fred's Famous Brunch Punch

1 6-ounce can frozen pineapple-orange juice concentrate
6 ounces gin or vodka
6 ounces apricot or peach brandy
1 6-ounce can cracked ice
6 ounces carbonated water

Put all ingredients in blender and blend until smooth.
Serve in champagne glasses.

YIELD: 4–5 SERVINGS

THE JUNIOR LEAGUE OF SAGINAW, MICHIGAN

Honeymoon Eggnog

3 eggs, separated
½ cup sugar
½ pint bourbon
½ pint heavy cream
½ pint milk

Beat egg yolks until stiff, add ¼ cup sugar and beat again. Pour bourbon slowly into yolks, stirring constantly. Add cream and milk.

Beat egg whites until stiff, and mix in remaining ¼ cup sugar. Fold into yolk mixture.

Chill thoroughly before serving.

YIELD: 2 SERVINGS

THE JUNIOR LEAGUE OF SAGINAW, MICHIGAN

Hot Mulled Cider

12 cups cider
1½ teaspoons whole allspice
2 tablespoons whole cloves
6 cinnamon sticks
1 cup brown sugar
2 oranges, sliced
1 lemon, sliced

Combine all ingredients in a large saucepan. Boil until the sugar is dissolved. Simmer to keep it hot.

Serve piping hot. (If desired, add as much Calvados, applejack, or whiskey as you wish. Add the liquor just before serving.)

YIELD: 12 SERVINGS

Tested, Tried, and True
THE JUNIOR LEAGUE OF FLINT, MICHIGAN

. . . .

Sweet Dandelion Wine

2 quarts dandelion blossoms, tightly packed
2 quarts boiling water
3 cups sugar
Juice of 1½ oranges
Juice of ½ lemon
¼ compressed yeast cake or envelope active dry yeast
1 slice rye toast

Pick only the young, early blooms of dandelions. Empty them into a 4-quart stoneware pot and pour the boiling water over them. Cover pot and let stand for 3 days.

Strain liquid through cheesecloth into a large saucepan, squeezing flowers dry. Add sugar and the fruit juices and simmer for 20 minutes over low heat.

Return mixture to the stoneware pot and let cool to lukewarm. Sprinkle yeast on top of a slice of rye toast. Place toast on top of mixture. Cover pot with cloth and keep at room temperature (65°–70°) for a week.

Strain wine into a 2-quart jug, plug loosely with a small piece of cotton, and store in a cool dark place for 3 weeks. Pour gently into a bottle; cap or cork tightly. Age for 5 months before serving.

YIELD: 2 QUARTS

THE JUNIOR LEAGUE OF SPRINGFIELD, ILLINOIS

Damson Plum Cordial

1 pound Damson plums
1 pound sugar
4/5 quart gin

Wash plums; slit and puncture skins. Place in half-gallon jar. Add sugar and gin. Stir daily until sugar is dissolved (3–4 days). Let stand 3–4 months.

Pour off liquid and serve in cordial glasses.
Make in early fall to serve at holiday parties.

YIELD: APPROXIMATELY 1 QUART

VARIATION:
Substitute 1 pound dried apricots for plums.

Be Our Guest
THE JUNIOR LEAGUE OF MILWAUKEE, WISCONSIN

Dayton Crème de Menthe

8 cups sugar
8 cups water
1 tablespoon essence of peppermint (available at pharmacies)
3 tablespoons vanilla
1 tablespoon green food coloring
1 pint 190-proof clear alcohol (available at liquor stores)

Mix all ingredients in a 1-gallon glass jar. Secure lid tightly. Place in a dark, cool place and let age for at least 3 weeks.

This makes a great homemade holiday gift when packaged in a pretty glass container. We rate it better than commercial and it keeps for years!

YIELD: 1 GALLON

Discover Dayton
THE JUNIOR LEAGUE OF DAYTON, OHIO

· · · · · · · · · · · · · · · · · ·

Planter's Punch

1 6-ounce can frozen pineapple juice concentrate
1 6-ounce can frozen lemonade concentrate
1 12-ounce can frozen orange juice concentrate
Water
1½ quarts bottled lemon juice
2 cups sugar
4½ fifths light rum
Cherries
Orange slices, halved

Dilute frozen juices as directed on cans. Combine with lemon juice and sugar. (Makes 1 gallon plus 1 pint juice mixture.) To each quart (4 cups) of juice mixture, add 1 bottle (4/5 quart) of rum.

Serve with lots of cracked ice and garnish with a cherry and an orange slice.

YIELD: ABOUT 2 GALLONS

Cincinnati Celebrates
THE JUNIOR LEAGUE OF CINCINNATI, OHIO

Order Information

Many of the recipes for *The Midwestern Junior League Cookbook* have been selected from the cookbooks published by the individual Junior Leagues. To obtain a particular League's own book of recipes, send a check or money order plus a complete return address to the appropriate address listed below. (Prices of all cookbooks subject to change.)

All proceeds from the sale of cookbooks will be used for charitable purposes.

Bluff City Cooks
The Junior League of Greater Alton, Inc.
P.O. Box 27
Alton, Illinois 62002
Price per copy: $5.95
Postage per copy: 50¢
Illinois residents add 30¢ sales tax per copy.
Make checks payable to: The Junior League of Greater Alton, Inc.

Peacock Pie and Other Perfections
The Junior League of Battle Creek, Michigan
143 Lakeshire
Battle Creek, Michigan 49015
Price per copy: $2.95
Postage per copy: 75¢
Make checks payable to: Junior League of Battle Creek, Inc.

The Cook's Book, published by The Junior League of Cedar Rapids, Iowa, Inc., is out of print and not available for sale.

Soupçon
The Junior League of Chicago, Inc.
1447 North Astor Street
Chicago, Illinois 60610
Price per copy: $8.95
Postage per copy: 95¢

Illinois residents add 45¢ sales tax per book.
Make checks payable to: The Junior League of Chicago, Inc.

Cincinnati Celebrates
The Junior League of Cincinnati, Inc.
Regency Square, Apt. 6-F
2334 Dana Avenue
Cincinnati, Ohio 45208
Price per copy: $6.50
Postage per copy: 75¢
Ohio residents add 30¢ sales tax per book.
Make checks payable to: Cincinnati Celebrates

Discover Dayton
The Junior League of Dayton, Ohio, Inc.
140 East Monument Avenue
Dayton, Ohio 45402
Discover Dayton is in the pre-publication planning stage. Further inquiries
may be directed to the above address.

Tested, Tried, and True
The Junior League of Flint, Inc.
310 East Third Street
Flint, Michigan 48502
Price per copy (postpaid): $7.00
Make checks payable to: The Junior League of Flint, Inc.

Cookbook
The Junior League of Grand Rapids, Inc.
1500 Wealthy Street, S.E.
Grand Rapids, Michigan 49506
Price per copy: $8.95
Postage per copy: 75¢
Michigan residents add 36¢ sales tax per copy.
Make checks payable to: The Junior League of Grand Rapids, Inc.

Be Our Guest
The Junior League of Milwaukee, Inc.
P.O. Box 17622
Milwaukee, Wisconsin 53217
Price per copy: $5.95
Postage per copy: 75¢
Wisconsin residents add 24¢ sales tax per copy.
Make checks payable to: Junior League of Milwaukee Cookbooks

Marigolds to Munch On
The Junior League of Peoria, Inc.
P.O. Box 3233
Peoria, Illinois 61614
Price per copy: $4.95
Postage per copy: 75¢
Illinois residents add 25¢ sales tax per copy.
Make checks payable to: Junior League of Peoria Cookbook

Gourmet Gab, published by The Junior League of Saginaw, Michigan, Inc., is out of print and not available for sale.

The Discovery Shop Cookbook
The Junior League of Sioux City, Inc.
417 Pearl Street
Sioux City, Iowa 51101
Price per copy: $3.00
Postage per copy: 60¢
Iowa residents add 9¢ sales tax per copy.
Make checks payable to: The Discovery Shop

Bestir Yourself, published by The Junior League of Toledo, Ohio, Inc., is out of print and not available for sale.

Sunflower Sampler
The Junior League of Wichita, Inc.
6402 East Twelfth
Wichita, Kansas 67206

Price per copy: $6.50
Postage per copy: $1.00
Kansas residents add 20¢ sales tax per copy.
Make checks payable to: Junior League of Wichita Cookbook

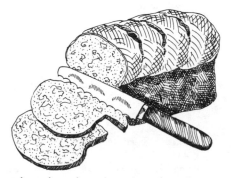

Index